Praise for *Google™ Web Toolkit Applications*

"Ryan clearly understands the GWT value proposition and how GWT integrates into a diverse web technology stack—and not just in a theoretical way. With the popularity of gpokr.com and kdice.com, Ryan can speak with the authority of concrete success."

—Bruce Johnson, creator of Google Web Toolkit

"This book distinguishes itself from other books on GWT in that it walks through the entire process of building several nontrivial GWT applications, not the toy applications that most books present."

—R. Mark Volkmann, Object Computing, Inc.

"*Google™ Web Toolkit Applications* is an excellent resource for any GWT developer. Solutions to challenges commonly encountered in GWT are presented through the design and development of actual applications. The applications developed throughout the text demonstrate best practices from simple UI design all the way to custom code generation, and are presented with little pretext about the amount of Java knowledge a given developer may have. Advanced concepts are not withheld but are presented in a way that will be understood by both novice and seasoned developers alike. Good application development practices and proper Model View Controller design is reinforced throughout the book, nearly guaranteeing that the reader will come away a better programmer. "

—Jason Essington, Senior Web/Java Engineer, Green River Computing

"Dewsbury's *Google™ Web Toolkit Applications* is a book for both experts and beginner programmers who want to discover this open source Java software development framework, as well as write Ajax applications. A very detailed book!"

—Massimo Nardone, Advisory IT Security Architect

D1537960

Google™
Web Toolkit
Applications

Google™ Web Toolkit

Applications

Ryan Dewsbury

PRENTICE
HALL

Upper Saddle River, NJ • Boston • Indianapolis • San Francisco
New York • Toronto • Montreal • London • Munich • Paris • Madrid
Capetown • Sydney • Tokyo • Singapore • Mexico City

The publisher offers excellent discounts on this book when ordered in quantity for bulk purchases or special sales, which may include electronic versions and/or custom covers and content particular to your business, training goals, marketing focus, and branding interests. For more information, please contact:

U.S. Corporate and Government Sales
(800) 382-3419
corpsales@pearsontechgroup.com

For sales outside the United States please contact:

International Sales
international@pearsoned.com

Visit us on the Web: www.prenhallprofessional.com

Library of Congress Cataloging-in-Publication Data
Dewsbury, Ryan.
   Google web toolkit applications / Ryan Dewsbury.
           p.   cm.
   Includes index.
   ISBN 978-0-321-50196-7 (pbk. : alk. paper)
   1. Ajax (Web site development technology) 2. Java (Computer program language) 3. Google. I. Title.
   TK5105.8885.A52D49 2007
   006.7'6—dc22

                                                    2007039396

ISBN-13: 978-0-321-50196-7
ISBN-10:   0-321-50196-9
Text printed in the United States on recycled paper at Courier in Stoughton, Massachusetts.
First printing, November 2007

*To Maura, for listening,
supporting something new,
and taking risks with me.*

Contents

Chapter 2   **User Interface Library Overview   37**

Preface

I've always had an interest in the nontechnical side of software development: the user experience. It started back when I was working on teams building the core of application servers in C++. We admired the beauty of the C++ language and its expressiveness. We made large, complex systems run seamlessly with elegant code. We marveled at our templating techniques, which made the C++ compiler churn out code just like a code generator would. Then I would leave work and was not able to mention a word of it without receiving blank stares in return.

I decided to find time to write a client-side application that would be as elegant to the user as well-written code can be for a developer. I chose to build an instant messenger application, mostly with C++, that combined the four major networks into one interface. At the time, instant messengers were becoming bloated with features—there were too many buttons distracting users from sending a simple text message. The instant messenger application I developed resulted in a much better user experience for instant messaging: instead of users downloading a 10MB application with a five-step installation process, I optimized the messenger to be 200K with a clean interface (much like the Google Talk messenger is today). As a result, it was downloaded over a million times.

While developing interfaces in C++ I was always impressed by the ease of creating a nice-looking interface on a web page. If you compare the code required to set a font in C++ to cascading style sheets, you'll see what I mean. Then Ajax started to become popular, producing web interface behavior similar to desktop interface behavior. Combine this with the ease

of making things look better with CSS, and you have a much better platform for interface development.

I was really impressed when I saw Google Maps for the first time. The user
experience was perfect. I simply typed `maps.google.com` into my
browser and I was instantly provided with a fully functional map application. I could drag the map around in different directions, traveling around
the world, zooming in and out without waiting for a page referesh. I had a
brief look at the technology needed to do this, specifically JavaScript, and
was disapointed. I knew there were limits to what you can build with Java-
Script. It would be nearly impossible to build large complex client-side
applications with it.

Then the Google Web Toolkit (GWT) was released, and I decided to try
writing an application using it. In only three weeks I had built the client
and server side for a poker application. I put it up at http://gpokr.com. You
could simply type the URL into your browser and be instantly presented
with a live poker game. No downloads, no installations, and the interface
could be styled nicely and easily with CSS. Scott Blum, Bruce Johnson, and
Joel Webber from the GWT team came by to do some "testing," and I had
the opportunity to thank them for building an incredible tool. I marveled
at being able to write elegant Java code that could be transformed into Java-
Script by the GWT compiler. I was really impressed by how GWT so solidly
let anyone create applications that delivered great user experiences.

After GWT's initial release, I found that its great abilities weren't clear to
many and that it would take a book with several real examples to illustrate
this. I had never written a book before, and to write one on a technology
that was not my specialty didn't seem quite right. But then again, nobody
specialized in GWT at this point. I believed enough in the technology to
give it a shot. To make up for my lack of experience and before writing any
of the chapters, I spent several months exclusively developing GWT applications to explore every part of GWT as well as every part of web technology that GWT could touch. Part II of this book presents five of these
applications.

What Is This Book About?

This book is about writing nontrivial Ajax applications to create great user
experiences using web technologies and Java development tools, with

GWT bridging the two. The book focuses primarily on the Google Web Toolkit, with an in-depth look at its library and tools. As a secondary focus, it covers software development techniques and patterns using Java, and how to apply Ajax application development with GWT. A terciary focus is on web technologies, including web standards and other Ajax libraries and APIs.

Who Should Read This Book?

I'm a developer who wrote this book for other developers. Software developers who need to create user-facing applications should read this book. Most of the code in the book is based on Java, but care is taken so that the book is accessible to a beginner with the language. If you don't know Java, you should familiarize yourself with the language before starting this book. Sun has great tutorials to get you started: http://java.sun.com/docs/books/tutorial/java/index.html.

GWT is not just an Ajax tool for Java developers. I think this view severely undercuts its true strength. Java developers will find using it easy; however, the technology is for any software developer who needs to build nontrivial Ajax applications. You could be a .NET, PHP, Ruby, or C++ developer. If you're one of these developers you would need to learn another language to build an Ajax application whether you use GWT or not. I recommend that you learn Java—starting with the previously mentioned tutorials from Sun, and GWT through this book and the GWT documentation at http://code.google.com/webtoolkit/documentation/—instead of JavaScript. As a result, you will save a substantial amount of time debugging and maintaining the application while creating a much better user experience.

Organization of This Book

This book has two parts. Part I gives you an in-depth introduction to using the Google Web Toolkit. You can use it as a reference for the GWT library or as a guide to using effective development techniques with GWT. Part II provides a thorough look at five nontrivial applications built with GWT. In this part you'll find development patterns, techniques, and subtleties used through application design and development. Each application in this part is designed to be a balance of GWT library usage, web service and technology interoperation, application design and architecture, and user interface design. As you read through these chapters, you can follow along and construct the applications on your machine. The chapters include most of the code, but you'll need to refer to the source code at www.gwtapps.com in certain instances that are identified.

Part I: Understanding the Google Web Toolkit

- Chapter 1, First Steps with the Google Web Toolkit, introduces web technologies, skill sets, and GWT, and includes a short tutorial on creating an Ajax game application.

- Chapter 2, User Interface Library Overview, details the user interface library that comes with GWT. This material consists mainly of notes and examples based on the usage of each widget.

- Chapter 3, Server Integration Techniques, describes several methods for integrating with server-side applications.

- Chapter 4, Software Engineering for Ajax, looks at Java tools for software development and how they apply to GWT development.

- Chapter 5, Using the Toolkit Effectively, covers some of the more advanced techniques of development with GWT, including CSS, code generation, internationalization, and performance.

Part II: Rich Web Applications by Example

- Chapter 6, Gadget Desktop Application, presents a gadget application with a rich drag-and-drop interface, persistence with cookies and Gears, along with using JavaScript APIs with GWT.

- Chapter 7, Multi-Search Application, shows how to create a search application that makes requests to many search engines. The application uses JavaScript Object Notation with Padding (JSONP) to communicate with Google, Yahoo!, Amazon, and Flickr.

- Chapter 8, Blog Editor Application, walks you through an application to manage blog entries across many blogs. This application integrates with the Blogger REST API using an HTTP proxy.

- Chapter 9, Instant Messenger Application, details a web page instant messenger based on GWT-RPC. It covers how to use an event-based protocol along with optimizing with Comet on Tomcat and Continuations on Jetty.

- Chapter 10, Database Editor Application, looks at a database manager for a traditional web page. The application explores advanced topics such as reading complex data structures from the server using Data Access Objects, code generation for easy XML and JSON, and integrating with PHP, Ruby on Rails, and Java with Hibernate.

Web Support

The web site for this book is located at www.gwtapps.com. It contains the source code and live demos for the sample applications, a forum for questions and error reports, and other useful reference material.

Acknowledgments

I thank the GWT team for creating such an interesting technology to write about. Also, thanks to the great people at Prentice Hall including John Wait, who had an inspirational interest in design and doing something different; Rebecca Greenberg for her excellent copyediting work; Chris Zahn for his attention to detail and enthusiasm; Raina Chrobak for keeping things organized and not freaking out over my constant TOC changes; and Julie Nahil for managing production.

Thanks to all of the reviewers—Sandy McArthur, Jason Essington, Bruce Johnson, Massimo Nardone, and Mark Volkmann—who found mistakes and made suggestions that made this a much better book.

Finally, thanks to the thousands of members of Gpokr and Kdice who tolerated a lack of updates and bug fixes for six months.

About the Author

Ryan Dewsbury has been involved with C++ and Java as a developer, architect, and consultant since 1998. Ryan spent several years helping build the system framework for a semiconductor manufacturing system. More recently, Ryan has been working to create great user experiences through cutting-edge software with a few web startup companies.

In between contracts Ryan spends time on independent software projects including Easy Message, which was acquired in 2004, and more recently Gpokr (http://gpokr.com) and KDice (http://kdice.com), two casual web-based games based on GWT.

About the Author

PART I

Understanding the Google Web Toolkit

1

First Steps with the Google Web Toolkit

This chapter traces the development of web technologies to help you understand how the Google Web Toolkit (GWT) fits into web application development technologies and tools. It shows how to build a simple Ajax application with the GWT and briefly explores GWT's library.

The Emergence of Ajax

In the early part of this century, after the dot.com bubble broke and as the browser wars died down, companies decided it was no longer lucrative to build web technology, and development ceased for many technologies that had earlier promised to be the way of the future. We were, however, left with the browsers and their somewhat common implementation of web standards.

Something fundamentally different started to take shape. Production of new web technology slowed down. Developers focused on creating clean HTML, using elegant cascading style sheets (CSSs) and adding touches of JavaScript. Software tool venders virtually stopped selling new technology that promised to wow users. We didn't need to constantly learn new things. Instead, we became experts at the technology that was resistant to a stock market crash.

This evolution of a "new web" focused on mastering the most basic foundations of web technology before adding another layer. Instead of building old things again with new technology, developers innovated with old technology. Nontechnical people enjoyed using web applications more than before, and in some cases these applications performed better than their desktop application counterparts. Maybe web applications now seemed a relatively lightweight load on a computer already bogged down with bloated installed software. Perhaps the design and usability of web interfaces had advanced with designers' solid understanding of CSS. Whatever it was, the new web felt good.

The web thrived with people-centric applications like blogs and social networks—applications perfectly suited to the web, with a document-like structure that users could search and view. However, administering these types of applications didn't seem so easy. Signing into a blog service to manage a blog entry followed the same document browsing structure, which made this task awkward: First users provided their credentials and waited for their account page to load, then selected the section they wanted to manage and waited for that page to load, and so on. This process involved loading a series of documents sequentially, which creates a tedious and an incongruent user experience. While sequentially loading pages is native to the web and perfect for many tasks, managing a blog effectively requires something completely different. For an interface like this to become usable it needs to be presented as a single responsive entity to the user. This was something older web technology wasn't able to provide.

The big breakthrough happened with the development of asynchronous JavaScript techniques, which eliminated web applications' painful page loading usability issues. Using these techniques, JavaScript makes requests to the server for data asynchronously to update the web page without causing a refresh. The previously laborious multipage web applications started to behave like seamless desktop applications, without pauses or complete interface refreshes between actions. The increased use of JavaScript also let developers put more programmatic logic in the client side of the application, which in turn reduced the load on the server: Data would only be loaded when necessary, and the client application could hold state information that previously had been handled on the server. And as an added bonus, improvements in usability were typically paired with impprovements in performance. While the techniques, dubbed **Ajax** (Asynchronous JavaScript and XML), initially seemed like a bit of a hack, they have largely been embraced by both web users and developers.

Using Ajax techniques to build web applications caused an important change in web application architecture. Web applications now used interfaces that weren't generated through templates on a web server but with JavaScript in the client's browser. The client side of the application became an application on its own that largely decoupled itself from the server. Developers had mastered the basic web technologies well enough to build full client-side applications with them—and in some cases not even needing a server for anything other than distributing the application. This unlikely job for web technologies stretched their abilities, but they performed the job much better than technologies developed by any one company. Applications built using Ajax were not seeing much competition: They were being developed, distributed, and adopted quicker than anything built with competing technologies, including those built with traditional desktop application development tools.

As the adoption of Ajax applications increased, competition and application complexity also increased, and development started to hit a scalability problem that other application development techniques handled with object-oriented design and powerful development tools. However, Ajax evolved out of technologies never meant to build applications, much less big applications, and there weren't any available tools to help build large applications with JavaScript in the way there are for desktop applications. Support emerged with frameworks, which provided better foundations for building applications (like Dojo, which is a community effort). But no matter how many libraries developed for building Ajax applications, Ajax was being used for something it was never designed to do.

Rethinking Web Applications

Writing Ajax applications' programmatic logic in JavaScript, an interpreted scripting language, makes it hard for developers to scale an application's size and complexity the way developers can with languages meant for desktop applications. Like Ajax, desktop applications have frameworks too. However, they often add more weight to the application and are often not the best answer to help scale an application. More importantly, desktop applications have software engineering tools, which have had much more time to mature than Ajax application tools. These software engineering tools mature faster too, since they're also used for server-side applications, which often are more complex and require even more engineering.

In addition to the absence of tools, JavaScript also lacks the language features that dramatically improve the ability to build complex applications, including certain object-oriented programming constructs and the ability to catch errors at compile time.

Many companies, having recognized both the success and limitations of Ajax applications, want to get in on the action and provide an alternative to Ajax for richer web experiences. Applications built with these technologies, including Ajax applications, can be classified as Rich Internet Applications (RIAs).

The following sections discuss several alternatives to using Ajax techniques to build RIAs. Time will tell whether any of these will gain enough momentum to become the de facto standard for RIAs, and regardless of how the battle between the technologies turns out, Ajax will most likely still be there. Based on web-standard technologies implemented by many vendors, its natural emergence and acceptance without the marketing push of a large company speaks for its goodwill. Instead of giving up on a technology that works, there must be a way to fix its problems without causing users of the applications to install yet another plugin tentatively supported by one company.

Adobe Flash and Flex

Adobe Flash has been the most successful browser plugin—it's installed on 98 percent of Internet-enabled desktops.[1] Its success stems from the relatively small download size of both the plugin and the SWF files that it plays, its fast animation performance, and its graphic-designer-friendly development tool used to construct SWF files.

Flash, already widely used as a player for advertisements and games, has more recently been used as a player for applications built with Adobe Flex, a software development kit for building Flash-based applications. Flex uses MXML (Multimedia eXtensible Markup Language) and ActionScript, along with an Integrated Development Environment (IDE), to build applications that compile down to SWF files. While the Flash development environment is geared toward use by graphic designers, Flex is geared

---

1. See www.adobe.com/products/player_census/flashplayer/.

toward software developers and provides data services such as remoting and messaging solutions to communicate to a Java 2 Enterprise Edition (J2EE) server. Refer to www.adobe.com/products/flex/ for more information on Flex.

Although developers can create impressive animated interfaces with Flash, its drawing foundations can cause usability issues when new custom controls used for application interfaces confuse users more familiar with native OS controls. Adobe may eventually overcome this problem much like the way Java has with the Standard Widget Toolkit (SWT).

Because Flash is being driven by a single company, it isn't standards based. As a result, Adobe will have competition for market share with the technology, making its future less stable than web technologies. For example, if Microsoft can put enough money into a competing product, it could bury Flash like Netscape before it.

Microsoft Silverlight

Microsoft has a long history of support for client application development for their Windows operating system. Their tools and documentation have always been very good and they have consistently made efforts of advancing web technology. However, many of their efforts have been in contrast with the democratic nature of the web. Microsoft initially didn't like Java applets delivering more advanced applications through the browser, and they decided to remove the Java Runtime Environment (JRE) from their Internet Explorer distribution and instead provide the ability to embed ActiveX objects, which use their proprietary Component Object Model (COM) technology. This decision introduced uncertainty in browser implementations, causing some browsers to have Java support while others supported ActiveX. This lack of standardization is the most probable cause for ActiveX browser plugins not being widely used today.

Microsoft learned from this mistake and now offers Silverlight (see http://silverlight.net/), based on their .NET technology, as a plugin for many browsers. Silverlight enables developers to build RIAs using development techniques more advanced than JavaScript. However, this solution, which benefits from good .NET Framework tools and support from Microsoft, does not have a wide distribution and is controlled by Microsoft's will instead of a standards organization.

Java FX

Java enjoyed a wide browser distribution early on with Java applets. These Java applets used the Java Runtime Environment inside the browser to provide more advanced programmatic functionality than HTML and Java-Script could provide. However, Java applets gained a reputation for slow loading and ugly interfaces when compared to Flash's quick downloads and impressive interfaces. Microsoft dropping support for Java applets in Internet Explorer sealed its fate in the browser.

As illustrated by the success of Flash and Ajax, developers want more programmatic functionality in the browser, and with Microsoft getting into the game with Silverlight, the timing may be right for Java to succeed in a second attempt at browser-based applications.

Sun Microsystems announced Java FX at JavaOne in May 2007, a few days after Microsoft announced Silverlight 1.1. The Java FX family of technologies helps create RIAs. At the time of this book's publication, Java FX consists of a Script and a Mobile module that run on a standard JRE, so it's too early to properly evaluate this solution.

Software Engineering for Ajax

Google released their toolkit with little fanfare, and although it was immediately *dugg* and *slashdotted*[2] as any new technology from them would be, it wasn't universally accepted as another Google great. Varying posts both praised and dismissed it, but the overall discussion was quiet. People seemed somewhat confused by the toolkit's place in the web landscape, as it takes a new approach to web application development. If you take the time to understand its place, I think you'll find the Google Web Toolkit the most powerful tool for creating Ajax applications.

That's a bold statement, so I suppose I should back it up. There are many great JavaScript libraries that help you build great Ajax applications. However, GWT fundamentally differs from these libraries by providing a wealth

---

2. To be *dugg* or *slashdotted* refers to a story making the front page at www.digg.com or http://slashdot.org, two technology-related social news sites.

of software engineering tools from Java to use for Ajax applications, instead of providing a feature-rich library (though its library has many features). You can also include any existing JavaScript libraries, and your application compiles down to be distributed as an Ajax application using only web standards that don't require any new runtimes or plugins. To the browser it appears like any Ajax application, but to the developer it is like building a regular desktop application. The improvement in development flexibility and productivity that benefits the developer eventually filters down to the user with a solid application with good usability. The Ajax application development process can leverage high-quality software engineering tools such as JUnit for test-driven development and IDEs like Eclipse that provide superior debugging support and compile-time error checking on the fly.

GWT contains many tools that assist with building Ajax applications, including a user interface library of widgets and panels, libraries to perform asynchronous server communication through HTTP or remote procedure calls (RPCs), tools to interoperate with other web applications using JavaScript, JSON, and XML, and access to a mature development environment for software engineering.

Building Rich Interfaces with Widgets and Panels

GWT provides a library of widgets and panels that you can use in the Java code of your Ajax application. They're constructed with HTML using JavaScript to handle events; when your application is compiled to JavaScript, the browser renders them just like a traditional web page, without requiring a single plugin or even the JRE.

The widgets in GWT give you programmatic control over well-defined user interface elements. Some of the widgets wrap the standard HTML tags, such as `img` for images and anchors for links, along with the controls that forms use, such as buttons and file upload boxes. You can also use more complex widgets not available through HTML tags, such as the `Tree` widget to display a tree control that you would typically see in desktop applications.

The toolkit also includes **panels**—widgets that assist with the layout of your application's interface. Panels follow strict rules for the arrangement of their child widgets so they look the same across all browsers.

It's important to note that widgets in GWT don't explicitly try to look like a desktop application; instead, they integrate well with the browser and aim to provide an experience familiar to users. In particular, a browser's history mechanism lets you handle the back and forward buttons and links naturally. Also, the application can integrate with any part of an existing HTML page, letting the application still look like a web page and while taking advantage of the vertical space that users expect to be available.

Getting Better Performance with Asynchronous Communication

Ajax applications improve web server performance by holding application state and relieving the server of this task. This means that instead of loading a new web page for each action, Ajax applications can execute several actions together on the client side and submit data as a batch only when necessary. They can also incrementally load data as the user browses through the interface instead of loading the entire dataset when the web page loads.

GWT provides an HTTP library to send and retrieve data from a server asynchronously, as well as an RPC implementation that connects to a Java servlet and makes invoking methods on the server as easy as making a local method call.

Providing Interoperation Through Web Standards and Web Services

The toolkit doesn't try to be a framework that you build applications on; it aims to be a set of tools that dramatically improve your ability to make Ajax applications. Part of accomplishing this involves leveraging the currently existing web standards and web services. Instead of committing to one technology, GWT's tools allow you to interoperate with any technology.

In particular, GWT provides JSON and XML libraries that let you translate between raw XML or JSON data and their corresponding library objects. GWT provides a way to connect your applications' layout and widgets to CSS to leverage this great styling technology and its wealth of graphic designer expertise. The toolkit lets you integrate with other existing JavaScript libraries by providing the JavaScript Native Interface (JSNI), a way to directly interact with JavaScript from Java and vice versa.

Speeding Development Using Java Tools

Perhaps GWT's best trick is its ability to bring real software engineering to Ajax application development without requiring any new plugin or JRE to be deployed to the clients. You can use all of the development tools for building Java applications to also create Ajax applications with GWT. These tools include IDEs like Eclipse, which lets you write your code and get immediate feedback about errors, compile your code to catch bugs before running the application, and debug your code by stepping through your application and inspecting variables as it runs. You can leverage JUnit to perform test-first development, where you write your test before you write the code to fulfill the test, and Ant to automate compilation and deployment.

The compile step also allows further enhancements to your application and its development process. For example, during the compilation step new code can be generated, reducing the amount of code you need to write manually. You can use this technique to generate code to automatically handle serialization of Java objects for GWT-RPC and to bundle several images into one image, thereby reducing HTTP round trips and decreasing application load time with the `ImageBundle` feature. The compilation process also provides a translation step where your code can be optimized by removing functions that aren't used, which reduces the size of the download. These types of optimizations would be much more difficult with regular Ajax applications built directly with JavaScript. The GWT team is also actively working on improving the compiler. You can easily add performance improvements available in new versions of the compiler to your application by simply upgrading to a new GWT version. For example, with GWT release 1.4 a simple recompile resulted in compiled JavaScript code that was 20 percent smaller than the same application compiled with GWT release 1.3. A smaller application size means the application loads faster in the client's browser.

Evaluating Your Background

Now that you know how the Google Web Toolkit fits into the web landscape, let's consider how your background fits with GWT. Although using GWT is fairly easy, there are several prerequisites to using it—and they may not be what you think. The following distinctions can help you understand the range of professionals who may find GWT useful. The most interesting thing about this discussion is that developers who specialize *less* in web technologies may find it easier to use the toolkit. Read these descriptions and see how you fit into these categories.

Web Designers

You build web sites and specialize in making them look good. You're interested in the Google Web Toolkit because it has the potential to add great Google-like[3] features to future projects. You're likely to have an understanding of popular web technologies like CSS, JavaScript, HTML, and Flash.

What to expect: You're likely to find using GWT very much unlike most things you've done before. However, you should be glad to know that GWT applications are styled entirely using CSS. Building Ajax application logic may seem complex, as you'll need to understand Java and object-oriented development first. You should learn about Java, possibly with one or more tutorials available at http://java.sun.com/docs/books/tutorial/. You should also familiarize yourself with an IDE like Eclipse. Also, Chapter 4 has several sections on using Eclipse to build applications with GWT.

Web Site Developers

You build web sites and know server-side programming like PHP, Rails, or JSP. You understand how traditional web applications work, including client-side technologies like HTML forms and JavaScript.

What to expect: Using the Google Web Toolkit is unlike most things you've done before, since the logic to build interfaces is not template based and is run on the client instead of being generated on the server. However, your understanding of client-server programming will come in handy, and you will find client-side programming with GWT easier than a web designer would.

---

3. Google first started pushing their applications forward with Ajax and set some standards as to how an Ajax application should behave. For example, Google Maps, Gmail, and Google Docs all have a simple interface that is responsive with asynchronous data updates.

Ajax Developers

You build web sites that can be classified as Ajax applications. You have a solid understanding of JavaScript and asynchronous programming techniques, and you may have used other Ajax frameworks.

What to expect: You may find it difficult to drop some of your JavaScript coding techniques in exchange for Java techniques. However, if you really feel the need to use JavaScript, GWT makes it easy with its JavaScript Native Interface. Your (mostly likely) intimate knowledge of document object model (DOM) and DHTML user interface development will help you understand how the GWT widgets are constructed and allow you to easily build custom GWT widgets.

Web Application Developers

You build web applications with more advanced server-side technology like J2EE, Swing, JSF, or ASP.NET. You probably have a little less understanding of client-side web technologies than web site and Ajax developers.

What to expect: You have the background to understand the benefits of quality software engineering tools and techniques in application development. However, you are familiar with thin clients, where the server generates the application's view. GWT lets you have a looser coupling between client and server with a heavier client. Thus, the server does less work and performs better. You may need to learn about user interface programming with GWT. It is not declarative like HTML, but more like AWT in Java or Windows Forms development in .NET, although its use of cascading style sheets for style information may be new to you.

Desktop Application Developers

You build applications that run on the desktop and that have rich responsive interfaces. You use object-oriented languages like .NET, C++, and Java and understand concepts like events, multithreading, and Model-View-Controller (MVC) design.

What to expect: Learning GWT should be easy for you, as it is designed to work the way you've worked in the past. The same skills you've learned to manage complex UIs also apply to GWT applications. You will learn how to build web applications with familiar tools and a familiar environment. However, you'll need to be aware of the restrictions of browser-based applications compared to desktop applications. Also, you'll need to understand how to use cascading style sheets to format your application.

The Importance of Application Development Skills

If your experience is with the web standards JavaScript and HTML, you may feel that GWT does not leverage them much (the web standard used extensively for GWT applications is CSS). In fact, you don't need to know much about JavaScript and HTML to use GWT. The real prerequisites are object-oriented application development methodologies.

So does this mean GWT doesn't use web technologies? Well, that's not entirely true. It's actually built on top of web technologies, and that's part of why the toolkit is so powerful.[4] However, the application developer using the toolkit doesn't directly use the web technologies, and therefore doesn't need to specialize in their intricate details. GWT hides the web technologies from the developer—unless you need them—and uses an abstraction as a familiar application framework in the Java language.

This may not seem to make much sense at first glance. Why would Google release a *web* toolkit for making web applications that doesn't utilize the web technology skills of the seemingly infinite number of web developers? Besides, browsers are starting to converge on their support for web standards, web developers have become familiar with any differences, the web is thriving, and Java had its chance on web pages as an applet but never caught on. The answer is threefold.

First, we are spoiled by desktop applications. These applications run locally on our computer and are relatively fast, responsive, and visually

---

4. You may see web technologies as poor technology and not a likely source of why GWT is powerful. The power, however, comes from support in modern browsers and many operating systems. Applications built on this technology can be easily deployed to more computers than applications built on any other technology.

rich. Traditional web technologies were built to create documents and not applications, so the web has an inherent document feel. It takes a lot of effort to make desktop-like user interfaces with these technologies. GWT provides a framework of widgets modeled after desktop application widgets. These widgets help create web applications that behave more like desktop applications and act less like documents. Okay, you may be thinking, this is exactly what Java applets did. And I'm sure you can remember the distinct look of Java applets on web pages, their slow loading times, and the confined boxes they would render in. However, because GWT is based on the same web technologies used to create traditional web pages, the feel is far different from a Java applet. Also, the applications can interact with the entire web page and blend in with the style of traditional sites.

Second, traditional web pages have a communication model that is tedious for applications. The web uses HTTP, a web protocol that communicates between Internet clients and servers. The basic method of HTTP is GET. Web browsers call GET on a web server and receive a web page back. This is how the web works over and over: getting a page at a time. Web sites have advanced from this document repository type of model to become more like applications by sending parameters to the server with the GET method so a dynamically generated document can be returned. This is more like an application because the result depends on user input, similar to a desktop application, but it can still be considered a traditional web application. A **traditional web application** can be defined as a web application that requires a full page refresh (another GET) with each user action. Solutions to this problem make traditional web applications act more responsive. The most widely implemented solution to do this, Ajax, uses a JavaScript object that asynchronously communicates with the server in the background, receives new information, and updates the page on the client without causing a full refresh. Ajax applications actually come very close to matching the behavior of desktop applications and thus have become very popular. However, it's stretching HTTP and JavaScript further than they were originally intended, and as a result the development becomes fairly complex. The Google Web Toolkit uses Ajax for its server communication but abstracts the complexity away from the developer with a friendly API.

Third, application development and JavaScript don't mix well. In general, Ajax applications have been successful, but the major downside is that Ajax has evolved out of technologies made for web pages, which typically have more content than code. Ajax applications suffer from a code management problem. The applications require more JavaScript code than any web page, and JavaScript lacks the code organization tools that most modern application development languages have. JavaScript development needs a lot of discipline (the downside of older application languages like C). This reliance on code discipline can be risky and error prone. GWT generates JavaScript code from Java code, allowing you to develop and debug well-organized frameworks in an established application development language.

The traditional application developer may suggest using nonweb technologies for client-server development. These frameworks exist and have had time to mature, but they lack web technologies as a foundation. Cascading style sheets, which provide a simple and centralized way to style visual elements, have matured quickly and are well known and well documented. The HTML document object model provides a way to dynamically manipulate visual elements and is also well known and documented. Applications using these technologies usually look quite a bit better, since designers find their styling technologies easier to use. In fact, the technologies have been moving to the desktop. Windows XP uses them in several places instead of the standard Windows controls (look at add/remove programs). Being a standard is a big plus: They are supported across browsers and operating systems, and they don't require a framework to be installed (like .NET Framework and JRE). Nearly every computer already has a modern web browser installed. In a sense, the browser is the new OS and the Google Web Toolkit is the compiler.

The case for GWT will be made in the long run. Ajax has already proven to be a good technological foundation for many applications, and GWT will help increase the quality of these applications as they become more complex. In the short term, you just need to learn how to use GWT to build an Ajax application. Fortunately, it's easy to get started.

A Quick Tutorial

The best way to get a feel for building applications with GWT is to run through a quick high-level view of building a simple application. This section shows you how to build an Ajax application, including how to start a

GWT project, customize the generated code, create a dynamic interface, and load data asynchronously from a server. The application we'll build, called Hangman, provides an interface to play a game which involves guessing a word. You have a limited number of guesses, and if they run out, you lose. If you guess the word before they run out, you win.

Starting a GWT Project

To use GWT you need to have Java Development Kit (JDK) version 1.4 or later installed on your machine. You can check to see if you have the proper version installed by running `javac -version` from a command prompt or terminal window, as shown in Figure 1-1.

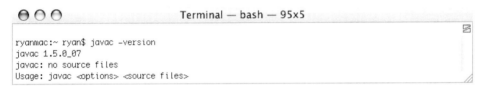

Figure 1–1.   Checking the version of the JDK installed

If you don't have at least JDK 1.4, you can download the JDK from the Sun Developer Network site at http://java.sun.com/javase/downloads.

You also need to have the Google Web Toolkit SDK installed on your machine. You can find this at http://code.google.com/webtoolkit/download.html.

The toolkit ZIP file is approximately 13MB. After you download it, extract the file to your preferred installation directory (no installer needed). You should add the installation directory to your path variable to make calling GWT's scripts easy from any directory. On Windows, you can do this by going to **Control Panel > System > Advanced > Environment Variables** and adding the installation path to the `PATH` variable. On OS X and Linux, you can add the path to the `PATH` variable using the `set` command or by setting the variable in a startup script. For example, as shown in Figure 1-2, I set the path variable on OS X in my .profile file in my home directory. Setting the path variable lets you execute the GWT scripts without specifying their full path, as illustrated in Figure 1-3.

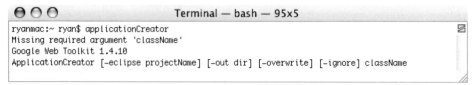

Figure 1–2.   Adding GWT to the `PATH` variable on OS X

```
ryanmac:~ ryan$ applicationCreator
Missing required argument 'className'
Google Web Toolkit 1.4.10
ApplicationCreator [-eclipse projectName] [-out dir] [-overwrite] [-ignore] className
```

Figure 1–3.   Running the `applicationCreator` script without specifying a path

To start using GWT to build an application, we first need to create a new project. The project is going to be for a Hangman Ajax application, so we'll use **Hangman** for the project name. Figure 1-4 shows creating the application's directory and then running GWT's `applicationCreator` script to generate the required files.

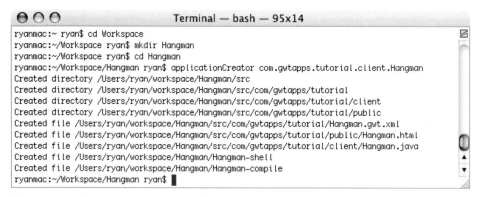

Figure 1–4.   Creating a new project called Hangman with `applicationCreator`

As shown in Figure 1-4, we ran the following command to generate these files:

```
applicationCreator com.gwtapps.tutorial.client.Hangman
```

The argument is the full Java path name for our GWT application. (If you're not already familiar with Java, you can learn about referencing Java

resources by looking at http://java.sun.com/docs/codeconv/html/
CodeConventions.doc8.html.) The Java path maps directly to a path in the
file system, as you can see in Figure 1-4. This technique helps you organize
your code into packages.

At this point the application is ready to run. GWT supports two run
modes: You can run the application in GWT's hosted browser using the
generated Hangman shell script, which is the method you use to test and
debug your application, or you can use the generated Hangman compile
script to compile the application to JavaScript and run it in any browser.
The **GWT hosted mode** runs your application in an environment controlled by GWT instead of the browser, allowing you to view log and error
messages and debug your application within a Java environment. This
contrasts to running your compiled application inside a browser as Java-
Script, where you rely on JavaScript error messages and there isn't debugging support. When you run the application in hosted mode using the
Hangman shell script, you see a GWT shell window that displays errors
and other logging messages, as illustrated in Figure 1-5, and a hosted
browser window loading the generated application, as shown in Figure 1-6.

That's all you need to do to start a GWT application project. You'll see in
Chapter 4 how you can speed up development by starting a project in an
IDE like Eclipse.

Figure 1–5. The GWT shell window

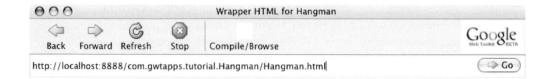

Hangman

This is an example of a host page for the Hangman application. You can attach a Web Toolkit module to any HTML page you like, making it easy to add bits of AJAX functionality to existing pages without starting from scratch.

Click me

http://localhost:8888/com.gwtapps.tutorial.Hangman/Hangman.html

Figure 1–6.   The hosted browser window

Customizing a Generated Application

To customize the generated application, we need to look at two of the generated files. The first, the host HTML page, acts as the starting point for your GWT application. When loaded into a browser, it includes the JavaScript that starts the application. In this case, the host HTML file, called Hangman.html, is located in `com/gwtapps/tutorial/public`. The contents of the file should look similar to the following:

```
<html>
   <head>
      <title>Wrapper HTML for Hangman</title>
      <style>
         body,td,a,div,.p{font-family:arial,sans-serif}
         div,td{color:#000000}
         a:link,.w,.w a:link{color:#0000cc}
         a:visited{color:#551a8b}
         a:active{color:#ff0000}
      </style>
      <script language='javascript'
         src='com.gwtapps.tutorial.Hangman.nocache.js'></script>
   </head>
   <body>
      <iframe src="javascript:''" id="__gwt_historyFrame"
         style="width:0;height:0;border:0"></iframe>
```

```
    <h1>Hangman</h1>

    <p>
       This is an example of a host page for the Hangman application.
       You can attach a Web Toolkit module to any HTML page you like,
       making it easy to add bits of AJAX functionality to existing pages
       without starting from scratch.
    </p>

    <table align=center>
       <tr>
          <td id="slot1"></td><td id="slot2"></td>
       </tr>
    </table>
  </body>
</html>
```

As you probably noticed, this looks like a typical HTML file. The HTML contents are responsible for most of you see when the hosted mode browser ran. You can see the Hangman title in a header tag and the paragraph with the explanation. The head section contains the `title` tag that places a title in the browser window's caption. A `style` tag holds CSS codes used to style the application, and a `script` tag loads the application source. You can see that the button in the browser does not have a matching tag in the body of the HTML. The button, which is part of the generated GWT application, attaches itself to tags within this file based on the `td` tag IDs.

The second important generated file is the Java file, which acts as the entry point to the application. This file, Hangman.java, is located in `com/gwtapps/tutorial/client/`. The generated code in this file should look like this:

```
/**
 * Entry point classes define <code>onModuleLoad()</code>.
 */
public class Hangman implements EntryPoint {

  /**
   * This is the entry point method.
   */
  public void onModuleLoad() {
    final Button button = new Button("Click me");
    final Label label = new Label();
```

```
button.addClickListener(new ClickListener() {
  public void onClick(Widget sender) {
    if (label.getText().equals(""))
      label.setText("Hello World!");
    else
      label.setText("");
  }
});

// Assume that the host HTML has elements defined whose
// IDs are "slot1" and "slot2". In a real app, you probably would not want
// to hard-code IDs. Instead, you could, for example, search for all
// elements with a particular CSS class and replace them with widgets.
//
RootPanel.get("slot1").add(button);
RootPanel.get("slot2").add(label);
  }
}
```

Notice that the `Hangman` class implements GWT's `EntryPoint` interface and its `onModuleLoad` method. You can build your interface and initialize your application with this method, which the application loads into the browser. The generated code creates `Button` and `Label` widgets and adds them to the `td` tags with the IDs `slot1` and `slot2`. It also adds a `ClickListener` to the button to handle a click event by changing the text in the `Label` widget. For now, concentrate on the concept and don't worry about these details; you'll learn about the `RootPanel` class, widgets, and handling events in Chapter 2.

Creating a Dynamic Interface

Next, we'll slim down the HTML host file to have one `div` tag that we'll connect to from Java code:

```
<html>
  <head>
    <title>Hangman</title>
    <style>
      body,td,a,div,.p{font-family:arial,sans-serif}
      div,td{color:#000000}
      a:link,.w,.w a:link{color:#0000cc}
      a:visited{color:#551a8b}
      a:active{color:#ff0000}
    </style>
```

```
    <script language='javascript'
        src='com.gwtapps.tutorial.Hangman.nocache.js'></script>
</head>
<body>
    <!-- OPTIONAL: include this if you want history support -->
    <iframe src="javascript:''" id="__gwt_historyFrame"
        style="width:0;height:0;border:0"></iframe>
    <h3>Hangman</h3>
    <div id="hangman"></div>
</body>
</html>
```

Notice that the body of the HTML has a `div` tag with the ID `hangman`. In the Java code we need to attach the Hangman application's user interface elements to this `hangman` tag. First, however, we need to decide what the interface will look like. If you're not familiar with the game, here's how it works. Players try to guess a phrase letter by letter. Each time the player guesses a letter that isn't in the phrase, the program adds one limb to a stick figure being hanged (apologies for the somewhat gruesome example). To win, you need to guess all of the letters in the phrase before the stick figure is fully drawn.

The interface needs a row of buttons that can be pressed to guess a letter, an image that can change based on the number of wrong guesses, and a label to display the phrase being guessed. Figure 1-7 shows a mockup of what the interface should look like.

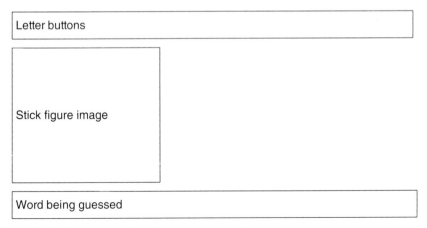

Figure 1–7. The layout of the Hangman application

We will use GWT to build this layout and place it inside the `div` tag with the `hangman` ID. To accomplish this we'll use one GWT widget for each of the boxes in Figure 1-7, and we can change the implementation in the `Hangman.java` file to the following:

```
public class Hangman implements EntryPoint {
    private FlowPanel letters = new FlowPanel();
    private Label wordLabel = new Label();
    private Image image = new Image();

    public void onModuleLoad() {
        //create interface
        RootPanel hangman = RootPanel.get("hangman");
        hangman.add(letters);
        hangman.add(image);
        hangman.add(wordLabel);
    }
}
```

We've created three widgets. The `letters` widget uses a `FlowPanel` and is added first. As mentioned earlier, a panel in GWT is a type of widget that can hold other widgets. A panel usually dictates a formal layout over its child widgets. For a `FlowPanel`, the internal layout is very similar to HTML. When we add child widgets in this case, they will create one button for each letter and flow from left to right; when there is no more horizontal space, the buttons will wrap to the next line. The `Image` widget wraps HTML's `img` tag and can display a single image. We'll use the same `Image` widget to switch between the stick figure drawings. The third and final widget, an instance of `Label`, just displays text.

You could run the application at this point, but we haven't added anything into the widgets so the browser would just display an empty page. So let's add a `startGame` method to the `Hangman` class and call the method from the `onModuleLoad` method. This new method sets up the state for the interface for starting a new game. We want the `startGame` method to be a separate method from the `onModuleLoad` method so users can start a new game without restarting the application. The following code sets up the initial game interface:

```
public void onModuleLoad() {
    //create interface
    RootPanel hangman = RootPanel.get("hangman");
    hangman.add(letters);
```

```
    hangman.add(image);
    hangman.add(wordLabel);

    startGame();
}

public void startGame(){
    //add letter buttons
    letters.clear();
    for( char letter = 'A'; letter <= 'Z'; letter++ ){
        final Button button = new Button(Character.toString(letter));
        button.addClickListener( new ClickListener(){
            public void onClick( Widget sender ){
                button.setEnabled(false);
                guess( button.getText().charAt(0) );
            }
        });
    letters.add( button );
    }
    //set initial image
    image.setUrl("hm1.gif");
}
```

The startGame method has a loop over each letter in the alphabet to create one Button widget per letter. The letter is set as the label on the button. We added a ClickListener to the button to handle the event when a user clicks it. Inside the ClickListener's onClick method the button is disabled so users can't select the same letter twice by mistake. Then the onClick method calls a method named guess to handle a letter guess from the user. In the remainder of the startGame method the Image widget's drawing is initialized to hm1.gif. We can use a simple pattern to reference new images when the user makes wrong guesses. For example, the next image after one wrong guess will be hm2.gif, the next hm3.gif, and so on.

Figure 1-8 shows the interface at this point with the letter buttons and the initial image.

The following code implements the rest of the game logic for this application:

```
private final int MAX_GUESSES = 6;
private int misses;
private char[] word;
private char[] visibleWord;
```

```
//set up a new word to guess
public void setWord( String newWord ){
    word = newWord.toUpperCase().toCharArray();
    visibleWord = new char[word.length];
    for( int i=0; i<word.length; i++ ){
        if( word[i] != ' ' )
            visibleWord[i]='_';
        else
            visibleWord[i]=' ';
    }
    wordLabel.setText( new String(visibleWord) );
}

//handle a guess from the user
public void guess( char letter ){
    boolean badGuess = true;
    boolean wordFinished = true;

    //check for matches for this letter
    for( int i=0; i<word.length; i++ ){
        if( word[i]==letter ){
            isibleWord[i] = letter;
            badGuess = false;
        }
        else if( visibleWord[i]=='_'){
            wordFinished = false;
        }
    }
    wordLabel.setText( new String(visibleWord) );

    if( wordFinished ){
        Window.alert( "Congratulations, you got the answer!" );
        startGame();
    }
    else if( badGuess ){
        misses++;
        image.setUrl("hm"+Integer.toString(misses+1)+".gif");
        if( misses == MAX_GUESSES ){
            Window.alert(
                "You ran out of guesses! The answer is "+ new String(word));
            startGame();
        }
    }
}
```

Notice the line in the guess method near the end when a bad guess has been made: the URL for the next image is calculated from the number of missed guesses. Figure 1-9 shows the seven images the application will use.

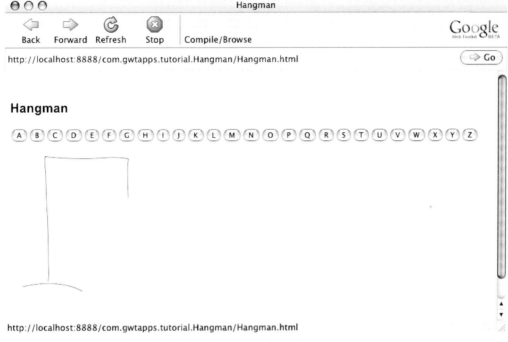

http://localhost:8888/com.gwtapps.tutorial.Hangman/Hangman.html

Figure 1-8.   User interface with the letter buttons and initial image

Figure 1-9.   The seven stick figure images

Using Asynchronous HTTP

So far we've set up an interface for this Ajax application using GWT widgets and declared some extra logic that makes the game work, but we haven't created the source of the game's words. This is a good opportunity to test loading data asynchronously from the server, which is one of the primary tasks of Ajax applications. GWT provides multiple ways to load data from the server, including asynchronous HTTP modules and an RPC module, along with different ways to parse structured data (e.g., JSON and XML). For this application we'll asynchronously load data from the server by using the `com.google.gwt.user.client.HTTPRequest` class, which is a simplified way to make asynchronous HTTP requests compared to GWT's HTTP module.

On the server we'll place a text file called `movies.txt` that contains a list of movies. Here is a sample of the file's contents:

```
The Godfather
The Shawshank Redemption
Pulp Fiction
Schindler's List
Casablanca
The Empire Strikes Back
The Lord of the Rings
One Flew Over the Cuckoo's Nest
...
```

We can use each movie listed in this file as a different phrase for the Hangman application. To get this data into the application, the `HTTPRequest`'s `asyncGet` method needs to be called with the file name as the first parameter. The second parameter needs to be an implementation of the `ResponseTextHandler` interface. After the application calls the `asyncGet` method, the `HTTPRequest` class requests the file from the server and the application code resumes executing in the client. When the server responds, the `HTTPRequest` class calls the `onCompletion` method in your `ResponseTextHandler` interface with the file contents as a parameter. Adding the following code to the `onModuleLoad` method of the `Hangman` class implements the asynchronous loading of the `movies.txt` file:

```java
private String[] words;

public void onModuleLoad() {

    //create interface
    RootPanel hangman = RootPanel.get("hangman");
    hangman.add(letters);
    hangman.add(image);
    hangman.add(wordLabel);

    //load words
    HTTPRequest.asyncGet("movies.txt", new ResponseTextHandler(){
        public void onCompletion(String responseText) {
            words = responseText.split("\n");
```

```
        startGame();
    }
  });
}
```

Notice that we added an array of strings as a field on the class. The `String.split()` method creates the array of strings from the file's contents, and uses a line break to denote where to split the string. In the `startGame` method we just need to randomly select one of the phrases from the `words` array:

```
setWord(words[Random.nextInt(words.length)]);
```

That's all that needs to be done! We've created a simple Ajax application with a dynamic interface and with data that's asynchronously loaded from the server. The final application should look like Figure 1-10 in the hosted mode browser.

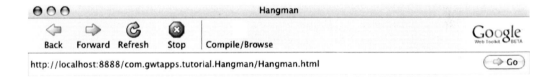

Figure 1-10. The finished application

Overview of Toolkit Packages

Although GWT's main advantage comes from using the Java language and its tools to build web clients on web-standard technology, you'll also appreciate its sizeable library of Java packages. The goal of these packages is the same as the purpose of the entire toolkit—to assist you in building dynamic browser-based applications—and they do a great job at this. This section briefly explores the GWT library. For more details, see Chapter 2 for user interfaces and Chapter 3 for server communication.

The library packages are in the `gwt-user.jar` file, which is located in the GWT installation directory. If you're not familiar with a **JAR** file, think of it as similar to a ZIP file for Java libraries: a file that contains a directory structure with many types of files, typically including compiled Java class files. All GWT projects require this file to run in hosted mode, because the JAR file contains a lot of the code that GWT applications are based on. When you set up your project or generate the scripts to run your project, this JAR file will be in the classpath. Since the GWT `applicationCreator` script sets up the classpath for you automatically, you don't have to worry much about this JAR file other than knowing that the GWT library code is in it. Even when you deploy your application to be used in a web browser, you don't need to include this file. GWT's compilation step compiles your code as well as any code that you've used from this library to JavaScript. GWT ensures that when your application is deployed and running in the browser, its only dependencies are web standards supported by all popular browsers, including Firefox, Internet Explorer, Safari, and Opera.

The `gwt-user.jar` file is a good place to start to look at the entire library that comes with GWT. Figure 1-11 shows the folder structure for the `gwt-user.jar` file for GWT 1.4.

In this directory structure you can see some of the major packages for the GWT library. The packages can be divided into five categories: user interface, server calls, data formats, JRE emulation, and utility. Figure 1-12 illustrates how the GWT library divides its functionality.

The packages in the user interface category, probably the biggest and most used category, deal with building and managing a dynamic user interface. Two packages contain the classes that help build user interfaces.

Figure 1–11.   The `gwt-user.jar` file's folder structure

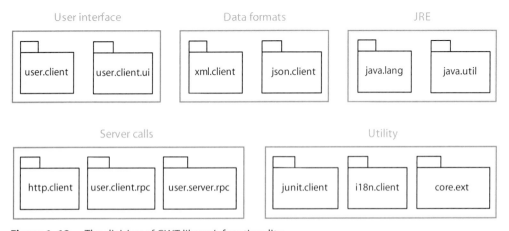

Figure 1–12.   The division of GWT library's functionality

- `com.google.gwt.user.client`

  This package provides basic access to a web browser's API for dynamically programming a web page, as well as a few other helper classes to
  access basic browser functionality. The DOM class in this package
  allows direct editing of a web document through its document object
  model. GWT widgets and panels, which are part of the next library in
  this list, use this library to construct themselves. You can also use this
  library to create custom widgets.

- `com.google.gwt.user.client.ui`

  In this package the toolkit prescribes a framework for building user
  interfaces that is very similar in design to Java's Abstract Window Toolkit (AWT). The package does a great job of helping to create and use
  dynamic and reusable user interface components. In this book we will
  build interfaces using this framework.

A second category of packages, server calls, helps us make remote calls to a server. These packages contain classes that help GWT applications communicate with the server.

- `com.google.gwt.http.client`

  This HTTP package creates a powerful browser-independent wrapper around the `XMLHttpRequest` object, which Ajax applications use for asynchronous communication.

- `com.google.gwt.user.client.rpc` and
  `com.google.gwt.user.server.rpc`

  These packages give applications the capability to communicate with the server through remote procedure calls. This library uses RPC communication relay calls from a Java-based interface to our server without requiring us to think about the protocol details. It also uses the web browser's `XMLHttpRequest` JavaScript object for its communication.

These two categories of packages cover the main two areas of functionality, dynamic user interfaces and asynchronous server communication, needed in a library to support an Ajax application. If you just want to create a dynamic interface, you only need the first set of libraries; if you just require asynchronous server communication, you only need the second set of libraries. You don't need to worry about selecting only the libraries you need. The GWT compiler knows which libraries you use in your application and is smart enough to only compile the code you need to JavaScript. This makes your application code as small as possible when you distribute it. This is another advantage of using the toolkit instead of other JavaScript frameworks; you wouldn't have the capability to reduce the libraries' size with the same level of granularity.

Let's continue looking at the available packages. The third category of packages provides your application with the capability to parse and construct data formats.

- `com.google.gwt.xml.client`

  This XML package gives your application the capability to parse an XML document and iterate over its contents through a document object model. You can also use this to construct a document object model and generate an XML document. Using this package with the

HTTP package allows you to send and receive XML documents to and from a server.

- `com.google.gwt.json.client`

  This JSON package is similar to the XML package, except the format is JSON instead of XML. JSON is a hierarchical data format similar to XML but lighter in weight (smaller). This library allows you to generate and parse JSON data.

The JRE emulation category contains a subset of the Java Runtime Environment library to assist with common programming tasks, including basic Java types, exceptions, and collections. The Java language comes with many libraries that assist in building many types of applications. Instead of creating more new libraries, GWT emulates two of the most often used libraries in the JRE. Emulating these libraries has the advantage of providing classes that developers may already be familiar with. It is considered emulation because the JRE classes are not used when a GWT application is deployed. Instead, the GWT compiler replaces usage of the JRE classes with equivalent JavaScript code.

- `java.lang`

  This package contains basic Java classes such as `Integer` and `String`.

- `java.util`

  The utility package provides many of the basic collection classes available with Java, including `Maps`, `Lists`, and `Sets`.

The final category of packages is a set of miscellaneous but important utility classes.

- `com.google.gwt.junit.client`

  This JUnit package provides classes to assist in writing unit tests for your application using JUnit.

- `com.google.gwt.i18n.client`

  GWT provides internationalization support, and this package provides classes to help access it.

- `com.google.gwt.core.ext`

  This extension package provides classes that help you extend the GWT compiler.

Note that these packages are entirely optional. You can choose any combination of packages to use in your application, and the GWT compiler ensures that only the code used is included in your compiled application. You aren't limited to using only the packages that ship with the toolkit; you can also include third-party libraries for use with GWT to extend your application's functionality. For example, the Gadget Desktop application in Chapter 6 uses the Google Gears GWT library to support integration with Google's local persistency browser plugin. However, I think you will find that the GWT library gives you substantial building blocks to build Ajax applications without using third-party packages.

Overview of GWT Applications

This book takes an application-centric view to using GWT. Often developers use Ajax as an addition to traditional document-based web pages. This is a perfectly viable use of Ajax, but you can use GWT to help solve problems with building larger complex Ajax applications. It does this well, and lets you develop Ajax applications that reach the complexity of desktop applications.

The rest of the chapters in Part I of this book provide an overview of GWT and how to use it effectively in your applications. The chapters in Part II describe how to build five different types of applications with GWT. Each application illustrates different ways to use GWT to interoperate with the web, and each also follows a different application pattern.

Common Application Patterns

This book uses five application patterns:

- The **Container** pattern is used for applications that have a plugin-like structure to support many smaller utility-like applications.
- The **Aggregator** pattern is used for applications that combine several usually discrete sets of data into one interface.
- The **Workspace** pattern is used for applications that provide a document and unobtrusive tools to work on it.
- The **Collaborator** pattern is used for applications that allow many users to get together and communicate.

- The **Manager** pattern is used for applications that provide an interface to access and manage a large set of data.

Sample Applications

The Gadget Desktop application in Chapter 6 follows the Container pattern. It has a flexible and dynamic user interface with drag and drop that contains several gadgets performing tasks such as downloading news through Really Simple Syndication (RSS), providing a weather report and displaying maps from Google Maps. The application illustrates how to integrate with other JavaScript libraries, such as Google Maps and Google Ajax Feed API, and how to provide client-side storage through browser cookies or Google Gears.

The sample application in Chapter 7, Multi-Search, follows the Aggregator pattern and lets you search multiple search engines using a single interface. The application illustrates how to load remote data in the client using JSON from Yahoo! Search, Google Base, Amazon Books, and Flickr.

The Blog Editor application in Chapter 8 follows the Workspace pattern and provides an interface to manage many blogs and blog entries without the typical page refreshes that blog services have with their standard interfaces. The application illustrates how to integrate with the Blogger API through a REST web service interface and how to build an HTTP proxy to bypass the browser's Same Origin policy.

In Chapter 9, the Instant Messenger application follows the Collaborator pattern and shows a way to integrate subtly with an existing web page to have its readers interact with each other through instant messages. It illustrates how to use the GWT-RPC library and how to provide an RPC-based event system where server-side events are pushed to the client.

The Database Editor application in Chapter 10 follows the Manager pattern and includes an interface to manage a large set of data for an existing traditional web application. The application illustrates how to incrementally load data from a server using action, REST, and RPC approaches. It shows how to integrate PHP scripts using the action-based approach, Ruby on Rails using a REST-based approach, and a Java servlet using GWT-RPC. It also demonstrates how you can write a code generator to automatically serialize Java objects to and from JSON and XML.

After reading these chapters and looking through the provided source code, you should have a solid understanding of how to build, manage, and maintain large complex Ajax applications using Java tools and GWT.

Summary

This chapter introduced the history behind the Google Web Toolkit, discussed application development on the web, and examined the skills required to build applications with GWT. The tutorial provided a taste of Ajax application development with GWT. The next four chapters will dig deeper into the GWT library and look at techniques that will help you effectively build applications with GWT.

2

User Interface Library Overview

The `com.google.gwt.user.client.ui` package contains classes that allow you to create dynamic user interfaces using techniques that have proven successful with other user interface frameworks such as Java's AWT. The classes in this package build upon a web browser's user interface features to provide dynamic reusable components that have the same behavior between supported browser implementations and versions. The GWT user interface library calls these components **widgets,** and they range from simple buttons and labels to more complex tab panels and tree views. Some of the widgets map directly to HTML elements that you would use in a regular web page, and some are composites of many HTML elements combined with scripting and event handling.

This book divides the different types of widgets into the following functional categories.

- **Static widgets,** which aren't very interactive, only change state as a result of some programmatic action from the application.

- **Form widgets** simply wrap the HTML elements that would typically be used for web forms, including text boxes and buttons.

- GWT provides **complex widgets,** which are new UI features for browsers using a composite of HTML tags and JavaScript event handling.

- The remaining four categories of widgets cover the panels. The **simple layout panels** and **complex layout panels** act as parents to other widgets. Each layout panel follows a unique layout pattern. The other panels,

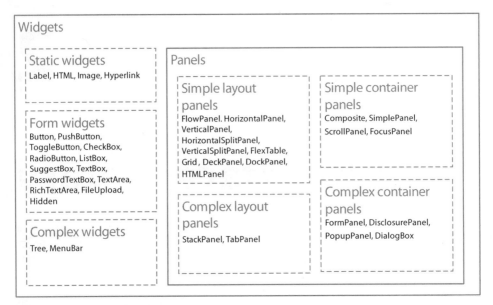

Figure 2–1.   GWT widgets by category

simple container panels and **complex container panels,** don't deal with layout but provide unique container functionality to their single child widget.

Figure 2-1 presents the widgets that come with GWT divided into their categories.

Static Widgets

These simplest types of widgets don't have any internal state or change dynamically on their own. They can still be part of a dynamic user interface in which the user interface code can change their properties and location at runtime, but they don't change as a result of user actions. These widgets include `Label`, `HTML`, `Image`, and `Hyperlink`.

Label

When you add a `Label` widget to a parent widget, it simply displays its non-HTML string. The following code shows how to add a `Label` to a container:

```
mainPanel.add( new Label("Signing in...") );
```

You instantiate the `Label` widget with the string that you want displayed. The parent container, in this case the `mainPanel` instance, determines where to place the label in the interface. The `Label` instance simply knows to fill its space. The code snippet, from the Instant Messenger sample application in Chapter 9, adds a `Label` instance to appear in the application during sign-in, as shown in Figure 2-2.

Figure 2–2.   The Signing in...label

A `Label` has a default CSS name set to `gwt-Label`, which lets you easily set the style for all labels in your application. For example, adding the following CSS to the style tag of the host HTML document or to a CSS file referenced from the host HTML document makes the label have a blue background with yellow writing:

```
.gwt-Label{ background-color:#008; color:#FF0; }
```

This change would cause the Instant Messenger application to display the "Signing in…" label, as shown in Figure 2-3 (minus the color, of course).

Figure 2–3.   The Signing in... label with different color background and text

Normally a label has its text justified to the left instead of centered as in Figure 2-3. The text is centered in this label because the parent widget has had its children's horizontal alignment set to center. We can also set the label's horizontal alignment using the class' setHorizontalAlignment method since Label implements the HasHorizontalAlignment interface. The following code sets the label's horizontal alignment to the right side:

```
Label signInLabel = new Label("Signing in...");
signInLabel.setHorizontalAlignment(HasHorizontalAlignment.ALIGN_RIGHT);
```

Using this code with the Instant Messenger sample application causes the label to be displayed on the right side, as shown in Figure 2-4.

Figure 2–4.   The label displayed on the right

Label also implements the HasWordWrap interface. Word wrap happens when the text doesn't fit in the horizontal space provided to the widget. In the default behavior, with word wrap on, words that don't fit wrap around to the next line. The setWordWrap method turns word wrap on by passing a value of true and off by passing a value of false. The two images in Figure 2-5, from the Blog Editor application in Chapter 8, first illustrate word wrap on and then word wrap off.

The Nature of
Asynchronous   view edit delete
Method Calls
The nature of asynchronous method calls requires the caller to pass
in a callback object that can be notified when an asynchronous call

The Nature of Asynchronous Method Calls   view edit delete
The nature of asynchronous method calls requires the caller to pass
in a callback object that can be notified when an asynchronous call

Figure 2–5.   Examples of word wrap on and word wrap off

A `Label` also implements the methods for the interfaces `SourcesMouseEvents` and `SourcesClickEvents` to support handling of mouse events and click events on the label (covered later in this chapter).

HTML

The `HTML` widget, another simple widget, is very similar to a `Label` but it can support and render `HTML`. In fact, it extends the `Label` widget, gaining its support for mouse events, click events, word wrap, and horizontal alignment. Using its default CSS name, `gwt-HTML`, allows you to customize CSS attributes in a fashion similar to that of the `Label` widget. In addition to `Label`'s functionality, the `HTML` widget implements the `HasHTML` interface, which has `setHTML` and `getHTML` methods to add and retrieve an HTML string. If you were to use HTML tags for `Label` in a string, it would render the tags as their textual values. The fact that `Label` disallows rendering of HTML actually makes `Label` a safer widget to use in your application. The problem with rendering HTML from a string is that you can't always be certain that it will exhibit the same behavior among browser versions, and if you don't know the value's source (it could be input by users), then it may render malicious HTML, including JavaScript. You should use GWT widgets and CSS to lay out and format your application, and to only use the `HTML` widget when necessary. If you do need to display HTML that will be generated by another application or entered by the user, then it should be checked for malicious tags.

The widget does come in handy for small pieces of HTML where creating a separate widget would be overkill. For example, in the Instant Messenger application, an `HTML` widget is used to display the user's message and name in bold:

```
HTML messageLabel = new HTML("<b>"+escapeHtml(contact.getName())+
    "</b>: "+escapeHtml(message));
```

You could also accomplish this by using a panel to hold two `Labels` and set the CSS value for the first label, representing the contact's name, to set in bold. This line of code, however, is much simpler, and we can be fairly certain the bold tag will render the same in all browsers. The message appended to the string in this case comes from the user, so proper precautions need to be made to avoid improper rendering or JavaScript injection.

Notice that the `escapeHtml` method is called for each of the strings added to the `HTML` widget. This method does not come with GWT but is essential when adding user-generated text. The implementation of this method is as follows:

```
public String escapeHtml(String maybeHtml) {
    final Element div = DOM.createDiv();
    DOM.setInnerText(div, maybeHtml);
    return DOM.getInnerHTML(div);
}
```

This code escapes any HTML characters in the string into HTML entities so they are displayed as text instead of being interpreted as tags, effectively preventing unwanted HTML rendering or script injection.

Image

The `Image` widget, another simple widget, is static just like the `Label` and `HTML` widgets. Instead of accepting a string and rendering it, the `Image` widget accepts a URL pointing to an image file and renders it. The widget wraps the `IMG` HTML tag, allowing you to use the tag as a widget in GWT's UI framework.

The Instant Messenger application in Chapter 9 uses the `Image` widget to display a user icon beside each contact name with the following code:

```
listTable.setWidget( row, 0, new Image("icon_user.gif") );
```

In this line of code the application creates the `Image` widget with a string for the image file's file name. Since the image file is not a full URL, the browser treats it as a path relative to the application's location (where the host HTML file is). The browser tries to retrieve this image from the same location as the host HTML file. You could also specify a relative path to a subdirectory:

```
listTable.setWidget(row,0, new Image("images/icon_user.gif") );
```

With this string the browser looks in the images directory under the location of the host HTML file. The URL could also be an absolute URL on the server:

```
listTable.setWidget(row,0, new Image("/images/icon_user.gif") );
```

Notice the addition of the first forward slash. This tells the browser to look on the same server as the host HTML file starting in the images directory. You could also specify the host file's server location:

```
listTable.setWidget(row,0, new Image("http://www.rdews.com/img/icon_user.gif") );
```

Regardless of the URL used, if the image file exists at the specified location, the browser renders the image. The image's container widget dictates the spot in the browser where the image appears. In the Instant Messenger application, the image appears to the left of the contact's name, as shown in Figure 2-6.

           🚹 Ryan

Figure 2–6.   The image appearing to the left of the contact's name

An `Image` widget also handles mouse and click events the same as the `Label` and `HTML` widgets since it supports the `SourcesMouseEvents` and `SourcesClickEvents` interfaces. It adds the capability to support load events through the `SourcesLoadEvents` interface. Handling the load event allows you to have code execute when the image has successfully loaded or if it fails for some reason. The following code removes the `Image` widget if it does not load properly so the broken image icon doesn't display:

```
final Image userIcon = new Image("icon_user.gif");
listTable.setWidget(row,0, userIcon );
userIcon.addLoadListener(new LoadListener() {

   public void onLoad(Widget sender) {
      //success!, do nothing
   }

   public void onError(Widget sender) {
      userIcon.removeFromParent();
   }
});
```

This code implements an instance of the LoadListener interface and its two methods. The application passes the LoadListener instance to the Image widget's addLoadListener method. When the load event occurs, the Image widget calls the appropriate method: onLoad if loading was successful or onError if loading failed. If this code looks a little foreign, don't worry; the section Event Interfaces later in this chapter explains this in more detail. At this point it is just important to understand that this functionality exists for an Image widget.

One common problem with images on HTML pages when used in a dynamic interface is that they take time to load, so the image is not visible immediately after it has been instantiated and added. This can be a little bit disorienting to users and may reduce their confidence in the application. Fortunately, the Image widget provides a static prefetch method that can be called to load an image based on its URL before it is actually used. When you add an image to the interface, the browser already has it available and this eliminates the loading delay. If you use images in your user interface, you may want to consider calling the prefetch method at the start of your application. The Instant Messenger application could prefetch the user icon like this:

```
Image.prefetch("icon_user.gif");
```

This method instantiates the image but doesn't add it to the document. This causes the browser to fetch the image. Then when the application creates an Image widget, the browser knows that this image is already available and doesn't need to load it.

Hyperlink

The Hyperlink widget is the most complex of the static widgets in that it has to handle the history and link problems with Ajax applications. The problem stems from Ajax applications running one dynamic document without refreshing the page. With traditional web applications, the link brings the user to a new document and the old one is removed from view. If this happened with an Ajax application, the application would unload and its state would be lost. The new document would replace the application, and if it had any state it would start from the beginning. This is obviously a usability problem, but it doesn't stop here—there's more. If the user, after clicking a link and arriving on a new page, did not want his Ajax application to end, he would click the back button to return to the application. However, the browser would restart the application and any progress the user had made would be lost.

GWT has taken a great step toward solving this usability issue, and it begins with the use of the `Hyperlink` widget. This widget implements a link that, when clicked, takes the user to another state within the application. Each `Hyperlink` can be a link to a specific state identified by a `String` token. As the user navigates through the application, he builds a history of states in the form of a list of tokens. The application developer must implement these states within the application and must be able to build a particular state based on its token.

This implementation works well with the back and forward buttons, since it uses the history tokens in the URL for the application. Every time the user clicks a link, the URL for the page has its token set to the token used for the `Hyperlink` widget. For example, the Multi-Search application in Chapter 7 uses the tokens as the search strings. Every time a user enters a search, the application creates a history token and forwards the browser to a new URL, which does not cause a page refresh but adds the URL to the browser history to work with the back and forward buttons. For a search for the term *GWT,* the URL for the Multi-Search application looks like this:

```
http://localhost:8888/com.gwtapps.multisearch.MultiSearch/index.html#GWT
```

If we then searched for *Java,* the URL would change to this:

```
http://localhost:8888/com.gwtapps.multisearch.MultiSearch/index.html#Java
```

Now if we click the back button, the URL would change back to the one with the GWT token, and GWT would notify our application that the *GWT* token is the current history token, and the application would know to load the search results for *GWT.*

The Instant Messenger application in Chapter 9 uses the `Hyperlink` widget for each contact name in the contact list, as shown in Figure 2-7.

The following code creates a `Hyperlink` in this application:

```
Hyperlink link = new Hyperlink( contact.getName(), contact.getName() );
```

Figure 2–7.   The `Hyperlink` widget used for contact names

This code creates a `Hyperlink` widget with the contact's name as the text for the link and the token as the contact's name. When the user clicks a contact, the current token changes to the contact name the user clicked. The application handles this token change by loading the chat window for this contact. If the user presses the back button, then the application loads the previous contact chat window.

Changes to the current token, whether invoked by clicks on a `Hyperlink` widget or by using the back and forward browser buttons, can be handled by implementing GWT's `HistoryListener` interface and its `onHistory Changed` method. To add a history listener to an application, you would call the `History.addHistoryListener` method. The following code shows how to handle a history token change in the Instant Messenger application:

```
public void onHistoryChanged( String historyToken ){
   Contact contact = contactList.getContact( historyToken );
   if( contact != null ){
      getChatWindowView( contact );
   }
}
```

As you can see, handling history token changes are fairly straightforward. This code expects the history token to be a contact name. The code tries to find the `Contact` instance for the name in the application's domain model objects. If a contact exists with a name that matches the token, then the application displays the contact's chat window.

The `Hyperlink` widget does a good job of using the browser link and history function in a way that is intuitive to users. However, this widget does not provide the capability to link to external resources. To create a link to an external resource, you need to use an HTML widget and add an anchor tag like this:

```
HTML externalLink = new HTML("<a href='http://www.rdews.com'>Ryan's Site</a>");
```

When a user clicks this link, the browser unloads the application and replaces it with the resource to which the link's URL points. If your application handles state properly using history tokens, then when a user returns by clicking the browser's back button, she will return to the application in the state where she left off.

You could also create your own external link widget using GWT's DOM class. For example, the Blog Editor application in Chapter 8 creates an external link widget to let users click on a link to view the blog or blog post hosted by an external blog service.

Form Widgets

Form widgets are simple widgets that are typically used with HTML forms. However, HTML forms follow the traditional web model where the form is submitted and the page is then refreshed with the result. Ajax applications try to eliminate this page refresh and typically submit data to a server asynchronously. The form widgets provided with GWT do not have to be used inside a HTML form and can be used in more flexible ways similar to their counterparts in desktop applications. The form widgets that come with GWT are `Button`, `CheckBox`, `RadioButton`, `ListBox`, `TextBox`, `PasswordTextBox`, `TextArea`, `FileUpload`, and `Hidden`. The 1.4 release of GWT adds several more form widgets of greater complexity, including `ToggleButton`, `PushButton`, `SuggestBox`, and `RichTextArea`.

Button

The `Button` widget wraps the HTML form input with the type button. In HTML, the `type` attribute is used on the generic `input` tag to specify the type of input. You add buttons to HTML pages using the following code:

```
<input type="button">
```

Buttons are commonly seen on forms to submit data, but with GWT you can use the button to invoke any action within your application. For example, the Multi-Search application in Chapter 7 uses a button to submit a search query similar to search buttons used for search engines, as shown in Figure 2-8.

Figure 2–8.   A Search button created using the `Button` widget

In this figure the button is on the right and does not include the search string text input. The following code shows how you can add the button to the application:

```
Button submitButton = new Button("Search");
searchPanel.add( submitButton );
```

This code creates the `Button` widget, supplying its text string for the button label and adding it to a parent container to be displayed. When a user presses the search button, the application handles the event and executes code that retrieves search results from multiple search engines. A traditional web application does this through a `form` tag that submits the form data, including the search string, to the server when the user presses the button. The server would then respond with the search results. With Ajax applications you can submit to the server asynchronously without refreshing the page. In this way you do not surround the form controls with a `form` tag, since its default behavior would be to refresh the page. Instead, your application handles the click event and uses one of GWT's server call libraries to submit a call to the server.

The `Button` widget class implements the `SourcesClickEvents` interface, which lets the application code handle click events. We can add a click listener to the button that calls a `doSearch` method for the Multi-Search application like this:

```
submitButton.addClickListener( new ClickListener(){
    public void onClick(Widget sender){
        doSearch();
    }
});
```

This widget and many of the other form widgets also support focus function-ality by implementing the `HasFocus` interface and `SourcesFocusEvents`. The events allow you to programmatically handle situations where the widget gets the keyboard focus or loses it. It's important to pay attention to focus handling when designing an interface since many users prefer to use the keyboard. We'll look at handling user interface-focused behavior later in this chapter.

`ToggleButton` and `PushButton`

The `ToggleButton` and `PushButton` widgets are two more types of but-tons in the user interface library that can be used similarly to the regular `Button` widget. A `ToggleButton` differs from a `Button` in that when it is clicked, it remains down until clicked again. A common example of this type of button is the bold button in a word processor. You click it once to turn it on and again to turn it off, toggling its state with each click. A `PushButton` acts the same as a `Button` but supports customization of its look based on its state.

Both of these buttons extend the `CustomButton` class, which provides the common functionality of displaying different button faces for different button states. A button face is simply an instance of the button's displayed content. The face can be text, HTML, or an image. Providing different faces for different button states allows you to create custom buttons that act like regular buttons. It may be tempting to create a new button from a simple image or text, but using this method usually lacks the subtleties in its states that make regular buttons very usable. A button typically can be enabled or disabled, which lets the user know when a particular command is available or not. For example, a button can display differently when a mouse hovers over it to indicate that it can be clicked, and a button can have a way to indicate to the user the button is down when it is clicked. To understand this usability issue, let's look at a regular button on Windows XP and also a hyperlink in a web page. Figure 2-9 shows three different states for a button on Windows XP. The first button illustrates the regular state, the second displays when the mouse is hovering over the button, and the third appears when the button is disabled.

Figure 2–9.   Three different states for a button

Textual buttons should exhibit similar functionality. Often web pages style their links to look different when a mouse hovers over them compared to when they have been clicked. Figure 2-10 shows three different states of a hyperlink in a web page. The first state, a regular hyperlink, has been styled to not be underlined; the second state occurs when the mouse hovers over the link and the underline appears, which signals the user that the button can be clicked; the third state displays when the link has been clicked and it's giving the user feedback that the click is working.

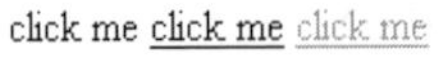

click me <u>click me</u> <u>click me</u>

Figure 2–10.   Three different states for a textual button

You can style these states for the hyperlinks using CSS, but if they're a GWT `Button` widget or just a regular button on the web page, these states are not available to be styled from CSS. This is where a `CustomButton`, either `ToggleButton` or `PushButton`, becomes useful.

The `CustomButton` implementations support six different button states. Each state can have a different button face and independent CSS styles defined. The button's content for the state's face can be text, an image, or HTML. The following list describes the six states available for a `CustomButton`.

- Button up—The idle state for a `PushButton` or the up state for a `ToggleButton`.

- Button down—The state when the mouse button is down on a `PushButton` or the down state for a `ToggleButton`.

- Button up, mouse hovering—The same as the button up state but occurring when the mouse is hovering over the button. This can be used to visually indicate to the user that the button is clickable.

- Button up, disabled—The same as the button up state but the button has been disabled with the `setDisabled` method. Often a button is grayed when in this state, which informs the user that it is not clickable.

- Button down, mouse hovering—For a `PushButton` this is the same as the button down state, since the mouse always hovers when the button is clicked. For the `ToggleButton` this is similar to the button up, mouse hovering state, since it similarly needs to inform the user that the button is clickable to return to the button up state.

- Button down, disabled—This state only occurs with the `ToggleButton`, since it can be down and disabled at the same time. A `PushButton` can't be clicked when disabled, so it can't enter this state.

At a minimum you need to have a face defined for the button up state. If you have no other faces defined, this face will be used for every state. The states follow a hierarchy to determine which face to show if one has not been defined. For example, if the button is in the button down, mouse hovering state and there is no face defined, it will use the button down face; if there is no button down face defined, it will use the button up face. Figure 2-11 shows the dependencies in this hierarchy.

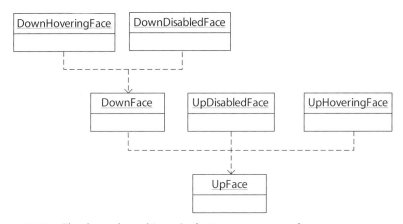

Figure 2–11. The dependency hierarchy for `CustomButton` faces

The Gadget Desktop application in Chapter 6 uses both `ToggleButtons` and `PushButtons` on each gadget's title bar. Figure 2-12 shows the title bars for gadgets. The arrow left of the title bar is a `ToggleButton`. It is in its down state in the first gadget and in the up state in the second. Notice how the image indicates the different states to the user.

Hello World

Figure 2–12. The title bar for gadgets using `ToggleButton` and `PushButton`

This application creates the `ToggleButton` like this:

```
ToggleButton minimizeButton = new ToggleButton(new Image("minimize1.gif"),
    new Image("minimize2.gif"));
```

Notice that the constructor takes two `Images`. This constructs the `ToggleButton` with one image for the up state and a different one for the down state. We could also use the `Face` class to adjust the content for each button's face. For example, the following code changes the down face for the button:

```
minimizeButton.getDownFace().setImage(new Image("minimize2.gif"));
```

You create the `PushButton` in the same way; it only differs from the `ToggleButton` in behavior.

Setting the content of these buttons for each available face with images, HTML, or text is not the only way to customize them. You can change the look of buttons for each state with CSS style names. When the button enters a state, the application attaches a new style name to it, which causes the browser to render new style information. Using style names with buttons, you can change backgrounds, borders, underlines, and more much in the same way you would for a hyperlink in a traditional web page. The style names are different for the `ToggleButton` and `PushButton` but follow a similar pattern, as you can see in Table 2-1.

Table 2–1 Style Names for `ToggleButton` and `PushButton`

Button state	ToggleButton	PushButton
Button up	gwt-ToggleButton-up	gwt-PushButton-up
Button down	gwt-ToggleButton-down	gwt-PushButton-down
Button up, mouse hovering	gwt-ToggleButton-up-hovering	gwt-PushButton-up-hovering
Button up, disabled	gwt-ToggleButton-up-disabled	gwt-PushButton-up-disabled
Button down, mouse hovering	gwt-ToggleButton-down-hovering	gwt-PushButton-down-hovering
Button down, disabled	gwt-ToggleButton-down-disabled	gwt-PushButton-down-disabled

Checkbox

The `Checkbox` widget wraps HTML's check box `input` tag. This button, much like the `Button` widget, supports focus behavior and click events, but it differs from the `Button` widget by having a state of being checked or not checked. The default is not checked, and if a user clicks it the state toggles to checked. You can programmatically set the state with the `setChecked` method by passing true for checked or false for unchecked. The source code for the Gadget Desktop application in Chapter 6, which you can find at www.gwtapps.com, has an additional To Do List gadget that uses a check box, as illustrated in Figure 2-13.

Figure 2–13.   A check box created using the `Checkbox` widget

Users can mark the check box for each item in the To Do list as completed or not. The following code creates a new `CheckBox` widget, adds it to its parent, and handles its `onClick` method:

```
final checkBox checkBox = new CheckBox();
row.setWidget(0,0, checkBox );
checkBox.addClickListener( new ClickListener(){
   public void onClick( Widget sender ){
      if( checkBox.isChecked() )
         label.addStyleName("ToDoList-Done");
      else
         label.removeStyleName("ToDoList-Done");
   }
});
```

The `onClick` method changes the label's CSS style to give it the strikethrough decoration when a user checks the `CheckBox` widget. To make things simpler, you don't need a label that is separate from the `CheckBox` widget. This example requires a separate widget because that application needs advanced editing. But if you just need a static label, you can set the text value on the `CheckBox` widget like this:

```
checkBox.setText( "check me" );
```

RadioButton

A `RadioButton` widget is the same as a `CheckBox` widget except that it belongs to a group of other `RadioButton`s and only one can be checked at a time. In a group of `CheckBox` widgets, users can check any, all, or none of them. Figure 2-14 shows an example of a radio button group that lets the user choose red, green, or blue.

○ red ◉ green ○ blue

Figure 2–14.   Radio buttons created using the `RadioButton` widget

In this example, green has been selected, but if the user clicks blue, blue is selected and green is deselected. This widget is ideal for situations where only one choice is valid. The following code implements this example:

```
RadioButton redButton = new RadioButton("colors", "red");
RadioButton greenButton = new RadioButton("colors", "green");
RadioButton blueButton = new RadioButton("colors", "blue");
panel.add( redButton );
panel.add( greenButton );
panel.add( blueButton );
```

The `RadioButton` widget extends the `CheckBox` widget, so it inherits all of the `CheckBox` widget's functionality, including the `setChecked/isChecked` methods, the focus behavior, and the client event handling.

ListBox

The `ListBox` widget in its most basic state does the same job as the `RadioButton` widget: it presents the user with a group of options of which he can only select one. The `ListBox`, however, contains all the options in one widget and has a different look than the `RadioButton` widget. In fact, it has two looks, as illustrated in Figure 2-15.

Figure 2–15.   The two different looks for the `ListBox` widget

The first look shows the options in a drop-down box. The selected option displays in the box, and when the user clicks the down arrow button the list selection is shown. The following code shows how you can create this style of list box:

```
ListBox colorList = new ListBox();
colorList.addItem("red");
colorList.addItem("green");
colorList.addItem("blue");
panel.add( colorList );
```

The second look for the `ListBox` shows a list of options with the selected option highlighted. It doesn't have a drop-down box, but if the list contains more items than can be viewed, then the list displays a vertical scrollbar to let users scroll to other items. To create a `ListBox` like this, you simply need to set the number of items that should be visible using the `setVisibleItemCount` method:

```
colorList.setVisibleItemCount(3);
```

Like the other form widgets, the `ListBox` widget supports both focus behavior and handling change events. Change events occur when the user changes the selected item. For example, the following code handles a change event on the `ListBox` widget and displays an alert box with the user's selection:

```
colorList.addChangeListener( new ChangeListener(){
    public void onChange( Widget sender ){
        int selectedIndex = colorList.getSelectedIndex();
        String selectedColor = colorList.getItemText(selectedIndex);
        Window.alert( "you selected " + selectedColor );
    }
});
```

This code displays the selected color in the alert box by getting the selected index using the `ListBox`'s `getSelectedIndex` method and then, using the index, retrieving the text for the item using the `getItemText` method.

SuggestBox

In some situations using a `ListBox` is not practical; for example, when you need to provide users with many options (imagine scrolling through a list of 1,000 options!). A common solution employed by many Ajax applications is to provide a text box with drop-down suggestions based on the word that you type. Google employs this usability technique for their Suggest search engine. When you start to type your search, you get a drop-down list of selections, as shown in Figure 2-16.

cana	
canadian tire	1,690,000 results
canada 411	3,970,000 results
canada post	339,000,000 results
canada	613,000,000 results
canada411	859,000 results
canada's wonderland	304,000 results
canadian idol	1,600,000 results
canadian dollar	24,900,000 results
canadian passport	1,510,000 results
canada revenue agency	2,000,000 results

Figure 2–16.   The suggest box for Google's Suggest search engine

GWT 1.4 has this type of functionality through the `SuggestBox` widget. The widget provides a rich pop-up box that highlights letters typed by the user in its suggestions. It also supports scrolling through the list with the keyboard or with the mouse. You can customize the look of the `SuggestBox` through its style names, which are set for the input box, the pop-up box, all of the items, and the currently selected item.

The `SuggestBox` takes a `SuggestOracle` instance that acts as the source of the suggestions. This differs from the `ListBox` widget's implementation, which you add the list items to. This separation of the source of suggestions from the `SuggestBox` widget is because the suggestions may not be as simple as a short static list; the suggestions may need to be generated from the server side of the application. For example, consider how Google's Suggest search engine implements this type of control. It would be impossible for the browser to store all of the possible suggestions for which someone could search. Instead, the browser makes asynchronous requests to the server to get suggestions based on what the user types. The `SuggestOracle` instance provides the application developer with a way to plug into the `SuggestBox` to provide dynamic results.

GWT provides a simple implementation of `SuggestOracle`, called `MultiWordSuggestOracle`, that stores its suggestions in the browser. The following code creates a `SuggestBox` using the `MultiWordSuggest Oracle` and a list of movies:

```
String[] words = responseText.split("\n");
MultiWordSuggestOracle oracle = new MultiWordSuggestOracle();
oracle.addAll(Arrays.asList(words));
SuggestBox sb = new SuggestBox(oracle);
```

This code, modified from the Hangman application in Chapter 1, takes the array of strings, converts it to a `List`, adds it to the `MultiWord SuggestOracle`, and then creates a new `SuggestBox`. Figure 2-17 shows the result.

re|

Rear Window
Requiem for a Dream
Reservoir Dogs
The Shawshank **Redemption**

Figure 2–17. Using the `SuggestBox` to search for a movie

By default, the suggest box pop-up is not styled. You need to manually add CSS to get the type of styles shown in Figure 2-17. These styles help identify the different parts of the pop-up. The following is their CSS:

```
.gwt-SuggestBox {}
.gwt-SuggestBoxPopup { border: 2px solid #C3D9FF; background-color:#E8EEF7; }
.gwt-SuggestBoxPopup .item { }
.gwt-SuggestBoxPopup .item-selected { background-color:#C3D9FF;}
```

As mentioned before, sometimes it's not practical to have all of the possible suggestions loaded in the browser. In this case the best option is to load the suggestions from the server. This requires significantly more work by the application developer. You first need to create your own specialization of the `SuggestOracle` class implementing the `requestSuggestions` method. For example, the following specialization implements the `requestSuggestions` method to call a PHP script:

```
public class RemoteSuggestOracle extends SuggestOracle {

  public void requestSuggestions(
     final Request request, final Callback callback) {
```

```
//get the query string
String query = request.getQuery();

//request the results from the server
HTTPRequest.asyncGet("movies.php?query="+query,
    new ResponseTextHandler(){
    public void onCompletion(String responseText) {

        //send the response back to the callback
        String[] words = responseText.split("\n");
        Response response = new Response(Arrays.asList(words));
        callback.onSuggestionsReady(request, response);
    }
});
  }
}
```

This code uses the `HTTPRequest` class to make an asynchronous call to the server. It is a very basic class, and I encourage you to use the HTTP module instead of the `HTTPRequest` class since this lets you handle errors properly. However, the `HTTPRequest` class is sufficient for this illustration of a `SuggestOracle`. The code sends the query to the PHP script on the server, which most likely would look up matching strings in a database with a SQL query that could look like this:

```
mysql_query("SELECT * FROM movies WHERE name LIKE '%".$query."%'");
```

This is actually a bit of PHP calling the `mysql_query` method to send the SELECT query to the database. The query looks for rows in the `movies` table that have a `name` column which contains the query string. Note that this isn't the complete PHP code; it's important to do proper error checking, and escaping to guard against SQL injection attacks.

You can implement a `SuggestOracle` not only by using a PHP script, but also in any server-side technology using GWT-RPC, HTTP with XML, or even JSONP.

TextBox

The `TextBox` widget encapsulates HTML's input tag with type input, which is the standard way to capture relatively small portions of text from the user. The Multi-Search application in Chapter 7 uses the `TextBox` widget to capture a search string from the user (see Figure 2-8).

This application implements this widget and adds to its container quite simply:

```
TextBox searchBox = new TextBox();
searchPanel.add( searchBox );
```

In this example, the user has the option of clicking on the button to submit the search string or pressing the Enter key. To implement support for pressing Enter, we need to handle the keyboard events that the TextBox supports. The following code adds a keyboard listener to the TextBox and checks for the Enter key:

```
searchBox.addKeyboardListener(new KeyboardListenerAdapter(){
    public void onKeyPress(Widget sender,char keyCode,int modifiers){
        if(keyCode == KEY_ENTER )
            doSearch();
    }
});
```

One of the parameters on the onKeyPress method is the key code of the key that the user just pressed. You can compare this code to characters or use some of the predefined constants defined on the KeyboardListener interface, like KEY_ENTER. This code calls the doSearch method when it encounters KEY_ENTER, which the application implements to submit the user's search query to several search engines.

Like the ListBox widget, the TextBox widget also supports change events and click events by implementing the SourcesChangeEvents and SourcesClick events interfaces.

PasswordTextBox

The PasswordTextBox widget works exactly the same as the TextBox widget except its contents are hidden from the user to protect sensitive data like passwords. Figure 2-18 shows what this widget looks like in Internet Explorer.

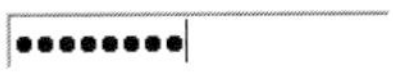

Figure 2-18. The PasswordTextBox widget's text box area

Typically this widget is used for signing into a service in combination with a `TextBox` widget for the user name and the `PasswordTextBox` widget for the password.

TextArea

The `TextArea` widget accepts text input from the user like the `TextBox` widget, but it also allows the text to span multiple lines. This widget is a better choice for larger sections of text. The Blog Editor application in Chapter 8 uses this widget to let users edit blog entries, as illustrated in Figure 2-19.

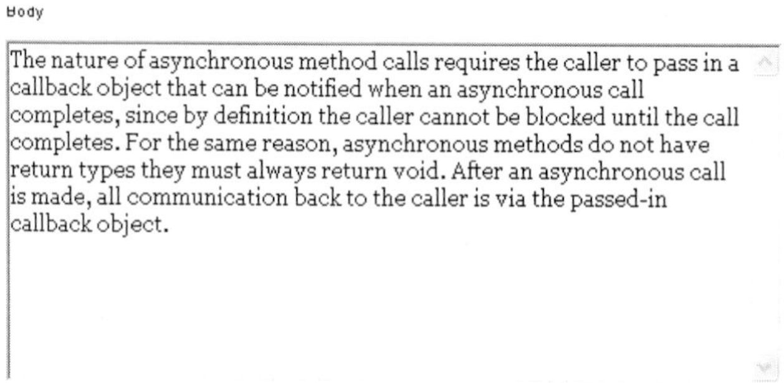

> Body
>
> The nature of asynchronous method calls requires the caller to pass in a callback object that can be notified when an asynchronous call completes, since by definition the caller cannot be blocked until the call completes. For the same reason, asynchronous methods do not have return types they must always return void. After an asynchronous call is made, all communication back to the caller is via the passed-in callback object.

Figure 2–19.   The `TextArea` widget provides a way to enter multiple lines of text

The following code adds the `TextArea` widget shown in Figure 2-19 to its container:

```
TextArea postContent = new TextArea();
postContent.setCharacterWidth(80);
postContent.setVisibleLines(20);
postPanel.add( postContent );
```

This code sets the width of the widget to 80 characters with the `setCharacterWidth` method and the height to show 20 lines with the `setVisibleLines` method. Alternatively, you can set the width and height of this widget with the `setWidth` and `setHeight` methods or the `height` and `width` properties in CSS.

This widget supports the focus behavior, click events, and change events that you've seen with the other form widgets.

RichTextArea

For a long time all text input into web applications was either plain text or marked-up text. There was no easy way to input rich text without worrying about markup, as we are familiar with in most modern word processors. Support for rich text editing unnaturally slipped into the browser starting with an Internet Explorer extension for FrontPage that allowed you to edit an HTML page. Then it was used as a rich text replacement for the textarea tag by putting the editable HTML page inside an iframe and sizing it to the size of a textarea. This rich text technique proved valuable and was eventually added to other browsers, but no implementation is exactly the same, and web developers find it extremely difficult to provide support without leveraging another mature JavaScript library that has already tackled the problem. Fortunately, the GWT 1.4 library has a rich text widget called RichTextArea that handles all of the browser differences automatically.

You can use the interface to the RichTextArea in a very similar way to the TextArea widget. It has getText and setText methods to get and set text within the control, but in the RichTextArea these methods still return plain text instead of rich text or HTML. The RichTextArea widget adds the getHTML and setHTML methods to get and set the rich text in the widget. Figure 2-20 shows how this works in the Blog Editor application discussed in Chapter 8.

In Figure 2-20 notice that the toolbar looks similar to commands in a word processor. This type of toolbar is essential for editing rich text, but it's not

Figure 2–20.   Editing a blog entry in rich text

part of the `RichTextArea` widget. The `RichTextArea` widget is simply the square text box in Figure 2-20. It is left up to the application developer to implement a toolbar. However, a fairly good toolbar called `RichText Toolbar` exists in the Kitchen Sink sample application that ships with GWT. This is the toolbar used in Figure 2-20 and the Blog Editor application.

If you need to interact more closely with the `RichTextArea`'s formatting, use its `getBasicFormatter` and `getExtendedFormatter` methods. These methods return formatters for the `RichTextArea`. Note that these methods may return `null` in some browsers. You will need to handle these cases in your code by simply not providing formatting in the browsers that fail. Most modern browsers, however, support both the basic and extended formatters.

FileUpload

The `FileUpload` widget encapsulates HTML's input tag with its type attribute set to file, which allows users to select a file from their local file system to be uploaded to the server. Browsers have strict security restrictions that disallow most interaction with the operating system, and the use of this widget is also fairly restrictive. The browser enforces a rule that only the file that the user selects can be submitted; it does not allow any programmatic way of selecting another file from the user's hard drive. Furthermore, the file is only sent to the server by the browser when the form is submitted. This means this widget has little value to an application that does not submit forms. However, GWT provides a `FormPanel` class that allows you to programmatically construct a form and asynchronously submit it to a web server without a page refresh. This is ideal for integrating with server-side scripts that were previously used with forms or for submitting files to the server in an asynchronous manner. We will look at the use of this widget in detail later in this chapter when we discuss the `FormPanel` widget.

Hidden

The `Hidden` widget also only has value when used with a `FormPanel` to submit a form asynchronously to the server. It represents a named value that will be submitted and that doesn't require the user to edit a visual representation.

Complex Widgets

Once browsers started to support JavaScript and dynamic HTML, we started seeing user interface widgets in web pages that did not have HTML tag equivalents. These widgets were created by compositing HTML tags together and handling user events through JavaScript to emulate more sophisticated widgets. With GWT you can also build these types of custom widgets, and the toolkit even comes with a few.

Tree

The `Tree` widget displays a hierarchical view of data that can be expanded and collapsed. Its behavior is based on similar tree widgets in desktop applications typically used for browsing files or outlining hierarchical data. GWT implements the tree view with HTML elements and dynamic JavaScript abstracted by an interface to support tree operations (this will be familiar to you if you have used a desktop version of a tree widget).

The `Tree` widget is best used to show an outline of hierarchical data. For example, Figure 2-21 illustrates using a `Tree` widget to show a list of databases as the first level in the hierarchy and a list of tables as the second level.

```
-  information_schema
      TRIGGERS
      USER_PRIVILEGES
      VIEWS
+  gp
   mysql
+  ppp
   test
```

Figure 2-21. The `Tree` widget shows data hierarchically

Instantiating a `Tree` widget is as simple as creating any other widget with GWT:

```
Tree treeList = new Tree();
mainPanel.add( treeList );
```

You can add data to a `Tree` widget in several ways. You can simply add string values directly to the tree:

```
treeList.addItem("first item");
treeList.addItem("second item");
treeList.addItem("third item");
```

Or you could add other widgets:

```
treeList.addItem( new Image("icon_user.gif") );
treeList.addItem( new HTML("<b>hello</b>") );
treeList.addItem( new CheckBox("check me") );
```

However, these methods only add items to the root level of the tree, which may be okay in some situations. The `Tree` widget does provide a way to add widgets to more than just the root level using `TreeItems`. You can also use these add methods to add new `TreeItem` instances. The `TreeItem` class represents one item within the tree, and its interface uses these same add methods, which support the creation of a multilevel tree. To add to the second level of the tree you would create a `TreeItem` instance, add it to the `Tree` widget, and then call the add methods on the instance to add new child items. The new items could also be `TreeItems` that have child items added to create subsequent levels in the hierarchy. For example, the following code iterates over a list of databases and their tables to create a `Tree` hierarchy similar to the `Tree` widget image in Figure 2-21:

```
for( Iterator it =d atabases.iterator(); it.hasNext();){
    Database database = (Database)it.next();
    TreeItem databaseTreeItem = new TreeItem( database.getName() );
    treeList.addItem(databaseTreeItem);
    for( Iterator it2 = database.getTable().iterator(); it2.hasNext();){
        Table table = (Table)it2.next();
        databaseTreeItem.addItem( table.getName() );
    }
}
```

Notice that the code adds the `databaseTreeItem` directly to the `treeList`'s `Tree` widget and adds the `tableTreeItem` to the `databaseTreeItem`, so that the item in the second level of the hierarchy appears beneath the database to which it belongs.

Also notice that the tree control's image displays several icons that guide the user how to use the widget. The application selected the database and table icons and displayed them as `Image` widgets. In GWT 1.3 and earlier, the `Tree` widget used the Plus and Minus icons, but they couldn't be embedded in the GWT library, so application developers had to make sure that these icons were deployed with the application.

If you're using GWT 1.3 you'll need to copy three images from the GWT distribution when using the `Tree` widget.

- tree_white.gif displays the whitespace that represents indent levels in the tree hierarchy.
- tree_open.gif displays as the icon next to an item when its children are visible.
- tree_closed.gif displays as the icon next to an item when its children are hidden.

Fortunately, GWT copies these files to the compilation directory along with your other application files. You can use any images for these three icons, but you must use these names for the `Tree` widget to pick them up properly.

In GWT 1.4 the `Tree` widget uses the `ImageBundle` functionality. This feature bundles images together in a single image during compilation, and lets you automatically include the default images in your deployment. You can override the default images by providing your own implementation of the `TreeImages` interface. The `TreeImages` interface is an image bundle that defines three images:

```
public interface TreeImages extends ImageBundle {
  AbstractImagePrototype treeOpen();
  AbstractImagePrototype treeClosed();
  AbstractImagePrototype treeLeaf();
}
```

The following code shows how to override this interface by using custom images with a `Tree` widget:

```
interface CustomTreeImages extends TreeImages {

  /**
   * @gwt.resource down.gif
   */
  AbstractImagePrototype treeOpen();
```

```
    /**
     * @gwt.resource right.gif
     */
    AbstractImagePrototype treeClosed();
}
CustomTreeImages images = (TreeImages)GWT.create(CustomTreeImages.class);
Tree tree = new Tree(images);
```

This code specifies the down.gif and right.gif images. Put these images in the same directory as this source code, or else use a full or relative path in the @gwt.resource annotation. The GWT compiler finds these images and bundles them in a single image for use at runtime. See Chapter 5 for more information on ImageBundle.

You can further customize the look of the Tree widget by using its CSS names. GWT adds the CSS name gwt-TreeItem-selected to an item in the tree when a user selects it. This lets you change the look of the item to tell the user that it is selected through CSS. For example, the following CSS sets the background of the selected item in a tree to a light blue:

```
.gwt-TreeItem-selected{ background-color:#def; }
```

In the database tree example described earlier, this CSS causes the selected item to look like the one in Figure 2-22.

Figure 2–22.   The selected item is highlighted

If you're using the Tree widget in an application that displays different views for the selection of each item, you'll need to receive events from the widget letting you know when the selection changes. To support this, the Tree widget implements SourcesTreeEvents, which allows you to add GWT's TreeListener instances to listen to events. The TreeListener interface looks like this:

```
public interface TreeListener extends EventListener {
    void onTreeItemSelected(TreeItem item);
    void onTreeItemStateChanged(TreeItem item);
}
```

GWT calls the first method, `onTreeItemSelected`, when a user selects an item in the tree. The second method, `onTreeItemStateChanged`, is called when a user opens the item's children for viewing or closes them. To handle these events, you implement this interface and its methods and then add the instance that implements them to the `Tree` widget like this:

```
treeList.addTreeListener(this);
```

In this case the class that implements the `TreeListener` interface calls the `addTreeListener` method to request the tree events.

MenuBar

The `MenuBar` widget, another complex custom widget that comes with GWT, is constructed from several HTML elements and JavaScript event handlers. It is based on desktop application menu bars that you commonly see at the top of an application or the top of your desktop. Like the `Tree` widget, the `MenuBar` displays a hierarchical list of data, but instead of listing the data vertically, it displays its data horizontally. The `MenuBar` differs further from a `Tree` widget by only displaying one branch at a time and only for the duration that the widget keeps the mouse focus. Furthermore, you typically use the `MenuBar` to hold a hierarchical list of application commands, while the `Tree` widget is usually used for application data.

To build a proper menu you need to add instances of the `MenuItem` class to the `MenuBar` widget. A `MenuItem` represents one clickable line on a menu. For example, the word *File* on the Eclipse menu is a menu item. If you open the File drop-down menu, each of the items listed vertically would also be `MenuItem`s. These are two different types of `MenuItem`s, and they differ by the way they behave after the user has clicked them. The first type opens a new menu when clicked, and the second kind executes some other command and causes the menu to close. To implement these two menu types, you can construct the `MenuItem` class with either a `Command` instance that executes when the user clicks the item or with another `MenuBar` object that displays when the user clicks the item.

As an example, let's create a File menu with New, Open, Save, and Close items and a Help menu with an About Item. The File and About menus will be `MenuItems` that sit on the main `MenuBar` and open one of the two other `MenuBars` when clicked. The other `MenuBars` for File and Help will contain the rest of the items that execute commands. For this example we will just use an empty `Command`, but you can place any code in the `execute` method of this class to customize the behavior that occurs when a user clicks a command. The following code builds the menu just described:

```
Command cmd = new Command() {
    public void execute() {
        //code to handle the command goes here
    }
};

MenuBar filemenu = new MenuBar(true);
filemenu.addItem("New", cmd);
filemenu.addItem("Open", cmd);
filemenu.addItem("Save", cmd);
filemenu.addItem("Close", cmd);

MenuBar helpmenu = new MenuBar(true);
helpmenu.addItem("About", cmd);

MenuBar menu = new MenuBar();
menubar.addItem("File", filemenu);
menubar.addItem("Help", helpmenu);
```

This code creates an instance of a `Command` interface with an empty `execute` method and three `MenuBar` instances. The File and Help menus are instantiated with the Boolean value `true` passed into the `MenuBar` constructor. This tells the `MenuBar` class that this instance will be vertical. If we leave this parameter blank or pass the Boolean value `false`, then the `MenuBar` will display horizontally. A horizontal menu is typically used across the top of an application. The two vertical menus are drop-down menus that open when the user clicks an item on the main menu. The code adds items to the menu bars with the `addItem` method. This method takes the value that will be displayed for the item as a first parameter and either an object that implements the `Command` interface or another menu as a second parameter. If you use a `Command` object, the `execute` method is called when the user clicks the menu item. This code uses `Command` objects to implement the events when the user clicks the New, Open, Save, Close, and About menu items. When another `MenuBar` is used as a second parameter to the `addItem` method, as when adding the File and Help menus to the main menu, a click on the item causes the new `MenuBar` to display.

If you placed this sample code in your application, it would display as a fairly plain-looking menu and would not give users enough hints that it is a menu that can be clicked. To enhance this you would use CSS styles, both to make the menu look more menu-like and to blend it in with the style of your application. For example, the following CSS gives the menu a desktop application look:

```
.gwt-MenuBar {
    background-color:#F3F5F6;
    border:outset 1px;
}
.gwt-MenuBar .gwt-MenuItem {
    font-size: 9pt;
    cursor:hand;
    cursor:pointer;
    padding:2px 5px 2px 5px;
    margin:0px;
}
.gwt-MenuBar .gwt-MenuItem-selected {
    background-color:#316AC5;
    color:white;
}
```

Running the sample code with these CSS styles produces a menu like the one shown in Figure 2-23.

Figure 2–23. CSS styles give menus more of a desktop application look

You can set three other CSS styles for the `MenuBar` widget: `gwt-MenuBar` for the horizontal or vertical `MenuBar` widget, `gwt-MenuItem` for one item in a `MenuBar`, and `gwt-MenuItem-selected` for the menu item in the `MenuBar` that is currently selected.

Simple Layout Panels

The widgets that we've covered up to this point represent the leaves of the user interface tree. That is, they are used at the bottom of a bigger structure which manages the layout of the application. This section looks at the layout widgets, also called panels, that come with GWT.

FlowPanel

The FlowPanel is one of the more basic panels that comes with GWT. If you're familiar with how HTML layout works, then you'll quickly understand this layout since it models itself after HTML layout. Its layout is also similar to how, in a text editor, words flow and wrap when they reach the edge of the page. The FlowPanel's child widgets display horizontally and then wrap to the next row down when there is not enough horizontal room left.

For example, the Gadget Desktop application in Chapter 6 has a menu at the top that displays a list of gadgets that can be added to the page. This application adds each item in the list as a link to a FlowPanel widget. The following code builds the panel:

```
FlowPanel gadgetsmenu = new FlowPanel();
for( int i=0; i< gadgetclasses.size();++i){
   GadgetClass gadgetclass = (GadgetClass)gadgetclasses.get(i);
   Hyperlink gadgetlink = new Hyperlink(gadgetclass.getName(),null);
   gadgetsmenu.add( gadgetlink );
}
```

When the list of available gadgets displays in the application, it spans horizontally, as shown in Figure 2-24.

HelloWorld Time Calendar To Do List News Playlist Weather

Figure 2–24.   Menu items appearing horizontally

When a user reduces the browser window and not all of the widgets can be displayed, the FlowPanel wraps the widgets around to the next line, as shown in Figure 2-25.

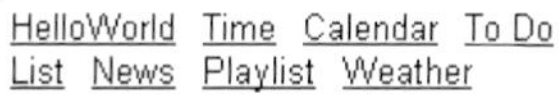

HelloWorld Time Calendar To Do
List News Playlist Weather

Figure 2–25.   Menu items wrapping to the next line

Note that this panel follows the HTML layout style for inline and block elements. **Inline elements** in HTML are elements that can be displayed in the same line as other elements. For example, text, hyperlinks, images, and form elements are all inline. A **block element,** however, does not share a horizontal space with other widgets. For the `FlowPanel` widget this is also true. All of the simple widgets used as inline widgets will wrap when used in the `FlowPanel`, but more complex widgets such as other panels, which are implemented with block HTML, will not share horizontal space and will be listed vertically and therefore will not wrap.

`HorizontalPanel` and `VerticalPanel`

`HorizontalPanel` and `VerticalPanel` are two more simple panels that behave just as their names suggest. The `HorizontalPanel` displays its child widgets horizontally and the `VerticalPanel` displays its child widgets vertically. The `HorizontalPanel` differs from the `FlowPanel` in behavior when the browser widow is too small to display the entire panel. Instead of wrapping its contents to the next line, `HorizontalPanel` continues to display its contents horizontally out of view, requiring the use of the browser's scroll bars for viewing. Similarly, when the `VerticalPanel`'s contents are out of view, they can be brought into view using the browser's scroll bars. The `VerticalPanel`'s contents can also be used inside a `ScrollPanel` widget (described later in this chapter) to limit their visible area to a region smaller than the browser window.

This book uses these panels in the sample applications since they are simple and their behavior is very predictable. Chapter 7's Multi-Search application uses a `HorizontalPanel` to display the search text box and the Search button (see Figure 2-26) and a `VerticalPanel` to display the search results (see Figure 2-27).

Figure 2–26.   Using the `HorizontalPanel` widget

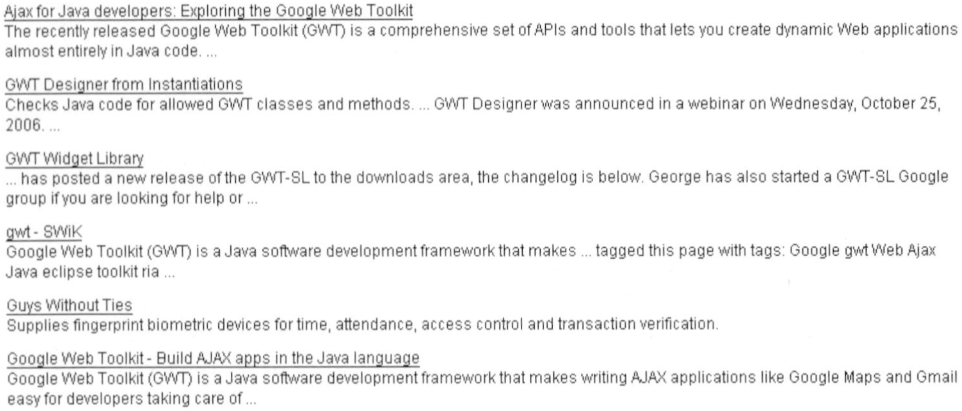

Ajax for Java developers: Exploring the Google Web Toolkit
The recently released Google Web Toolkit (GWT) is a comprehensive set of APIs and tools that lets you create dynamic Web applications almost entirely in Java code. ...

GWT Designer from Instantiations
Checks Java code for allowed GWT classes and methods. ... GWT Designer was announced in a webinar on Wednesday, October 25, 2006. ...

GWT Widget Library
... has posted a new release of the GWT-SL to the downloads area, the changelog is below. George has also started a GWT-SL Google group if you are looking for help or ...

gwt - SWiK
Google Web Toolkit (GWT) is a Java software development framework that makes ... tagged this page with tags: Google gwt Web Ajax Java eclipse toolkit ria ...

Guys Without Ties
Supplies fingerprint biometric devices for time, attendance, access control and transaction verification.

Google Web Toolkit - Build AJAX apps in the Java language
Google Web Toolkit (GWT) is a Java software development framework that makes writing AJAX applications like Google Maps and Gmail easy for developers taking care of ...

Figure 2–27. Using the `VerticalPanel` widget

Notice that the `VerticalPanel` used here does not contain simple widgets as its child widgets. Since panels are also widgets in GWT, we can use panels inside other panels. In this case we have a `VerticalPanel` inside another `VerticalPanel`.

Building these panels is straightforward, simply requiring a call to the `add` method for each child widget that is to be added.

HorizontalSplitPanel and VerticalSplitPanel

It's often hard to predict the size of content in a web application. Traditional web pages benefited from the flexibility of the default HTML layout, which automatically wrapped content to the next line. When you start to deal with more complex Ajax widgets, this wrapping is sometimes no longer possible and you need to find a different solution. GWT provides two split panels, `HorizontalSplitPanel` and `VerticalSplitPanel`, to help you adjust the interface to create a customized fit for content.

A **split panel** is a panel that can contain two child widgets and provides an area in between to adjust their relative size with the mouse. The `HorizontalSplitPanel` lays out the child widgets horizontally, and the `VerticalSplitPanel` lays out the child widgets vertically.

The Database Editor application in Chapter 10 uses a `Horizontal SplitPanel` to divide the tree content from the workspace content, as

Figure 2–28. A HorizontalSplitPanel dividing the tree and the workspace views

shown in Figure 2-28. It's difficult to predict the horizontal size of the tree content or how much of it the user would like to see. In this application the split panel gives the user the ability to customize its interface.

Using the split panels is very straightforward. You can set the split position relative to the top widget for a VerticalSplitPanel or the left widget for a HorizontalSplitPanel using the setSplitPosition method. Then, to set the child widgets, you use setLeftWidget and setRightWidget for the HorizontalSplitPanel or setTopWidget and setBottomWidget for the VerticalSplitPanel. The following code shows how the Database Editor application uses HorizontalSplitPanel:

```
HorizontalSplitPanel mainPanel = new HorizontalSplitPanel();
mainPanel.setSplitPosition("250px");
mainPanel.setLeftWidget( tree );
mainPanel.setRightWidget( workspace );
```

FlexTable and Grid

The FlexTable and Grid widgets, both based on HTML's table tag, display child widgets in a grid spanning vertically and horizontally. The Grid widget is an HTML table that enforces an explicitly set number of rows and cells for each row. The FlexTable, as its name implies, is more flexible, allowing cells to be added as needed, rows to have a variable number of cells, and cells to span multiple rows or columns.

Both implementations share a lot of their functionally, which you implement through the HTMLTable superclass. You can add content to cells with both widgets through the `setHTML`, `setText`, or `setWidget` methods. These methods take a row and column number to specify the destination in the table, along with the content to add. For the `Grid` widget you can only call these methods for an existing cell or an exception will be thrown.

The Database Editor application in Chapter 10 uses the `FlexTable` widget, since tables are perfect for rendering rows in a database. Figure 2-29 shows an example of a table from a database rendered in GWT's `FlexTable` widget:

CHARACTER_SET_NAME	DEFAULT_COLLATE_NAME	DESCRIPTION	MAXLEN
big5	big5_chinese_ci	Big5 Traditional Chinese	2
dec8	dec8_swedish_ci	DEC West European	1
cp850	cp850_general_ci	DOS West European	1
hp8	hp8_english_ci	HP West European	1
koi8r	koi8r_general_ci	KOI8-R Relcom Russian	1
latin1	latin1_swedish_ci	cp1252 West European	1
latin2	latin2_general_ci	ISO 8859-2 Central European	1

Figure 2–29.   Using the `FlexTable` widget

The table is also styled so that there are noticeable headers for each column. Both the `Grid` and the `FlexTable` widget allow you to style individual cells, rows, or columns using CSS. The table in Figure 2-29 was constructed based on an instance of the application's `Table` class, an object in the application's model representing a table in the database, and an instance of the application's `Page` class, another model object representing one page of rows in the table:

```
FlexTable rows = new FlexTable();
rows. setStyleName("tableViewBrowse");

//add column headers
rows.getRowFormatter().setStyleName(0, "tableViewBrowseHeaders");
    for( int i=0;i< table.getFieldCount(); ++i ){
        Field field = table.getField(i);
        rows.setText(0, i, field.getName());
}

//add rows
for( int i=0;i< page.getRowCount(); ++i ){
    String[] row = page.getRow(i);
```

```
for( int j=0;j< row.length; ++j ){
    rows.setText( i+1, j, row[j] );
    rows.getRowFormatter().setStyleName( i+1, "tableViewBrowseRow" );
  }
}
```

Notice that in this code the header row's style name is set by getting the row formatter from `FlexTable` and passing the row number and the style name as parameters. This allows you to specify the formatting for the header using CSS. The application uses the row formatter again for each row of data in the table so they can have their own style. Use the following CSS to get the style shown in Figure 2-29:

```
.tableViewBrowseHeaders{ font-size:8pt; color:#ccc; font-weight:bold }
.tableViewBrowseRow{ font-size:8pt;  border:1px solid #eee;}
.tableViewBrowse{ border-spacing:0px;border-collapse:collapse;}
.tableViewBrowse td{ padding:3px; border:1px solid #eee;padding-right:10px;}
.tableViewBrowseHeaders td{ border:0px;border-bottom: 1px solid #888;}
```

This CSS simply uses the style names set for the header and the data rows to specify their styles, which specify the borders and font styles.

The row formatter for tables has many other methods that allow you to customize the table on a per row basis, including alignment, width, height, visibility, and more. GWT also has a cell formatter that you can retrieve with the `getCellFormatter` method that allows you to customize the table on a per cell basis. The `FlexTable` widget also provides a `FlexCellFormatter` helper object retrieved through its `getFlexCell Formatter` method, which lets you set the row or column span for individual cells. When you set this to a value more than one, the cell will span more than one column or row. For example, Figure 2-30 shows cell A spanning two rows and cell B spanning three columns.

Tables can be further customized to exhibit more complex user interface behavior through the `TableListener` interface. You implement this interface in your application when you want to handle the user clicking on a cell in the table. For example, if you were using a table widget to display a list of files and wanted to allow the user to select one, you would probably want to set the selected row to be highlighted to give feedback to the user like that shown in Figure 2-31.

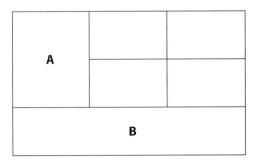

Figure 2-30.   Cells can span more than one row or column

Name	Size	Modified
another.html	1 kb	10/10/06 14:24 EDT
test.html	1 kb	10/10/06 14:22 EDT
asfsdfasfsadf.html	1 kb	10/10/06 14:25 EDT

Figure 2-31.   The selected row is highlighted

You can do this by adding an instance of the `TableListener` interface to the `Grid` widget so that its style information can be changed when clicked:

```
filelist.addTableListener( new TableListener(){
    public void onCellClicked(SourcesTableEventssender, int row, int cell){
        filelist.getRowFormatter().removeStyleName(selected, "selected");
        selected = row;
        filelist.getRowFormatter().addStyleName(selected, "selected");
    }
});
```

This code simply removes the `selected` style from the previously selected row and adds it to the currently selected row. In the CSS we can change the row's background to a blue highlight.

```
.selected {
    background-color:#316AC5;
    color:#FFFFFF;
}
```

DeckPanel

The DeckPanel widget is a layout panel that can have multiple child widgets but can only display one at a time. The interface lets you flip through each child widget like different pages in a book. The best example of its use is in the TabPanel class, which uses a DeckPanel to display each page corresponding to the selected tab. You can also use the widget on its own, like in Chapter 9's Instant Messenger application. This application uses the DeckPanel widget to display a Sign In view and a Contact List view. Users see the Sign In view when the application first loads, and when the user signs in, the view changes to the contact list. Figure 2-32 shows the application's Sign In view sitting in a DeckPanel widget.

Figure 2-32.   The sign-in in a DeckPanel widget

When the user signs in, the DeckPanel switches to the Contact List view, as shown in Figure 2-33.

As you can see, both views take up the same space provided by their DeckPanel parent, but only one is displayed at a time.

Constructing this widget is easy. For example, the DeckPanel widget for the Instant Messenger application looks like this:

```
DeckPanel mainPanel = new DeckPanel();
mainPanel.add( signIn );
mainPanel.add( contactListView );
mainPanel.showWidget(0);
```

Figure 2-33.   After sign-in, the DeckPanel widget switches to the Contact List view

This code creates a DeckPanel widget and adds the two child widgets. Then it calls the DeckPanel's showWidget method to set the visible child widget to the first one added. To switch to the second child widget, you would just call showWidget with the second child's index:

```
mainPanel.showWidget(1);
```

DockPanel

The DockPanel widget implements a layout common in desktop applications: child panels are docked to the edges of the panel and a main child occupies the remaining space. For example, the Mail sample application that comes with GWT uses a DockPanel widget to get the layout behavior of a desktop e-mail client (see Figure 2-34).

In this sample application the DockPanel widget is the outer layout widget with the top welcome panel, left shortcut panel, and the right mail list panel as children. The application adds the children to the DockPanel widget using layout constants to define their locations. The top welcome panel uses the DockPanel.NORTH constant, the left shortcut panel uses the DockPanel.WEST constant, and the right mail list panel uses the DockPanel.CENTER constant. The following code builds this layout:

```
DockPanel outer = new DockPanel();
outer.add(welcomePanel, DockPanel.NORTH);
outer.add(shortcuts, DockPanel.WEST);
outer.add(mailListPanel, DockPanel.CENTER);
outer.setWidth("100%");
```

Figure 2–34. `DockPanel` used to create the layout of a mail desktop client

As you can see, the top and left panels are located at the edges of the layout. The right panel is set to the center, which means it will occupy the remaining space in the panel. As a browser window grows, the child windows also grow to fill the new space in the `DockPanel` widget. Child widgets added with the `DockPanel.NORTH` or `DockPanel.SOUTH` constant grow and shrink horizontally, and their height remains the same. Child widgets added with the `DockPanel.EAST` or `DockPanel.WEST` constant grow and shrink vertically, and their width remains the same. There can only be one child added with the `DockPanel.CENTER` constant, and it grows and shrinks both vertically and horizontally to fill the rest of the space in the `DockPanel` left by the child widgets on the edges.

The resulting behavior is ideal for situations where the user focuses on the center child. The `DockPanel` widget ensures that the center child takes up the maximum amount of space and leaves just enough room for the edge children, which typically hold commands to operate on the center child widget.

HTMLPanel

An `HTMLPanel` widget is similar to the `HTML` widget in that it can render an `HTML` string, but it also supports attaching other widgets as children tags within the `HTML`. You may consider using this widget when you have some complex `HTML` that you want to render which surrounds another

GWT widget and does not have a straightforward implementation using GWT widgets. However, it's preferable to use GWT widgets to render user interface elements to avoid exposing any security problems or encountering browser inconsistencies. You may also consider using this widget when you have asynchronously retrieved an HTML segment and want to render it and attach a GWT widget.

For example, the following code creates some HTML to make a round corner background for a child widget:

```
HTMLPanel panel = new HTMLPanel(
    "<div style='background-image:url(top.gif)'></div>"+
    "<div id='inner' style='background-image:url(back.gif)'></div>"+
    "<div style='background-image:url(bottom.gif)'></div>");
panel.add(anotherWidget,"inner");
```

This code renders the HTML and then adds the child widget using the HTMLPanel's add method specifying the id of the element. In this case the ID, "inner", acts as the parent.

Complex Layout Panels

The layout panels we've looked at up to this point have been relatively simple in that they just have an algorithm for arranging their child widgets on the page. GWT provides a couple more panels, StackPanel and TabPanel, to assist with the layout for your application. These provide the simple layout behavior of the previous panels, but have controls that let you dynamically change the layout of the children.

StackPanel

The StackPanel widget uses a layout similar to VerticalPanel in that it renders its children vertically, but it only displays one at a time, allowing others to be opened by clicking on its header section. Each child widget has a header section that you can set when adding children to the panel. Figure 2-35 shows how the Mail sample application that comes with GWT uses the StackPanel widget.

This sample application constructs the StackPanel widget by adding the three child widgets, which are TreeList widgets, and supplying the

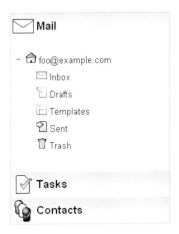

Figure 2–35.   The `StackPanel` shows the selected header section's child

header text. The header text can either be plain text or HTML. The example in Figure 2-35 uses HTML to render an image to the left of the text.

You can use CSS styles to style the headers in the `StackPanel` widget. You can set the styles for the entire `StackPanel` widget using the `gwt-StackPanel` name, the headers using `gwt-StackPanelItem`, and the currently selected header using `gwt-StackPanelItem-selected`. The GWT sample Mail application uses this CSS to style its `StackPanel`:

```
.gwt-StackPanel .gwt-StackPanelItem {
   background-image: url(gray_gradient.gif);
   background-repeat: repeat-x;
   background-color: #EEEEEE;
   cursor: pointer;
   cursor: hand;
}
```

This CSS sets the background image to be the gray gradient that you see in the header section of the `StackPanel` in Figure 2-35. It also sets the cursor to be the hand cursor to hint to the user that the area is clickable.

TabPanel

The `TabPanel` widget is similar to the stack panel: It displays one of its child widgets at a time and provides controls to select the child to display. It differs from the other panels through its implementation by not being part of the panel class hierarchy. Instead, it is a composite of other widgets, displaying a `TabBar` along the top and a `DeckPanel` to fill the bottom that implements panel behavior.

The `TabBar`, another widget like the `DeckPanel` widget, can be used for other implementations outside the `TabPanel` widget. For example, the `TabPanel` widget displays the `TabBar` above the `DeckPanel`, but you may want to provide an implementation which displays the `TabBar` at the bottom.

The `TabBar`'s behavior is to simply display a horizontal row of tabs that users can select. It implements `SourcesTabEvents` so that its clients can listen to its events, which include when a tab is selected. It also provides CSS style names for its tabs so they can be styled. The style names include `gwt-TabBar` to style the entire bar, `gwt-TabBarFirst` to style the area of the bar on the far left before any tab, `gwt-TabBarRest` to style the right side of the tab bar after all tabs, `gwt-TabBarItem` to style tabs which are not selected, and `gwt-TabBarItem-selected` to style the selected tab. The style names allow for very flexible styling. For example, Figure 2-36 illustrates using background colors to style tabs to have a look similar to that used in the Gadget Desktop application in Chapter 10.

Figure 2–36. Background colors used to style the tabs

In Figure 2-36, the selected tab has a lighter color than the other tab. The following CSS gives the tabs this look:

```
.gwt-TabBar .gwt-TabBarItem{
    padding:10px;
    margin-right:10px;
    cursor: hand;
    background-color:#ddd;
}
.gwt-TabBar .gwt-TabBarItem-selected{
    background-color:#f5f5f5;
}
```

You can also use images to style the tabs to look more like a desktop application. Figure 2-37 illustrates this as an update to the look of the Gadget Desktop application.

Figure 2-37.   Tabs styled to look more like a desktop application

This example uses the CSS `background-image` attribute to set the backgrounds for different sections of the `TabBar` widget:

```
.gwt-TabBar{
    background-image:url(tab-rest.gif);
    background-repeat: repeat-x;
    background-pos:bottom;
    padding-top:3px;
    width:100%
}
.gwt-TabBar .gwt-TabBarFirst { width:10px; }
.gwt-TabBar .gwt-TabBarItem {
    background-image:url(tab.gif);
    background-repeat:no-repeat;
    width:126px;
    height:27px;
    font-size:8pt;
}
.gwt-TabBar .gwt-TabBarItem { padding:5px; }
.gwt-TabBar .gwt-TabBarItem-selected {
    background-image:url(tab-selected.gif);
}
```

Even though both of these examples use the `TabBar` style names, they do not use the `TabBar` widget directly; instead, they use the `TabPanel` widget. It would be redundant to duplicate these style names for the `TabPanel`.

The `TabPanel` handles the tab selection events from the `TabBar` to display the appropriate page. This saves you from doing this work; you just need to set up the child widgets with their tab name using `TabPanel`'s add method. The Database Editor application's `TabPanel` is constructed like this:

```
TabPanel tabPanel = new TabPanel();
tabPanel.add( browsePanel,"Browse" );
tabPanel.add( structurePanel,"Structure" );
tabPanel.setWidth("100%");
tabPanel.selectTab(0);
```

After you add the child widgets to the panel, you call the `selectTab` method to tell the `TabPanel` to bring the widget with the given index to the foreground.

Simple Container Panels

Container panels differ from layout panels in that they do not control the layout of child widgets; instead, they provide added functionality as a container of a single child widget. Simple container panels include `Composite`, `SimplePanel`, `ScrollPanel`, and `FocusPanel`.

Composite

The `Composite` widget's usefulness lies more in code organization than in anything the user of the application will notice. Use a `Composite` widget when you want to build a single reusable component and hide its implementation from the rest of the application. When used in the application and added to a parent panel, it acts as if only its child widget were there.

The sample applications in this book use the `Composite` widget for the views in Model-View-Controller design. The views extend `Composite` and expose interfaces for other views and the controller to use while hiding the widget implementations. This design technique allows applications to change their widget structure without needing to modify other sections of the application.

As an example, let's look at the `SignInView` for the Instant Messenger application in Chapter 9. First, the `SignInView` is declared as extending the `Composite` class:

```
public class SignInView extends Composite
{
```

Then in the class constructor the view sets up its layout starting with calling the `Composite` widget's protected `initWidget` method with the main child widget for the view:

```
private VerticalPanel mainPanel = new VerticalPanel();
public SignInView( )
{
    initWidget( mainPanel );
```

The constructor would typically then continue building the layout of child widgets. Having the `VerticalPanel` hidden from the code that uses this class allows us to modify the implementation without affecting other code.

Another example of a `Composite` widget, GWT's `TabPanel` widget, exposes an interface that is intuitive to use and uses the `Composite` widget to hide the internal implementation.

SimplePanel

The `SimplePanel` widget is much like the `Composite` widget except it has a representation in the interface, which can have its own CSS styles such as a border, and it has a public method, `setWidget`, to set the child widget.

The `SimplePanel` widget is an abstract class, which means you can't instantiate it directly, but you can use it as a superclass to build new widgets. GWT uses it in many panels, including the rest of the panels discussed in this section, as a superclass.

ScrollPanel

The `ScrollPanel`, a container panel that extends `SimplePanel`, adds the capability to scroll over the child widget when the child becomes too big to display in the area designated for the panel. The Instant Messenger application in Chapter 9 uses this panel as a container to the chat history list in its Chat window, as shown in Figure 2-38.

In this example you can see the right side of the `ScrollPanel` as indicated by the visible vertical scroll bar. The child widget of the `ScrollPanel` is a

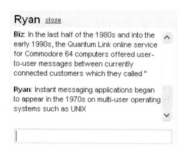

Figure 2–38.   `ScrollPanel` in action

`VerticalPanel` that contains the instant messages as its children. To get the vertical scroll bar working in this example, the height of the `Scroll Panel` needs to be set to a constant value. When the `VerticalPanel` grows larger than this constant value, the scroll bar will appear to let users scroll the unseen area into view. The following code constructs the `ScrollPanel` in this example:

```
ScrollPanel conversationScroller = new ScrollPanel();
conversationScroller.setHeight("150px");
conversationScroller.setWidget( conversationPanel );
```

The widget also contains methods that assist with the control of the scroll position, making a child component visible, and controlling the visibility of the scroll bars. You can find additional information about each method in the GWT documentation at http://code.google.com/webtoolkit/documentation/gwt.html.

FocusPanel

A `FocusPanel` is a `SimplePanel` that adds the capability to handle various events from its children. It supports click, focus, keyboard, and mouse events. You can also set this panel to have a tab index, which is a spot that the focus stops on when the user presses the Tab key, and you can explicitly set its focus.

Complex Container Panels

Complex container panels also can only have a single child widget, but they provide more complex behavior than simple container panels. Complex container panels include `FormPanel`, `DisclosurePanel`, `PopupPanel`, and `DialogBox`.

FormPanel

The `FormPanel` wraps HTML's `form` tag and provides the capability to submit form data to the server from GWT widgets using the browser's form submitting capability. Typically the browser's form submitting capability is not used in Ajax applications since it causes the page to refresh. However, the `FormPanel` in GWT uses a technique that allows you to have a form in your application and have it submit without refreshing the page. Your application then receives notification when the form is submitted and when a response is returned from the server by implementing the `FormHandler` interface.

All of the widgets outlined earlier in the Form Widgets section that implement the `HasName` interface can be used in a form. They require the `HasName` interface because the HTML `form` tag requires a name for each submitted value. This name is passed with its value to the server when submitted, and the server uses the name-value pairs to execute the request. For example, the following code creates a `FormPanel` to submit a sign-in request to the web server:

```
//create the form panel, set its action and method
final FormPanel form = new FormPanel();
form.setAction("/signin");
form.setMethod(FormPanel.METHOD_POST);

//set the main widget for the panel to a vertical panel
VerticalPanel panel = new VerticalPanel();
form.setWidget(panel);

//create the username field
TextBox tb = new TextBox();
tb.setName("username");
panel.add(tb);
```

```
//create the password field
PasswordTextBox ptb = new PasswordTextBox();
ptb.setName("password");
panel.add(ptb);

//create the Submit button
panel.add(new Button("Submit", new ClickListener() {
    public void onClick(Widget sender) {
        form.submit();
    }
}));

//add a form handler
form.addFormHandler(new FormHandler() {
    public void onSubmitComplete(FormSubmitCompleteEvent event) {
        Window.alert(event.getResults());
    }

    public void onSubmit(FormSubmitEvent event) {
        if (tb.getText().length() == 0 || ptb.getText().length() == 0 ) {
            Window.alert("The fields must not be empty.");
            event.setCancelled(true);
        }
    }
});
```

This code first creates a `FormPanel` instance and sets its action and method. A form's action is the URL destination of the server-side script that will handle the form submission. You need to call `setMethod` to set the HTTP method, either GET or POST, that should be used to post the form data. In this example we chose POST instead of GET. The difference between using these two methods for form submission is that GET submits the form data in the URL and POST submits the data in the HTTP request's body.

After the `FormPanel` is created, the form fields are added. Since the `FormPanel` widget is a simple panel, it can only have one child. This allows you to select any layout panel to manage the layout of your fields. In this example we use the `VerticalPanel` widget so our fields will span vertically. We create the username field as a `TextBox` widget and the password field as a `PasswordTextBox` widget and then add them to the `VerticalPanel`. Then the Submit button is created with a click listener that submits the form by calling the `FormPanel`'s `submit` method.

Finally, a `FormHandler` instance is added to the panel to listen for form events. Two events may occur when using the form panel. The first is `onSubmit`, which occurs just before the form is submitted to the server. You can use this event to validate the field data on the form and cancel the submission if necessary. In this case we check the form to make sure the fields are not empty. If either is empty, we alert the user and cancel the submission through the `setCancelled` method on the event object. The other event, `onSubmitComplete`, occurs when the server returns a response from the form submission.

It is important to note that browsers have security restrictions that don't allow you to read the results of a form submitted to another domain. If you do submit these results to another domain, you may not be able to read the results of the query or determine if the submission was successful or not.

DisclosurePanel

Web applications often have interfaces that are designed to scroll vertically. As the amount of data that needs to be displayed on a single page increases, vertical scrolling becomes more of a hassle. As a solution to vertical scrolling, GWT provides the `DisclosurePanel`.

The `DisclosurePanel` is a container panel that has one content widget and can have a header defined. It toggles the content's visibility when a user clicks the header. This allows portions of data that scroll vertically to be categorized into sections that can then be hidden with a single click, thereby freeing up vertical space for other sections.

The Multi-Search application in Chapter 7 uses the `DisclosurePanel` to provide a simple way to hide a search engine's search results to view other results, as shown in Figure 2-39.

Figure 2-39 shows the search engine's name used as a header, along with a down-facing arrow image indicating that the `DisclosurePanel` is open. When a user clicks on the header of the `DisclosurePanel`, the content is hidden and a different image is displayed. In this case, the arrow points to the right instead of down. The following code creates this type of disclosure panel:

Figure 2–39. `DisclosurePanel` used to hide search results

```
DisclosurePanel mainPanel = new DisclosurePanel(
    searchResultImages, engine.getName(),true );
mainPanel.setContent(results);
```

Notice that the constructor's first parameter is a field called `searchResultImages`. This field is an instance of an `ImageBundle` interface that the `DisclosurePanel` uses to display the images in the header. Two images need to be defined for the `DisclosurePanel` by implementing GWT's `DisclosurePanelImages` interface:

```
public interface DisclosurePanelImages extends ImageBundle {
  AbstractImagePrototype disclosurePanelOpen();
  AbstractImagePrototype disclosurePanelClosed();
}
```

The Multi-Search application uses the following code to define this interface and provide images for the `DisclosurePanel`:

```
static public interface SearchResultImages extends DisclosurePanelImages {
    /**
     * @gwt.resource minimize1.gif
     */
    AbstractImagePrototype disclosurePanelOpen();

    /**
     * @gwt.resource minimize2.gif
     */
    AbstractImagePrototype disclosurePanelClosed();

}
public static SearchResultImages searchResultImages = (SearchResultImages)
GWT.create( SearchResultImages.class );
```

Notice that the interface extends the `DisclosurePanelImages`' interface so it can be used in the `DisclosurePanel`. The code provides annotations for the two methods that point to the images that should be used. This code creates an instance of the interface using the GWT deferred binding `GWT.create` method. This may seem somewhat complex, but using image bundles in your applications greatly improves performance. This code bundles all of the images together in a single image during the GWT compilation step and downloads them as a single bundle when the application is loaded in a browser. For more information on image bundles, see Chapter 5.

PopupPanel

The `PopupPanel` widget is a `SimplePanel` displayed on top of the existing interface. Desktop widgets with similar behavior include tooltips, which appear when the mouse hovers over a widget, or the drop-down part of a list box, which appears when the user clicks the widget. In GWT the `PopupPanel` displays vertical menus after the user has clicked a `MenuItem`, and the `DialogPanel` uses it as a superclass. The Blog Editor application in Chapter 8 uses the `PopupPanel` to display the hosted version of a blog entry after the user clicks the `view` link on the entry, as illustrated in Figure 2-40.

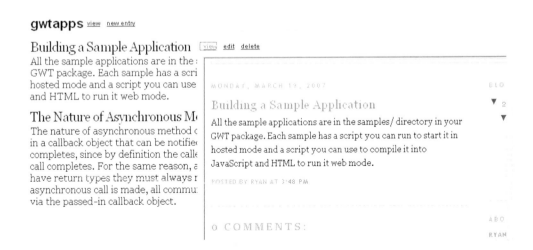

Figure 2-40.   A `PopupPanel` displaying a blog entry

In this figure the `PopupPanel` sets a `Frame` as its widget and sets the `Frame`'s URL to the hosted URL for the blog entry. Figure 2-40 shows the panel after a user clicked the View button, and it is set up to be visible right below the View button. In this example, when the `PopupPanel` loses focus, it disappears. The Blog Editor application uses the following code to build this `PopupPanel`:

```
public class HostedBlogView extends PopupPanel {
    public HostedBlogView( String url, Widget sender ) {
        super(true);
        Frame frame = new Frame(url);
        frame.setWidth("100%");
        frame.setHeight("100%");
        setWidget(frame);
        setPopupPosition(
            sender.getAbsoluteLeft(),
            sender.getAbsoluteTop()+sender.getOffsetHeight());
    }

}
```

The code extends the `PopupPanel` as its own class so that it can be reused in different parts of the application. In the constructor, the superclass constructor passes true for the autohide parameter. This enables the functionality in the `PopupPanel` that causes the panel to hide itself when it loses focus. Then the `Frame` widget is created and set as the main widget in the `PopupPanel`. The panel's pop-up position is set using the `PopupPanel`'s `setPopupPosition` method, with the widget's location supplied in the constructor argument as parameters. This widget is created when the user clicks on the view button:

```
private class ViewClickListener implements ClickListener {
    public void onClick( Widget sender ) {
        new HostedBlogView(entry.getLink(),sender).show();
    }
}
```

In this click listener a new instance of the `HostedBlogView` class is created (the `PopupPanel`), with the entry's link and the widget that was clicked as constructor parameters. Then the `show` method is called, which displays the `PopupPanel`.

DialogBox

The `DialogBox` widget extends the `PopupPanel`, inheriting its pop-up behavior, and adds a dragable caption bar to the top. This widget is modeled after modal dialog boxes found in desktop applications. A modal dialog requires the user's interaction before any further interaction can occur with the rest of the application.

Figure 2-41 shows an example[1] of the `DialogBox` widget used in the Gpokr GWT application (see http://gpokr.com).

In this example the dialog is created after the user clicks on the Change Table button in the top, right corner. The user cannot interact with any part of the application except the widgets, which are children of the dialog. When the user is done with the dialog, after selecting a table and clicking Go or Cancel, the application hides the dialog and the user can resume interacting with the application.

The code used to create and show the dialog is in the click listener for the Change Table button:

```
changetable.addClickListener(new ClickListener() {
    public void onClick(Widget sender){
        new ChangeTableDialog().show();
    }
});
```

The `ChangeTableDialog` class uses the `DialogBox` as a superclass so it inherits its `show` and `hide` methods. The application calls the dialog constructor immediately before it calls `show`. This is where it builds its layout and sets the title of the dialog box:

```
ChangeTableDialog(){
    setText( "Change Table" );
    VerticalPanel vpanel = new VerticalPanel();
    setWidget( vpanel );
```

---

1. This is a GWT application I wrote to test the toolkit shortly after its release in May 2006. The dialog box here is implemented with a `TabPanel` for the Ring and Sit n Go tabs. The list is a `Grid` widget inside a `ScrollPanel`.

Figure 2–41.   The `DialogBox` widget creates a modal dialog box

The constructor continues to set up the dialog's layout, starting with a `VerticalPanel` widget as the root. The class handles the click events of the Go and Cancel buttons to execute a table change and hide the dialog:

```
Button gobutton = new Button( "Go" );
gobutton.addClickListener( new ClickListener(){
   public void onClick(Widget sender){
      hide();
      loadTable( selectedTable );
}});

Button cancel = new Button( "Cancel" );
cancel.addClickListener( new ClickListener(){
```

```
   public void onClick(Widget sender){hide();}
});
```

The `DialogBox` widget has two preset style names: `gwt-DialogBox` for the frame of the dialog box and `Caption` for the caption bar on the dialog box. The preceding examples use these two styles to give the dialog box and caption a background image and set the size of the caption font. The following code shows the CSS styles used:

```
.gwt-DialogBox {
   border: 1px solid #748299;
   background-color: white;
   background-image: url(back.jpg);
   background-repeat:repeat-x;
   background-position:bottom;
}
.gwt-DialogBox .Caption {
   background-color: #C3D9FF;
   background-image: url(titlebar.gif);
   background-repeat:repeat-x;
   padding: 10px;
   font-weight: bold;
   color: white;
   cursor: default;
}
```

User Interface Framework Glue

The widgets in GWT follow common designs and share interfaces to allow easy understanding, development, and extension. This section covers this glue that binds widgets together. It is divided into two categories: event interfaces and feature interfaces.

Event Interfaces

Handling events is a core part of any user interface code. On one side you have the application's controller populating the interface with data, and on the other side the user is interacting with the user interface widgets. It's this second side where an event model comes in handy. The model chosen to implement user interface events with GWT widgets follows the observer pattern.

The **observer pattern** is a design pattern where the observer—your application code—observes the state of a subject, the user interface. When the subject's state changes, the observer is notified. Using this pattern allows you to decouple your application code from the subject. In other words, the subject does not need to know the details of your application to call methods on it. The pattern is typically implemented with the subject holding a collection of observers that are iterated over to call a notify method on each observer when a state change occurs. The notify method is usually a method on an interface provided by the subject that the observer implements. The UML diagram in Figure 2-41 illustrates this relationship.

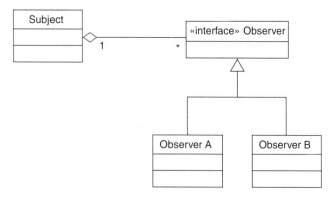

Figure 2–42.   UML diagram of subject-observer relationship

In GWT, the subject would be a widget like the Button widget, the observer interface for the click events on the button is the ClickListener interface, and the observer implementation would be provided by your application code. For example, the following code builds the button and ClickListener just described:

```
//create a button
Button subject = new Button("click me");

//implement a ClickListener
ClickListener observer = new ClickListener(){
    public void onClick( Widget sender ){
        Window.alert( "I've been clicked" );
    }
});

//add the ClickListener to the button to receive click events
subject.addClickListener( observer );
```

Some observer interfaces have multiple event methods, which means you need to have an implementation, even just an empty one, for each method to follow the rules of implementing Java interfaces. Some of the observer interfaces are large, which makes you tediously implement many empty methods just to handle one event. For these situations GWT provides an adapter class to let you implement only some of the methods on the observer interface. GWT's KeyboardListenerAdapter is an example of an adapter class for the KeyboardListener interface, which has three methods. Since the adapter is a class that implements each method as empty, you simply need to override the methods for the events you want to handle. The following code shows the implementation of the KeyboardListenerAdapter in GWT:

```
public class KeyboardListenerAdapter implements KeyboardListener {

   public void onKeyDown(Widget sender, char keyCode, int modifiers){}

   public void onKeyPress(Widget sender, char keyCode, int modifiers){}

   public void onKeyUp(Widget sender, char keyCode, int modifiers){}
}
```

The Multi-Search application in Chapter 7 uses the KeyboardListener-Adapter to handle the onKeyPress event from a TextBox widget. The following code shows the use of the KeyboardListenerAdapter in that application:

```
searchBox.addKeyboardListener( new KeyboardListenerAdapter(){
   public void onKeyPress( Widget sender, char keyCode, int modifiers){
      if(keyCode == KEY_ENTER )
         onSearch();
   }
});
```

Notice that only one method needs to be implemented from the KeyboardListener interface. These adapter classes save you from writing a lot of unneeded code when handling events.

On the subject side of the observer pattern, GWT uses a consistent design to implement events that include a subject interface and a subject helper collection. If you will be developing new widgets and implementing events, it's important for you to understand how they are implemented in GWT. Each subject interface represents one type of event grouping that the subject supports. For example, the subject implements the `Sources-ClickEvents` interface for click events. Since many widgets have click events, this interface can be shared between them. The interface simply has methods that allow the application code to add and remove listeners:

```
public interface SourcesClickEvents {
    void addClickListener(ClickListener listener);
    void removeClickListener(ClickListener listener);
}
```

When widgets implement one of these interfaces, they relay events to the listeners typically using a collection helper class. For click events GWT has a `ClickListenerCollection`. These helper collections simply keep track of all the listeners and provide firing methods for each event. For click events, the `ClickListenerCollection` has the method `fireClick`:

```
public class ClickListenerCollection extends Vector {
    public void fireClick(Widget sender) {
        for (Iterator it = iterator(); it.hasNext();) {
            ClickListener listener = (ClickListener) it.next();
            listener.onClick(sender);
        }
    }
}
```

This method is implemented by iterating over the collection of listeners and calling the `onClick` method for each one.

The reason for this design is to promote code reuse. The collection helper classes can be reused for each widget that supports click listeners. Another added benefit of sharing the source's interface between widgets is that it allows code to be written that generically operates on a widget supporting a specific type of event.

These patterns that implement events using an observer pattern are consistently repeated throughout GWT. Table 2-2 outlines the available event types and their interfaces.

Table 2–2 GWT Event Types and Their Interfaces

Events	Observer Classes	Subject Classes	Supporting Widgets
onChange	ChangeListener	ChangeListenerCollection SourcesChangeEvents	ListBox PasswordTextBox TextArea TextBox
onClick	ClickListener	ClickListenerCollection SourcesClickEvents	Button CheckBox FocusPanel HTML Hyperlink Image Label ListBox PasswordTextBox RadioButton TextArea TextBox
onFocus onLostFocus	FocusListener FocusListenerAdapter	FocusListenerCollection SourcesFocusEvents	Button CheckBox FocusPanel ListBox PasswordTextBox RadioButton TextArea TextBox Tree

(continued)

Table 2-2 GWT Event Types and Their Interfaces *(Continued)*

Events	Observer Classes	Subject Classes	Supporting Widgets
onKeyDown onKeyPress onKeyUp	KeyboardListener KeyboardListenerAdapter	KeyboardListenerCollection SourcesKeyboardEvents	FocusPanel PasswordTextBox TextArea TextBox Tree
onError onLoad	LoadListener	LoadEventsCollection SourcesLoadEvents	Image
onMouseDown onMouseEnter onMouseLeave onMouseMove onMouseUp	MouseListener MouseListenerAdapter	MouseListenerCollection SourcesMouseEvents	FocusPanel HTML Image Label
onMouseWheel	MouseWheelListener	SourcesMouseWheelEvents	FocusPanel HTML Image Label
onPopupClosed	PopupListener	PopupListenerCollection SourcesPopupEvents	DialogBox PopupPanel
onScroll	ScrollListener	ScrollListenerCollection SourcesScrollEvents	ScrollPanel
onCellClicked	TableListener	SourcesTableEvents TableListenerCollection	FlexTable Grid
onBeforeTabSelected onTabSelected	TabListener	SourcesTabEvents TabListenerCollection	TabBar TabPanel
onTreeItemSelected onTreeItemStateChanged	TreeListener	SourcesTreeEvents TreeListenerCollection	Tree

Feature Interfaces

The design of the widgets in GWT follows interface-based design practices, so writing code to interfaces is preferred over using a class. This helps decouple your application from the library implementation. For example, the Gadget Desktop application in Chapter 6 takes advantage of this type of development and has a `DockableWidget` that supports dragging to and from any panel that supports the `HasWidgets` interface. This allows the `DockableWidget`'s code to be fairly generic and workable with many panels. The alternative, to work with individual panel interfaces, would mean custom code for each type of panel.

Here is a snippet of code from the `DockableWidget` that uses the `HasWidgets` interface:

```
if( containerWidget instanceof HasWidgets &&
    absCenterX >= containerWidget.getAbsoluteLeft() &&
    absCenterX <= containerWidget.getAbsoluteLeft() +
    containerWidget.getOffsetWidth() &&
    absCenterY >= containerWidget.getAbsoluteTop() &&
    absCenterY <= containerWidget.getAbsoluteTop() +
    containerWidget.getOffsetHeight() ){
    if( containerWidget != parentWidget ){
        ((HasWidgets)containerWidget).add( this );
    }
    for( Iterator it = ((HasWidgets)containerWidget).iterator();
        it.hasNext() && switchWith == null;){
```

As you can see, this code operates on the `HasWidgets` interface. First it checks to see if the container is an instance of the `HasWidgets` interface and uses the `instanceof` operator to avoid casting an exception. Then it casts the `containerWidget` to the interface and calls its methods. The actual implementation of the `containerWidget` can be any widget that supports `HasWidgets`, which includes all of the panels in GWT.

You can see another example of using interface-based design in GWT's implementation of the `FormPanel`. The code is written so that each widget added to the form panel that will have its data included in the form submission implements the `HasName` interface.

Table 2-3 outlines the feature interfaces that come with GWT, excluding the event interfaces outlined in the previous section.

Table 2–3   GWT Feature Interfaces (Excluding Event Interfaces)

Feature	Methods	Supporting Widgets

`HasAlignment`	`getHorizontalAlignment`
	`getVerticalAlignment`
	`setHorizontalAlignment`
	`setVerticalAlignment`
		`DockPanel`
		`HorizontalPanel`
		`HTML`
		`Label`
		`VerticalPanel`

`HasCaption`	`getCaption` `setCaption`	

`HasFocus`	`getTabIndex`
	`setAccessKey`
	`setFocus`
	`setTabIndex`
		`Button`
		`CheckBox`
		`FocusPanel`
		`ListBox`
		`PasswordTextBox`
		`RadioButton`
		`TextArea`
		`TextBox`
		`Tree`

`HasHorizontalAlignment`	`getHorizontalAlignment` `setHorizontalAlignment`	`HTML` `Label`

`HasName`	`getName`
	`setName`
		`CheckBox`
		`FileUpload`
		`Hidden`
		`ListBox`
		`PasswordTextBox`
		`RadioButton`
		`TextArea`
		`TextBox`

`HasText`	`getText`
	`setText`
		`HTML`
		`Label`
		`PasswordTextBox`
		`TextArea`
		`TextBox`

`HasVerticalAlignment`	`getVerticalAlignment` `setVerticalAlignment`	

Feature	Methods	Supporting Widgets

`HasWidgets`	`add`
	`clear`
	`iterator`
	`remove`
		`All Panels`
		`Tree`

`HasWordWrap`	`getWordWrap` `setWordWrap`	`HTML` `Label`

`IndexedPanel`	`getWidget`
	`getWidgetCount`
	`getWidgetIndex`
	`remove`
		`DeckPanel`
		`FlowPanel`
		`HorizontalPanel`
		`StackPanel`
		`TabPanel`
		`VerticalPanel`

Summary

GWT provides a fairly large user interface library in its `com.google.gwt.user.client.ui` package. The widgets and panels provide a browser-independent foundation for Ajax application user interfaces that extends what is currently available through plain HTML. Following the design that many Java user interface developers are familiar with, it provides a rich event system and a solid structuring model.

This chapter divided the widgets into four major categories. For widgets, the categories include the static widgets—labels, images, HTML, and hyperlinks—which provide the most basic but necessary elements in an interface; form widgets, which give users the ability to select and input information to the application; and complex widgets, which provide more advanced navigation and interface organization. In terms of panels, there are the simple and complex layout panels that help you create a solid structure for the application's interface, and simple and complex container panels that provide extra functionality for sections of the application's interface.

When building Ajax applications with GWT, it's good to be familiar with the widgets available in the toolkit so that you can create the most effective Ajax interface.

3

Server Integration Techniques

Ajax applications are a nice blend of desktop applications and traditional web applications. They have responsive interfaces like desktop applications and easy distribution like traditional web applications. They also, like traditional web applications, have great support for integrating with server-side technologies. This chapter looks at the many options and techniques you can use to integrate your GWT application with server technologies. We start by looking at basic integration techniques, including using the standard Ajax asynchronous HTTP request to load simple text or HTML from the server. Then we discuss loading more complex data from the server and leveraging the Google Web Toolkit's XML and JSON libraries. After looking at data formats, we explore how to integrate with third-party servers through JavaScript APIs, JSONP, and an HTTP proxy. The chapter ends with a section on more advanced server integration techniques, including using REST and GWT-RPC.

This chapter gives you an overview of these techniques. For more information on them, see the sample application chapters in Part II, which look at these techniques in greater detail.

Basic Server Integration Techniques

Traditional web applications operate on a thin client model with the server doing most of the work. The client side typically consists of just some HTML codes marking up data for display in a browser. These documents become part of the interface for interacting with the server-side application when they give the user the ability to request specific URLs or submit data through forms. The most basic web application is a data browser in which the user can click through data from the server. More sophisticated applications allow the user to interact with the data model by submitting data. Ultimately you would develop the entire application on the server, and the client simply uses the browser's features to display the application's interface.

The browser's features that let the client interact with the server in these traditional web applications are its ability to request data over HTTP and submit data through forms. This section looks at integrating GWT applications with traditional server-side web applications through basic server integration techniques.

Asynchronous HTTP Requests

An Ajax application's core capability is being able to asynchronously make calls to the server to obtain data and avoid a page refresh. One way you can accomplish this is by using different JavaScript objects for different browsers when creating an Ajax application in JavaScript. With GWT, you simply need to use the classes in the HTTP library and GWT handles the browser details.

In Chapter 1 you saw a brief example of an asynchronous HTTP request with the Hangman tutorial, where the application downloads a simple text file from the server when it starts. This example used a simplified `HTTPRequest` class to download the data. However, it is preferable to use the HTTP library instead since it has more support for handling error situations.

The HTTP library is in the `com.google.gwt.http.client` package in the gwt-user.jar file. To use this package in your code, you need to add the package to your GWT module file with the `inherits` XML element like this:

```
<inherits name="com.google.gwt.http.HTTP"/>
```

Having applications make calls to the server using this library is relatively straightforward and follows the Observer pattern described in Chapter 2. You start with a `RequestBuilder` instance to set up the details of your request, such as the URL and header parameters. Then you send the request with the `sendRequest` method providing the post data, if needed, and an instance of the `RequestCallback` interface as parameters. When the request completes, the `RequestCallback` instance either has its `onError` method called if the server call failed or its `onResponse Received` method called if the call was successful. When the HTTP library calls the `onResponseReceived` method it provides a `Response` object for the application to consider. The response contains the body of data sent from the server along with status text, the status code, and a list of HTTP headers.

The type of data you post to the server or receive from the server can be in any format, but since GWT provides libraries for constructing and parsing JSON and XML, consider these formats first. You could also integrate with older server scripts which previously accepted form submissions. In this case you would construct your post data following the standard form encoding (see the next section for an example of this method).

The Database Editor application in Chapter 10 uses the HTTP library to send and receive XML from the server. The following code, taken from this application, illustrates how to use the HTTP library to post data to and read data from the server:

```
//create a new GET request for the database table XML feed
RequestBuilder builder = new RequestBuilder(
    RequestBuilder.GET, "/databaseEditor/feed/"+database.getName());

try{
    //send the request
    builder.sendRequest( null, new RequestCallback(){
        public void onError(Request request, Throwable exception){
            //log the error
            GWT.log( "error", exception );
        }

        public void onResponseReceived(Request request, Response response){
            //check the status code
            int statusCode = response.getStatusCode();
            if( statusCode == 200 || statusCode == 201 ){
                //make the call to parse the response
```

```
            parseTableXML( response.getText() );
        }
    }
 });
}
catch (RequestException e){ GWT.log( "error", e); }
```

In this code the HTTP request does not post any data, indicated by the null first parameter in the `sendRequest` method call, but expects a response in the form of XML data. The application receives the response in the `onResponseReceived` implementation of the `RequestCallback` method by calling the `getText` method on the `Response` instance. (The next section discusses how to read and write structured formats like JSON and XML.)

As you can see, it's fairly easy to make server calls with the HTTP package. It can be tempting to make server calls to third-party servers since there are many free web services available, but browsers impose a fairly severe security restriction, called the Same Origin policy, to prevent this. This policy basically states that you cannot make calls to servers other than the server the HTML document originated from. Of course there are ways to get data from other servers and bypass this restriction. The Multi-Search application in Chapter 7 shows one method using `script` tags, and the Blog Editor application in Chapter 8 illustrates another way using a server-side proxy. The next section looks at these two techniques.

Another limitation of using HTTP specifically with GWT is that you can only use two kinds of HTTP requests, GET and POST. This restriction is due to a bug in the Safari browser that will not allow any other HTTP request method. If you do not want to provide support for Safari, you can extend the `HTTPRequest` class to allow other HTTP methods. The Blog Editor application uses the DELETE and PUT methods by passing these methods in the `X-HTTP-Method-Override` header. The Database Editor application requires DELETE and PUT methods to interact with a REST-based Ruby on Rails server. Instead, the application uses the POST method with the Rails `_method` parameter set to the intended HTTP method.

A third restriction with asynchronous HTTP is the two connection limit per domain. This restriction, dictated by the HTTP protocol, prevents flooding servers with connections. This means that you can only have two pending asynchronous requests at any time. A third request must wait until one of the first two completes. This two connection limit doesn't only apply to asynchronous HTTP requests from your application, but also to any resource being loaded from the server on the same domain, including script files and images. You could run into a performance issue if, for example, two large image files are being downloaded, taking up both of the connections, and you try to load XML data asynchronously. You can work around problems with large files taking up a connection by putting them in a subdomain. For example, if you use images.yourdomain.com, you automatically have two more connections available. Be careful not to move your asynchronous requests to a domain other than the one the application was loaded from or you'll bump into the Same Origin policy restriction.

Working with Plain Text and HTML

First let's look at how to integrate an Ajax application with a server inter-face that produces existing HTML. Ajax applications can use the browser's asynchronous HTTP functionality to fetch data from the server over HTTP at any time. Typically you use this to request XML, but any format is possi-ble. With an existing traditional web application you may already have HTML fragments available on the server that you could asynchronously load and display in an Ajax application. For example, let's look at loading an existing HTML page from the server to display as a tooltip as an addi-tion to the Instant Messenger application in Chapter 9.

First, we need to create a test HTML fragment that will be stored on the server called ryan.html:

```
<b>Ryan</b><br/>
Software Developer<br/><a href="http://www.rdews.com">http://www.rdews.com</a>
```

This basic HTML will display my name in bold, my profession, and then my web site as a link. We can store one file like this for each person and fetch the person's file asynchronously when it's needed. We can simply create a tooltip of the HTML when the user clicks on a Contacts icon in the Instant Messenger application, as illustrated in Figure 3-1.

In this example the Instant Messenger application is an Ajax application that loads existing HTML data asynchronously from the server and displays

Figure 3–1.   Displaying asynchronously loaded HTML as a pop-up

it dynamically as part of the application. The following code performs this task:

```
icon.addClickListener(new ClickListener(){
    public void onClick( Widget sender ){
        try{
            RequestBuilder requestBuilder = new RequestBuilder(
                RequestBuilder.GET,
                GWT.getModuleBaseURL()+"/"+contact.getName()+".html" );
            requestBuilder.sendRequest( null, new RequestCallback(){
                public void onError(Request request, Throwable exception){
                    /*ignored*/
                }
                public void onResponseReceived(
                    Request request, Response response){
                    if( response.getStatusCode() == 200 ){
                        PopupPanel popup = new PopupPanel(true);
                        popup.setStyleName("popup");
                        popup.setWidget( new HTML(response.getText()));
                        popup.setPopupPosition( icon.getAbsoluteLeft(),
                            icon.getAbsoluteTop()+ icon.getOffsetHeight());
                        popup.show();
                    }
                }
            });
        }catch( Exception e){ /*ignored*/ }
    }
});
```

This code adds a click listener to the icon, which implements the `onClick` event to use GWT's HTTP library to make an asynchronous request to the server for an HTML document with the icon contact's name. If the request is successful, when there is an existing HTML document for the contact, the code creates a `PopupPanel` widget holding the HTML contents of the requested document and displays it beneath the icon.

This technique, loading existing HTML documents from the server, is one basic integration method with the server and can help a client Ajax application leverage resources from an existing server application.

Integrating with Traditional Server-Side Script Technologies

Most existing web applications are more than a collection of HTML documents or fragments. They commonly run on scripting engines that produce HTML dynamically on the server from user input or data from a database. When requesting data from a script, it is often transparent to the user or client developer that a script is being used. For example, the HTML fragment in the previous section could have been generated by a script that first retrieved the data from a database and then generated the resulting HTML to be returned to the user. Other times an application needs to accept data from the user through a script. The script would take data submitted by the user through a form submission and process the data, often validating the data and then inserting the data into a database.

This means there are three possible behaviors for a server-side script from a client application's perspective.

- The script accepts parameters from the client and generates a response.
- The script accepts a request from the client and then fetches data from a database and generates a response.
- The script accepts data submission from the client and processes the data or inserts it into a database.

GWT provides tools that allow Ajax applications to interact with all three of these types of script behaviors. Let's look at the first two behaviors, where the script generates a response from client parameters or from the database, since they are commonly used together. We'll modify the Instant Messenger pop-up example from the previous section, where users click on a contact icon to display an HTML information page. In this case, instead of requesting different HTML documents stored on the server, we will request the document from a single PHP script providing the contact's name as a parameter. If you're familiar with building server-side scripts, then you are familiar with GET and POST parameters. These parameters, which can be sent across an HTTP request using GET or POST, are name-value pairs separated by the & (ampersand) symbol. GET requests send the parameters in the URL after the ? (question mark) symbol. POST requests send the parameters as part of the request body after the HTTP headers. Most server-side scripts, including PHP, have support for automatically parsing these parameters and placing them in a data structure that makes each value easily accessible.

Our PHP script will be called getContact.php and will accept a name parameter. It will build the contact HTML similar to the ryan.html file shown previously, except it will support the ability to generate HTML for many contacts. To request the HTML for a contact, you would make a request for the script with the name attribute like this:

```
getContact.php?name=ryan
```

The PHP script to accept the parameter and generate the HTML looks like this:

```php
<?php
    $contacts['ryan'] = array(
        'name' => 'Ryan',
        'job' => 'Software Developer',
        'website' => 'http://www.rdews.com');
    $contacts['biz'] = array(
        'name' => 'Biz',
        'job' => 'Cat',
        'website' => 'http://www.cat.com');

    $contact = $contacts[$_GET['name']];
?>

<b><?=$contact['name']?></b><br/>
<?=$contact['job']?><br/>
<a href="<?=$contact['website']?>"><?=$contact['website']?></a>
```

This PHP first generates an associative array of data that has information for two different contacts. Typically this type of data would be loaded from a database. The code selects the contact requested by using the GET parameter and looking up the name in the contacts array. Then the script plugs the values from the selected contact into the HTML output. It's not important that you know PHP to understand this. This example just demonstrates how to use GWT to integrate with existing form-handling server-side scripts. This example integrates with a server-side script that accepts a GET parameter.

On the client side, we simply need to change the request URL to point to the PHP script like this:

```
RequestBuilder requestBuilder = new RequestBuilder(
RequestBuilder.GET,
GWT.getModuleBaseURL()+"/getContact.php?name="+
URL.encodeComponent( contact.getName() ) );
```

Notice that this code uses the parameter submission format for GET requests of placing the parameters at the end of the URL following the ? character. The code adds the parameters with their names and if there were more than one we would separate them with the & character. It's important to use GWT's URL.encodeComponent method, which encodes any characters that may get in the way of interpreting the URL and its parameters. For example, if the name had an & symbol in it, this would cause the PHP parameter parser to interpret it as the start of the next set of variables. Instead, the server interprets encoded parameters correctly. GWT also provides the URL.encode method, which is used for other parts of the URL that are not in the parameter part.

You can submit data to a script that would normally process a form submission in a similar way. Typically HTML form tags have a couple of important parameters, named action and method, for communicating with the server. The action attribute specifies the script URL where the form will submit its values. The method attribute specifies which HTTP method to use, GET or POST. The form uses the same type of parameter encoding that was mentioned earlier. Let's look at an example of submitting data via a POST request to a script that would normally receive form submissions.

We'll start by looking at the form's HTML you could use to submit data to a registration script:

```
<form name="input" action="register.php" method="post">
   Username: <input type="text" name="user"><br/>
   Email: <input type="text" name="email"><br/>
```

```
    Password: <input type="password" name="password"><br/>
    <input type="submit" value="Submit">
</form>
```

The form has `register.php` as its action, `post` as its method, and takes three parameters. This means that when the form is submitted, an HTTP POST request will be made to register.php with the form input values as parameters. The actual data submitted by the browser will look like this:

```
POST /register.php HTTP/1.1
Content-Type: application/x-www-form-urlencoded

username=ryan&email=ryan%40rdews.com&password=secret
```

This scaled-down version of what is sent illustrates the important pieces. The first section, the HTTP protocol, starts with the POST request followed by HTTP headers. You can see that the POST request asks for the `register.php` script from the HTTP server. It has a Content-Type header set to `application/x-www-form-urlencoded`, which tells the script what kind of data is being posted. When PHP sees this as the content type, it knows to parse the content as form parameters that it provides to PHP in an array. Other server scripting languages, such as JSP, perform the same task. The parameter list follows the header in the parameter encoding we've been using, which consists of name-value pairs separated by the `&` character. Notice that the `@` symbol in the e-mail value is encoded. The server-side script engine will automatically decode this value before the register.php script processes it.

When the server runs the `register.php` script, it would typically validate the data and create a new row in the database. We're not really interested in how this is done, but rather how to integrate with this script from an Ajax application without having to change the server-side script.

There are two options to integrate with a script like this. The first involves constructing an HTTP request manually and submitting the values to the server, similar to the GET request we constructed earlier. The second involves using GWT's `FormPanel` to create a form interface and to use the browsers' form-submitting functionality to submit the data. Using the `FormPanel` requires less work with the lower-level HTTP request, but it requires an interface. If you are going to create an interface for the form anyway, this is probably the way to go. Otherwise you can still submit data to the form with the first method we looked at. Let's look at the implementation for the first method.

Submitting POST data to a script that would normally accept POST data from a form is fairly straightforward. You do this exactly the same as the previous example using the GET method, except you don't submit the parameters through the URL, but as POST data. The GWT HTTP library allows POST data to be submitted in the `sendRequest` method. You also need to set the Content-Type HTTP header so the server-side script knows the format of the POST data. The following code implements the POST submission to the request.php form:

```
//build the data to post
StringBuffer postBuilder = new StringBuffer();
postBuilder.append("username=" );
postBuilder.append( URL.encodeComponent( username ) );

postBuilder.append("&email=" );
postBuilder.append( URL.encodeComponent( email ) );

postBuilder.append("&password=" );
postBuilder.append( URL.encodeComponent( password ) );

try{
   //create and submit the request
   RequestBuilder requestBuilder = new RequestBuilder( RequestBuilder.POST,
      GWT.getModuleBaseURL()+"/register.php" );
   requestBuilder.sendRequest( postBuilder.toString(), new RequestCallback(){
      public void onError(Request request, Throwable exception){
         /*ignored*/
      }

      public void onResponseReceived(Request request, Response response){
         /*ignored*/
      }
   });
}catch( Exception e){ /*ignored*/ }
```

This method allows you to integrate with existing scripts and programmatically submit data to them. The other method, using the `FormPanel`, presents a user interface and uses an underlying form tag to do the submission. However, the `FormPanel` does not cause a page refresh as a typical form tag would. It submits its data to a hidden form so the Ajax application can continue running without a refresh.

The following code creates a `FormPanel` which submits the same data to the register script:

```
//create the form panel, set its action and method
final FormPanel form = new FormPanel();
form.setAction("/register.php");
form.setMethod(FormPanel.METHOD_POST);

//set the main widget for the panel to a vertical panel
VerticalPanel panel = new VerticalPanel();
form.setWidget(panel);

//create the username field
TextBox tb = new TextBox();
tb.setName("username");
panel.add(tb);

//create the e-mail field
TextBox tb = new TextBox();
tb.setName("email ");
panel.add(tb);

//create the password field
PasswordTextBox ptb = new PasswordTextBox();
ptb.setName("password");
panel.add(ptb);

//create the Submit button
panel.add(new Button("Submit", new ClickListener() {
   public void onClick(Widget sender) {
      form.submit();
   }
}));
```

This code does not programmatically submit the data, but instead it waits for the user to input the data and click the Submit button. The data submitted is the same as the previous example. To the `register.php` script, both form submission techniques look the same.

A server-side web application built with these types of server-side scripts works with HTML forms and can be called an **action-based web application.** The word *action* comes from the `action` attribute on the HTML form tag, which points to the location of the server-side script. The Database Editor application in Chapter 10 includes a detailed example on how to integrate with an action-based PHP web application.

Using Data Format Libraries

You've seen that integrating with traditional web applications on the server typically involves reading HTML or plain text and making calls to server-side scripts using form encoding. However, HTML is a markup language for rendering data for viewing and it isn't well structured for using programmatically. Also, form encoding is not ideal for more complex data structures that are hierarchical. More advanced web applications have more robust ways to send and receive data from the server. The two most common formats for sending and receiving more complex data structures on the web are XML and JSON, both of which have libraries in GWT to build and parse their formats. These formats can be paired with asynchronous HTTP requests to send and receive structure data to and from a server.

Reading and Writing XML

XML is a very important data format on the web and it is a large part of many Ajax applications (XML put the *X* in Ajax). Typically, Ajax applications build their interface with dynamic JavaScript and asynchronously load data from the server in XML format. This technique allows Ajax applications to operate on the data in many dynamic ways, which leads to much richer client applications than the traditional web model, where the server prerenders data to be displayed statically in the browser. XML has syntax similar to HTML, but it differs greatly in how it can be used by applications. While you can use HTML to mark up data for specific rendering in a browser, XML marks up data to describe its meaning to applications. For example, doing a search for books on the Amazon.com web page returns a list of books formatted in HTML and rendered in a browser so it can be easily read by the user. If an application made the same request and received a list of books in HTML format, it would have a difficult time understanding or being certain of what the data meant. Furthermore, if Amazon decided to change their presentation in HTML, the structure would change and potentially confuse an application reading the data. This is where XML excels. If Amazon were to return a list of books in XML format (and they do provide this service), an application could read the XML and know exactly how to interpret the data. XML gains this quality by being a self-describing format; that is, each piece of data has extra information attached describing what it is. For example, the Blog Editor application in Chapter 8 returns a blog entry from the Blogger service in XML format looking like this:

```
<entry>
    <id>tag:blogger.com,1999:blog-6153289560998349310.post-4077746181889447434</id>
    <published>2007-03-08T19:08:00.000-08:00</published>
    <updated>2007-04-12T08:59:46.568-07:00</updated>
    <title type='text'>The Nature of Asynchronous Method Calls</title>
    <content type='html'>The nature of asynchronous method calls requires the
caller to pass in a callback object that can be notified when an asynchronous call
completes, since by definition the caller cannot be blocked until the call
completes. For the same reason, asynchronous methods do not have return types;
they must always return void. After an asynchronous call is made, all
communication back to the caller is via the passed-in callback object.</content>
    <link rel='alternate' type='text/html' href='http://gwttest.blogspot.com/2007/
03/test.html'></link>
    <link rel='self' type='application/atom+xml' href='http://
gwttest.blogspot.com/feeds/posts/default/4077746181889447434'></link>
    <link rel='edit' type='application/atom+xml' href='http://www.blogger.com/
feeds/6153289560998349310/posts/default/4077746181889447434'></link>
    <author><name>Ryan</name></author>
</entry>
```

As you can see, the syntax is similar to HTML except the tags describe the data they contain. When an application receives this, it can easily determine the different parts of data. For example, the Blog Editor application parses this blog entry using the GWT's XML library with the following code:

```
//parse and get the root element
Element entryElement = XMLParser.parse( xml ).getDocumentElement();
entry.setTitle( getElementText( entryElement, "title" ) );
entry.setContent( getElementText( entryElement, "content" ) );

//find the link elements in the document
String editLink = "";
NodeList links = entryElement.getElementsByTagName("link");
for(int j=0;j<links.getLength();j++ ) {
   Element linkElement = (Element)links.item(j);
   String rel = linkElement.getAttribute( "rel" );
   if( rel.equals("alternate") )
      entry.setLink( linkElement.getAttribute("href") );
   else if( rel.equals("edit") )
      editLink = linkElement.getAttribute("href");
}
entryEditLinks.put( entry, editLink );
```

Parsing data with the XML library always starts with a call to the static parse method on the `XMLParser` class. The return value, a `Document` instance, represents the data that was parsed. The document holds a document object model, making it easy to programmatically iterate over the parsed data. Following XML rules, the document contains one root element, which you can access with the `getDocumentElement` method. In this case the document element is the entry element you saw in the XML data just shown. Each tag in the XML data has a corresponding `Element` instance in the document object model. The `Element` class exposes some methods that allow the application to retrieve its tag name, its attributes, and any child nodes contained in the tag. Note that the previous code uses a helper method to access an `Element`'s child text, called `getElementText`:

```
// gets the text in the first child element with a given name
private String getElementText( Element item, String value ) {
    String result = "";
    NodeList itemList = item.getElementsByTagName(value);
    if( itemList.getLength() > 0 && itemList.item(0).hasChildNodes()) {
        //assuming there is one text node
        //ideally this should iterate over the child nodes and
        //concatenate the text
        result = itemList.item(0).getFirstChild().getNodeValue();
    }
    return result;
}
```

Note that not all objects in the document object model are elements. Attributes, textual data, and many other node types can also be part of an XML document. All of these objects have their own classes in GWT's XML library, which are subclasses of the `Node` class. The UML diagram in Figure 3-2 shows the structure of the XML document object model as implemented by GWT's XML library.

In this book we use the `Document`, `Element`, and `Text` classes to access XML data. You can find additional information about the other entities in the XML document object model at www.w3.org/DOM/.

In the blog entry example, the XML is parsed based on its structure. Parsing creates an instance of the document object model that represents the parsed data. The document object model for the parsed data looks something like Figure 3-3.

The code simply navigates through this hierarchy using GWT's XML library and retrieves the required data, which in this case is the data needed to build the `Entry` object from the application's model.

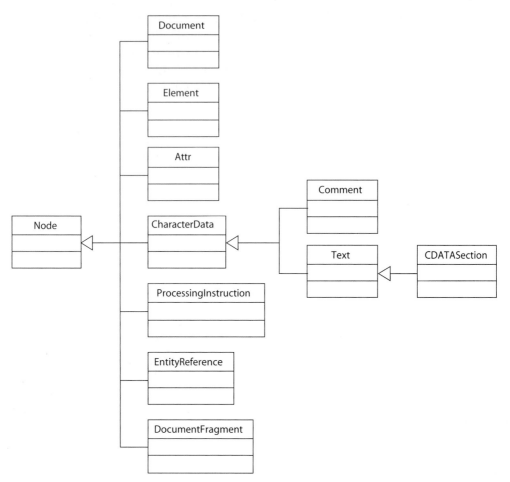

Figure 3–2. The structure of the XML document object model as implemented by GWT's XML library

The reverse operation is also part of the XML library. You can build a document object model using the same objects and then convert the model to a string. This is most commonly used when you need to communicate with a server by sending structured XML data. The Blog Editor application uses this feature to send XML data to the Blogger service to create a new blog entry and to also update an existing blog entry. It uses the same format that was used in the previous example. The following is a code snippet from this example and shows the XML generated prior to sending it to the server:

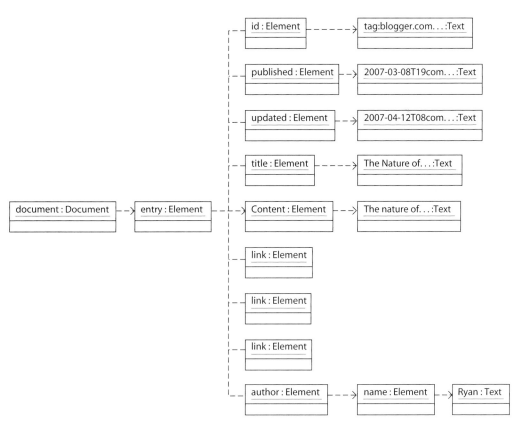

Figure 3–3.   Document object model for the blog example after parsing a string

```
Document document = XMLParser.createDocument();
Element entryElement = document.createElement("entry");
Element titleElement = document.createElement("title");
Element contentElement = document.createElement("content");
Text titleText = document.createTextNode( entry.getTitle());
Text contentText = document.createTextNode( entry.getContent() );
document.appendChild(entryElement);
entryElement.setAttribute("xmlns","http://www.w3.org/2005/Atom");
entryElement.appendChild(titleElement);
entryElement.appendChild(contentElement);
titleElement.appendChild(titleText);
contentElement.setAttribute("type","html");
contentElement.appendChild(contentText);
String xml = document.toString();
```

This code creates each node in the document object model using the create methods on the `Document` class. It creates the hierarchy structure by using the `appendChild` method to add child nodes to parents. Then it sets XML attributes using the `Element` class' `setAttribute` method. When the document object model is fully constructed, the code calls the `document.toString()` method to convert the model to an XML string.

Reading and Writing JSON

GWT also comes with a JavaScript Object Notation (JSON) library for parsing and constructing JSON strings. The JSON data format, like XML, is hierarchical and self-describing, but it differs from XML in its size and syntax, which many consider one of its advantages over XML. Its other advantage is that it is easily parsed with the JavaScript `eval` function:

```
var jsonString = "{'Title':'Ajax for Java developers'}";
var obj = eval( jsonString );
alert( obj.Title );
```

In this JavaScript code, the JSON-encoded string is passed to the `eval` function, which returns a JavaScript object version of the parsed string. With this easy support for this format in JavaScript, it makes a natural addition to GWT.

Let's briefly go over the format for JSON, starting with a comparison to XML. The structure of XML is divided into elements, attributes, and text, whereas the JSON's structure is divided into objects, arrays, and values. Table 3-1 presents a comparison of the two formats for formatting the same type of data.

Table 3–1   XML Versus JSON Formatting of the Same Data

XML	``` <entry> <title type='text'>The Nature of Asynchronous Method Calls</title> aScript Object Notation, (of the document object model that repre- sents the parsed data. sed Ruby server. ##################<author> <name>Ryan</name> </author> </entry> ```

JSON	```
	{
	    "entry":{
	        "title":"The Nature of Asynchronous Method Calls",
	        "author":{
	            "name":"ryan"
	        }
	    }
	}
	``

The syntax differences begin with the delimiters. JSON uses curly braces to begin and end an object, names its attributes using quoted strings, and presents their value with a colon. The value can either be another object, a string value or other simple data type, or an array. The savings in size come from the format not needing to repeat named data the way XML does with start and end tags. The data typing system in JSON is also stronger than the data type system in basic XML (excluding Schemas, which are not automatically supported in GWT). A simple JSON value can be a Boolean, number, string, or null. Figure 3-4 illustrates the data types available in JSON through GWT's JSON library.

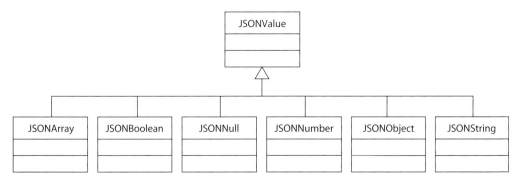

Figure 3–4.   Data types available in JSON

This JSON library is in the `com.google.gwt.json.client` package. It is not automatically included with your application, so you need to add the following line to your project's module file to use it:

```
<inherits name="com.google.gwt.json.JSON"/>
```

The library's object model is similar to the XML document object model in that they both use several classes to build a hierarchical model as a result of parsing data. To parse JSON data, you use GWT's `JSONParser` class' parse method, passing in the JSON string. The return value is a `JSONValue` representing the root of the object structure for the parsed data. The Multi-Search application in Chapter 7 parses JSON search results returned from several search engine services. The following code snippet from this application shows parsing the search results from Yahoo! with the JSON library:

```
//parse the string and get the ResultSet object
JSONObject j = (JSONObject)JSONParser.parse(json);
JSONObject feed = (JSONObject)j.get("ResultSet");
```

```
//iterate over the Results array
JSONArray entries = (JSONArray)feed.get("Result");
for( int i=0; i< entries.size(); ++i ) {
   JSONObject entry = (JSONObject)entries.get(i);
   JSONString title = (JSONString)entry.get("Title");
   JSONString url = (JSONString)entry.get("Url");
   JSONString summary = (JSONString)entry.get("Summary");
   if( url != null ) {
      getView().addSearchResult( new SearchEngineResult( title.stringValue(),
         url.stringValue(), summary.stringValue() ) );
   }
}
```

The code first parses the json variable, which is a string of the JSON data, and receives a JSONObject instance back. The example shows how to get several different types of JSON values back from the parsed data and how to iterate over the values in a JSONArrary. The code creates a new SearchEngineResult, a domain model object for the application, for each search result it finds in the JSON data.

This code was simplified to not check the type of each JSON value. This means if the value is not the type expected, the application will throw a ClassCastException. To avoid this exception, you could check the type of the JSONValue object using its type identification methods. For example, to check the type of the value returned when retrieving the search result title, you would use code like this:

```
JSONValue value = entry.get("Title");
if( value.isString() ){
   JSONString title = (JSONString)value;
```

Converting GWT's JSON values to a JSON string is as simple as calling the toString method on the value.

JSON may have a couple of benefits over XML, but XML is much more widely used, understood, and has a greater array of tools and technologies built on top of it. So why use JSON? If you're building a new system that does not integrate with other systems that use XML for integration, then you may want to consider JSON. Keep in mind that this may limit your capability to integrate with other systems. JSON is increasing in popularity due to its use in Ajax applications, but it will most likely not gain the usage that XML has. You may also use JSON to load data remotely through a script tag on a web page, effectively bypassing the browser's Same Origin policy restriction. This is the reason for using JSON in the Multi-Search application. This application has the capability to load external JSON data sources through the script tag without a server-side proxy. We look at this method, called JSONP (JSON with Padding) in the next section.

Third-Party Server Integration

One of the most common sayings in software development is "Don't reinvent the wheel." This applies to web application development as well, especially because there are a vast number of free or low-cost third-party web services available. They provide a well-defined way for your application to integrate with their service. Many of the sample applications in this book integrate with third-party servers. The Gadget Desktop application in Chapter 6 integrates with Google Maps, Yahoo! Weather, and the Google Ajax Feed API using JavaScript APIs. The Multi-Search application in Chapter 7 integrates with Google Base, Yahoo! Search, Amazon Books, and Flickr using JSONP. And the Blog Editor application in Chapter 8 integrates with the Blogger web service using an HTTP proxy. This section looks at the techniques used in these applications.

The Same Origin Policy

Typically you can't communicate with third-party servers from a client-side Ajax application because of the Same Origin policy applied by web browsers. This policy states that your JavaScript can only access data that shares its server origin. This is a really good thing to have. Without it, it would be possible for JavaScript from another domain running in another window to change the HTML in the current window. You could never be certain that what you were looking at actually originated from the domain shown in the browser's location field. With the policy in place, we know for sure that what we are viewing was sent by the domain we are browsing.

For Ajax applications, this also means that data can't be asynchronously downloaded from other domains; we can only load data from the server from which the browser loaded the application. This is an unfortunate restriction given the wealth of web services available to Ajax applications.

Using JavaScript APIs

The Same Origin policy doesn't restrict importing scripts from third-party servers using the HTML script tag. This doesn't mean it's perfectly safe. If you do load third-party JavaScript API's from another source, you have to trust that the third party would not send your application malicious code. There are quite a few JavaScript libraries available for inclusion into Ajax applications that come from large companies that would not jeopardize their reputation by providing malicious code. Google and Yahoo! are two of these companies.

The Gadget Desktop application uses the Google Ajax Feed API to load RSS feeds from third-party sites. When including JavaScript APIs you should follow the instructions provided in the API documentation. Typically this involves adding a `script` tag to the HTML file that you want to use the API on. For a GWT application, you can add the API to your host HTML page's `head` tag. For example, the following code adds the Google Ajax Feed API to the Gadget Desktop application:

```
<head>
    <title>GWT Applications - Gadget Desktop</title>
    <script type="text/javascript" src="http://www.google.com/
jsapi?key=ABQIAAAACeDba0As0X6mwbIbUYWv-RTb-
vLQlFZmc2N8bgWI8YDPp5FEVBQUnvmfInJbOoyS2v-qkssc36Z5MA"></script>
    <script type="text/javascript">
        google.load("feeds", "1");
    </script>
```

This HTML code loads the JavaScript code from Google when the HTML page is loaded. The JavaScript code is then available to be used by your GWT application. However, the code is in JavaScript and your application is in Java, so you need to use GWT's JavaScript Native Interface (JSNI). (For more on JSNI, refer to Chapter 5.) Using JSNI you can access the functions provided by the loaded JavaScript API.

Other examples of communicating with third-party servers through Java-Script APIs include using the Google Maps API in the Gadget Desktop application. You also use this API by loading its code through a `script` tag and accessing the methods through JSNI. The loaded JavaScript code handles loading map data from the Google servers asynchronously.

Using JSONP

You can also use `script` tags to load more structured data like JSON from third-party sites. JSON can be automatically interpreted by a JavaScript compiler, so it is a natural format to use for transmitting structured data through `script` tags. Essentially, using a `script` tag to load structure data from a third-party site bypasses the Same Origin policy restrictions imposed by the browser. In fact, the Multi-Search application uses JSONP to load data from Google, Yahoo!, Amazon, and Flickr without any server-side implementation.

To do this, the GWT Application adds a `script` tag to the HTML document, which causes the browser to load the script from the supplied URL. The third-party server receives a request for the URL and generates JSON output wrapped by a `callback` method. When the browser finishes receiving the remote script file, the browser runs the file in its JavaScript interpreter. Since the file is JSON data wrapped by a call to a `callback` function, the `callback` function is called in the browser. Before the GWT application adds the `script` tag, it needs to add a `callback` function with the expected name in order to receive the call when the script completes loading. This is an asynchronous process much like the asynchronous HTTP request. Figure 3-5 illustrates this sequence.

For an implementation of a GWT JSONP class called `JSONRequest`, see the Multi-Search application.

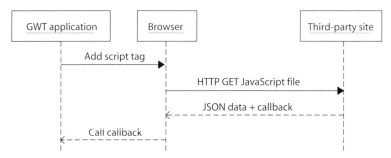

Figure 3–5.   Loading remote data using JSONP

Using an HTTP Proxy

For server interaction more complex than simply fetching data, you'll need to create a server component for your application and to choose a server integration technique to communicate with your server. Your server acts as a proxy to the third-party server by relaying a request from the client Ajax application to the server. The Blog Editor application uses a simple HTTP proxy servlet to relay REST-based API calls to the Blogger service. Since the blogger API requires us to use many HTTP commands, including GET, POST, PUT, and DELETE, and post XML-formatted data, our only option is to connect to the Blogger server from our server. For a detailed example of an HTTP proxy, see the Blog Editor application.

Advanced Server Integration Techniques

So far you've seen techniques to integrate your GWT application with traditional action-based web applications, simple asynchronous HTTP, and third-party server integration. These techniques all have their uses, but they are fairly basic in their level of integration. For more complex applications there is typically a more complex server, and consequently integration becomes more complex. Relying on forms or a simple asynchronous HTTP request class to handle the complexity can lead to unmanageable code. This section looks at advanced techniques to integrate with stateless servers using a REST interface or GWT-RPC, starting with the difference between a stateful server and stateless server.

Stateful Servers

The traditional web application model is based on HTTP, which is a stateless protocol. This means that one request has no relation to another request; the server treats them as distinct requests. However, it's possible for applications built on HTTP to hold application state, and many do to create a meaningful application. For example, consider a web e-mail application like Hotmail. You could be writing your e-mail and need to upload a photo. Clicking the Upload button brings you to a new page to upload a file. Once you upload the file, the web application returns you to the e-mail you were working on. In this example the web server has remembered the state of the application and is able to guide your browser through the required steps. This type of application state is usually stored on the server, accessed through a cookie or URL parameter, and called a *session.* Although GWT provides client-side application developers with tools to let you improve the functionality of the client-side application to the point where it doesn't need to rely much on server-side state, there will still be situations where an application may need to integrate with a stateful server.

A GWT application can act like a traditional web application to a stateful server using HTML forms, and can also enhance the user experience using client-side stateful information. Also, many early RPC implementations, in particular XML-RPC, were based on a stateful server application. The client would operate on server-side data—one remote call at a time. You can also accomplish this with GWT applications by using the XML and HTTP libraries.

Figure 3-6 illustrates how a GWT application interacts with a stateful server.

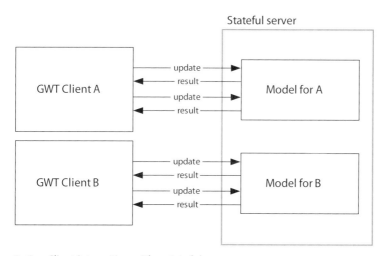

Figure 3–6.   Client interaction with a stateful server

This is also how traditional web application development works. The server holds a state, or model, for each client. The client can interact with that state with small incremental changes. This model applies to both traditional HTML forms over HTTP and XML RPC.

Although this is the predominant architecture for web applications, you should only use this when necessary. Heavier Ajax applications that can hold some of the server-side state for their session can improve performance dramatically. This solution is described next. Note that in some situations a stateful server is perfectly valid. The Instant Messenger application requires a stateful server since the clients share the application state. Each client must know what other clients are logged on to the server. This state cannot be pushed to the clients. There must be a common entity between the clients to hold the common session state.

Integrating with Stateless Servers

The stateful web server application is an effect of the thin client architecture. In terms of performance, it is not ideal for servers to manage the state of small user actions, but since HTML clients lack any ability to maintain state, with the web page being refreshed after each action, there are few alternatives. However, Ajax applications give us the ability to build heavier client applications which can hold application state much better and allow the user's actions to be isolated in the client until they absolutely need to be committed to the server in a larger transaction style request. When dealing with remote requests, fewer but larger transactions perform much better than many small ones. It's a common mistake not to consider this when designing remote interfaces, especially when there are nice RPC libraries, like the GWT-RPC library, which allow you to quickly write interfaces as you would write a local interface in your application. Think of each method call to the server as a single transaction. Smaller units of work should be performed within the client without interaction with the server. Figure 3-7 illustrates the communication between a stateless server and a rich client.

Web application models are slowly moving toward this architecture. Replacing XML-RPC is SOAP, an application communication protocol that tries to solve the problem of XML-RPC being too closely coupled with the server-side implementation. Instead of procedure calls, the interaction is based on messages that follow this model, which is more stateless and transactional than a remote call model. Another stateless web architecture for communicating with a server is called REST (representational state transfer). In this architecture, applications treat the server as a set of stateless resources identified by URLs and modified by HTTP methods. The Blog Editor application in Chapter 8 is a good example of a GWT applica-

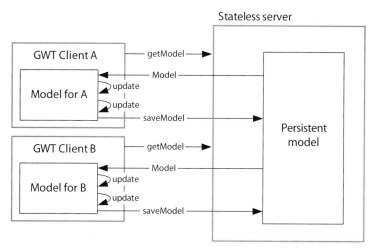

Figure 3–7.   Client interaction with a stateless server

tion communicating with a stateless server based on REST. The application loads all of the blog data in one transaction when the application starts, which enables the user to use the application to operate on the data. Additional server interaction is only required when users click the Save or Delete button. Even when users select to create a new blog entry, the application doesn't contact the server until users save the new entry. This application has dramatically fewer round-trip calls to the server than the HTML forms equivalent application would. For example, at www.blogger.com you would need several HTTP requests just to browse through the interface to get to an editor to add a new entry. The Database Editor application in Chapter 10 also follows this stateless REST-based architecture.

You can't always choose which architecture to use when integrating with a server, since the server most likely is already running with its own interface. But if you are considering building a server application with a GWT application as a client, then you should be looking at moving most of the application state to the client so the application will scale better.

Using GWT-RPC

GWT extends a browser's capability to asynchronously communicate with the server by providing a remote procedure call (RPC) library. In general, remote procedure calls aim to simplify the task of making calls to the server by providing you with an interface of methods that can be called similarly to regular method calls. The calls then get marshaled (converted to a stream of data) and sent to the remote server. When the server receives the marshaled data, it unmarshals it and invokes the method on the server.

In GWT, the RPC library is divided into two packages: the com.google .gwt.user.client.rpc package used for client-side RPC support and the com.google.gwt.user.server.rpc package used for server-side RPC support. The client side provides interfaces that you can use to tag your application interface that you'll use for RPC. When you compile your client project to JavaScript using the GWT compiler, the code required to do the RPC marshaling is generated based on the interfaces you tagged. The Instant Messenger application in Chapter 9 uses GWT-RPC, and the following code declares the interface to be a RPC interface:

```
public interface MessengerService extends RemoteService{
    void signIn( String name );
    void signOut();
    ArrayList getEvents();
    void sendMessage( Contact to, Message message );
}
```

The RemoteService interface is an empty GWT-RPC interface that tells the GWT compiler that marshaling code should be generated for this interface. You must implement this interface on the sever side.

The server-side package for RPC is built to be used in a Java servlet container such as Tomcat or Jetty. Fortunately, GWT's hosted browser comes with an embedded Tomcat server, which allows us to easily test and debug the server-side RPC from an IDE like Eclipse. The server-side package contains one class that you extend to implement the server-side RPC interface. The Instant Messenger application defines the server-side class as follows:

```
public class MessengerServiceImpl
    extends RemoteServiceServlet implements MessengerService {
        public void signIn( String name )
        {
        }

        public void signOut()
        {
        }
```

```
public ArrayList getEvents()
{
}

public void sendMessage( Contact to, Message message )
{
}
}
```

The class simply extends GWT's `RemoteServiceServlet` and implements the methods on the RPC interface just described. You can easily
install this servlet for testing in the hosted browser by adding the following
line to the project's module file:

```
<servlet path="/messenger"
class="com.gwtapps.messenger.server.MessengerServiceImpl"/>
```

The `path` attribute represents the servlet's callable location on the server,
and the `class` attribute specifies the servlet class name to install.

When it's time to deploy to a servlet container outside of the GWT hosted
browser, you'll need to follow a few steps to get things set up. For Tomcat,
you need to install it in the web applications directory as a new web application with the directory structures shown in Figure 3-8.

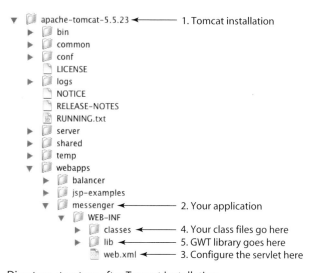

Figure 3–8.   Directory structure after Tomcat installation

Let's look at the five steps shown in Figure 3.8. First, you need to locate the installation directory for Tomcat. Second, you need to create your application directory under the webapps directory. Third, you need to set up your web.xml file in the WEB-INF directory for your application. For the Instant Messenger application, this file looks like this:

```
<?xml version="1.0" encoding="UTF-8"?>
<web-app>
    <servlet>
        <servlet-name>messenger</servlet-name>
        <servlet-class>com com.gwtapps.messenger.server.MessengerServiceImpl
        </servlet-class>
    </servlet>
    <servlet-mapping>
        <servlet-name>messenger</servlet-name>
        <url-pattern>/messenger</url-pattern>
    </servlet-mapping>
</web-app>
```

Fourth, copy your `servlet` class to the class' directory in the WEB-INF directory. Finally, copy the gwt-servlet.jar file to the lib directory in the WEB-INF directory. The gwt-servlet.jar file has the GWT classes required to support the server-side RPC. You could use gwt-user.jar instead, but gwt-servlet.jar is smaller and therefore preferred. Deployment can be automated by using a build tool such as Ant.

Whether you have the servlet running in GWT's embedded Tomcat or in another installation, the client-side code used to make RPC calls is the same. The client code needs to create a proxy instance that will receive the method calls from the client and marshal them to the server. When the server has completed the call it returns a response to the client-side proxy. The proxy then relays this to the client application through the `Async` `Callback` interface. For this asynchronous method call system to work, you need to create a second interface for use on the client side that handles return values differently. For the Instant Messenger application, the interface looks like this:

```
public interface MessengerServiceAsync {
    void signIn( String name, AsyncCallback callback );
    void signOut( AsyncCallback callback );
    void getEvents( AsyncCallback callback );
    void sendMessage( Contact to, Message message, AsyncCallback callback );
}
```

Notice that the interface is very similar to the `MessengerService` interface; the only differences are that there aren't any return values and it requires an extra `AsyncCallback` parameter for each method. This setup allows the proxy to return the RPC method's return value from the server in your implementation of the `AsyncCallback` interface. For example, the `getEvents` method uses the following callback:

```
private class GetEventsCallback implements AsyncCallback {
    public void onFailure(Throwable throwable) {
        GWT.log("error get events",throwable);
    }
    public void onSuccess(Object obj) {
        ArrayList events = (ArrayList)obj;
        for( int i=0; i< events.size(); ++i ) {
            Object event = events.get(i);
            handleEvent( event );
        }
    messengerService.getEvents( this );
    }
}
```

The proxy calls the `onFailure` method when the call to the server fails. The proxy calls the `onSuccess` method when the method call returns successfully. In this instance the return value is an array of events which are iterated over in the `onSuccess` handler. The RPC library automatically marshals and unmarshals this return value, along with the parameter values for method calls. You can even create new classes to send as method parameters to the server or to receive from the server as return values. For example, the Instant Messenger application uses the `Contact` class to transfer data to and from the server:

```
public class Contact implements IsSerializable {
    private String name;
    public Contact(){}
    public Contact( String name ) {
        this.name = name;
    }
    public String getName() {
        return name;
    }
}
```

GWT requires that classes implement the `IsSerializable` or `Serial izable` interface and a constructor with no arguments for GWT-RPC to transfer instances of the class to and from the server. The `IsSerializable` interface is defined by GWT and has no methods; it just acts as a tag to signal the GWT complier that it needs to generate marshaling code for this class.

Before making a method call to the server, the client application needs to create the proxy instance. It does this using the `GWT.create` deferred binding mechanism. You simply make a call to `GWT.create` with the parameter being the class for the RPC interface you want to make calls on:

```
MessengerServiceAsync messengerService =
(MessengerServiceAsync) GWT.create( MessengerService.class );
```

Instead of returning an instance of the RPC interface, this method creates the proxy object that will facilitate RPC communication with the server. The proxy will support two interfaces. One interface, as seen in the preceding code, is the asynchronous version of the RPC interface requested. The other interface is GWT's `ServiceDefTarget` interface. This second interface allows you to set the URL for the remote service that implements the RPC interface. For the Instant Messenger application the URL is set like this:

```
ServiceDefTarget endpoint = (ServiceDefTarget) messengerService;
endpoint.setServiceEntryPoint( GWT.getModuleBaseURL() + "messenger" );
```

This code sets the URL using the `setServiceEntryPoint` method and passing the base URL for the application with the servlet name appended.

Don't worry if this seems fairly complicated; it's really not. Once you have these basics set up, you can easily build rich interfaces with the server. It's worth the small setup costs to gain the productivity in the long run. You can constantly add new methods and data types nearly as straightforwardly as you would for local Java applications.

Figure 3-9 shows an overview of the instances involved with a GWT-RPC implementation for the `MessengerService` in the Instant Messenger application:

You can find a more detailed explanation and further development with GWT-RPC in Chapter 9.

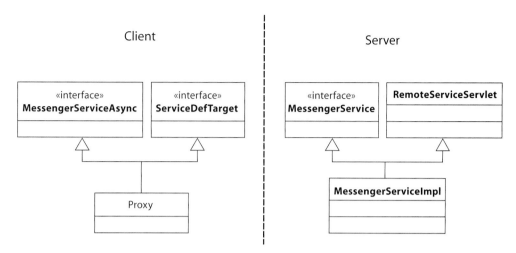

Figure 3–9.   Client and server instances in a GWT-RPC implementation for the `MessengerService`

Summary

This chapter reviewed the many ways that an Ajax application can communicate with servers. The common Ajax technique of asynchronously loading data from the server is a simple method to load data that works well. You can easily load and interpret plain text, HTML, XML, and JSON in your GWT application. You can communicate back to the server using form encoding in the same way traditional web applications communicate with the server. You can leverage third-party services through JavaScript APIs and JSONP without relying on a server-side implementation. In addition, you can perform more advanced interaction with third-party services using a server-side implementation as a proxy. For more advanced projects, you need to use a well-defined interface with the server. GWT's RPC implementation provides an easy way to create a well-defined server interface.

This chapter gave you an overview of these techniques; the sample applications explore these techniques in greater depth. The Gadget Desktop application in Chapter 6 looks at loading JavaScript APIs to interact with third-party services. Chapter 7's Multi-Search application uses JSONP to communicate with four different search services. Neither of these applications relies on any server-side implementations. The Blog Editor application in Chapter 8 interacts with the Blogger web services, which requires richer integration and uses a server-side proxy. The Instant Messenger application in Chapter 9 uses GWT's RPC to create a collaborator-style application with which clients can communicate with each other through the server. The last application in the book, the Database Editor application, explores integrating with three different server-side implementations—PHP, Ruby on Rails, and a Java servlet with Hibernate—using three different server integration techniques, including actions, REST, and GWT-RPC.

4

Software Engineering for Ajax

Perhaps the greatest advantage of using the Google Web Toolkit to build Ajax applications is having the capability to leverage advanced software engineering. JavaScript was never meant to be used to build large applications. It lacks language features that assist in code organization and compile-time type checking. It also lacks mature tools for building large applications, such as automation, integrated development environments, debugging, and testing. This chapter looks at how to use the Java software engineering tools in GWT to build nontrivial high-quality Ajax applications.

Setting Up the Development Environment

To build applications with GWT, you need the Java Development Kit (JDK) 1.4 or greater. Many other Java tools can also assist with your development, such as an IDE like Eclipse or a build tool like Ant. All of these tools bring a lot of value to the process of building Ajax applications. It is important to note that users don't need any of these tools to use your application. They do not even need to have Java installed on their computer; they only need a reasonably modern web browser like Firefox, Internet Explorer, Safari, or Opera. The GWT compiler compiles your application so it conforms to web-standard technology.

Installing the Java Development Kit

The JDK, a package provided by Sun Microsystems, includes the Java Runtime Environment (JRE), which is required to run Java programs on your computer, and command line developer tools which let you compile Java classes to create code that can run. The JDK is on Sun's web site at http://java.sun.com/javase/downloads.

You can choose from several options to download, but the minimum you need is the JDK without anything else bundled. Some options come with NetBeans or Java EE, but these are not required. There is also a download option for JRE, but this does not include the developer tools that you need.

Once you download the JDK (approximately 50MB), you need to install it. On Windows, the download is an executable file that runs the installation. Install the JDK with all the default options.

Installing the Google Web Toolkit

The GWT complements the JDK by adding the ability to compile your Java code to JavaScript so that it can run in a web browser without the Java Runtime Environment. Think of the GWT as another compiler to run Java on a new platform—your web browser. It also provides a hosted mode browser that lets you take advantage of Java's powerful debugging features, just like you would debug a normal Java application. JavaScript debugging tools are primitive compared to what Java and GWT allow you to do. You can find the Google Web Toolkit SDK at http://code.google.com/webtoolkit/download.html.

On Windows, the GWT zip file is approximately 13MB. After you download it, extract the file to your preferred installation directory. On Mac and Linux you can extract the download using this `tar` command:

```
tar xvzf gwt-mac-1.3.3.tar.gz
```

Let's look inside the distribution. The following list gives you a brief overview of the important files that come with GWT.

- gwt-user.jar

  This is the GWT library. It contains the Java classes that you use to build your application with GWT. Your application uses this file when you run it in hosted mode, but this file is not used when your application is deployed, since your application code and the code used in this file are translated to JavaScript.

- gwt-servlet.jar

  This stripped down version of gwt-user.jar has the classes required for the server side of your application. It is much smaller than gwt-user.jar and better for deployment since it does not contain the GWT classes that are required for hosted mode.

- `applicationCreator`

  This script produces the files required to start a GWT application. The generated files produce a runnable bare-bones GWT application.

- `projectCreator`

  This script generates project files for an Eclipse GWT project.

- `junitCreator`

  This script generates a starter test case along with scripts that start the tests in web mode and hosted mode.

- `i18nCreator`

  This script generates an interface based on a properties file for internationalizing an application.

With only the JDK and GWT installed, you can write, run, and compile web-based applications.

For convenience, you should put the GWT installation directory on your path so that you can call the GWT scripts without specifying the full installation path each time. For example, if you installed GWT to c:\code\gwt (this is a Windows path; for Mac and Linux you would similarly use your install path), you would add this to your PATH variable. Then at a command line you can run the `applicationCreator` script inside your application directory without specifying the script's full path, as shown in Figure 4-1.

```
C:\Projects>mkdir gwtapps

C:\Projects>cd gwtapps

C:\Projects\gwtapps>applicationCreator com.gwtapps.examples.client.HelloWorld
Created directory C:\Projects\gwtapps\src
Created directory C:\Projects\gwtapps\src\com\gwtapps\examples
Created directory C:\Projects\gwtapps\src\com\gwtapps\examples\client
Created directory C:\Projects\gwtapps\src\com\gwtapps\examples\public
Created file C:\Projects\gwtapps\src\com\gwtapps\examples\HelloWorld.gwt.xml
Created file C:\Projects\gwtapps\src\com\gwtapps\examples\public\HelloWorld.html

Created file C:\Projects\gwtapps\src\com\gwtapps\examples\client\HelloWorld.java

Created file C:\Projects\gwtapps\HelloWorld-shell.cmd
Created file C:\Projects\gwtapps\HelloWorld-compile.cmd

C:\Projects\gwtapps>_
```

Figure 4–1. Running the `applicationCreator` script for a GWT project

Running this script creates the application named HelloWorld in the current directory. It also generates scripts that let you run the application. You can run this application by just typing the following line:

```
HelloWorld-shell
```

Running this generated script causes GWT to load its hosted browser, which in turn loads the generated application. The hosted browser displays the default generated application, as illustrated in Figure 4-2.

You can also compile the application so that it can be used in a standard browser using the generated HelloWorld-compile script, as seen in Figure 4-3.

The compile script builds the HTML and JavaScript files, which you need to deploy the application, and copies them to the www directory in your application directory, as shown in Figure 4-4.

The generated application can be run in any browser by simply loading the host file. In this HelloWorld application, the host file is named HelloWorld.html. Loading this file in Firefox, as shown in Figure 4-5, results in the same application as in GWT's hosted browser in Figure 4-2, with the major difference being the lack of any Java dependency.

So you can see that the minimum environment for building web applications with GWT is small, only requiring GWT and the JDK to be installed. However, you'll be able to speed up the development process by using

Figure 4–2. Running the default generated project in hosted mode

```
C:\Projects\gwtapps>HelloWorld-compile
Output will be written into C:\Projects\gwtapps\www\com.gwtapps.examples.HelloWo
rld
Copying all files found on public path
Compilation succeeded
```

Figure 4–3. Compiling the project from the command line

Figure 4–4. The files generated from compiling a GWT project

Figure 4–5. The default project compiled and running in Firefox

many of the available Java tools. For example, an IDE like Eclipse is usually used to speed up Java development.

Installing Eclipse

Eclipse is an open source IDE developed in Java and supported by major technology companies including IBM. An IDE allows you to write, organize, test, and debug software in an efficient way. There are many IDEs for Java, and you can use any of them for GWT development. If you do not have a Java IDE installed, I suggest using Eclipse since it works very well and has support with the GWT scripts to help integration.

Eclipse lets you write, organize, test, and debug your GWT Ajax applications in a productive way. It has great support for the Java language, including refactoring and content assist.[1] You can develop using many languages through plugins with Eclipse by taking advantage of Eclipse's rich plugin framework, but the most widely used language is Java. You can find the Eclipse download at www.eclipse.org/downloads.

---

1. Content assist is an Eclipse feature that suggests or completes what you are currently typing. It automatically appears, and you can activate it when needed by pressing Ctrl+Spacebar.

Select the Eclipse SDK from this page. After you download the file (approximately 120MB), extract the file to your preferred installation directory. On Windows, the default location for the file eclipse.exe is in the root of the installation directory; you may want to create a shortcut to the file since you will be using it frequently to edit and debug your code.

Adding Projects to Eclipse

When you first load Eclipse, you are prompted by the dialog box shown in Figure 4-6 for the workspace location. This is the location on your computer that will hold your projects.

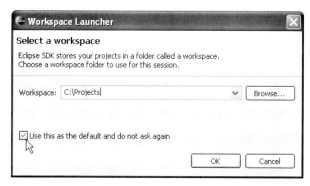

Figure 4–6.   Loading a workspace in Eclipse

Figure 4-6 shows setting the workspace to C:\Projects and selecting the check box to save this as the default workspace, so the next time Eclipse opens this workspace is automatically loaded. Since this is a new workspace, when the main Eclipse window loads it will not have any projects listed in its Package Explorer. At this point we could start building a project manually in Eclipse for the HelloWorld application built earlier in this chapter, but GWT gives us a shortcut with the `projectCreator` script shown in Figure 4-7.

This creates an empty project that references GWT and can be easily loaded into Eclipse. To load the GWT project into Eclipse, choose **File > Import** to display the Import dialog box, shown in Figure 4-8.

```
C:\Projects\gwtapps>projectCreator -eclipse GwtApps
Created directory C:\Projects\gwtapps\test
Created file C:\Projects\gwtapps\.project
Created file C:\Projects\gwtapps\.classpath

C:\Projects\gwtapps>
```

Figure 4–7.   Creating a project with the `projectCreator` script and the `-eclipse` flag

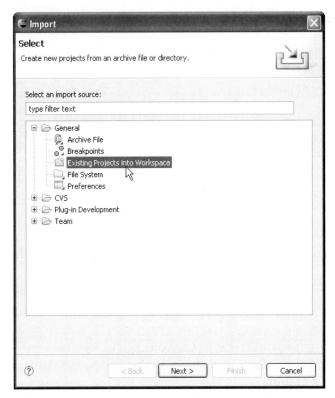

Figure 4–8.   Step 1 of importing a generated GWT project into Eclipse

In the Import dialog, select **Exiting Projects into Workspace** and then click **Next**. The next page of the Import dialog, shown in Figure 4-9, lets you select the projects you want to import.

In this dialog you first need to select the location of your project files. The dialog then presents the list of possible projects that you can import. Figure 4-9 shows the GwtApps project that we created with the GWT `projectCreator` script. Make sure this project is checked and then click **Finish.**

Figure 4–9. Step 2 of importing a generated GWT project into Eclipse

At this point Eclipse loads the project into the Eclipse workspace, and the HelloWorld application is listed under Package Explorer, as shown in Figure 4-10, since it was generated in the Projects directory.

You can add other applications to this project using the `application Creator` script, but since we're in Eclipse now we can take advantage of the `-eclipse` option with the script. When the HelloWorld application was run this option was not specified, so we do not have any Eclipse-specific files that allow you to launch the application from Eclipse. So let's run the `applicationCreator` script again, this time specifying the `-eclipse` option, as shown in Figure 4-11.

If you're creating a new application for use in Eclipse, you do not need the `-overwrite` option. This example used this option to overwrite the previously generated application, which did not have Eclipse support. Notice in Figure 4-11 that the new file HelloWorld.launch was created. This launch

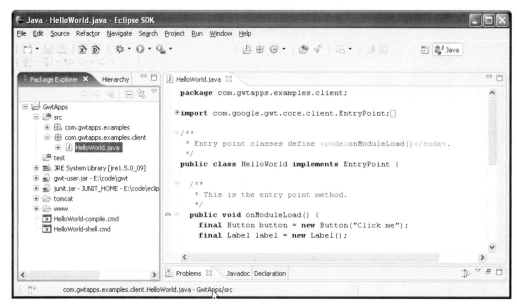

Figure 4–10.   The generated GWT project in the Eclipse IDE

```
C:\Projects\gwtapps>applicationCreator -eclipse GwtApps -overwrite com.gwtapps.e
xamples.client.HelloWorld
Overwriting existing file C:\Projects\gwtapps\src\com\gwtapps\examples\HelloWorl
d.gwt.xml
Overwriting existing file C:\Projects\gwtapps\src\com\gwtapps\examples\public\He
lloWorld.html
Overwriting existing file C:\Projects\gwtapps\src\com\gwtapps\examples\client\He
lloWorld.java
Created file C:\Projects\gwtapps\HelloWorld.launch
Overwriting existing file C:\Projects\gwtapps\HelloWorld-shell.cmd
Overwriting existing file C:\Projects\gwtapps\HelloWorld-compile.cmd

C:\Projects\gwtapps>
```

Figure 4–11.   Creating an application for use in Eclipse

file allows you to select the **Debug** or **Run** command options for the HelloWorld application inside Eclipse. To see this change in Eclipse, refresh
your project (right-click on the project and select **Refresh**), and then run
the HelloWorld application in Debug mode by clicking on the Debug icon
(see the bug icon on the toolbar in Figure 4-12). If your application isn't
listed in the debug drop-down box, which shows a list of recently
debugged configurations, you'll need to click **Debug...** in the drop-down
menu to load the Debug dialog. You'll find the launch configuration for
the HelloWorld application under Java Application.

The application will load in GWT's hosted mode browser, and you can
interact with it while still being connected to the Eclipse IDE. This means

Figure 4–12.   Running a GWT application in the Eclipse debugger

you can set breakpoints, change code, and perform other Eclipse functions while your application is running. The ability to do this shortens the code-test cycle dramatically and its ease promotes heavy testing.

Attaching GWT development to Eclipse, or any other Java IDE, is a giant step forward for Ajax application development. Let's look at some of the details of writing code with Eclipse.

Writing Java Code in Eclipse

Eclipse has many tools for writing Java code that provide hints and constraints on what is possible, shortcuts for common tasks, and refactoring functions for large code changes. Of course, you don't have to use these tools to produce Ajax applications with GWT, but they make writing Java code a lot easier.

Creating Classes in Eclipse

First, let's look at Eclipse's tools for creating classes. Eclipse lets you create new classes or interfaces by clicking on the New Class icon on the top toolbar (shown in Figure 4-13). After clicking on the New Class icon, a drop-down menu presents a list of options. For a new class you need to click **Class** in the drop-down menu.

Clicking this icon displays a New Java Class dialog box that prompts you for the information required to create a class. This method is faster than writing a Java class file from scratch and it ensures that everything

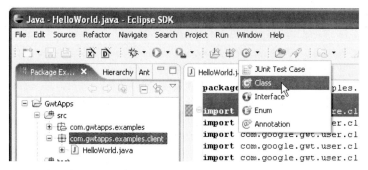

Figure 4–13. Creating a new class

required to be in the file will be there and will be correct. Notice in Figure 4-13 that the `com.gwtapps.examples.client` package is listed. This is where the new class will go. When the New Java Class dialog appears, it displays this package as the default package.

New Java Class

Java Class
Create a new Java class.

Source folder:	GwtApps/src	Browse...
Package:	com.gwtapps.examples.client	Browse...
☐ Enclosing type:		Browse...

Name:	HelloWorldView
Modifiers:	⦿ public ◯ default ◯ private ◯ protected
	☐ abstract ☐ final ☐ static
Superclass:	Composite Browse...
Interfaces:	Add...
	Remove

Which method stubs would you like to create?
☐ public static void main(String[] args)
☐ Constructors from superclass
☑ Inherited abstract methods
Do you want to add comments as configured in the properties of the current project?
☐ Generate comments

[Finish]   [Cancel]

Figure 4–14. The New Java Class dialog in Eclipse

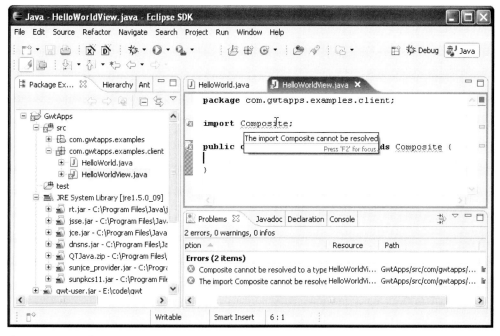

Figure 4–15. The new Java class in the Eclipse IDE

In this dialog, the name `HelloWorldView` is specified as the class name for the new class. The superclass is set to Composite. Clicking **Finish** creates the file and a usable Java class inside, as shown in Figure 4-15.

Actually, the new Java class isn't quite usable yet. We've specified a superclass that doesn't exist. Notice how Eclipse has unobtrusive indicators that let you know something is wrong. The Package Explorer has an X in a red square on the new Java file and on every parent node in the tree up to the project. If we had the project node closed, we would still know that there is an error somewhere in the project. Eclipse also displays a problems list at the bottom that shows a list of errors and warnings in the workspace. It also has the new problems listed. Double-clicking on any of the errors in this list brings you directly to the location of the error in an Eclipse Editor window. In this case there are two errors and the Editor window for the new Java class file is open. Inside the Editor window you can see a further indication of errors. On the right side of the Editor window red marks represent the location of the error within the file.

The file representation for this vertical space is the same scale as the vertical scroll bar. So if this was a bigger file and there were errors, you could quickly locate them by moving the scrollbar to the location of one of the red marks to see the error in the Editor window. Inside the Editor window, error icons display on the left side and the actual code producing the error has a jagged red underline. Furthermore, when you hover the mouse over the code with the error, a tooltip displays an error message, in this case "The import Composite cannot be resolved." The problem is that we selected just the simple class name as the superclass in the New Java Class dialog, but Eclipse requires the full class name. Often it's hard to remember the full class name for a class, but Eclipse helps us here as well. We can have Eclipse automatically suggest the full class name by clicking on the error and selecting the **Source > Add Import** command, as shown in Figure 4-16.

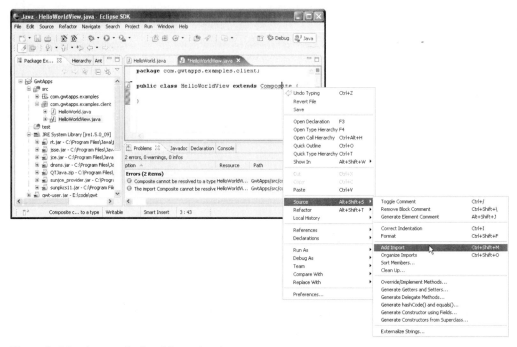

Figure 4–16. Automatically adding a Java import

Alternatively, you could use the keyboard shortcut Ctrl+Shift+M to run the Add Import command. Eclipse automatically adds the required import information. In situations where there is more than one matching import, Eclipse presents you with a choice, as shown in Figure 4-17.

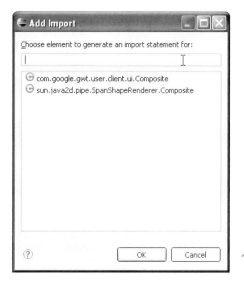

Figure 4–17.   Eclipse presents a list of matching import packages

Choosing the GWT Composite class as the import fixes the errors and all of the error indications go away. Eclipse provides this type of early warning of errors for any compile-time errors instantly, instead of having to wait until you compile to get this feedback, as is typical with typed languages. Eclipse updates the IDE with this information as you develop, so you can catch errors immediately after they are created.

Using the Eclipse Java Editor

Now let's look at some of the unique features of the Eclipse Java editor. We'll start by adding some code to the constructor of the `HelloWorld View` class. We can save some typing and generate the constructor by choosing **Source > Generate Constructors from Superclass...**, as shown in Figure 4-18. Eclipse can also automatically suggest items from the Refactor menu if you press Ctrl+L when the cursor is on a section of code. For example, if you implement an interface on a class but have not yet written the methods that must be implemented, you can press Ctrl+L for the suggestions and Eclipse presents a command to automatically implement the required methods.

Syntax may be all the compiler needs to understand code, but adding code syntax coloring in the editor makes it much easier for us to read the Java

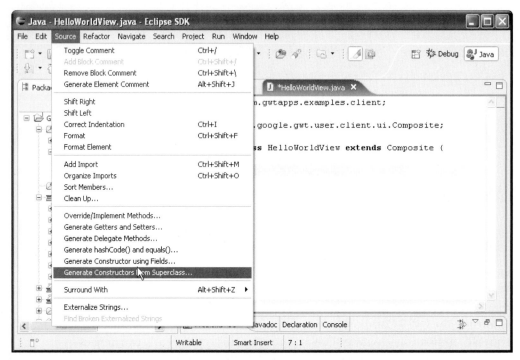

Figure 4-18.   Automatically creating a class constructor

code, as illustrated in Figure 4-19. The default syntax coloring in Eclipse uses a bold purple font for Java keywords like class, super, extends, and public, a green font for all comments, a blue font for fields, and a blue italic font for static fields.

Now let's create a `HorizontalPanel` in the constructor and add a couple widgets to it. As you type, Eclipse watches for errors. After you type the word `HorizontalPanel` it will appear as an error, because the class has not been imported. Use the same technique as before to import it (Ctrl+Shift+M or **Source > Add Import**). When you start typing to call a method on the panel, Eclipse's content assist feature displays a list of method suggestions, as shown in Figure 4-20.

```
public class HelloWorldView extends Composite {

    public HelloWorldView() {
        super();
        // TODO Auto-generated constructor stub
    }
}
```

Figure 4-19.   An automatically generated constructor

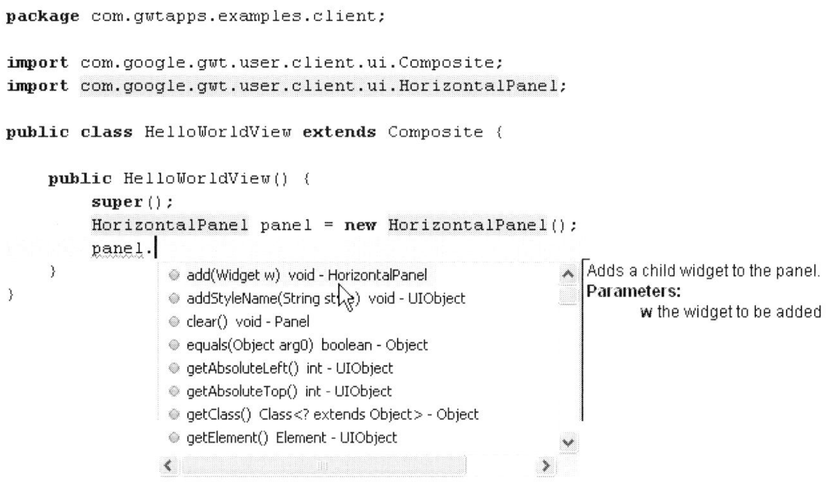

```
package com.gwtapps.examples.client;

import com.google.gwt.user.client.ui.Composite;
import com.google.gwt.user.client.ui.HorizontalPanel;

public class HelloWorldView extends Composite {

    public HelloWorldView() {
        super();
        HorizontalPanel panel = new HorizontalPanel();
        panel.|
    }
}
```

⊚ add(Widget w) void - HorizontalPanel	Adds a child widget to the panel.
⊚ addStyleName(String st⯈) void - UIObject	**Parameters:**
⊚ clear() void - Panel	w the widget to be added
⊚ equals(Object arg0) boolean - Object	
⊚ getAbsoluteLeft() int - UIObject	
⊚ getAbsoluteTop() int - UIObject	
⊚ getClass() Class<? extends Object> - Object	
⊚ getElement() Element - UIObject	

Figure 4–20.   Content assist in Eclipse

Eclipse automatically shows the suggestions, or you can force them to display by pressing Ctrl+Spacebar. In this case we want the add method, but we can also get an idea of the other methods available. In a way, content assist not only helps speed up typing and locating method names, but it also acts as an educational tool for the class you're using. Instead of leafing through documentation, you can pick up quite a bit of information about a library through this feature.

Another way to educate yourself about a class you're using is to use the editor's Ctrl+Click feature, shown in Figure 4-21. Using Ctrl+Click on a variable, class, or method in the editor takes you to its source in the Eclipse editor. For example, if you click on a variable name, the editor takes you to the variable declaration. If you click on a class name, it takes you to the class' Java file, and if you click on a method, it takes you to the method declaration. This allows you to browse your source code with the same convenience and efficiency as browsing the web. This even works with classes in the GWT library, since the GWT jar file contains the Java source code.

When you can't find what you're looking for while browsing your code, Eclipse provides rich support for searching. First of all, there is a simple single file Find/Replace command which you can access from the Edit menu or by pressing Ctrl+F. This is a standard find and replace feature that you find in most editors. On top of this single file find, Eclipse provides a rich multifile search feature that you can access from the Search menu or by pressing Ctrl+H. Figure 4-22 shows the Search dialog.

```
public class HelloWorldView extends Composite {

    public HelloWorldView() {
        super();
        HorizontalPanel panel = new HorizontalPanel();
        panel.add( new Button("Click Me") );
        panel.add( new Label("Hello World") );
    }
}
```

Figure 4–21.   Using Ctrl+Click to browse source code

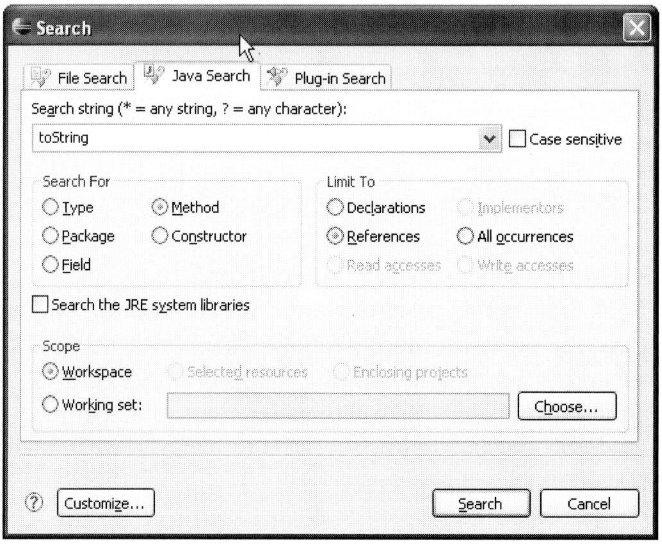

Figure 4–22.   Searching in Eclipse

The first tab in the Search dialog, File Search, lets you search for any string within any files in your workspace. The second tab, Java Search, provides a more restrictive search since it has an understanding of the Java language. In this tab you can search for specific instances of a certain string. For example, the dialog in Figure 4-22 shows searching for toString when it's being called as a reference. This search would ignore any other occurrence of toString, such as toString declarations or any comments.

The file search also allows you to replace matching values across files. This is helpful for refactoring code. For example, you could replace all occurrences of HelloWorld in our project files with MyFirstApp.

Eclipse provides refactoring support beyond multiple file search and replace. For example, you can change the name of the HelloWorld class

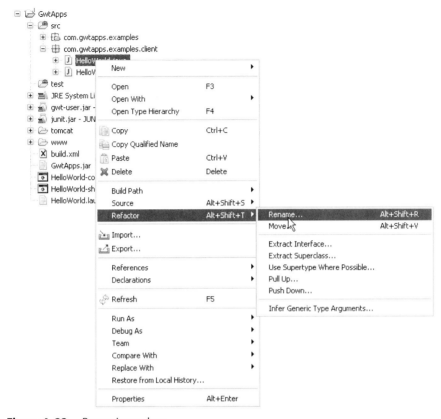

Figure 4–23. Renaming a class

to `MyFirstApp` with the **Refactor > Rename** command, as shown in Figure 4-23.

When you make changes through the Refactor menu, Eclipse ensures that references using the original value are also changed. This method is less error prone than doing a search and replace. Eclipse has many more time-saving refactoring commands, and you can easily find them by checking the Refactor context menu for any item, including highlighted code.

Eclipse also has many more features that can help you write your code. Even though they may not seem like dramatic productivity features, as you start using more of them you'll find yourself writing code faster and with fewer frustrations. Writing code is only one piece of the application development puzzle that Eclipse enhances. The next piece we'll look at is its debugging support.

Debugging in Eclipse

Eclipse provides a nice environment for debugging a running Java application. When you run a GWT application in hosted mode, Eclipse runs it as a Java application and you can debug it within Eclipse. This ability to debug a browser-based web application is a huge advancement for the Ajax development process.

Earlier in this chapter you saw that an Eclipse launch configuration can be automatically created by the GWT `applicationCreator` script by using the `-eclipse` option when creating the application. You can launch the application in hosted mode from Eclipse using either the Run or Debug command. When launched, the application runs in the hosted mode browser. In Debug mode, the hosted mode browser is connected to Eclipse and can use Eclipse's debugging commands.

First, let's look at breakpoints. Breakpoints allow you to set a location within your code where, when reached, the application running would break and pass control to the debugger. This lets you inspect variables or have the application step through the code line by line to analyze the program flow. To see how this works, add a breakpoint to the HelloWorld application on the first line of the button's `ClickListener.onClick` method by right-clicking on the left margin of that line in the editor and selecting **Toggle Breakpoint**, as shown in Figure 4-24.

You'll see the breakpoint added represented by a blue circle in the margin. Alternatively, you can double-click the same spot in the margin to toggle the breakpoint. Now when you debug the application, Eclipse will break into the debugger when it reaches the breakpoint. In this case it will happen when you click on the button. Start the debugger by opening the Debug menu from the Bug icon on the toolbar and selecting HelloWorld, as shown in Figure 4-25.

When the HelloWorld application opens in the hosted mode browser, click on its Click Me button to see Eclipse display the debugger. You should see Eclipse in the Debug perspective, as shown in Figure 4-26.

This is the view you should become familiar with if you are going to be building an Ajax application of any decent size. It provides you with a working view of exactly what is going on in your application. If your appli-

Figure 4–24.   Setting breakpoints

Figure 4–25.   Starting the debugger

cation exhibits strange behavior, you can set a breakpoint to see exactly what is happening. If you are a JavaScript developer, this type of debugging tool may be new to you and seem somewhat complex. However, it is definitely worth the effort to learn how to use it properly, since it will save you a lot of time when finding bugs. Instead of printing out and analyzing logs, you can set a breakpoint and step through the program one line at a time, while checking variable values, to determine what the bug is.

Let's briefly look at some of the tools in the Debug perspective. First of all, there are the controls that sit above the stack. The Resume and Terminate buttons are the green triangle and red square, respectively. Resume lets the program continue running. In Figure 4-26 it is stopped on the breakpoint. The Terminate button ends the debug session. You typically end your program by closing the hosted mode browser windows; however,

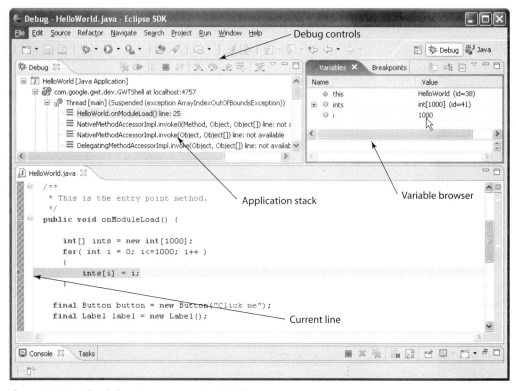

Figure 4–26.   The debugging perspective in Eclipse

when you are in a breakpoint, the application has stopped and you cannot access the interface of the hosted mode browser. The only way to end the program in this case is to use the Terminate button. The yellow arrows next to the Resume and Terminate buttons are used for stepping through the application. Taking a step when the application has stopped on a break-point executes one step. This allows you to see how one step of code affects any variables. It also lets you inch your way through the program and at a slow pace see how it flows. The first step button, Step Into, takes a step by calling the next method on the current line. Typically this will take you to another method and add a line to the stack. You would use this button when you want to follow the program flow into a method. To avoid stepping into another method, use the next step button, Step Over, which executes the current line, calls any methods, and stops on the next line in the cur-rent method. The third yellow arrow button, Step Return, executes the rest of the current method and returns to the calling method, where it stops.

Underneath the debug controls is the calling stack.[2] This is actually a tree that lists threads in the Java application with their stacks as children. The stacks are only visible if the thread is stopped on a breakpoint. Ajax applications are single threaded, so we only need to worry about the one thread and its stack. When we hit the breakpoint in the `onClick` method, the single JavaScript thread displays its method call stack with the current method highlighted. You will find the stack particularly helpful to see when and how a method is called. You can click on other methods in the stack to look at their code in the editor. When you browse the stack like this, the Debug perspective adjusts to the currently selected line on the stack. For example, the editor will show the line in the selected method where the child method was called. It will also adjust the Variables view to show the variables relevant to the currently selected method.

The Variables view lists local and used variables in the current method. The list is a columned tree that lets you browse each variable's contents, and if it is an object, displays its value in the second column. An area on the bottom of the view displays text for the currently selected variable using its `toString` method.

Sometimes stepping through an application with breakpoints isn't enough to find and fix problems. For example, an exception may occur at an unknown time, and placing a breakpoint would cause the debugger to break perhaps thousands of times before you encountered the exception. This is obviously not ideal. Fortunately, Eclipse provides a way to break into the debugger when a specific exception occurs. To add an exception breakpoint you simply need to choose **Run > Add Java Exception Breakpoint**. This displays the dialog shown in Figure 4-27.

In this dialog you select the exception you'd like to break on. The list is a dynamically updating list filtered by the text entered. Figure 4-27 shows breaking on Java's `ArrayIndexOutOfBoundsException`. After clicking on **OK**, you can see that the breakpoint was added by looking at the Breakpoints view in the Debug perspective shown in Figure 4-28.

---

2. A **calling stack** is a list of methods calls in an application, where each item on the stack is a method preceded by its calling method. So, for example, when a method completes, control returns to the calling method on the top of the stack.

Figure 4–27.   Adding an exception breakpoint

Figure 4–28.   The list of breakpoints in Eclipse

To test this, let's write some code that will cause an index to be out of bounds:

```
public void onModuleLoad() {
    int[] ints = new int[1000];
    for( int i = 0; i<=1000; i++ ){
        ints[i] = i;
    }
}
```

Now when running the application in Debug mode, Eclipse breaks when this code tries to write to the 1,001st `int` in the array (if you bump into another out-of-bounds exception when trying this, press the Resume button). Figure 4-29 shows the Debug perspective stopping on the exception breakpoint.

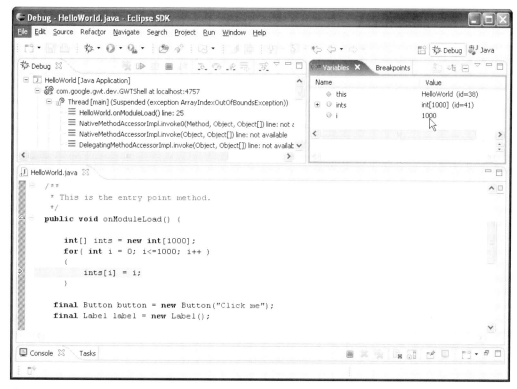

Figure 4–29.   Breaking into the debugger on an exception

Notice that the current line is the line where the out of bounds exception occurs. The value of `i` can be seen in the variables window as `1000` (arrays start at 0, so index 1,000 is the 1,001st item and over the bounds which was set at 1,000 items). The benefit of this type of breakpoint is that we did not need to step through 1,000 iterations of the loop to see where the problem is. Of course this is a trivial example, but you can apply this technique to more complex examples that exhibit similar behavior.

Now that we know we have a bug in our HelloWorld code, we can use another great feature of Eclipse that allows us to update the code live and resume the application without restarting. With the application stopped at the exception breakpoint, let's fix the code so that it looks like Figure 4-30.

We've set the comparison operation to less than instead of less than or equals, and removed the 1,000 value to use the `length` property of the array. Save the file, resume the application, and then click the Refresh button on the hosted mode browser. You'll see that the application runs the

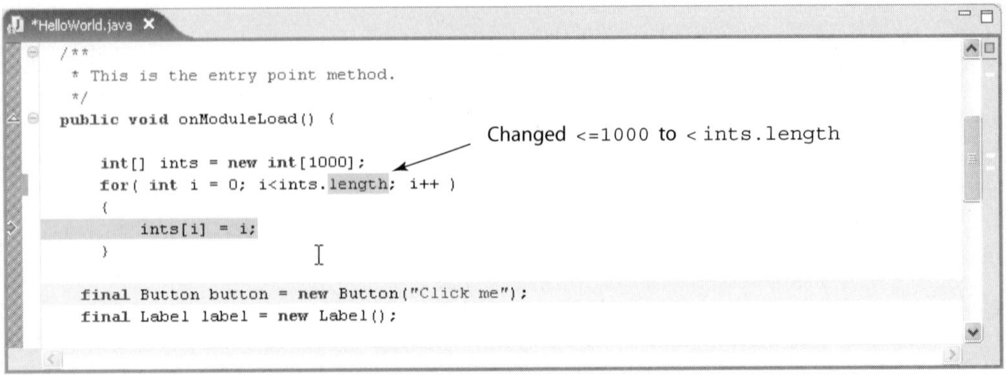

```
/**
 * This is the entry point method.
 */
public void onModuleLoad() {
                                        Changed <=1000 to < ints.length

    int[] ints = new int[1000];
    for( int i = 0; i<ints.length; i++ )
    {
        ints[i] = i;
    }

    final Button button = new Button("Click me");
    final Label label = new Label();
```

Figure 4–30.   Fixing the code while debugging

new fixed code and does not encounter the exception. This technique saves quite a bit of time which would otherwise be spent restarting the hosted mode browser. Also, reducing breaks in your workflow helps keep your mind on the task at hand.

Organizing Your Application Structure

When you generate an application using GWT's `applicationCreator` script, the script creates files and directories that follow a recommended structure. Each application that you create shares your Projects directory. Figure 4-31 shows how the directory looks for the HelloWorld generated application. Figure 4-32 shows the directory result after running the `applicationCreator` again and adding the new application, HelloWorld2, to the same Eclipse project used for HelloWorld. Notice that new scripts were created for the HelloWorld2 application. The `applicationCreator` script creates the application source files in the src directory, and shares this directory with the first HelloWorld application, as shown in Figure 4-33.

The source code is organized in standard Java package structure. Since we created the application as com.gwt.examples.HelloWorld2, the script generates the source files in the `src/com/gwt/examples` directory. This directory structure technique is a nice way of organizing Java modules and applications. It allows you to add packages and give them a unique location in the source tree, avoiding overwriting other classes that may be in a different package but have the same name. It also gives you a unique way to refer to a class from Java code.

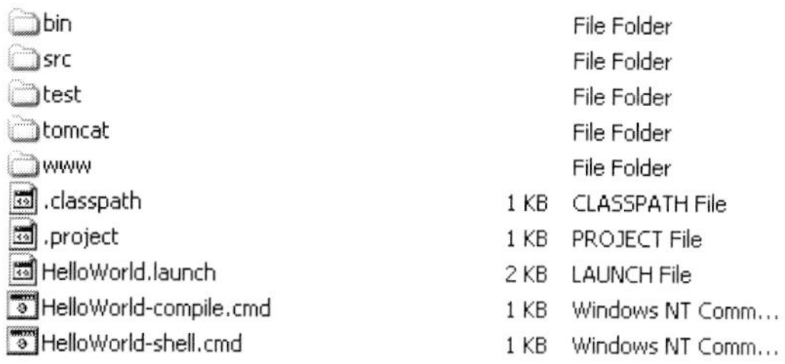

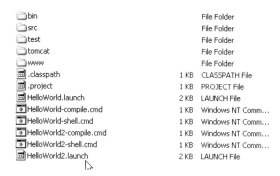

Figure 4–31. Directory structure for the HelloWorld application

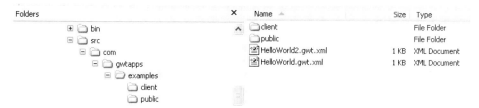

Figure 4–32. Directory structure after adding a new application

Figure 4–33. Two applications sharing the same source directory

Each generated GWT application has a module file and other source files in the client subdirectory and public subdirectory. Figure 4-33 shows the module file for HelloWorld2, HelloWorld2.gwt.xml. This file specifies the application's configuration options for the GWT compiler. The generated module file looks like this:

```
<module>
    <!-- Inherit the core Web Toolkit stuff.                    -->
    <inherits name='com.google.gwt.user.User'/>
```

```
<!-- Specify the app entry point class.                    -->
<entry-point class='com.gwtapps.examples.client.HelloWorld2'/>
</module>
```

This is the minimum specification that the application needs to run. The GWT compiler needs to know the class that acts as the entry point to the application, specified with the `entry-point` tag, and it needs to use the `com.google.gwt.user.User` module for its user interface. When you need to use other modules in your application you specify their location here. The module file has many more configuration options, all of which are outlined on the GWT web site at http://code.google.com/webtoolkit.

Now let's look inside the public folder shown in Figure 4-34. For each generated application, the script creates a new HTML host file in the public directory. The GWT compiler considers files placed in the public directory to be part of the distribution. In other words, when you compile your application, GWT will copy all of the files in this directory to the www output directory. For example, we could move the CSS from inside the HTML host file to a separate CSS file and place it in this directory. Other common files you might place in this directory are images that are used in the application's user interface.

Name ▲	Size	Type
HelloWorld2.html	2 KB	HTML Document
HelloWorld.html	2 KB	HTML Document

Figure 4–34.   The public folder holding the static application files

The generated Java source file for the applications is found in the client directory, as shown in Figure 4-35. When the GWT compiler compiles the Java source to JavaScript, it compiles the Java files in this directory. Any files outside of this directory will not be compiled to JavaScript, and if you use them you will get an exception when compiling or running in hosted mode. However, using the `inherits` tag in your module file tells the GWT compiler to use another module.

Name ▲	Size	Type
HelloWorld2.java	2 KB	JAVA File
HelloWorld.java	2 KB	JAVA File

Figure 4–35.   The client directory holding the files that will be compiled to JavaScript

The GWT compile automatically includes subdirectories and packages in the client directory without inheriting a module. This is useful for organizing subcategories of code within your application. For example, many of the sample applications in this book use a model-view-controller (MVC) architecture and keep the model and view in subpackages. Figure 4-36 shows this type of organization for Chapter 7's Multi-Search sample application. You can use this to organize your client-side code into categories other than model and view.

Figure 4–36.   MVC organization inside the client directory

There may be situations where you'll have application code that shouldn't be compiled to JavaScript and shouldn't be in the client directory; for example, when writing server-side code in Java, perhaps using a GWT RPC servlet. The common place to put this server-side code is in a server directory. For example, the Instant Messenger application in Chapter 9 places the servlet class in the server subdirectory, as shown in Figure 4-37. Since this is outside of the client directory, the GWT compile ignores the code when compiling the client. Typically the GWT compiler will not be able to compile server-side code since it usually uses packages that aren't emulated by GWT and would not be useful in a browser.

Figure 4–37.   Server-side code is placed outside the client directory

The reverse is possible, however. The server classes can use classes in the client directory as long as they don't rely on browser features. The Instant Messenger application does this to share the Java classes that are used to transmit data over RPC between the client and the server.

Finally, when you're ready to deploy your application, you run the generated compile script. GWT copies all of the files used for distribution, including the generated JavaScript files and all of the files in the public directory, to the applications directory inside the www directory. The compiler names the application's directory with the full module name, as shown in Figure 4-38.

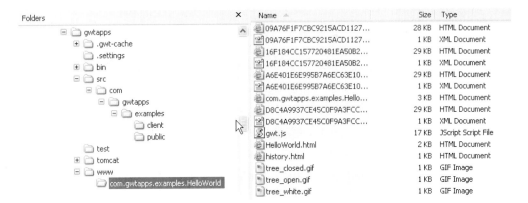

Figure 4–38. The GWT writes the compiled and static files to the www directory

Testing Applications

Having the capability to build Ajax applications with Java gives you many tools that let you maintain larger applications with less work. One very important aspect of maintaining a large application is being able to easily create unit tests for most, if not all, functionality. This need comes from a common problem with software development: the code size grows to a point where small changes can have cascading effects that create bugs.

It has become common practice to incorporate heavy testing into the development cycle. In the traditional waterfall development cycle you would write code to a specification until the specification was complete. Then the application would be passed to testers who would look for bugs. Developers would respond to bug reports by fixing the bugs. Once all the bugs were fixed, the product would be shipped. Figure 4-39 illustrates the steps in traditional software development testing.

The problem encountered with this type of development cycle is that during the bug finding and fixing phase, code changes can easily cause more

Figure 4–39.   Old-style testing = bad

bugs. To fix this problem, testers would need to start testing right from the beginning after every code change to ensure new bugs weren't created and old bugs didn't reappear.

One successful testing methodology has developers write automated unit tests before they write the features. The tests cover every use case of the new feature to be added. The first time the test is run, it will fail for each case. The development process then continues until each test case in the unit test is successful. Then the unit test becomes part of a test suite for the application and is run before committing any source code changes to the source tree. If a new feature causes any part of the application to break, other tests in the automated test suite will identify this problem, since every feature of the application has had tests built. If a bug is found at this point, it is relatively easy to pinpoint the source since only one new feature was added. Finding and fixing bugs early in the development life-cycle like this is much easier and quicker than finding and fixing them at the end. The test suite grows with the application. The initial investment in time to produce the unit tests pays off over the long run since they are run again on every code change, ensuring each feature's health. Figure 4-40 illustrates this process.

In practice, when comparing this approach to the one illustrated in Figure 4-39, there is a large time saving from finding bugs earlier and less of a need for a large testing team since the developer is responsible for much of the testing.

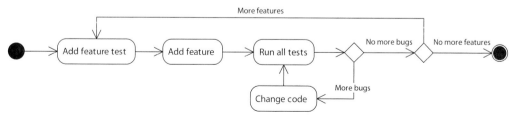

Figure 4–40.   Test-first testing = good

This technique is relatively novel for client-side web applications. Testing is reduced to usability testing and making sure that different browsers render pages properly with traditional web applications. This is one of the great things about HTML. It's a declarative language that leaves little room for logical bugs. It's easy to deploy HTML web pages that work (browser-rendering quirks aside). However, using JavaScript introduces the possibility of logic bugs. This wasn't too much of a problem when JavaScript was being used lightly, but for Ajax applications heavily using JavaScript, logical bugs are somewhat of a problem. Since JavaScript is not typed and does not have a compile step, many bugs can only be found by running the application, which makes the creation of unit tests difficult. Furthermore, it is difficult to test an entire application through its interface. Many simple bugs, such as trying to call an undefined function, cannot be caught without running the program and trying to execute the code that has the bug, but by using Java you could catch these bugs immediately in the IDE or at compile time. From a testing perspective, it does not make sense to build large Ajax applications with JavaScript.

Using JUnit

JUnit is another great Java tool that assists in creating an automated testing for your application. It provides classes that assist in building and organizing tests, such as assertions to test expected results, a test-case base class that allows you to set up several tests, and a mechanism to join tests together in a test suite. To create a test case for JUnit you would typically extend the `TestCase` class, but since GWT applications require a special environment, GWT provides a `GWTTestCase` class for you to extend.

Let's walk through the creation of a test case for the Multi-Search application in Chapter 7. The first step is to use the GWT `junitCreator` script to generate a test case class and some scripts that can launch the test case. The `junitCreator` script takes several arguments to run. Table 4-1 outlines each argument.

To run this script for the Multi-Search application we can use the following command:

```
junitCreator -junit E:\code\eclipse\plugins\org.junit_3.8.1\junit.jar -module
com.gwtapps.multisearch.MultiSearch -eclipse GWTApps
com.gwtapps.multisearch.client.MultiSearchTest
```

Table 4–1 `junitCreator` Script Arguments

Argument	Description	Example
`junit`	Lets you define the location of the junit jar file. You can find a copy in the plugin directory of your Eclipse installation.	`-junit E:\code\eclipse\plugins\org.junit_3.8.1\junit.jar`
`module`	Specifies the GWT module that you'll be testing. It is required since the environment needs to run this module for your test.	`-module com.gwtapps.multisearch.MultiSearch`
`eclipse`	Specifies your Eclipse project name if you want to generate Eclipse launch configurations.	`-eclipse GWTApps`
	The last argument should be the class name for the test case. You would typically use the same package as the one being tested.	`com.gwtapps.multisearch.client.MultiSearchTest`

```
C:\gwtapps-ws\gwtapps>junitCreator -junit E:\code\eclipse\plugins\org.junit_3.8.
1\junit.jar -module com.gwtapps.multisearch.MultiSearch -eclipse GWTApps com.gwt
apps.multisearch.client.MultiSearchTest
Created directory C:\gwtapps-ws\gwtapps\test\com\gwtapps\multisearch\client
Created file C:\gwtapps-ws\gwtapps\test\com\gwtapps\multisearch\client\MultiSear
chTest.java
Created file C:\gwtapps-ws\gwtapps\MultiSearchTest-hosted.launch
Created file C:\gwtapps-ws\gwtapps\MultiSearchTest-web.launch
Created file C:\gwtapps-ws\gwtapps\MultiSearchTest-hosted.cmd
Created file C:\gwtapps-ws\gwtapps\MultiSearchTest-web.cmd
```

Figure 4–41. Using `junitCreator` to generate a test case

Figure 4-41 shows the output from this command. The script created two scripts, two launch configurations for launching the test in web mode or hosted mode, and one test case class that is stored in the test directory. In Eclipse the test case class will look like Figure 4-42.

The generated test case has two methods. The first, `getModuleName`, is required by GWT and must specify the module that is being tested. The `junitCreator` script has set this value to the Multi-Search module because it was specified with the module command line argument. The second method, a test case, is implemented as a simple test that just asserts that the value true is true. You can build as many test cases as you like in this one class.

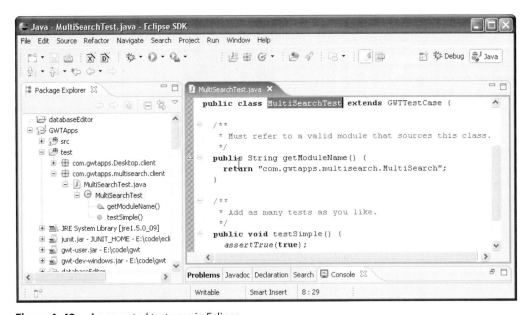

Figure 4–42. A generated test case in Eclipse

You can run the tests by running the scripts generated by `junitCreator`. Alternatively, you can launch JUnit inside Eclipse for a visual representation of the results. Running inside Eclipse also lets you debug the JUnit test case, which can greatly assist in finding bugs when a test case fails. Since `junitCreator` created a launch configuration for Eclipse, we can simply click the Run or Debug icons in the Eclipse toolbar and select the `Multi SearchTest` launch configuration from the drop-down menu. After launching this configuration, the JUnit view automatically displays in Eclipse. When the test has completed, you will see the results in the JUnit view, as shown in Figure 4-43. Notice the familiar check marks, which are displayed in green in Eclipse, next to the test case indicating that the test case was successful.

Figure 4–43.   Running a JUnit test case from Eclipse

Now let's create a test case for each type of search engine that the application uses. Adding the following code to the test class creates four new tests:

```
protected MultiSearchView getView(){
    MultiSearchView view = new MultiSearchView( new MultiSearchViewListener(){
        public void onSearch( String query ){}
    });
    RootPanel.get().add( view );
    return view;
}

protected void doSearchTest( Searcher searcher ){
    searcher.query( "gwt" );
}
```

```
public void testYahoo() {
    doSearchTest( new YahooSearcher( view ) );
}

public void testFlickr() {
    doSearchTest( new FlickrSearcher( view ) );
}

public void testAmazon() {
    doSearchTest( new AmazonSearcher( view ) );
}

public void testGoogleBase() {
    doSearchTest( new GoogleBaseSearcher( view ) );
}
```

The first two methods, getView and doSearchTest, are helper methods for
each test in this test case. The getView method simply creates a view, the
MultiSearchView defined in the application, and adds it to the RootPanel
so that it is attached to the document. Then the doSearchTest method
sends a query to a Searcher class implementation. Each test case instantiates a different Searcher implementation and sends it to the doSearchTest
method. When JUnit runs, each test case runs and submits a query to the
respective search engine. Figure 4-44 shows what the result looks like in
the Eclipse JUnit view.

If any search failed by an exception being thrown, then the stack trace for
the exception would display in the right pane of this view and a red X icon
would display over the test case.

The problem with this test case is that it doesn't verify the results. JUnit
provides many assertion helper methods that compare actual results to

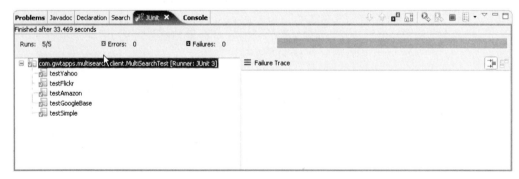

Figure 4–44.   Running several tests in one test case

expected results. However, in this case our results are asynchronous; that is, they don't arrive until after the test case completes. GWT provides help with this since much of Ajax development is asynchronous with the `delayTestFinish` method.

To use this method we need to have a way of validating an asynchronous request. When we have validated that an asynchronous request is complete, then we call the `finishTest` method. In the case of the Multi-Search test, we will validate when we receive one search result. To do this we need to hook into the application to intercept the asynchronous event. This requires a bit of knowledge about the application and may seem a little obscure otherwise. We will create a **mock object,** which is an object that pretends to be another object in the application, to simulate the `SearchResultsView` class. By simulating this class we will be able to extend it and override the method that receives search results. The class can be declared as an inner class on the test case like this:

```
private class MockSearchResultsView extends SearchResultsView {
    public MockSearchResultsView( SearchEngine engine ){
        super(engine);
    }

    public void clearResults(){}

    public void addSearchResult( SearchEngineResult result ){
        assertNotNull(result);
        finishTest();
    }
}
```

The class overrides the `addSearchResult` method, which one of the `Searcher` classes calls when a search result has been received from the server. Instead of adding the result to the view, this test case will use one of JUnit's assert methods, `assertNotNull`, to assert that the search engine result object is not null. Then it calls the GWT's `finishTest` method to indicate that the asynchronous test is complete.

To run this test we need to change the `doSearchTest` method on the test case to insert the mock view and tell JUnit to wait for an asynchronous response:

```
protected void doSearchTest( Searcher searcher ){
    searcher.setView(
        new MockSearchResultsView(searcher.getView().getEngine()));
```

```
    searcher.query( "gwt" );
    delayTestFinish(5000);
}
```

In this code we set the view of the searcher to the mock view that we've created, and then call the `delayTestFinish` method with a value of 5,000 milliseconds (5 seconds). If the test does not complete within 5 seconds, it will fail. If the network connection is slow, you may want to consider a longer value here to properly test for errors.

Running these tests at this point tests the application code in the proper GWT environment and with asynchronous events occurring. You should use these testing methods as you build your application so you have a solid regression testing library.

Benchmarking

When using GWT to create Ajax applications, taking user experience into consideration almost always comes first. Part of creating a good user experience with an application is making it perform well. Fortunately, since GWT has a compile step, each new GWT version can create faster code, an advantage that you don't have with regular JavaScript development. However, you probably shouldn't always rely on the GWT team to improve performance and should aim at improving your code to perform better. Starting with release 1.4, GWT includes a benchmarking subsystem that assists in making smart performance-based decisions when developing Ajax applications.

The benchmark subsystem works with JUnit. You can benchmark code through JUnit by using GWT's `Benchmark` test case class instead of `GWTTestCase`. Using this class causes the benchmarking subsystem to kick in and measure the length of each test. After the tests have completed, the benchmark system writes the results to disk as an XML file. You can open the XML file to read the results, but you can view them easier in the benchmarkViewer application that comes with GWT.

Let's look at a simple example of benchmarking. We can create a benchmark test case by using the `junitCreator` script in the same way we would for a regular test case:

```
junitCreator -junit E:\code\eclipse\plugins\org.junit_3.8.1\junit.jar -module
com.gwtapps.desktop.Desktop -eclipse GWTApps com.gwtapps.desktop.client.
CookieStorageTest
```

In this code we're creating a test case for the cookie storage feature in Chapter 6's Gadget Desktop application. The application uses the `Cookie Storage` class to easily save large cookies while taking into account browser cookie limits. In this test we're going to measure the cookie performance. First, we extend the `Benchmark` class instead of `GWTTestCase`:

```
public class CookieStorageTest extends Benchmark {

    public String getModuleName() {
        return "com.gwtapps.desktop.Desktop";
    }

    public void testSimpleString(){
        try {
            CookieStorage storage = new CookieStorage();
            storage.setValue("test", "this is a test string");
            assertEquals( storage.getValue("test"), "this is a test string" );
            storage.save();
            storage.load();
            assertEquals( storage.getValue("test"), "this is a test string");

        } catch (StorageException e) { fail(); }
    }
}
```

You can run this benchmark from the Eclipse JUnit integration or the launch configuration generated by the `junitCreator` script. The test simply creates a cookie, saves it, loads it, and then verifies that it hasn't changed. The generated XML file will contain a measurement of the time it took to run this method. At this point the benchmark is not very interesting. We can add more complex benchmarking by testing with ranges.

Using ranges in the benchmark subsystem gives you the capability to run a single test case multiple times with different parameter values. Each run will have its duration measured, which you can later compare in the benchmark report. The following code adds a range to the cookie test to test writing an increasing number of cookies:

```
public class CookieStorageTest extends Benchmark {

    final IntRange smallStringRange =
        new IntRange(1, 64, Operator.MULTIPLY, 2);

    public String getModuleName() {
        return "com.gwtapps.desktop.Desktop";
    }
```

```
/**
 * @gwt.benchmark.param cookies -limit = smallStringRange
 */
public void testSimpleString( Integer cookies ){
    try {
        CookieStorage storage = new CookieStorage();
        for( int i=0; i< cookies.intValue(); i++){
            storage.setValue("test"+i, "this is a test string"+i);
            assertEquals( storage.getValue("test"+i),
                "this is a test string"+i );
        }
        storage.save();
        storage.load();
        for( int i=0; i< cookies.intValue(); i++){
            assertEquals( storage.getValue("test"+i),
                "this is a test string"+i );
        }
    } catch (StorageException e) { fail(); }
}
public void testSimpleString(){
}
}
```

This code creates an `IntRange`. The parameters in the `IntRange` constructor create a range that starts at one and doubles until it reaches the value 64 (1, 2, 4, 8, 16, 32, 64). GWT passes each value in the range into separate runs of the `testSimpleString` method. GWT knows to do this by the annotation before the method, which identifies the parameter and the range to apply.

Notice that there is also a version of the `testSimpleString` method without any parameters. You need to provide a version of this method with no arguments to run in JUnit since it does not support tests without parameters. The benchmark subsystem is aware of this and is able to choose the correct method.

After running this code we can launch the benchmarkViewer application from the command line in the directory that the reports were generated in (this defaults to the Projects directory):

```
benchmarkViewer
```

The benchmarkViewer application shows a list of reports that are in the current directory. You can load a report by clicking on it in the list. Each

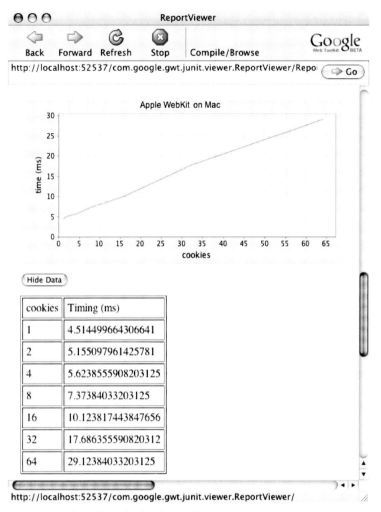

Figure 4–45.   Benchmark results for the cookie test

report contains the source code for each test along with the results as a table and a graph. Figure 4-45 shows the result of the testSimpleString test.

The benchmark system also recognizes beginning and ending methods. Using methods like these allows you to separate set up and take down code for each test that you don't want measured. For example, to define a setup method for the testSimpleString test, you would write the following code:

```
public void beginSimpleString( Integer cookies ){
    /* do some initialization */
}
```

Building and Sharing Modules

Each GWT module is not necessarily a full application, but it can be used as a reusable library for other applications instead. The GWT module structure, also used for applications, gives you the tools necessary to package your module and share it with other applications. In fact, GWT itself is divided into several modules, as you've seen with the user interface, XML, JSON, HTTP, and RPC modules, so you've already used the process of importing other libraries.

Using Modules

GWT modules are distributed as jar files that you can include in your application by adding them to your project's classpath and inheriting their project name in your application's module file. This is the same process that you use to include the GWT library classes in your application. In this case GWT automatically adds the module jar file, gwt-user.jar, to your project's classpath when you generate the project using the GWT `createProject` script. The `createApplication` script then generates a module XML file for your application and automatically adds the `com.google.gwt.user.User` module to it. When we generate the module XML file for the Gadget Desktop application in Chapter 6, we get the following XML:

```
<module>
    <inherits name='com.google.gwt.user.User'/>
    <entry-point class='com.gwtapps.desktop.client.Desktop'/>
</module>
```

This module file tells the GWT compiler how to compile the application to JavaScript. The `inherits` element tells the compiler that we are using classes from the `name` module, which will also need to be compiled to JavaScript. We can continue to add modules from gwt-user.jar since the file is are already on the classpath. For new modules in other jar files, we first need to add the jar to the classpath. In Eclipse, you can do this by going to the project's Properties dialog and selecting the Libraries tab from Java Build Path, as shown in Figure 4-46.

From here you can add and remove jar files. Notice that gwt-user.jar is already in the list. For the Gadget Desktop application we add the `gwt-google-apis` library to the project to use the Gears module from it. First,

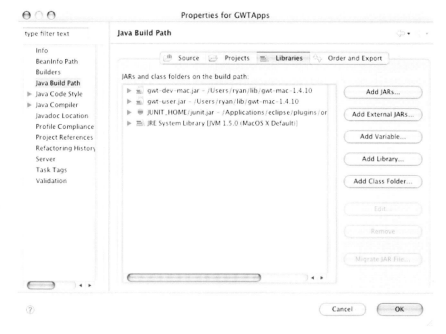

Figure 4–46.   Editing the build path in Eclipse

we add the `gwt-google-apis` jar to this list, and then the application's module XML file inherits the Gears module like this:

```
<module>
    <inherits name='com.google.gwt.user.User'/>
    <inherits name='com.google.gwt.json.JSON'/>
    <inherits name='com.google.gwt.xml.XML'/>
    <inherits name='com.google.gwt.gears.Gears'/>
    <entry-point class='com.gwtapps.desktop.client.Desktop'/>
</module>
```

Notice also that this project imports the JSON and XML modules which are already in the gwt-user.jar file. If you miss this step—adding the `inherits` tag to your application's module file—you will get an error from the GWT compiler that it can't find the module that you're using.

Creating a Reusable Module

If you've built a GWT application, you've already built a reusable module. The only difference is that your application has specified an entry point and can be turned into a GWT application loaded on its own in the GWT

hosted mode browser or web browser. You could reference the application's module file from another application to reuse its components.

You create a module the same way you create an application, using GWT's
`applicationCreator` script. You may want to use the `ant` flag with this
script to build an ant file that will automatically package your module in a
jar file for distribution.

The module structure of GWT is hierarchical using inheritance. For example, if you write a module that inherits GWT's User module, then any module or application that uses your module also automatically inherits
GWT's User module. This is an important feature, since it allows the users
of your module to automatically get all the requirements to run. GWT
takes this concept further and lets you also inject resources into modules
to ensure CSS or other JavaScript libraries are automatically included.

For example, if you were creating a module of widgets that required
default CSS to be included, you could reference this in the module XML
like this:

```
<module>
    <inherits name='com.google.gwt.user.User'/>
    <stylesheet src="widgets.css"/>
</module>
```

The widgets file would need to be included in your module's public files,
and when other modules inherit your module they would automatically
get the widgets.css file without directly including it.

You can similarly include JavaScript in your module using the `script` tag
like this:

```
<module>
    <inherits name='com.google.gwt.user.User'/>

    <!-- Include google maps -->
    <script src="http://maps.google.com/
maps?file=api&amp;v=2&amp;key=ABQIAAAACeDba0As0X6mwbIbUYWv-RTb-
vLQlFZmc2N8bgWI8YDPp5FEVBQUnvmfInJbOoyS2v-qkssc36Z5MA"></script>
</module>
```

This tag is similar to the `script` tag that you would use in your HTML file
to include a JavaScript library, except that this file would be automatically
included with every module that includes this module.

As of GWT 1.4 you can use image bundles to include resources with your reusable modules. Image bundles allow you to package several images together into a single image for deployment. If you use an image bundle within your module, applications that use your module will automatically generate the single image. In Chapter 6, images bundles are used to build the Gadget toolbar in the Gadget Desktop application.

Sharing a Compiled Application (Mashups)

Sometimes you'd like to share your compiled JavaScript application for use on other web sites. As of GWT 1.4, other web sites can easily load your application using the cross-site version of the generated JavaScript. The cross-site version has -xs appended to the package name for the JavaScript file name, and you can find it in the www directory after compiling an application. For example, to include the Hangman application developed in Chapter 1, you would use the following `script` tag:

```
<script language='javascript' src='http://gwtapps.com/hangman/
com.gwtapps.tutorial.Hangman-xs.nocache.js'></script>
```

Notice that this line differs from the line found in the original host HTML page for the application; it has the addition of -xs in the filename and is loading the script from the `gwtapps.com` domain.

Each application that you share may have additional requirements for integration on another site. In the Hangman example, the application looks for an HTML element with the ID `hangman`, so anyone including this on their site would need to also have the following HTML in the location where they'd like the Hangman application to show up:

```
<div id="hangman"></div>
```

Deploying Applications

Deploying a GWT application can be as easy as deploying a regular web page. A simple GWT client is made up of HTML and JavaScript files that can be copied to a directory on a web server and loaded into a browser. For example, the Gadget Desktop application in Chapter 6 does not use any server-side code, so its files for deployment are simply its JavaScript files, several image files, and the host HTML file. You can install this application on any web server simply by copying the files.

Deploying to a Web Server

You've seen how to set up development environments with Java tools, run the GWT scripts, and use the GWT jar files, but for a client-side application these files are left on the development machine. You simply need to run the GWT compile script, or click the Compile button in the GWT hosted mode browser, to generate the files needed for deployment. For example, compiling the Gadget Desktop application can be done from the command line. Or it can be compiled from the hosted mode browser, as shown in Figure 4-47. GWT places these files in a directory named after your application inside the www directory for your project, as you can see in Figure 4-48. This is the file list that you would copy to a directory on your web server.

Figure 4–47. Compiling your application from the GWT hosted mode browser

Deploying a Servlet to a Servlet Container

If you are using GWT-RPC, you will need to deploy your service implementation to a servlet container. Although the GWT hosted mode browser runs

Figure 4–48. The GWT compiler places the files to deploy in www

an embedded version of Tomcat, deploying to a regular Tomcat instance is somewhat different. If you are deploying to Tomcat, you'll need to add your application to its webapps directory. Figure 4-49 outlines the steps to add your application to Tomcat's directory structure.

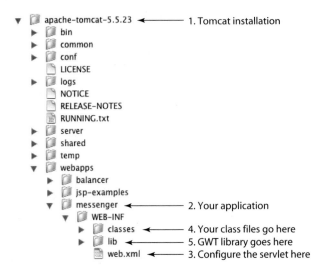

Figure 4–49.   Steps to deploy your application to Tomcat

Let's look at the five steps shown in Figure 4-49. First you need to locate the installation directory for Tomcat. Second, you need to create your application directory under the webapps directory. Third, you need to set up your web.xml file in the WEB-INF directory for your application. For the Instant Messenger application, the file looks like this:

```
<?xml version="1.0" encoding="UTF-8"?>
<web-app>
    <servlet>
        <servlet-name>messenger</servlet-name>
    <servlet-class>com.gwtapps.messenger.server.MessengerServiceImpl</servlet-class>
    </servlet>
    <servlet-mapping>
        <servlet-name>messenger</servlet-name>
        <url-pattern>/messenger</url-pattern>
    </servlet-mapping>
</web-app>
```

Fourth, copy your servlet class to the class' directory in the WEB-INF directory. Finally, fifth, copy the gwt-servlet.jar file to the lib directory in the WEB-INF directory. The gwt-servlet.jar file has the GWT classes required to support the server-side RPC. You could use gwt-user.jar instead, but gwt-servlet.jar is smaller and therefore preferred. Deployment can be automated by using a build tool such as Ant.

Automating Deployment with Ant

As you can see from the previous section, deployment to a server container often involves many steps of compiling code, copying files, and creating directories. When a task involves many steps like this, it is best to automate the process. Ant is the ideal Java tool for automating build tasks like this. With it you can accomplish all of the previous steps of deploying a GWT web application with one Ant step.

Ant is a command line tool that accepts an XML build file. The build file contains a list of build targets with steps to accomplish build tasks. There is rich support for different types of steps, including copying files, creating directories, and compiling code. The Ant system is also extensible, so you can develop new steps or add new steps from other developers.

Let's run through an example of how to build a GWT application for use on a servlet container with Ant. First, verify that you have Ant installed and in your path. You should be able to type `ant -version` at the command line, as shown in Figure 4-50.

Figure 4–50.   Verifying Ant is on your system

If you don't have Ant installed, you can download it from http://ant.apache.org. After ensuring that Ant is installed on your development machine, you can write a build.xml file for a project. The following is the build.xml file we will use:

```
<project default="deploy">
    <property name="gwtpath" value="/Users/ryan/lib/gwt-mac-1.4.10"/>
    <property name="gwtapipath" value="/Users/ryan/lib/gwt-google-apis-1.0.0"/>
    <property name="targetdir" value="${basedir}/www/${app}"/>
```

```
<property name="wwwdir" value="${basedir}/www"/>
<property name="srcdir" value="${basedir}/src"/>
<property name="bindir" value="${basedir}/bin"/>

<path id="classpath">
    <pathelement location="${gwtapipath}/gwt-google-apis.jar"/>
    <pathelement location="${gwtpath}/gwt-user.jar"/>
    <pathelement location="${gwtpath}/gwt-dev-mac.jar"/>
    <pathelement location="${srcdir}"/>
    <pathelement location="${bindir}"/>
</path>

<target name="compile-gwt">
    <java classname="com.google.gwt.dev.GWTCompiler" fork="true">
        <classpath refid="classpath"/>
        <jvmarg value="-XstartOnFirstThread"/>
        <arg value="-out"/>
        <arg value="${wwwdir}"/>
        <arg value="${app}"/>
    </java>
</target>

<target name="compile" depends="compile-gwt">
    <mkdir dir="${targetdir}/WEB-INF/classes"/>
    <javac srcdir="${srcdir}"
        destdir="${targetdir}/WEB-INF/classes"
        excludes="**/client/*.java">
        <classpath refid="classpath"/>
    </javac>
</target>

<target name="deploy" depends="compile">
    <mkdir dir="${targetdir}/WEB-INF/lib"/>
    <copy todir="${targetdir}/WEB-INF/lib" file="${gwtpath}/gwt-servlet.jar"/>
    <copy tofile="${targetdir}/WEB-INF/web.xml"
        file="${basedir}/${app}.web.xml"/>
</target>
</project>
```

 The file begins by defining a project element with a default target. This
target is run when one is not specified on the command line. The first few
elements inside the `project` tag are property definition elements. You
can place variables in these elements that will be reused throughout the
build file. For example, in this file we have the source directories and jar
directories set for use later. Inside the attributes you can see how the properties can be referenced with the ${name} format. Before the targets are
defined in the file, we set a path element. This element lists the jar files

and directories that are on the classpath. We use this classpath later and can refer to it by its ID.

The first target, `compile-gwt`, runs the GWT compiler on our GWT module. The module is not specified in this target. Instead the `${app}` placeholder is used. We have not defined this as a property, but we can pass in this variable as a command line argument. This gives the build file the flexibility of being used for more than one application. Running this target generates the compiled JavaScript files for the application and copies all of the public files used for the project to the www directory.

The second target, `compile`, uses the regular javac compiler to compile all of the other Java class files. These are class files that will be needed on the server and will include the GWT-RPC service servlet if one is used. The Ant script copies these class files to the www directory under WEB-INF/ classes. This is the standard location for class files for a servlet container web application.

The final target, `deploy`, copies the required GWT library, gwt-servlet.jar, to the WEB-INF/lib directory. This is the standard location for jar files for a servlet container web application. The target also copies a predefined web.xml file to the www directory. The web.xml file is required to describe the servlets in the web application.

Running the task for the Instant Messenger application in Chapter 9 results in the output shown in Figure 4-51. Once this is complete, we should have a www directory that is ready to be used in a servlet container, and which follows the conventions for servlet containers for file names and locations, as illustrated in Figure 4-52.

Figure 4–51. Compiling and deploying with Ant

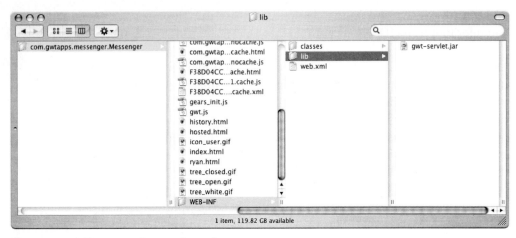

Figure 4–52.   The output from an Ant script

Summary

GWT simplifies real software engineering for Ajax applications. This was really lacking when attempting to build substantial applications based on JavaScript. Using Eclipse to write and debug applications can substantially increase development productivity. Java organization and modularization help you decouple application parts and leverage existing code. Testing and benchmarking using JUnit helps ensure that your applications are of high quality and perform well. When it's time to deploy your application, Ant can automate any tedious tasks. Overall, the ability to leverage the vast range of mature Java software engineering tools is a significant part of creating great Ajax applications with GWT.

5

Using the Toolkit Effectively

The previous chapters discussed the three main areas of GWT development, including the user interface library, server integration, and software engineering. With this knowledge you can create substantial high-quality Ajax applications. However, there are a few more things that fall outside of these categories that help you use GWT to its full potential. This chapter looks at several subjects that will help you use the toolkit effectively, including creating elegant interfaces with CSS, extending the toolkit, internationalizing your applications, and improving performance.

Using Asynchronous Programming

Traditional object-oriented programming typically involves sequential operations. You organize your code into objects and methods which are called sequentially in a hierarchy of code. Often application developers familiar with this type of programming initially have a little bit of trouble with asynchronous programming. Asynchronous programming involves making requests and receiving responses at any point later in the program execution. Writing software using asynchronous constructs often changes the way you write code. In situations with sequential programming in which you would write a complete method to accomplish a certain task, with asynchronous programming you would instead need to break the task up into smaller tasks that are executed as asynchronous events happen. Figure 5-1 illustrates the difference between these two models.

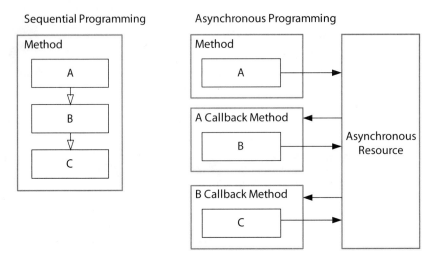

Figure 5-1. Sequential versus asynchronous programming

Sequential programming is relatively simple compared to asynchronous programming, primarily because the application provides a response after each method call. This allows you to make decisions in your code immediately after you have made a call. The result is you can put all of the code required to accomplish one process in one method. This is a useful organization technique which helps code readability and maintainability. With asynchronous programming, you need to break apart processes in your code that rely on a request's response to an asynchronous resource. The resulting code becomes fragmented and hard to read and maintain.

One option to clean up code with asynchronous programming in regular applications is to use blocking on asynchronous operations. Blocking basically causes the current thread of execution to wait—not continue with the method—until the asynchronous resource has responded. The resulting code can be contained in one method and the result looks like sequential programming. The problem with this technique is that it ties up a thread, which may cause the application to appear frozen if the threading is not handled properly. Furthermore, this method is not an option for browser-based applications, which rely on asynchronous features such as resources accessible over HTTP and user interactions. Browser-based applications written with JavaScript, including GWT, only have one thread to execute on. So you can't use blocking operations.

There could be situations where you perform a large amount of computation sequentially which will tie up the only thread available and cause the application interface to freeze. In this case you should break the processing up into smaller steps so the interface has a chance to react. In these instances you are taking sequential processing and forcing it to be asynchronous. GWT provides a tool to do this, the `IncrementalCommand` class. We'll look at this in the Improving Performance section in this chapter.

As you can see, asynchronous programming is essential for Ajax applications. Fortunately, the Java language has some features that greatly assist with the organization of asynchronous code.

Typically, applications receive asynchronous responses in some sort of callback method. Java does not have a way of passing method pointers around, so it usually accomplishes this through interfaces. The provider of the asynchronous resource defines a public interface that you would implement if you needed an asynchronous response. When asynchronous events occur, the event source calls a method on the provided interface instance. Figure 5-2 illustrates this model, which follows the Observer design pattern.

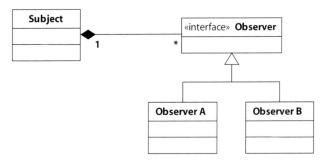

Figure 5–2.   The Observer design pattern

For asynchronous programming, the subject represents the asynchronous resource, and the observer interface represents the interface provided by the asynchronous resource's API. The provided interface allows the application to handle asynchronous events. The observer implementations are your application's handlers for the asynchronous events.

In GWT we see this type of asynchronous programming a lot in the user interface for handling interface events. Application view classes register themselves with the GWT widgets, which in turn handle events from the browser. To register for events, they pass an observer interface implementation into an `addListener` method. Java provides a couple of features, local classes and anonymous classes, that help reduce the work and code fragmentation for implementing these types of interfaces.

A **local class** is a class that you can define inside another class. The class acts similarly to member variables in that you can set its scope to be private, public, or protected. Instances of local classes are contained in an instance of the encapsulating class. This means that inside the local implementation you can write code that accesses members or methods in the encapsulating class. For example, the following code implements a ClickListener interface as a local class:

```
public class AppView extends Composite {

    private class AClickListener implements ClickListener {
       public void onClick(Widget sender){
          aLabel.setText("Clicked");
       }
    }

    private Label aLabel = new Label("Click Me");

    public AppView(){
       initWidget(aLabel);
       aLabel.addClickListener( new AClickListener() );
    }
}
```

In this code a Label widget is created and added to the AppView, then the local class AClickListener is added as a click listener for the label. When the user clicks the label, the click listener has its onClick method called. Notice how the local class can access the aLabel member variable of the encapsulating class. This is possible because Java associates the local class with the instance of the encapsulating class that instantiated it. Using this technique saves you from creating new Java class files for each asynchronous interface you want to implement. Instead the code is close to its related code and therefore easier to read and maintain. Of course, you could also implement the ClickListener interface on the AppView class, but this would not be as nice if you needed to handle clicks from multiple sources.

Java provides another feature, called anonymous classes, that helps bring code that handles asynchronous events closer to the initial asynchronous request. Anonymous classes can be declared and instantiated inside of methods as an expression. They do not have a name and cannot be used anywhere else in the application. For example, the preceding code can be written using anonymous classes like this:

```
public class AppView extends Composite {

   private Label aLabel = new Label("Click Me");

   public AppView(){
      initWidget(aLabel);
      aLabel.addClickListener( new ClickListener(){
         public void onClick( Widget sender ){
            aLabel.setText("Clicked");
         }
      });
   }
}
```

This code implements the `ClickListener` interface and instantiates an instance of it in the same line that uses the interface as a parameter for the `addClickListener` method. This cleans up the code even more and makes it easier to read. The downside to using this feature is that implementing this code in the method means it can only be used in this single location. You cannot use this interface implementation when you need to share asynchronous event handlers between multiple calls.

It may seem that you never need to use multiple calls for any single interface when looking at user interface handlers. Typically user interface handlers just need to be added once to listen to many user interface events. With network handlers this is much different. There is typically only one response per request, which means you may want to reuse the interface implementation for other requests. In this case you would need to use a local class implementation instead of an anonymous class implementation.

In the Blog Editor sample application in Chapter 8, the startup process of communicating with the Blogger web service involves several steps that span multiple asynchronous requests. Unfortunately, it's hard to read the code and understand the sequence of tasks in the process; external documentation of the process is probably needed. However, the result is an application that performs well while waiting for the process to complete on the server. The sample applications use many asynchronous programming techniques with GWT. Table 5-1 outlines all of the possible locations where asynchronous programming is required in GWT.

Table 5–1 Asynchronous Features in GWT

Asynchronous Feature	Description	Used in…
User Interface Events: `ChangeListener`, `ClickListener`, `Command`, `FocusListener`, `HistoryListener`, `KeyboardListener`, `LoadListener`, `MouseListener`, `PopupListener`, `ScrollListener`, `TabListener`, `TableListener`, `TreeListener`, `WindowCloseListener`, `WindowResizeListener`	The user interface is an asynchronous resource. The user interacts with the application at unknown intervals, which requires asynchronous programming techniques.	Used in every sample application in this book since they are fundamental for user interface development.
HTTP Requests: `com.google.gwt.http.client`	The HTTP library provides classes that let you build an HTTP request and receive a response by implementing a `ResponseCallback` class.	Used in the Blog Editor and Database Editor applications.
Form Submission: `FormPanel`, `FormHandler`	The `FormPanel` submits a request to the server using a hidden frame, which is loaded asynchronously. When the loading is complete, a method on the `FormHandler` implementation is used.	Used in the Database Editor application.
GWT-RPC: `com.google.gwt.user.client.rpc`, `com.google.gwt.user.server.rpc`	Each method call that is performed with the GWT-RPC implementation is an asynchronous call that requires an `AsyncCallback` implementation to receive the result.	Used in the Instant Messenger application for each request to the instant messenger server.

Handling the Back Button

A common problem with many Ajax applications is that they do not handle a page change well. Since Ajax applications typically don't refresh the page but still change their state, their state can be lost when the page is refreshed or when the user navigates away from the page using the back button. With traditional web applications users know how to browse a web site by clicking on links and using the back button to return to the previously viewed page. When these same users, familiar with links and the back button, use an Ajax application to browse whatever data the application is providing, they may use the back button to return to the previously viewed data. If the Ajax application is not handling this back button explicitly, it will unload and return to the previous web page. Then when users realize what has happened and try to go back, they return to the application in its original state. Any progress they may have made is lost.

It's far too much to ask for Ajax application users to become familiar with this quirk or to expect browser developers to invent an option for Ajax applications. Instead, Ajax applications need to provide reasonable handling of these usability situations.

GWT provides a nice solution that uses the browser's history feature paired with the HTML anchor. Everyone is familiar with browser history and using the back and forward buttons. The browser remembers the previous pages users have been to, and if they click back to a previous page, they can return by clicking the forward button. Users aren't as familiar with the HTML anchor, but web developers know it well. An anchor is the a tag you use in HTML to make a clickable link. It's usually referred to as a hyperlink, and anchor usually refers to a link within the same page. In HTML you can label a section in your page like this:

```
<a name="anyName">any spot in the page</a>
```

And then link to the spot using this:

```
<a href="#anyName">go to the spot</a>
```

When a user clicks on the hyperlink, the browser scrolls the page so the focus is on the anchor with the name *anyName*. The browser remembers this as an item in its history, but the browser does not refresh the web page since the link is within the current page. If a user clicks on a series of these internal links, he could then browse backward through the document with the back button without any refresh. Furthermore, the user could right-click on one he likes and select to open it in a new window at the anchor location.

To provide this support, the browser keeps track of these internal links by altering the URL of the page with the # symbol. For example, when the user clicks on the preceding hyperlink, the URL changes to this:

```
http://www.yourdomain.com/index.html#anyName
```

Notice that the browser appends the anchor name and the # symbol to the URL. When the user opens this URL in another window, the browser loads the index.html page and then sets the focus to the anyName location.

GWT implements its history feature using this anchor behavior in the browser. The `Hyperlink` widget can only be instantiated with a token string value, the name of the anchor, that represents the application's state after the user clicked the hyperlink. This integrates well with the existing functionality of the browser's back and forward buttons as well as the ability to open links in a new window. When the user moves forward in the application by clicking links, the application does not refresh itself and can keep track of its state. When the user presses the back button, the application receives an event that the state has changed to a previous one, based on an anchor token value, and can adjust its state to reflect the change. When a user opens the Ajax application in a new window based on a token, the application can process that token to render the appropriate state.

To implement this ability in your application, you need to come up with a model of an application state that can be represented by a string token. For example, in the Multi-Search application in Chapter 7, the state is represented by the user's search string. Each time a user performs a search, the application enters a token into the browser history. Clicking back then returns to a previous search, a common behavior for regular search engine web pages. The Database Editor application in Chapter 10 uses the tokens to represent the current view that is displayed. As the user browses through data, the application adds tokens to the browser's history. The user can easily return to the previous view with the back button. This behavior will be familiar to users familiar with browsing data on traditional web pages and being able to return to the previous set of data with the back button.

After you determine the correct granularity of states for your history tokens, you simply need to use GWT's `History` class to manage and receive events from the browser's history stack. New history tokens can be added using the `History.addToken` method, which is the same as the user clicking on a `Hyperlink` widget. This action adds the # symbol and the token as the current URL. For example, the following code shows how the Multi-Search application adds a history token after the user submits a search query:

```
private void onSearch(){
    String query = searchBox.getText();
    if( query.length() > 0 ){
        History.newItem(query);
    }
}
```

As you can see, the code simply gets the search query from a `TextBox` widget and adds the query string to the browser's history as a token.

The second half of implementing browser history in your application is to respond to changes in the history stack. You do this by implementing GWT's `HistoryListener` interface and adding the listener to the `History` class. The `History` interface is a simple interface with only the `onHistoryChanged` method:

```
public interface HistoryListener {
    void onHistoryChanged(String historyToken);
}
```

When you implement this interface, the application must change its state to reflect the state represented by the history token provided. In the Multi-Search application this token is the search string, so the application retrieves the search results based on this string. The following code shows the implementation of this in the Multi-Search application:

```
History.addHistoryListener( new HistoryListener(){
    public void onHistoryChanged(String historyToken){
        listener.onSearch(historyToken);
    }
});
```

This code adds the `HistoryListener` interface to the `History` class and has the `onHistoryChanged` event handled by submitting the history token to an `onSearch` function as a search query (the application controller handles this `onSearch` method to request search results from various search engines).

Creating Elegant Interfaces with CSS

You build interfaces with HTML declaratively with few rules and no compilation step, making it easy to experiment. The result of this freedom leads to interesting and creative interfaces, but it's not entirely good. The lack of rules in the HTML documents causes them to be messy, difficult to read, and hard to maintain. When you need to change similar elements across many HTML files, you're left with the tedious and error-prone task of manually updating each one. You can use Cascading Style Sheets (CSSs) to share these styles between applications.

Connecting GWT Widgets to CSS

Let's look at the CSS in the generated HTML host for the HelloWorld application in Chapter 4:

```
<style>
   body,td,a,div,p{font-family:arial,sans-serif}
   div,td{color:#000000}
   a:link,.w,.w a:link{color:#0000cc}
   a:visited{color:#551a8b}
   a:active{color:#ff0000}
</style>
```

The generated CSS is included in the HTML document's `style` tag. As an alternative, we could copy the contents of the tag, not including the `script` tag itself, to an external file called HelloWorld.css. The file would need to be in the public directory so that the compilation step will include the file in the deployment. The HTML file can then import the CSS file by adding this `link` tag in the head section:

```
<link rel="stylesheet" type="text/css" href="HelloWorld.css" />
```

Yet another way to handle this is to embed the CSS code in the compiled module itself. We'll look at how to do this later in this chapter.

The structure of CSS consists of a list of rules, each of which has one or more selectors followed by their style properties surrounded with curly braces. The selector chooses the elements in the HTML document that the styles will apply to. In this case the selector is choosing all elements based on their tag names. CSS also allows selecting elements based on their class attribute or their ID. Using GWT's widgets we don't know for certain which elements are being used, so instead we have to set attributes on the widgets. GWT uses the element's class attribute, which it calls the widget's style name. Every widget has three methods that let you set its style name.

- `setStyleName`

  This method sets the style name to be used for the widget. If the widget had any previous style names, they are removed.

- `addStyleName`

  This method adds a style name to the widget. Widgets can have multiple style names, so if there were any previous style names applied they are kept.

- `removeStyleName`

  This method removes one style name from the widget and leaves any others.

The sample applications in Part II of this book use these methods; this way, the widgets used in these applications can be styled from CSS. For example, the `TitleCommandBar` widget, used in the Blog Editor and Database Editor applications, sets its style names in its constructor:

```
public TitleCommandBar( String title ){
    initWidget( titlePanel );
    titlePanel.setWidth("100%");
    setStyleName("gwtapps-TitleBar");
    titleLabel = new Label( title );
    titleLabel.setStyleName("gwtapps-TitleBarTitle");
    titleLabel.setWordWrap( false );
    titlePanel.add( titleLabel );
}
```

The `TitleCommandBar` sets its style name to `gwtapps-TitleBar` and has a `Label` child which has its style name set to `gwtapps-TitleBarTitle`. In CSS we can adjust the look of this widget throughout the application easily with just a couple lines:

```
.gwtapps-TitleBar{
    border-bottom:1px solid #ddd;
    margin-top:20px;
    width:500px;
}
.gwtapps-TitleBarTitle{
    font-size:16pt;
    font-weight:bold;
}
```

When the browser renders the application, every `TitleCommandBar` widget will have a gray border along its bottom, a 20-pixel margin, and be 500 pixels wide. The title label in each `TitleCommandBar` widget will have a bold 16-point font. The following images show the Blog Editor's blog titles in a `TitleCommandBar` widget using the CSS just specified:

gwtbeta view   new entry

gwtapps view   new entry

Figure 5–3.   `TitleCommandBar` widgets styled with CSS

Notice that in the CSS the selectors have a dot in front of the style name. Without a dot they would be considered as referring to element names. With a dot, they refer to class names, or GWT's style names. You'll see all of the GWT style names starting with a dot when referring to them from CSS.

In the generated HTML host for the HelloWorld application, the rules don't use a dot and instead refer to element names. Since widgets in GWT are implemented using HTML elements, these rules still apply to them. However, you don't always have control or knowledge of how the widgets are implemented on HTML elements, so using element names is not a very powerful way to style your application. It is somewhat useful in the generated code for HelloWorld to set a font for the entire application using the common HTML tags that would contain text. For example, the first rule selects five HTML tags by their tag names as a comma-delimited list, then applies the `font-family` property with the value `arial,sans-serif`. This rule causes all body, td, a, div, and p tags, which are commonly used to contain text, to use the `arial` font if available, and if not then to use `sans-serif`. After these rules, the remaining CSS in the Hello World application contains rules for setting the color of text for selected `elements`. Other than these basic styles set for all HTML tags, you should use GWT's style names to format your application.

Being able to connect GWT widgets to CSS styles using the `addStyle Name` and `setStyleName` methods is all you need to do to apply styles to your application. The rest of this section outlines the commonly used styling properties that can be set.

Specifying Colors

Let's start by looking at the different value formats for CSS properties for color. In the HelloWorld CSS. the `div` and `td` tags have their font color set:

```
div,td{color:#000000}
```

This sets the CSS color property #000000, which is the hexadecimal RGB notation for a specific color. The red value is 00, and the green and blue values are both also 00. When the red, green, and blue color values are mixed, they produce a unique color. In this case the color is black. Each RGB hexadecimal value must be between 00 and FF; FFFFFF, the maximum value, is white and 000000, the minimum value, is black. Values in between can produce a wide variety of colors. For a table of values, see http://www.gwtapps.com/colors.html. You can also use any of the HTML or CSS standard color names shown in Table 5–2.

Shades of gray can easily be created by using an equal amount of each color. For example, `#CCCCCC` is a light gray and `#333333` is a dark gray.

Specifying Units

CSS has additional number and values formats. For example, you can explicitly set the width of an item with the `width` property. The value of the property can be represented in many formats. The most commonly used are a pixel format and a percent format:

```
div { width: 250px }
p { width: 50% }
```

Table 5–2 The 16 standard HTML color names, along with CSS color names

Standard	Red colors	Green colors	Blue colors
Aqua	IndianRed	GreenYellow	Aqua
Black	LightCoral	Chartreuse	Cyan
Blue	Salmon	LawnGreen	LightCyan
Fuchsia	DarkSalmon	Lime	PaleTurquoise
Green	LightSalmon	LimeGreen	Aquamarine
Gray	Crimson	PaleGreen	Turquoise
Lime	Red	LightGreen	MediumTurquoise
Maroon	FireBrick	MediumSpringGreen	DarkTurquoise
Navy	DarkRed	SpringGreen	CadetBlue
Olive		MediumSeaGreen	SteelBlue
Purple	**Pink Colors**	SeaGreen	LightSteelBlue
Red	Pink	ForestGreen	PowderBlue
Silver	LightPink	Green	LightBlue
Teal	HotPink	DarkGreen	SkyBlue
White	DeepPink	YellowGreen	LightSkyBlue
Yellow	MediumVioletRed	OliveDrab	DeepSkyBlue
	PaleVioletRed	Olive	DodgerBlue
White colors		DarkOliveGreen	CornflowerBlue
White	**Orange colors**	MediumAquamarine	MediumSlateBlue
Snow	LightSalmon	DarkSeaGreen	RoyalBlue
Honeydew	Coral	LightSeaGreen	Blue
MintCream	Tomato	DarkCyan	MediumBlue
Azure	OrangeRed	Teal	DarkBlue
AliceBlue	DarkOrange		Navy
GhostWhite	Orange	**Brown colors**	MidnightBlue
WhiteSmoke		Cornsilk	
Seashell	**Yellow colors**	BlanchedAlmond	**Purple colors**
Beige	Gold	Bisque	Lavender
OldLace	Yellow	NavajoWhite	Thistle
FloralWhite	LightYellow	Wheat	Plum
Ivory	LemonChiffon	BurlyWood	Violet
AntiqueWhite	LightGoldenrodYellow	Tan	Orchid
Linen	PapayaWhip	RosyBrown	Fuchsia
LavenderBlush	Moccasin	SandyBrown	Magenta
MistyRose	PeachPuff	Goldenrod	MediumOrchid
Grey colors	PaleGoldenrod	DarkGoldenrod	MediumPurple
Gainsboro	Khaki	Peru	BlueViolet
LightGrey	DarkKhaki	Chocolate	DarkViolet
Silver		SaddleBrown	DarkOrchid
DarkGray		Sienna	DarkMagenta
DimGray		Brown	Purple
LightSlateGray		Maroon	Indigo
SlateGray			SlateBlue
DarkSlateGray			DarkSlateBlue
Black			

In this code the `div` tag is set to 250 pixels wide and the paragraph is set to 50 percent of its parent. Note that all GWT widgets have a `setWidth` method that takes a string. The value that you pass to the string has the same format options as the CSS values. Table 5-3 outlines the different options for length units in CSS.

Table 5–3   CSS Length Units

Unit Type	Example	Description
Centimeters Millimeters Inches	5cm 50mm 1in	These are regular length units which tell the browser the physical length displayed on the screen. This format is not very reliable due to operating systems' poor definitions for actual screen resolutions.
Points	12pt	This is a standard measurement for fonts that you are probably familiar with from using a text editor. There are 72 points to an inch.
Em	1.5em	An em unit is relative to the default font size for the element. For example, if the font size is 12pt, then 1em is equal to 12pt and 1.5em is equal to 18pt.
Pixels	11px	A pixel measurement represents an actual pixel on the screen.
Percentage	50%	The percentage measurement is relative to the size of the element's parent.

You can use these measurement values, along with the color values, for many CSS properties. There are other value formats, but these are the most often used.

Using Font Properties

CSS provides many properties that you can use to adjust the style of text. Table 5-4 outlines these properties. Using the font properties you are able to quickly set text styles throughout your application.

Using Text Properties

After setting the font, you may want to set text properties that don't affect the font properties. Table 5-5 outlines the properties CSS provides for text.

Table 5–4   CSS Font Properties

Property	Example	Description
font-family	font-family: Arial, sans-serif	Specifies a list of fonts for rendering the contained text. The first font in the list is used. If it is not available the next font is used, and so on. You can specify individual font names like Arial or font families like sans-serif or monospace.
font-weight	font-weight: bold font-weight: normal	Font weight is most commonly used to make text bold. However, there are other options that allow you to set varying degrees of weight.
font-size	font-size: 12pt font-size: 11px font-size: 1.2em	The font size can be set using this property and one of the CSS length units. Alternatively, you can use the values small, medium, large, etc.
font-style	font-style: italic font-style: normal	The font style attribute is primarily used to set a font to be italicized.
font	font: bold 1.5em Arial, sans-serif	The font property is used to set many values at once.

Table 5–5   CSS Text Properties

Property	Example	Description
line-height	line-height: 12px line-height: 2	This property sets the line height, which represents the spacing between lines in a paragraph of text. The default line height is 1, which is equal to the font size.
vertical-align	vertical-align: top vertical-align: middle	The vertical alignment of text sets where the text (or image) is located relative to its parent.
word-spacing letter-spacing	word-spacing: 0.5em letter-spacing: -1px	These properties adjust the spacing between words and letters.
text-transform	text-transform: uppercase text-transform: capitalize	This property allows you to transform the capitalization of text.
text-decoration	text-decoration: underline; text-decoration: line-through;	The text decoration sets how lines are used with text. This is typically used to underline text, but you can also set text to look like it's crossed out with a line through it.

Using Margin, Border, and Padding Properties

CSS does not only allow you to format text, it also lets you format larger container elements in HTML. It divides tag types into two categories, inline and block. Inline tags include text and images and can share the same space horizontally in the browser. Block tags cannot share a line; they cause any subsequent tags to be displayed on the next line. The `div` and `table` tags are examples of block tags. When using GWT's widgets you don't have to worry much about the distinction between block and inline tags since the widgets provide a layout abstract on top of HTML. However, when working with CSS, you run into these concepts. In general, you can think of the GWT panels as being block tags, and the simple widgets and form widgets as being inline tags. The reason for the distinction is that not all CSS properties apply to inline tags. For example, you can't set the margin on an inline tag.

CSS provides several properties for managing the style of block-level elements, including padding, border, and margin. These apply to the box area that a tag, or widget, occupies. Figure 5-4 shows how these three properties relate to the box that the widget occupies.

The margin is the outermost space outside the border for the widget. This space separates this widget from any neighboring widgets. The border space can have a color and style and acts as a visible indication of the widget's boundaries. The padding is the space between the border and the

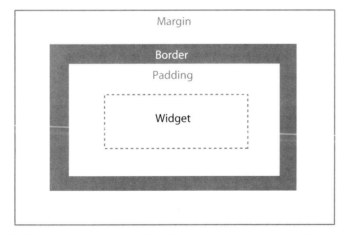

Figure 5–4. How margin, border, and padding properties relate to each other

contents of the widget. For example, for a `Label` widget with a paragraph of text and a border, it probably wouldn't look nice to have the border touching the text. Having padding between the text and the border would give the widget a cleaner look. The widget itself is at the center of this model. It can have width and height properties that set its size. The margin, border, and padding areas wrap the widget outside of its set size.

Table 5-6 outlines the properties that apply to the inside of this box model.

CSS Examples

Let's look at how these attributes are used in a sample application. The view in the application uses a `TabPanel` to display two different child views. The `TabPanel` styles its tabs to look like desktop application tabs, as illustrated in Figure 5-5.

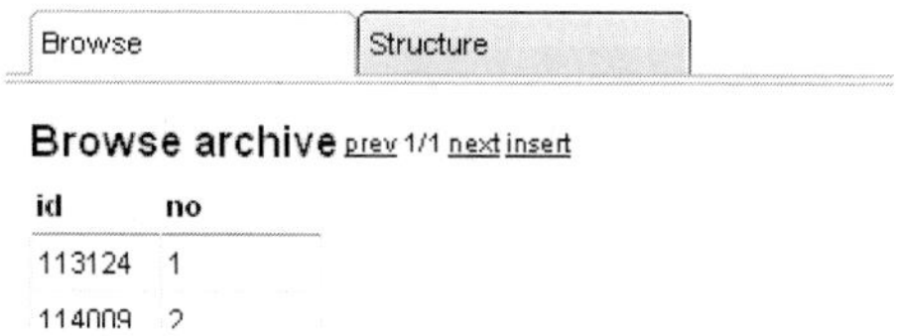

Figure 5–5. A tab panel with its tabs styled to look like a desktop application

Without any styling, these tabs would have black text on a white background. There would not even be any separation between the tabs or between the tabs and the current page. The following CSS sets the style for the tabs in Figure 5-5:

```
.gwt-TabBar{
    background-image:url(tab-rest.gif);
    background-repeat: repeat-x;
    padding-top:3px;
    width:100%
}

.gwt-TabBarFirst {
    width:10px;
}

.gwt-TabBarItem {
    background-image:url(tab.gif);
```

Table 5-6 CSS Block Properties

Property	Example	Description
margin margin-top margin-right margin-bottom margin-left	margin: 5px margin: 5px 0px 10px 3px margin-top: 5px margin-right: 0px margin-bottom: 10px margin-left: 3px	The margin properties allow you to set the margin length values for all of the sides or for selected sides only.
border-color	border-color: #555555	This property sets the color of the border. You must also set a size for the border since the default border size is 0.
border-width	border-width: 1px	The border width is the width of the border line. This is typically measured in pixels.
border-style	border-style: solid border-style: dotted border-style: outset	The border style is the type of line that is used for the border. It is usually solid, but it can be dashed, dotted, or any another available line style.
border border-top border-right border-bottom border-left	border: 1px solid #555555 border: 1px 0px 2px 0px border -top: 1px solid #55555 border -right: 0px border -bottom: 2px border -left: 0px	The border property lets you set all of the border properties in one line. You can also set different widths for the border sides with this property. Properties to format the border on an individual side are also available.
padding padding-top padding-right padding-bottom padding-left	padding: 5px padding: 5px 0px 10px 3px padding-top: 5px padding-right: 0px padding-bottom: 10px padding-left: 3px	The padding properties allow you to set the spacing size between the widget and its border.
background-color	background-color: #FF0000	This property set the background color. The color is shown behind any foreground elements in the widget and the border. It does not display in the margin space.
background-image background-repeat	background-image: url(back.gif) background-repeat: no-repeat; background-repeat: repeat-x; background-repeat: repeat-y;	These properties allow you to display an image in the background for the widget and how it is repeated horizontally and vertically. This property is used to set background tabs in the Database Editor application in Chapter 10.

```
      background-repeat:no-repeat;
      width:126px;
      height:27px;
      font-size:8pt;
      padding:5px;
}


.gwt-TabBarItem-selected {
      background-image:url(tab-selected.gif);
}
```

This code sets the tab bar with an image that runs horizontally in its background to divide the tabs from the viewable page. It uses the `background-image` CSS property to display this line and the `background-repeat` property to repeat the image horizontally. The width of the tab bar is set to 100 percent, so this image spans the entire width of the container widget. The tab on the tab bar, which has the style name `gwt-TabBarItem`, has its background set to the image of a tab without any repeats. The size of the tab is set to the size of the image, and the tab is given a padding of 5px so the text is not directly touching the edge of the tab. A selected tab has a lighter background image to give the user feedback when a tab is selected.

This example shows you how to use several of these properties together, and illustrates how pairing CSS with a dynamic interface can be a simple yet powerful method of styling an application.

Using the Cursor Property

The final CSS property that is useful when developing interfaces with GWT is the `cursor` property. This property allows you to change the cursor that is used for the mouse when it hovers over a widget. For example, in the Gadget Desktop application in Chapter 6, the cursor is set to a move cursor when the mouse hovers over the dragable section of a desktop gadget, as shown in Figure 5-6. Changing the cursor like this gives the user a hint that the gadget can be moved. The following CSS changes the cursor in this application when the mouse hovers over the title label for the gadget:

```
.gwtapps-GadgetContainerTitle {
      cursor: move;
      font-weight:bold;
      color: #678
}
```

Figure 5-6.   The CSS move cursor

CSS also has several other cursors you can use. For example, you can change the cursor to the hand cursor that is typically used automatically when the mouse hovers over a hyperlink. The Gadget Desktop application uses the hand for the `EditLabel` widget to signal the user that the label is clickable, as shown in Figure 5-7. The following CSS creates this effect:

```
.gwtapps-EditLabel{
   cursor: hand;
   cursor: pointer;
}
```

Figure 5-7.   The CSS hand pointer cursor

This CSS code actually sets the cursor twice, because different browsers use different CSS names for the hand cursor. Using both names ensures that the hand cursor will be displayed in all browsers.

A third cursor used throughout the sample applications in this book is the progress cursor in the `LoadingPanel` widget. This is a great cursor for Ajax applications because it lets the user continue to interact with the application but indicates that work is being done asynchronously. Figure 5-8 shows this cursor, which is a composite of the pointer image and the hour-glass image.

Table 5-7 lists the available cursor values for use in CSS along with their corresponding images.

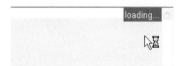

Figure 5–8. The CSS progress cursor

Table 5–7 CSS Cursor Types

Cursor	Example	Cursor	Example
default		not-allowed	
crosshair		col-resize	
hand/pointer		row-resize	
move		e-resize, w-resize	
text		ne-resize, sw-resize	
wait		nw-resize, se-resize	
help		n-resize, s-resize	
progress			

Extending the Toolkit

It's important to note that GWT does not aim to be a framework but rather a toolkit. This means that it does not want to prescribe a way to build applications but rather provide a set of tools that assists in building applications. The toolkit opens up the capability for you to access technologies outside of the toolkit, including HTML, CSS, and JavaScript, and also to extend the tools in the toolkit.

Building New Widgets

You've seen how it's possible to build new widgets through composition by attaching other widgets together. Sometimes, however, you need to create a new widget that does not extend an existing widget. To do this you employ the same techniques that are used to build basic Widgets in GWT.

GWT provides a DOM class, which allows you to make calls to the browser's document object model. The browser's document object model exposes functions that let you manage the current document, including creating new tags and inserting them. You can use these functions to compose new widgets based on a set of HTML tags. New widgets can automatically hook into GWT's event system using the `sinkEvents` method. This results in a new widget that is not dependent on another GWT widget. In the Blog Editor application in Chapter 8 we create a new widget called the `Link` widget. This widget provides your application with a widget that wraps HTML's a tag to create an external link, since the `Hyperlink` widget is only used for internal links. Let's look at this example.

First, the `Link` class is declared and extends GWT's widget so that it inherits basic widget functionality:

```
public class Link extends Widget{
```

In the `Link`'s constructor a new anchor tag is created and set as the widget's main element using the `setElement` method. Doing this connects the widget's base class to an anchor tag so that all other widget methods apply to this new element. The following is the code for the constructor:

```
public Link(){
    setElement( DOM.createAnchor() );
    sinkEvents( Event.ONCLICK | Event.MOUSEEVENTS );
    setStyleName("gwtapps-Link");
}
```

Notice the code also calls the `sinkEvents` method. Calling this method tells the widget's base class which events we are interested in receiving. The events to sink are passed into the method as an OR list.[1] The third line in the constructor simply sets a default style name for the widget.

---

1. The | symbol is a bitwise OR operation that is used to combine multiple constants into one integer value. Each constant typically represents a 1 value for one bit position. Combining them like this creates a single value that represents the selected constants.

To set values for the widget we implement setter methods, which use the DOM class to set attributes on the widget's element:

```
public void setText(String text) {
    DOM.setInnerText(getElement(), text);
}

public void setLink( String link ){
    DOM.setAttribute(getElement(), "href", link );
}
```

In this code the `setText` method uses the DOM's `setInnerText` method to set the text that will appear inside the anchor tag. The link is changed using the DOM's `setAttribute` method to set the widget's element's `href` attribute.

The new widget should also provide proper interfaces for the events that it will be receiving. First it should implement the event sources interfaces and use the event listener helper collections:

```
public class Link extends Widget
    implements SourcesClickEvents, SourcesMouseEvents {
    private ClickListenerCollection clickListeners;
    private MouseListenerCollection mouseListeners;
```

In this code we've changed the widget declaration to declare the implementation of the event interfaces. We've also set two private collection variables that will hold the listeners for the events. To add listeners to the widget, the client would need to call the appropriate add listener method, which is implemented like this:

```
public void addClickListener(ClickListener listener) {
    if (clickListeners == null) {
        clickListeners = new ClickListenerCollection();
    }
    clickListeners.add(listener);
}

public void addMouseListener(MouseListener listener) {
    if (mouseListeners == null) {
        mouseListeners = new MouseListenerCollection();
    }
    mouseListeners.add(listener);
}
```

Finally, the widget needs to distribute incoming events to the listeners. To do this it needs to override the widget's `onBrowseEvent` method:

```
public void onBrowserEvent(Event event) {
    switch (DOM.eventGetType(event)) {
        case Event.ONCLICK:
            if (clickListeners != null)
                clickListeners.fireClick(this);
        break;
        case Event.ONMOUSEDOWN:
        case Event.ONMOUSEUP:
        case Event.ONMOUSEMOVE:
        case Event.ONMOUSEOVER:
        case Event.ONMOUSEOUT:
            if (mouseListeners != null)
                mouseListeners.fireMouseEvent(this, event);
        break;
    }
}
```

As you can see, the helper collections do most of the work of distributing the events. Once this is complete we have a new widget built like the simple widgets are built in GWT, without dependencies on other widgets.

Using the JavaScript Native Interface

There will be occasions when you won't be able to access everything you need from the browser to extend GWT. The DOM implementation is not fully complete. This is partly due to browser incompatibilities. GWT provides the JavaScript Native Interface (JSNI) to give you direct access to the browser's JavaScript functions and objects.

This flexibility is very useful, although you need to be more cautious with it. The GWT tools work hard to be tools that work the same across different browser implementations. By accessing JavaScript directly, you are opening up your application to browser incompatibilities. You'll need to do extra testing to be certain that your JSNI code works in multiple browsers.

Writing a method in pure JavaScript is easy with GWT's JSNI. You simply need to declare the method as native and provide its JavaScript implementation within a comment. For example, the following Java method executes JavaScript to cause a browser's alert window to display:

```
public static native void alert(String msg) /*-{
   $wnd.alert(msg);
}-*/;
```

Notice that $wnd is used instead of the browser's window object. The reason for this is that GWT runs the JavaScript in a hidden frame. The window object would be the window for the hidden frame and not the window that the user is viewing. GWT provides the $wnd object to reference the actual window object that the user is viewing. Similarly, there is a $doc object for the real document object.

GWT also provides a way for JavaScript to call a Java method. The method signature is somewhat complicated when written in JavaScript. It uses the following form:

```
[instance-expr.]@class-name::method-name(param-signature)(arguments)
```

You specify the instance-expr part to access a nonstatic method. Its value should be the instance you will be calling the method on. The class-name part is the full class name of the class with the method you are calling. The method-name part is the method name to be called, and the param-signature part is an encoded list of parameters types. Table 5-8 outlines how to specify these encoded parameter types.

Table 5–8 Signature Encodings for Java Types

Java Type	Signature to Use
boolean	Z
byte	B
char	C
short	S
int	I
long	J
float	F
double	D
any class: java.lang.String	Lclass/name ; Ljava/lang/String;
array array of Strings array of ints	[type [java/lang/String; [I

The final part, the arguments part, is where you pass the actual argument values in the method.

The Multi-Search application in Chapter 7 uses JSNI to extend GWT to get the ability to retrieve data from remote servers, bypassing the browser's Same Origin policy. The application defines a JSON request class, which creates a new `script` tag and sets up a JavaScript callback through JSNI. The class defines a static `get` method used by the application to make a call for a remote script resource:

```
static public void get(
String url, String callbackName, JSONRequestHandler handler ){
   createCallbackFunction( handler, callbackName );
   Element scriptElement = DOM.createElement("script");
   DOM.setAttribute(scriptElement, "type", "text/javascript");
   DOM.setAttribute(scriptElement, "src", url );
   DOM.appendChild(RootPanel.get().getElement(), scriptElement);
}
```

You can see that this method uses the DOM class to set up a `script` tag, set its URL, and append it to the document. This causes the browser to start the request for the remote script. Before the request is sent, the code sets up a callback method using `createCallbackFunction`. This is a JSNI method on the class that sets up a JavaScript method, which will be called by the remote script when it completes loading, and then calls a callback method on a Java interface. The method is implemented like this:

```
private native static void createCallbackFunction(
   JSONRequestHandler obj, String callbackName ) /*-{
   tmpwin = $wnd;
   tmpcallback = function( j ) {
obj.@com.gwtapps.client.util.JSONRequestHandler::onRequestComplete(Ljava/lang/
String;)( j.toJSONString() );
   };
   eval( "tmpwin."+callbackName+"=tmpcallback" );
}-*/;
```

This function sets up a callback function that exists on the window object, and that is based on the name passed in as a parameter. Notice how the Java string can automatically be used as a JavaScript string in the `eval` function, which allows us to evaluate JavaScript in string format. The Java-Script of the method creates a new function, which is the callback that the remote script calls, and defines the implementation of that function as a call to a method on the `JSONRequestHandler` Java interface. The instance that implements this interface is passed into this method as the first parameter.

Providing Cross-Browser Support

One of the great advantages of using GWT is that it supports the same functionality across standard browsers, eliminating the need for you to write separate code to handle browser quirks. If you are extending the toolkit, then you should make your extensions browser-independent. GWT provides a mechanism that lets you automatically use different code for different browser platforms.

The mechanism is also used internally by GWT classes to support multiple platforms. It basically allows you to select different class implementations based on a single class name for different browser types. The differences can be specified in your project's module XML file using the `replace-with` element. For example, GWT needs to provide a different implementation for the `TextBox` widget when run on Internet Explorer. In the `Text Box.gwt.xml` module file in the GWT library, you will find the `replace-with` element replacing a class implementation with another class based on the browser:

```
<replace-with class="com.google.gwt.user.client.ui.impl.TextBoxImplIE6">
    <when-type-is class="com.google.gwt.user.client.ui.impl.TextBoxImpl"/>
    <when-property-is name="user.agent" value="ie6"/>
</replace-with>
```

In this code the `replace-with` class attribute specifies the class to use, and its child elements specify the conditions that have to be true for it to be replaced. The first child element is the `when-type-is` element with its class variable set to the class to replace. The second child element, the `when-property-is` element, has the name attribute `user.agent` and the value attribute `ie6`. These values restrict this replacement to occur only when the browser type is Internet Explorer (the `ie6` value is also used for Internet Explorer 7). This XML code in the module file effectively swaps in a different implementation for a different browser.

You can use this technique in your module as well, and it is best paired with the Strategy design pattern. The Strategy design pattern lets you choose different behavior for part of your application. It has a context class that can use one of several strategies to implement its behavior. Figure 5-9 shows the structure of the Strategy design pattern.

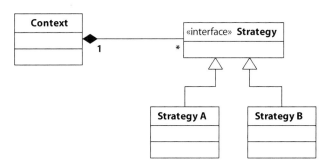

Figure 5-9.   The Strategy design pattern

For the preceding TextBox widget example, the context is the TextBox widget and the available strategies are the TextBoxImpl class or the TextBoxImplIE6 class. The TextBox widget only uses one of these classes, selecting it depending on the browser version.

In the source code for the Gadget Desktop application in Chapter 6 you'll find a Flash widget to play an MP3 file in the Playlist gadget. The Flash widget uses this technique to support the two different ways that browsers support Flash. Internet Explorer uses the object tag, while other browsers use the embed tag. Let's look at how this is implemented. First, refer to the UML diagram in Figure 5-10 to see the structure of the Strategy design pattern that supports this.

The widget, called FlashPanel, displays a flash file and holds an instance of a FlashPanelImpl class. The class can either be the base FlashPanelImpl

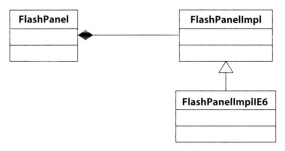

Figure 5-10.   Structure of the FlashPanel widget

class, holding the functionality for non-Internet Explorer browsers, or it can be a `FlashPanelImplIE6` class, which holds the functionality specifically for Internet Explorer. The XML elements need to be added to the module file to tell the GWT compiler which implementation to use:

```
<replace-with class="com.gwtapps.client.ui.FlashPanelImpl">
    <when-type-is class="com.gwtapps.client.ui.FlashPanelImplIE6"/>
    <when-property-is name="user.agent" value="ie6"/>
</replace-with>
```

This tells the GWT compiler to use the `FlashPanelImplIE6` class when the browser type is Internet Explorer. Note that the replacement does not occur for explicit instantiations of the class; instead, you need to use GWT's deferred binding mechanism with the `GWT.create` method. You can see how to use this by looking at the code for the `FlashPanel` widget:

```
public class FlashPanel extends Composite {
    private FlashPanelImpl impl =
    (FlashPanelImpl) GWT.create(FlashPanelImpl.class);

    public FlashPanel(String url, int width, int height, String flashVars ) {
        initWidget( impl.initWidget(url,width,height,flashVars) );
    }
}
```

The `FlashPanel` widget has one private member variable, the `FlashPanelImpl` implementation. Using the `GWT.create` method with the class value for the panel causes the proper implementation class to be created for the current browser. Then, in the widget's constructor, the `initWidget` method is called on the constructor to create the flash element that is appropriate for the current browser. For non-Internet Explorer browsers this is implemented as an embed tag like this:

```
public class FlashPanelImpl {
    Widget initWidget( String url, int width, int height, String flashVars ){
        HTML flashCode = new HTML();
        flashCode.setHTML( "<embed"+
            " height='"+height+"' width='"+width+"' "+
            " src='"+url+"'"+
            " flashVars='"+flashVars+"'"+
            " quality='high'"+
            " wmode='transparent'"+
            " align='absmiddle'"+
            " allowScriptAccess='sameDomain'"+
```

```
        " type='application/x-shockwave-flash'"+
        " pluginspage='http://www.macromedia.com/go/getflashplayer' />" );
        return flashCode;
    }
}
```

This base implementation creates the `embed` tag and adds it to an HTML widget. This widget is returned and used as the main widget for the `FlashPanel`. For Internet Explorer we need to use the `object` tag instead:

```
public class FlashPanelImplIE6 {
    Widget initWidget( String url, int width, int height, String flashVars ){
        HTML flashCode = new HTML();
        flashCode.setHTML( "<object "+"height='"+height+"' width='"+width+"'"+
            " classid='clsid:d27cdb6e-ae6d-11cf-96b8-444553540000'"+
" codebase='http://fpdownload.macromedia.com/pub/shockwave/cabs/flash/
swflash.cab#version=6,0,0,0'"+
            " align='absmiddle'"+
            " VIEWASTEXT>"+
                "<param name='wmode' value='transparent' />"+
                "<param name='allowScriptAccess' value='sameDomain' />"+
                "<param name='flashVars' value='"+flashVars+"' />"+
                "<param name='movie' value='"+url+"' />"+
                "<param name='quality' value='high' />"+
            "</object>" );
        return flashCode;
    }
}
```

As you can see, this method leads to a well-structured way of handling browser inconsistencies. This solution's architecture also excludes other browser implementations from the compiled JavaScript code, which reduces the final compiled code size. With other Ajax applications using pure JavaScript typically you would not have this flexibility and would have to combine code to handle all browsers together.

Using Other JavaScript Libraries

While the list of GWT modules available to integrate into your application is growing, there is a far greater—and will most likely always be—number of pure JavaScript libraries available. Using JSNI it is possible to integrate other libraries into your existing code.

With traditional JavaScript you include other libraries into your application simply by using the `script` tag and referencing the other library's URL. You use this same method with GWT applications, except that you write pure JavaScript code to interact with the library, while with a GWT application you interact with the library through JSNI methods.

One example of adding external JavaScript code to your library would be to use a JavaScript library to encode a password for authenticating with a server. Passwords are commonly sent in plain text and use HTML forms to authenticate with a web application's server. This makes it easy for anyone to intercept the transmission and read the password. Using a hash of the password instead, paired with a challenge value from the server, can provide increased security for the password.[2] This technique is used by Yahoo! for their non-SSL logins.

Writing a secure hash function may seem like a simple task, but it has several problems that need to be overcome for it to be considered secure, fast, and correct. Writing one in JavaScript is even harder because of browser differences. Fortunately, secure and correct JavaScript implementations have been tested in major browsers. Specifically, there is an implementation made available by Paul Johnston at http://pajhome.org.uk/crypt/md5/.

Let's write a quick login scheme which uses Paul's MD5 JavaScript library. The most secure way to do this is to have the server generate a random value, called a challenge, which is passed to our application.[3] Our application then uses the value with the user's password with the MD5 hash function to calculate a hash. The hash is then sent back to the server for authentication. The server performs the same task (MD5 is widely available in server libraries) and compares its result. If they are equal, then the user is authenticated; otherwise the user isn't authenticated. Figure 5-11 shows how this sequence works.

---

2. This technique helps fix eavesdropping problems where someone may listen to the transmission and intercept the password. However, it is not completely secure, since it is still possible for someone to modify the transmission because the HTTP data source is not securely validated. Using SSL is the best solution for true security.

3. The challenge causes the hash sent by the client to be different each time. Otherwise, an eavesdropper could simply pick up the hash and use it to authenticate at another time.

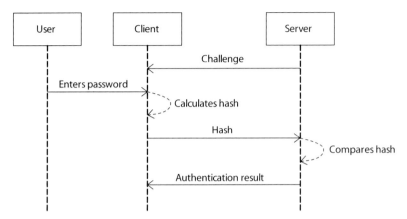

Figure 5–11.   Authentication using a hash

Now let's look at the client-side code to produce the hash. First we need to include the script library with MD5 functions in the head section of our host HTML page:

```
<script language="javascript" src="http://pajhome.org.uk/crypt/md5/md5.js">
</script>
```

This makes the library's MD5 hash functions available to our application through JSNI. Next we can create an MD5 Java class that has methods to access the JavaScript functions:

```
public class MD5 {
   public native static String getHexHMACMD5(
      String password, String challenge ) /*-{
      return hex_hmac_md5(password, challenge)
   }-*/;
}
```

This class just wraps one of the functions from the library. You can add other methods that use more functions from the library. In this case the method, hex_hmac_md5, takes a value and a challenge and produces an MD5 hash result. The method returns the result. Now we can simply create this hash from our application code using this method:

```
String hash = MD5.getHexHMACMD5( password.getText(), challenge );
```

This technique of using JSNI to integrate with external JavaScript libraries can also be used with libraries that have a user interface. For example,

Google Maps provide a JavaScript API to embed a map on a web page. Google's map user interface is very interactive and connects to a great map system on their servers. It would be a lot of work to create a widget with this functionality from scratch, so it makes sense to integrate with their JavaScript library. Let's run through a quick example of how to create a widget based on Google Maps.

The first step is to get an API key and include the script source in your application's host HTML file:

```
<script src="http://maps.google.com/
maps?file=api&amp;v=2&amp;key=ABQIAAAACeDba0As0X6mwbIbUYWv-RTb-
vLQlFZmc2N8bgWI8YDPp5FEVBQUnvmfInJbOoyS2v-qkssc36Z5MA" type="text/javascript"></
script>
```

This code points to the JavaScript library for Google Maps and has an extra parameter, `key`, which represents the API key for your application. I generated the key used here for the domain localhost:8888, which you can use while testing your application. You will, however, need to get your own API key for the domain you will deploy your application on.

The next step is to create a new widget class. In this case we will extend the `HTML` widget, since Google Maps attaches itself to an existing `HTML` tag. First we'll create a new `div` tag within the widget with a unique ID. Then we'll use JSNI to initialize a map to display within the `div` tag. The JSNI method will return the newly created JavaScript map object, which you use later to call additional functions on the map. The following is an example of a `GoogleMap` widget:

```
public class GoogleMap extends HTML{
    private static int nextId = 0;
    private JavaScriptObject map;

    public GoogleMap(){
        String id = "map"+(++nextId);
        setStyleName("gwtapps-GoogleMap");
        setHTML("<div id='"+id+"'></div>");
        RootPanel.get().add( this );
        map = initMap(id);
    }

    public void setCenter( final double lon, final double lat ){
        setCenterImpl( map, lon, lat );
    }
```

```
private native static JavaScriptObject initMap( String id ) /*-{
   var map = new $wnd.GMap2( $doc.getElementById(id) );
   return map;
}-*/;

private native static void setCenterImpl(
   JavaScriptObject map, double lon, double lat )/*-{
   map.setCenter(new $wnd.GLatLng(lon, lat), 13);
}-*/;
}
```

Notice that the constructor first sets up an ID which it uses for the ID of the contained `div` tag. The class adds itself to the application's `RootPanel` since the `GoogleMap` initialization requires that the `div` be in the document object model. Then the constructor calls the `initMap` method, which is a JSNI method that creates a new `GMap2` object, a JavaScript class that provides the map functionality. Note that the `$wnd` name references the names from the Google Maps library, since the library was loaded on the application's host page window. A second JSNI method is defined, `setCenterImpl`, which calls the `setCenter` function on the map object in JavaScript.

You can extend this widget to provide the full API for Google Maps as needed. You can find a full implementation of the Google Maps API written for GWT at http://sourceforge.net/projects/gwt/.

You can easily use the widget defined here by applications as part of GWT's widget framework. For example, in the Gadget Desktop application in Chapter 6, the `GoogleMap` widget is used inside a `GoogleMaps` gadget like this:

```
GoogleMap map = new GoogleMap();
initWidget( map );
map.setCenter( 37.4419, -122.1419 );
```

This code creates the `GoogleMap` widget, adds it to a `Composite` widget using its `initWidget` method, and centers it on the longitude and latitude values. This results in a Google map that integrates well inside a GWT application, as shown in Figure 5-12.

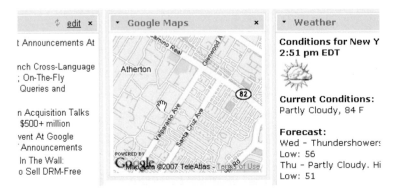

Figure 5–12.   Another JavaScript library integrating into a GWT application

Internationalizing Applications

Applications built for web distribution are commonly distributed globally and therefore often require translation of text strings and formatting styles to different languages. This translation process is called **internationalization** (i18n).[4] GWT provides classes to help internationalize an application in the com.google.gwt.i18n.client package.

It's possible to use two different techniques to provide internationalization with GWT applications. Both techniques follow the architecture of moving all strings that need to be translated outside application code and into a properties file or in the HTML host file as JavaScript. The external file is usually clean from syntax and easily readable by translators, who do not need to be familiar with Java code. This also makes it easy to localize your application by switching between property files without any code changes.

Your application simply accesses all of its constants or locale-sensitive data through an interface. The interface does not change between locales, so your application code remains the same. GWT connects the interface with a property file at compile time. When your application is loaded, GWT selects the version compiled for the selected locale. Figure 5-13 outlines this relationship.

---

4. i18n is the commonly used short form for internationalization. The *I* and the *N* refer to the first and last letters, and *18* refers to the 18 letters in the middle.

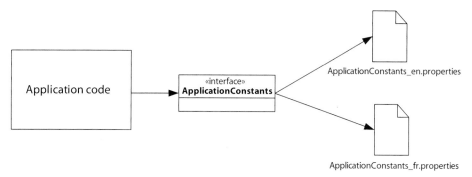

ApplicationConstants_en.properties

ApplicationConstants_fr.properties

Figure 5–13.   The constants used are hidden from the application code

Declaring Constants

The interface can be one of two types: a constant's interface or a message's interface. The constant's interface extends GWT's `Constant` interface and has one method without parameters for each constant value. The name of the method maps to the name of the method in the property file. For example, we could have a file called DesktopConstants.properties for the Gadget Desktop application in Chapter 6 with the following content:

```
appTitle = GWT Desktop
editLabel = edit
```

These are name-value pairs; the name maps to the method name on the constant's interface and the value is the return value from the method. The `DesktopConstants` interface in this case would look like this:

```
public interface DesktopConstants extends Constants {

String appTitle();
String editLabel();
}
```

You can use the interface inside a GWT application by instantiating it through the `GWT.create` method like this:

```
DesktopConstants constants =
    (DesktopConstants)GWT.create(DesktopConstants.class );
Window.alert( constants.appTitle() );
```

The GWT compilation process automatically handles connecting the values in the property files with the interface. It can even perform code optimizations where it moves the constant value inline to where it's used, thereby eliminating a method call.

This method also has the advantage of being type-safe and strongly bound based on a name. The compiler catches any type errors or name errors at compile time or in your IDE. This is better error checking when compared to a dynamic property implementation where values are held in a map (GWT's `Dictionary` class provides this type of implementation and has other advantages). Table 5-9 outlines the different types of values GWT supports for constants in a property file.

Obviously, constants are limited to one constant value that cannot change after the application has compiled. There are usually many locations where this type of value is required, and you can use the `Constants` interface to take advantage of the compile-time type checking. However, there are often situations when you need to localize messages that are not entirely constant. Typically these types of messages have some variable values involved. GWT provides the `Messages` interface to deal with this.

Table 5–9   Constant Types

Type	Description	Example
`String`	A regular string	`editLabel = Hello World`
`String[]`	An array of strings declared as a comma-delimited list. Use \\, to escape a comma.	`buttonLabels = new, edit, save`
`int`	An integer	`timeout = 30`
`float`	A floating point value	`price = 65.00`
`double`	A double-sized floating point value	`max = 1.7976931348623157E308`
`boolean`	A true or false value	`debugMode = false`

`Map`	A map of other properties declared as a comma-separated list	`newLabel = new`
		`editLabel = edit`
		`saveLabel = save`
		`buttonLabels = newLabel, editLabel,`
		`saveLabel`

Declaring Messages

The Messages interface shares the same localization infrastructure as the Constants interface, but differs in that it supplies the interface with string-based localized and parameterized messages. Each method on the interface can accept a number of typed parameters, which are converted to strings and used as part of a message from a properties file.

The properties file for messages looks similar to the properties file for constants, but doesn't have the same range of types, only allows strings, and has parameter placeholders. Each message must have the same number of parameter placeholders as the number of parameters its corresponding method on the messages interface has. GWT enforces this at compile time.

So, for example, we can create a messages property file similar to the DesktopConstants properties file, but we can add a couple of parameters like this:

```
appTitle = GWT Desktop, Version {0}.{1}
editLabel = edit
```

We've simply changed the title to have the version number. The parameters' placeholders are written as the parameter number surrounded by curly braces. The interface for this messages property file extends GWT's Messages interface and provides a method for each line in the property file. A message with two parameter placeholders must have a method with two parameters. The DesktopMessages interface looks like this:

```
public interface DesktopMessages extends Messages {
    String appTitle( int majorVersion, int minorVersion );
    String editLabel();
}
```

We create this interface, like the Constants interfaces, with the GWT.create method:

```
DesktopMessages messages =
(DesktopMessages)GWT.create(DesktopMessages.class );
Window.alert(messages.appTitle(1,0) );
```

Figure 5-14 shows a window with the parameterized message that the code displays.

Figure 5–14.   Showing a dialog box with a message generated by the `Messages` interface

The `Messages` and `Constants` interfaces are part of the i18n library, so you need to inherit this module in your application module file like this:

```
<inherits name="com.google.gwt.i18n.I18N"/>
```

It is a little extra work to maintain this type of structure, but it pays off when you localize your application and need to maintain property files for different locales. GWT also provides a script that will generate a constants or messages property file and scripts to automatically generate the Java interfaces based on the properties in the file.

Localization Tools

Adding new messages or constants can be a tedious task, since you first need to add them to the property file and then to the interface. When writing the code for the interface, you can easily make an error that slows the process down even more. GWT provides some scripts to automatically perform this task.

First you need to use the `i18nCreator` script to generate a messages or constants property file and an interface-generating script. For example, the following executes the script to create a messages file for the Gadget Desktop application:

```
i18nCreator -eclipse GwtApps -createMessages
com.gwtapps.Desktop.client.DesktopMessages
```

The `eclipse` flag tells the script to create an Eclipse launch configuration that will generate the `DesktopMessages` interface based on the properties in its property file. The `createMessages` flag tells the script to create a `Messages` interface instead of a `Constants` interface. To create a

```
C:\gwtapps-ws\gwtapps>i18nCreator -eclipse GwtApps -createMessages com.gwtapps.D
esktop.client.DesktopMessages
Created file C:\gwtapps-ws\gwtapps\src\com\gwtapps\Desktop\client\DesktopMessage
s.properties
Created file C:\gwtapps-ws\gwtapps\DesktopMessages-i18n.launch
Created file C:\gwtapps-ws\gwtapps\DesktopMessages-i18n.cmd
```

Figure 5–15. The output from running the `i18nCreator` script

`Constants` interface you simply leave this flag out. The final argument to the script is the name of the `MessagesInterface`. Running this script gives the output shown in Figure 5-15.

Note that three files were created: the DesktopMessages.properties file, which will hold our parameterized messages; the DesktopMessages-i18n.launch file, which allows us to generate the `DesktopMessages` interface from the property file through Eclipse; and the `DesktopMessages-i18n` script, which allows us to do the same from the command line. Looking inside the DesktopMessages.properties file you will find a sample message:

```
#sample message property to be translated in language-specific
#versions of this property file
#this message takes a single argument, which will replace the {0}
welcome: Welcome. The current time is {0}.
```

At this point we don't have a `DesktopMessages` interface, but we can easily generate one using the launch configuration in Eclipse called `Desk topMessages-i18n`. If you click on the Run button in the Eclipse toolbar, you will see this launch configuration in the list, as shown in Figure 5-16. Clicking on the Run button launches the script, which generates the `DesktopMessages` interface from the properties file. After running the script, the DesktopMessage.java file appears in the Desktop package, as you can see in Figure 5-17.

The script will generate the interface and methods based on the properties in the property file. Notice that the `generate` method also has the proper number of parameters. You can repeat this process as your property file grows to easily build the corresponding interface file. This process also applies to a `Constants` interface.

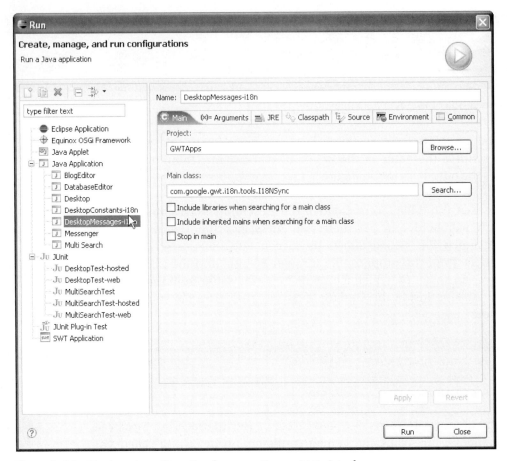

Figure 5–16. The launch configuration for generating an i18n interface

Managing Locales

The structure of Messages and Constants interfaces connecting the property files sets up a foundation for managing localized data for a range of locales. By using Messages and Constants interfaces in your application you can hide the actual locale the application runs in from your application code. The locale management occurs outside your code. Each interface will have one or more property files associated with it. During the compile step, GWT generates one set of code per locale and automatically inserts the property values for locales.

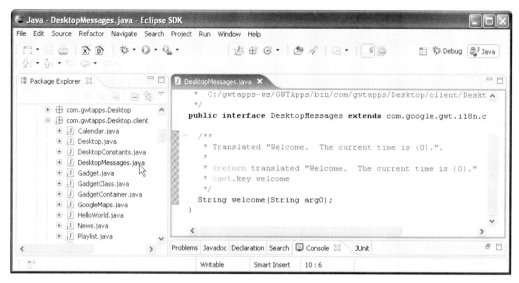

Figure 5–17.   A generated i18n interface

In the previous example, you saw a property file for messages called Desktop Messages.properties and a property file for constants called DesktopConstants .properties. These are considered default property files, and they act as a baseline for other localized property files. When you set a specific locale, the application uses constants or messages from that locale. If the locale's property file doesn't have a constant or message defined, then the default property file is used. This allows you to specify only the constants or messages you need in the localized property files.

To build a property file for a specific locale, you use the name of the interface followed by the locale identifiers:

```
DesktopConstants_en_GB.properties
```

This follows the format of `Type_x_Y.properties`, where `x_Y` is the locale name, `x` is the ISO language code, and `Y` is the ISO country code. In this case the language code is `en` for English and the country code is `GB` for Great Britain. You do not have to specify a country if you want the properties to apply to a specific language regardless of country. The following property file would be used for English:

```
DesktopConstants_en.properties
```

When GWT compiles the code for en_GB, it uses the constants from DesktopConstants_en_GB.properties, DesktopConstants_en.properties, and DesktopConstants.properties, where the constants in the more specific files take precedence. This allows you to specify only the constants that you need to for each country and language, reducing duplicate property declarations.

You also need to specify which locales your application uses. This is done in your module file. To support the preceding locales, add these lines to the Desktop module file:

```
<extend-property name="locale" values="en"/>
<extend-property name="locale" values="en_GB"/>
```

When the GWT compiler sees these two locales, it knows to generate the localized Constants or Messages interfaces for each locale.

The final step to localize an application is to specify the locale to be used at runtime. GWT provides two ways to specify the locale. The first uses a meta tag in the host HTML file for the application. This acts as a default locale for the application. For example, to make the locale en, specify this in the head tag of the host HTML file:

```
<meta name="gwt:property" content="locale=en">
```

The second way you can specify a locale, which can be used along with the preceding method, is as a URL parameter. The parameter name needs to be locale, and the value is the locale to be used. If both a locale URL parameter and a meta tag value are specified, the URL parameter locale takes precedence. This lets you treat the meta tag locale as a default. The following is an example of a URL specifying en_GB as a locale:

```
http://localhost:8888/com.gwtapps.Desktop.Desktop/index.html?locale=en_GB
```

Using the Dictionary

The Dictionary class provides the simplest way to move string values outside application code, but it does not provide any method of localization—it can't change the set of values based on a selected locale. You can use this class to integrate with existing localization systems outside of GWT, or to simply retrieve constants from outside the application.

The `Dictionary` class works simply by allowing the application to retrieve a dictionary object by name and then retrieve any value based on a key. Instead of specifying the values in a properties file, they are specified as JavaScript in your application's HTML host file. For example, when you add the following JavaScript to the application's HTML host file, the Java-Script's values are accessible from the `Dictionary` class:

```
<script language="javascript">
   var DesktopConstants = {
      appTitle: "GWT Desktop",
      editLabel: "edit"
   };
</script>
```

To access these values you first need to retrieve the `DesktopConstants` dictionary and then call its `get` method:

```
Dictionary constants = Dictionary.getDictionary("DesktopConstants");
Window.alert( constants.get("appTitle") );
```

Notice that instead of using an interface, a `String` key retrieves the value. This is a little less efficient than using the `Constants` interface, because the GWT compiler can't inline the constant value and must do a key-based lookup. The benefit of this class over the `Constant` interface is that you can change your parameters without needing to recompile your code.

Generating Code

One of the biggest differences between GWT Ajax applications and plain JavaScript Ajax applications is the compile step needed for GWT Ajax applications. The compile step lets you transform the code base before deployment to make it smaller and more efficient, or to include more functionality. Fortunately, the toolkit provides the ability to plug into this compile step to extend it. This section illustrates how to do this.

Using Generated Code

Although the GWT web site doesn't include information about generating code during the compile step, the library has several examples of the process. The `ImageBundle` functionality, the GWT feature that bundles many images into one to reduce HTTP round trips, is an example. For the application developer, implementing an image bundle is very simple. You simply need to define a Java interface with a method for each image and then create an instance of the interface using the GWT.create method. For example, the Gadget Desktop application in Chapter 6 shows how to create an ImageBundle to bundle the images used in the title bar for each gadget. The implementation looks like this:

```
static public interface TitleBarImageBundle extends ImageBundle{
    /**
     * @gwt.resource close.gif
     */
    public AbstractImagePrototype closeIcon();

    /**
     * @gwt.resource minimize1.gif
     */
    public AbstractImagePrototype minimize1Icon();

    /**
     * @gwt.resource minimize2.gif
     */
    public AbstractImagePrototype minimize2Icon();

    /**
     * @gwt.resource refresh.gif
     */
    public AbstractImagePrototype refreshIcon();
}
public static TitleBarImageBundle titleBarImages =
(TitleBarImageBundle) GWT.create( TitleBarImageBundle.class );
```

This code defines the file name of each image file with the gwt.resource annotation before each method. Then the code creates an instance of the interface using the GWT.create method with the interface class as a parameter. Calling each method returns the correct image. The following code shows how to add an image to a PushButton:

```
PushButton closeButton =
new PushButton(titleBarImages.closeIcon().createImage());
```

What happens here that you don't see in this code is that during compilation the GWT compiler combines each image listed in the interface together into one big image. When you distribute the application, you only distribute the one image, which reduces the HTTP round trips used, in this case by 3. For an application with many images, this is a large optimization while the code to implement it is short, clear, and easy to maintain. A GWT code generator performs the magic that provides this nice development experience.

You can find other examples of code generators within GWT following a similar pattern in the GWT-RPC implementation, where you define RPC interfaces and the code generator builds the serialization and deserialization code automatically. GWT also uses code generators with the internationalization interface, where code is generated to bring messages from property files that represent different locales as return values from a Java interface.

Beyond providing a nice way to clean up your code, GWT code generators also provide a way to optimize your code. It is common in modern programming languages to try to push as much processing as possible to compile time instead of having it occur at runtime. For example, if you declare a variable equals 24*60*60 in your code, the compiler can translate this into the value 86,400 before running the code, saving processing at runtime. With GWT code generation you can similarly perform processing at compile time to improve runtime performance.

Writing a Code Generator

Let's look at how to write a code generator for GWT. The first step is to declare a class that extends `com.google.gwt.core.ext.Generator`. It is important that this class does not go into your .client package. Instead, put it outside of your .client package in a .rebind package to follow the GWT convention. For example, it could go in `com.gwtapps.rebind` for the gwtapps sample packages. Then you need to implement the `generate` method as:

```
public String generate( TreeLogger logger, GeneratorContext ctx,
    String requestedClass) throws UnableToCompleteException
```

The compiler calls the `generate` method for each class or interface that matches the type defined for your generator. For example, the image bundle generator matches implementations of the `ImageBundle` interface.

To tell the compiler which interface or class to match to this generator, you need to add a `generate-with` element to your module XML file like this:

```
<generate-with class="com.gwtapps.rebind.XMLSerializableGenerator">
<when-type-assignable class="com.gwtapps.client.util.xml.XMLSerializable"/>
</generate-with>
```

This example defines a generator called XMLSerializableGenerator to be used for every instance of `XMLSerializable`. The generator can then generate custom XML serialization for each `XMLSerializable` class.

The actual code generation code written inside the `generate` method can become fairly complex. It is a difficult task to generate code since the generated code doesn't have the same development tool support as regular Java. For example, Eclipse does not provide you with code completion or error checking for writing code-generation code. Often the generated code is built from Java strings and the IDE treats it as such. However, the tradeoff for generated code makes this difficulty worth it. Not having to write serialization code for each RPC method when using GWT-RPC saves a lot of development and debugging time. The Database Editor application in Chapter 10 uses a code generator to provide reflection methods for selected classes, which saves quite a bit of code creation and maintenance that would otherwise be spent writing serialization code. The generation example in the Database Editor is fairly complex, so we will go through a simplified example in this section.

To illustrate how to implement a generator, we'll write a `generate` method that takes the matched type and generates a class with a new method. The following steps outline this procedure.

1. Implement a generator class that extends `Generator`. Make sure the new class is not in a client package that is going to compile to JavaScript.

2. Add the `generates-with` element to your module XML file to match the generator to a specific type.

3. Implement the `generate` method.

   a. Create a unique name for the new generated class.

   b. Use the `GeneratorContext` to create a new `PrintWriter` for the new class name.

    c. Use `ClassSourceFileComposerFactory` to start building the class imports and superclass, and to create a `SourceWriter` from the `PrintWriter`.

    d. Use the `SourceWriter` to write Java source code to the new class.

    e. Use the newly created class name as the return value for the `generate` method.

During the generation of code in the `generate` method you can use GWT's reflection classes to obtain information about all of the types that are being compiled. For the image bundle generator, the code iterates over the methods on the matched `ImageBundle` interface to determine which images to include in the bundle. GWT defines several classes that represent type information for the Java classes being compiled, including `JClassType`, `JMethod`, `JField`, `JPackage`, and others. You can start reading these values in your code using GWT's `TypeOracle`. To get a reference to the `TypeOracle` in your `generate` method, you need to call the `getTypeOracle` method on the `GeneratorContext` instance, which is passed into the method as a parameter. The following code gets an instance of the `TypeOracle` and requests a type based on a specified name:

```
TypeOracle typeOracle = context.getTypeOracle();
JClassType type = typeOracle.getType(typeName);
```

You can then use the methods on the `JClassType` instance to read more information from the class.

Writing the `generate` Method

In our simple example of a `generate` method, we produce a new class that has an extra method that creates a list of the field names for the class. The following code is the source of the `generate` method for this example:

```
public class ExampleGenerator extends Generator {
    public String generate(TreeLogger logger, GeneratorContext context,
        String requestedClass) throws UnableToCompleteException{
        //get the type oracle
        TypeOracle typeOracle = context.getTypeOracle();
        assert (typeOracle != null);
```

```
try {
    //get the class type and fields
    JClassType type = typeOracle.getType(requestedClass);
    JField[] fields = type.getFields();

    //build the subclass name
    String className = type.getName().replace('.', '_') + "_generatedExample";
    String packageName = type.getPackage().getName();

    //create print writer
    PrintWriter printWriter = context.tryCreate(logger,
    type.getPackage().getName(), className );
    if (printWriter == null) {
        return null;
    }

    //create source writer
    ClassSourceFileComposerFactory composerFactory =
        new ClassSourceFileComposerFactory( packageName, className );
    composerFactory.setSuperclass(requestedClass);
    composerFactory.addImplementedInterface(
        ExampleFieldsImpl.class.getName());
    SourceWriter srcWriter = composerFactory.createSourceWriter(
        context, printWriter);
    if (srcWriter == null) {
        return null;
    }

    //write the new method to the class
    srcWriter.println("public String getFieldString(){");
    srcWriter.indent();
    srcWriter.print("return \"");
    for( int i=0; i< fields.length; ++i ){
        srcWriter.print(fields[i].getName()+" ");
    }
    srcWriter.println("\";");
    srcWriter.outdent();
    srcWriter.println("}");

    //commit the writer and return the new class name
    srcWriter.commit(logger);
    return composerFactory.getCreatedClassName();

}
catch (NotFoundException e) {
    logger.log(TreeLogger.ERROR, "Unable to find required type(s)", e);
    throw new UnableToCompleteException();
}
}
}
```

Note that the `generate` method follows the steps outlined earlier to create a new class. It also uses the `TypeOracle` to get the `JClassType` and the list of fields in the class. Then the code creates a new class and implements a new method that returns a string of the fields in the class. To apply this `generate` method to classes, we first need to add the `generate-with` element to our application's module XML file like this:

```
<generate-with class="com.gwtapps.rebind.ExampleGenerator">
    <when-type-assignable class="com.gwtapps.client.util.ExampleFields"/>
</generate-with>
```

This code tells the compiler that the `ExampleGenerator` should be invoked for each class that can be assigned to the `ExampleFields` interface. This interface is a tag interface that has nothing defined on it:

```
public interface ExampleFields {}
```

We use this interface to tag the classes that we want to run the generator on. Then the generator creates a new class using our class as a subclass and implements the `ExampleFieldsImpl` interface, which adds the `getFieldString` method:

```
public interface ExampleFieldsImpl {
    String getFieldString();
}
```

The generated class then implements this method as returning a list of the fields in the class as a string. Let's look at a sample class that the code generator would apply to:

```
class AnExampleClass implements ExampleFields{
    String name;
    String description;
}
```

In this code we've tagged the class as an `ExampleFields` class so that the `ExampleGenerator` is invoked for it and generates the new class. To use the new class in our code, we need to instantiate this class using GWT's `GWT.create` method:

```
AnExampleClass exampleClass =
    (AnExampleClass)GWT.create(AnExampleClass.class );
ExampleFieldsImpl exampleClassFields = (ExampleFieldsImpl)exampleClass;
String fields = exampleClassFields.getFieldString();
```

In this code the class returned is still an instance of `AnExampleClass`, since the generated class uses it as a superclass. Since it is actually an instance of the generated class, we can cast the class to the `Example FieldsImpl` interface and use the generated `getFieldString` method.

What you don't see here is the generated code; this is part of the advantage of using code generators. The generated code can become quite complex, but this technique hides from application developers. For this example, however, the generated code is fairly simple:

```
package com.gwtapps.databaseeditor.client;

public class DatabaseEditor_AnExampleClass_generatedExample extends
com.gwtapps.databaseeditor.client.DatabaseEditor.AnExampleClass implements
com.gwtapps.client.util.ExampleFieldsImpl {
  public String getFieldString(){
    return "description name ";
  }
}
```

We will look at a more advanced example of code generation in the Database Editor application in Chapter 10. The generator creates code that allows several serializers for JSON and XML formats in this application to automatically serialize specified objects.

Improving Performance

Simply using GWT to build Ajax applications gives you a free boost over building with JavaScript. The GWT compiler goes through optimizations when compiling Java to JavaScript which would be difficult to do by hand. However, there are a few things about GWT development that you need to know to get a high-performing Ajax application. This section looks at handling long processing, reducing HTTP round-trips with `ImageBundle`, and several techniques to cache and compress the application files on the server.

Handling Long Processing

As you saw in the asynchronous programming section at the beginning of this chapter, Ajax applications only have one thread to execute on. This thread is shared by the user interface, which means if you have any long processes or blocking calls the user interface will become unresponsive. Fortunately, HTTP requests are nonblocking and use an asynchronous model. But you may run into a situation where you need to perform CPU-intensive processing that will cause the user interface to become unresponsive. This is a drawback of Ajax applications, but you can work around this by using GWT's `IncrementalCommand`.

The `IncrementalCommand` interface works similarly to the `Command` interface in that it has one `execute` method you need to be implemented:

```
public interface IncrementalCommand {
    boolean execute();
}
```

You can use the interface with GWT's `DeferredCommand` mechanism. `DeferredCommand` allows you to add commands to the browser's message queue to be executed after pending events. It may not be obvious when to use `DeferredCommand`, so as an example let's look at a situation where it's used in the Gadget Desktop application's `DockableWidget`. The `DockableWidget` handles the `onMouseMove` event to determine if a dragging widget can be docked at its current location, and if it can, the widget being dragged swaps spots with another widget. During the swap, the code also swaps mouse listeners, which causes a problem because the mouse listener collection is being iterated over to send `onMouseMove` events. So instead of performing the swap in the `onMouseMove` event, it is deferred to be done after the event completes. The following code shows how to defer the command:

```
DeferredCommand.addCommand( new Command(){
    public void execute() {
        swapChild();
    }
});
```

You use `IncrementalCommand` in the same way, but instead of being executed once, it is executed many times until the `execute` method returns false. This allows user interface events to be handled in between invocations of the `execute` method and protects your application from becoming unresponsive during long processing.

As an example, the following code adds an incremental command that processes 100 things at a time:

```
class ProcessThings implements IncrementalCommand{
    Iterator things;

    public ProcessThings( Iterator things ){
        this.things = things;
    }

    public boolean execute() {
        for( int i=0; i<100 && things.hasNext(); ++i ){
            Object thing = things.next();
            /* process thing */
        }
        return things.hasNext();
    }
}
DeferredCommand.addCommand(new ProcessThings(collectionOfThings.iterator()));
```

Using `ImageBundle`

As GWT is to JavaScript, `ImageBundle` is to images. GWT's image bundle feature groups images used in an application into a single image, which reduces the number of round-trips to the server. This may not sound substantial, but it's a big performance improvement. Keep in mind that as Ajax applications become more complex, they use more images for their interface or toolbar buttons. These images need to be loaded one by one for their display. Users get the feeling that the application's interface is being constructed before their eyes as the images show up one by one as the application loads. Also, remember that your server can only have two HTTP connections at a time, which makes image loading a sequential process. Packaging all of the images in one file not only results in them appearing at the same time, but also causes the application to load remarkably faster. In addition, the image bundles are given a name that is a hash of their contents. This may not be a readable file name, but the browser can cache this file forever. (See the next section on caching to get your server to tell clients to cache these files.) This means that the second time your application loads, the browser doesn't even need to check for a new version of the images. New images are only loaded when there is a new version of your application, when the application then points to an image bundle with a different hash value. Another benefit of the image bundle is modularization: Images can be easily bundled with modules to be included with the applications that use them.

So how does this work? To build an image bundle, you create an interface that extends ImageBundle and implements one method per image. Each method returns an AbstractImagePrototype object and has an annotation that points to the image's location in your source code. If the image is in the same path as the interface, you simply need the filename. The Gadget Desktop application uses an ImageBundle to bundle the images for the GadgetContainer title bar:

```
static public interface TitleBarImageBundle extends ImageBundle {

    /**
     * @gwt.resource close.gif
     */
    public AbstractImagePrototype closeIcon();

    /**
     * @gwt.resource minimize1.gif
     */
    public AbstractImagePrototype minimize1Icon();

    /**
     * @gwt.resource minimize2.gif
     */
    public AbstractImagePrototype minimize2Icon();

    /**
     * @gwt.resource refresh.gif
     */
    public AbstractImagePrototype refreshIcon();
}
```

When GWT compiles this application, it finds this interface and the referenced image files and combines them into a single image file for distribution. Then the GWT compiler generates code to implement the methods on the interface to return AbstractImagePrototype instances. Each AbstractImagePrototype references one image in the image bundle and can construct Image widgets for using the image in the interface. You can create an instance of your image bundle interfaces using GWT deferred binding like this:

```
TitleBarImageBundle titleBarImages = (TitleBarImageBundle) GWT.create(
TitleBarImageBundle.class );
```

Then you can add `Image` widgets to your interface using the image bundle's methods like this:

```
PushButton refreshButton = new PushButton(
titleBarImages.refreshIcon().createImage() );
```

This code creates a new `PushButton` widget with the `refresh.gif` image as the button's main image.

When you compile your application, you get a new `ImageBundle` image file in the www directory for your application, as shown in Figure 5-18. Figure 5-19 shows the images bundled together, and Figure 5-20 shows the images in the interface.

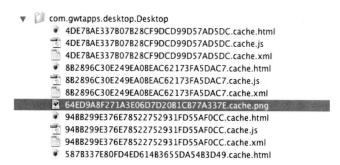

Figure 5–18.   The image bundle file

Figure 5–19.   The images bundled together

Figure 5–20.   The images in the interface

Caching on Apache

Notice that the compiled JavaScript files for your application have names that are hash values. This hash value of the source code is unique for each new build of the application, which means that the client can cache these files forever. Typically browsers will unnecessarily check if there is a newer version of these files on the server every time the application is loaded. You can add an HTTP header to tell the browser that these checks are not necessary and that these files can be cached forever. You can also cache the image bundle files forever since their generated names are also a unique hash of the image files. If you change any image in the bundle, it receives a new name.

If you're distributing your application on an Apache server, you can use the mod_header module to set a Cache-control header value for your GWT files. The following code, when added to the Apache configuration file, adds a Cache-control header to each request for a file that matches *.cache.*:

```
<IfModule mod_header.c>
   <FilesMatch "*.cache.*">
      Header set Cache-control max-age=31536000
   </FilesMatch>
</IfModule>
```

The header specifies the maximum age of the file to be 31,536,000 seconds, or 1 year, causing the GWT files to be cached for a sufficiently long time.

Caching on a Servlet Container

If you're using a servlet container directly (Tomcat, Jetty, Resin, etc.), you can create a filter that performs a similar task, but there is not a readily available header module to use. Instead, you will have to create a filter that adds the Cache-control header to files that match the *.cache.* pattern. Creating a filter for your servlet container is fairly straightforward. You simply need to create a new class that implements the Filter interface and implement the doFilter, init, and destroy methods. Then in the filter you can add the Cache-control header to the response. The following implementation of a filter adds the Cache-control header to a request for a file that matches ".cache.":

```
public class CacheFilter implements Filter {
   private FilterConfig filterConfig;


   public void doFilter( ServletRequest request, ServletResponse response,
      FilterChain filterChain) throws IOException, ServletException {
```

```
    HttpServletRequest httpRequest = (HttpServletRequest)request;

    String requestURI = httpRequest.getRequestURI();
    if( requestURI.contains(".cache.") ){
       HttpServletResponse httpResponse = (HttpServletResponse)response;
       httpResponse.setHeader("Cache-Control","max-age=31536000" );
    }
    filterChain.doFilter(request, response);    }

 public void init(FilterConfig filterConfig) throws ServletException {
    this.filterConfig = filterConfig;
 }

 public void destroy() {
    this.filterConfig = null;
 }
}
```

You can use this filter to add the `Cache-control` header to any file that matches " `.cache.` ". To configure this filter for GWT files you need to add the following to your web.xml file:

```
<filter>
    <filter-name> CacheFilter </filter-name>
    <filter-class>com.gwtapps.server.CacheFilter </filter-class>
</filter>
<filter-mapping>
    <filter-name>CacheFilter </filter-name>
    <url-pattern>/*.html</url-pattern>
</filter-mapping>
<filter-mapping>
    <filter-name>CacheFilter </filter-name>
    <url-pattern>/*.png</url-pattern>
</filter-mapping>
```

You can see in this XML that the filter is configured to point to the `Cache-Filter` class. Then in the `filter-mapping` elements we apply the filter to files that match the HTML files and PNG image files. This causes the servlet container to pass files with these extensions through the filter first before continuing to process the request. If the files contain " `.cache.` " then the filter adds the `Cache-control` to tell the browser to cache these for a long time.

Compression on Apache

You can make additional performance improvements to your application by compressing the JavaScript files on the server. Using `gzip` to compress the JavaScript files, you are likely to see up to a 70 percent reduction in size of these files. This means that you save up to 70 percent bandwidth distributing your application files, and the clients receive the files faster.

Apache supports this compression using automatic content negotiation. When a browser requests a file, it sends the type of compression it supports. If the client supports `gzip` and there is a `gzip` version of a file on the server, then the server sends that file. The client browser then decompresses the file before using it. To `gzip` your JavaScript files, simply run the following command:

```
gzip *.cache.*
```

Compression on a Servlet Container

Servlet containers typically don't have the same content negotiation that Apache has. Tomcat, however, supports a compression option that can be added to the `Connector` element in the server.xml configuration file like this:

```
<Connector port="8080" redirectPort="8443" acceptCount="20" compression="on" />
```

This option causes Tomcat to use `gzip` compression on all HTML and XML files for every web application. For more fine-grained support for compression you can create a filter that compresses selected files.

A compression filter needs to check to see that the browser supports `gzip` compression, and then forward requests to a `gzip` version of the file. The filter implementation that does this looks like this:

```
public class GZIPFilter implements Filter {
    private FilterConfig filterConfig;


    public void doFilter(ServletRequest request, ServletResponse response,
        FilterChain filterChain) throws IOException, ServletException {
        HttpServletRequest httpRequest = (HttpServletRequest)request;
```

```
//skip gzipped files
String requestURI = httpRequest.getRequestURI();
if( !requestURI.endsWith(".gz") ){

    //check for gzip support
    String acceptEncoding = httpRequest.getHeader("accept-encoding");
    if( acceptEncoding != null && acceptEncoding.indexOf("gzip") != -1){

        //forward to .gz file
        try{
            RequestDispatcher rd =
filterConfig.getServletContext().getRequestDispatcher(requestURI+".gz");
            rd.forward(request, response);
            return;
        } catch( ServletException e){ /*continue*/ }
    }
}
filterChain.doFilter(request, response);
}

public void init(FilterConfig filterConfig) throws ServletException {
    this.filterConfig = filterConfig;
}

public void destroy() {
    this.filterConfig = null;
}
}
```

This code checks the browser support for `gzip` files by verifying that the `accept-encoding` request header has the value `gzip`. Then the filter forwards the request to a version of the file with a `.gz` extension. If the file does not exist, an exception is thrown and the filter continues to the originally requested file. To use this filter you simply need to add it to your web.xml file and specify the file pattern that it will apply to:

```
<filter>
    <filter-name>GZIPFilter</filter-name>
    <filter-class>com.gwtapps.server.GZIPFilter</filter-class>
</filter>

<filter-mapping>
    <filter-name>GZIPFilter</filter-name>
    <url-pattern>*.html</url-pattern>
</filter-mapping>
```

Summary

This chapter introduced you to various aspects of writing effective applications with GWT. Each technique discussed provided information that, while not critical knowledge required to build applications with GWT, is essential to effectively use GWT in many situations. The chapter helped you to understand and adjust to asynchronous programming. It described how the browser's back button, which commonly breaks both traditional web applications and many Ajax applications, is handled properly in a GWT application. The CSS section provided an overview of the CSS properties that you can use to style a GWT interface. The chapter also covered some of the more advanced topics in GWT, including extending the toolkit, internationalization, generating code, and improving performance. With the tips found in this chapter along with the GWT library overview and software engineering techniques described in the previous chapters, you are now ready to look at the nontrivial Ajax application examples in Part II of this book.

PART II

Rich Web Applications
by Example

6

Gadget Desktop Application

This chapter looks at using GWT tools and its widgets, and considers application design techniques, including the Container Application pattern, the Abstract Factory design pattern, and a model-view-controller architectural pattern to build a nontrivial Ajax application: the Gadget Desktop. The interface uses GWT's user interface library to create the application's layout with panels, behavior with widgets and events, and look and feel with CSS and images. The application does not have a server-side component and focuses on client-side application development in the browser. This chapter illustrates the level of complexity that is easily obtainable and manageable through design techniques for Ajax applications written using GWT.

Functionally, the Gadget Desktop is an application you can use to customize and organize a number of gadgets inside your browser's desktop area. It's similar to many Ajax start page applications, including Netvibes, Pageflakes, My Yahoo!, and Google Start Page. You use the Gadget Desktop as a starting location when you begin to browse the web. It acts as a summary for many things and also as a gateway to frequently used services. It's richly customizable. Instead of prescribing the services and content that you view as a traditional web portal would, it lets you choose them and arrange them they way you like in pages and columns. You can try using a version that represents the end result of the work in this chapter that is running at http://desktop.gwtapps.com.

As you read through this chapter and Chapters 7–10, you can follow along and construct the Gadget Desktop application on your machine. Most of the code is presented in this chapter, but you'll need to refer to the source code for this chapter at www.gwtapps.com in certain instances that are identified.

Using the Container Application Pattern

Many developers are familiar with using design patterns to solve recurring software design problems. We'll use many design patterns[1] throughout the sample applications in this book. We can also use a similar method of identifying patterns to solve design problems at a higher application level, often involving architectural and user experience problems. For the Gadget Desktop application we use the Container Application pattern described in this section.

As features are added to an application, the code size grows and becomes harder to maintain. Each new feature adds many new potential points of failure between the code that implements the feature and the application. The Container Application pattern addresses this growth by decoupling the features from the application through a uniform interface, which allows easy and predictable feature integration.

The pattern is typically used in applications that need to be optimized for customizable or unpredictable growth in features. Many applications also use this pattern to have dynamically extensible features through a plugin system. For example, Eclipse uses the Container Application pattern to provide a flexible, customizable, and extensible development environment. As a result its code base is maintainable, since it doesn't have intimate integration with the vast range of plugins available.

Applications that use this pattern are decoupled from each feature by providing a basic set of interfaces that the features implement. The interfaces can be used to integrate with various aspects of the application such as the user interface, persistency, or application-specific functionality. Figure 6-1

---

1. These design patterns are from *Design Patterns: Elements of Reusable Object-Oriented Software* by Erich Gamma, Richard Helm, Ralph Johnson, and John Vlissides (Addison-Wesley, 1995).

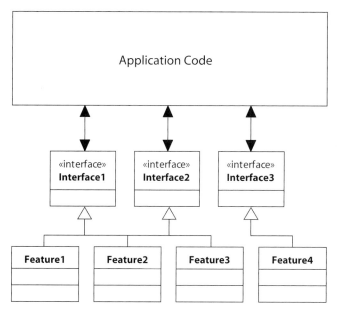

Figure 6–1.   The Container Application pattern

illustrates the structure of an application following the Container Application pattern.

Applications that follow this pattern act as containers to the features. The features can be plugins that complement the application's primary functionality, like plugins in Eclipse, or utilities that perform their own tasks independently of the application itself. In this latter case, the application becomes a pure container with its only purpose being to support a common foundation for the set of utilities. The Gadget Desktop uses the Container Application pattern in this way.

Designing the Model

The Gadget Desktop application organizes its parts into a model-view-controller (MVC) architecture. This is a great way to logically organize the application code, as many Java developers know. To keep the source code parts physically separated from each other, we'll place all model classes in the `com.gwtapps.desktop.client.model` package, all view classes in the `com.gwtapps.desktop.client.view` package, and all controller classes in the `com.gwtapps.desktop.client` package. Since all of these packages are children of the Gadget Desktop application's client package, they will all have their code compiled to JavaScript by the GWT compiler.

In MVC architecture the model is the data that the application operates on. For the Gadget Desktop application, the model is made up of the desktops gadgets. We'll place all of the code to support building gadgets for the application in the model package. This gadget's framework will provide services to the gadgets to facilitate easy instantiation by the view, and easy control, including persisting their state, by the controller.

Using the Abstract Factory Pattern

When writing a new gadget, we should make it as easy as possible to add it into the code. Using GWT we can leverage Java's ability to build application logic through well-designed object-oriented techniques and design patterns. We'll use an Abstract Factory design pattern for the Gadget Desktop. By using this pattern we can generically create and manage many different gadgets using the same code. Figure 6-2 helps visually illustrate how we implemented this pattern in the Gadget Desktop.

The classes on the left side of Figure 6-2 represent the factories and definitions of the instances on the right side of the diagram. Each gadget in the Gadget Desktop has a corresponding `GadgetClass` object that provides

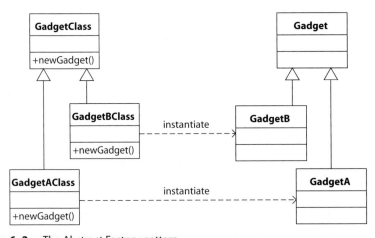

Figure 6–2.   The Abstract Factory pattern

generic access to the static methods for the gadget, such as the `newGadget` method that creates a new `Gadget`. Let's look at the code that acts as the foundation for this structure.

Making the `GadgetClass` Class

To implement the model we first need to create a `GadgetClass` class:

```
public abstract class GadgetClass {
    private String name;
    static private List classes = new ArrayList();

    //define some static methods to access all instances
    static public void addClass( GadgetClass gclass ){
        classes.add( gclass );
    }

    static public List getClasses(){
        return classes;
    }

    // constructor
    public GadgetClass( String n){
        name=n;
    }

    public abstract Gadget newGadget();

    public String getName(){
        return name;
    }
}
```

The class is fairly simple; it holds a static list of all available `GadgetClass` instances and the name of the gadget it represents. The static list allows the application to iterate over the available gadgets defined through their `GadgetClass` instances. The `GadgetClass` holds the static information for a gadget, which the application may need to use before creating a new gadget, such as the gadget's name. More information about gadgets can be placed on this class to implement other preinstantiation behavior.

The class also has an abstract method called `newGadget`. This is the factory method that returns a new instance of a gadget.

Every gadget that we write must create a class that extends this class and add it to the list of available gadget classes. The Gadget Desktop application initializes this list with the available gadgets in the `onModuleLoaded` method. Then in the application's view, defined in the `DesktopView` class, we can iterate over the list and display a button in the menu for each gadget with the label as the name attribute from the gadget's `GadgetClass`. When clicked, the button calls the creator method `newGadget`. Figure 6-3 illustrates how the view can generically handle many gadgets through instances of `GadgetClass`.

Figure 6–3.   The application's view generically displaying gadgets using `GadgetClass` instances

Let's look at the code that implements this. We'll start in the `onModule Loaded` method in the `Desktop` class. This is where we initialize the `GadgetClass` instances. In the following code we use dummy classes to illustrate the framework:

```
public void onModuleLoad(){
    GadgetClass.addClass( new GadgetAClass() );
    GadgetClass.addClass( new GadgetBClass() );
    GadgetClass.addClass( new GadgetCClass() );
    RootPanel.get("DesktopView").add( new DesktopView() );
}
```

This code sets up the list of `GadgetClass` instances so that they can later be used by the application's view, which we'll look at a little later. For now, let's continue with the `Gadget` class from the application's model.

Making the Gadget Class

The Gadget class is a simple class that each gadget will need to extend. Note that this is different from the GadgetClass class. Confused? This is similar to the relationship between a Java object and its class object. The class object holds static information that the application can use to reflect on the class. The object represents an instance of the class at runtime. Likewise, an instance of Gadget is one particular instance of a gadget and it has its gadget definition information, including its name stored in an instance of a GadgetClass.

The Gadget class is the class that the GadgetClass' newGadget method returns, and it represents a single instance of a gadget running in the application. The class is placed in the model package even though it has a user interface. This is a bit unusual, but this application just happens to operate on user interface elements as its model. The following code shows the implementation of this class:

```
public abstract class Gadget extends Composite{
    GadgetClass gadgetclass = null;
    HashMap userprefs = new HashMap();

    public Gadget( GadgetClass gc ){
        gadgetclass=gc;

        //set default preferences
        for( int i=0; i<gc.getUserPrefsCount(); ++i ){
            UserPref up = gc.getUserPref(i);
            userprefs.put( up, up.getDefaultValue() );
        }
    }

    public GadgetClass getGadgetClass(){
        return gadgetclass;
    }

    public String getTitle(){
        return gadgetclass.getName();
    }

    public void refresh(){
    }

    public Object getUserPrefValue( UserPref up ){
        return userprefs.get( up );
    }
```

```
    public void setUserPrefValue( UserPref up, Object value ){
        userprefs.put( up, value );
    }
}
```

The class is fairly simple, extending GWT's `Composite` widget, a widget that forwards all calls and events to its single child widget. It has a `refresh` method that can be implemented by derived classes. This method aims to support a Refresh button on the gadget's title bar. Some gadgets may not need to be refreshed, so the base implementation leaves this empty. The rest of the code in this class deals with user preferences. Before we build a sample gadget, we'll look at how user preferences for gadgets work.

Making Easy User Preferences

Gadgets have configurable options, called **user preferences,** that are values users can change after a gadget is created. They are saved with the instance of the gadget, so that when the user returns to the application the gadget displays in a similar manner. The controller uses the user preferences to implement persistence, and the view uses them to implement a view to edit a gadget's preference values. Figure 6-4 shows a URL of an RSS feed for an RSS gadget as an example of a user preference. In this `News` widget users can automatically display the list of preferences after clicking the Edit button, which switches to a Done button after being clicked. In this case there is one preference —the feed URL.

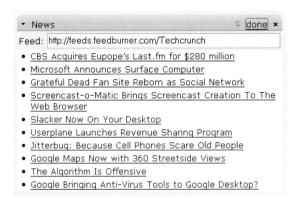

Figure 6–4.   The RSS feed user preference

Let's look at how to implement these preferences within the gadget's framework. Each gadget has a fixed set of preferences. They are not dynamic, so it makes sense to define the gadget's preferences on its `GadgetClass` object. Each instance of a gadget for a particular class uses the same set of preferences, although each gadget could have a unique set of values. So the `Gadget` class will hold a list of the user preference values. Let's look ahead briefly to see how the `News` gadget defines its feed URL preference in its `GadgetClass` definition:

```
static public class Class extends GadgetClass {
    static UserPref feed = new UserPref(
        "Feed", "http://feeds.feedburner.com/Techcrunch");

    public Class(){
        super("News", true);
        addUserPref(feed);
    }

    public Gadget newGadget(){
        return new NewsGadget(this);
    }
}
```

This class is defined as an inner class on the `News` gadget. One `UserPref` instance is defined with a name and a default value. Then in the class constructor the preference is added to a list of preferences. This is fairly straightforward from the gadget developer's point of view.

The gadget's framework stores the value for the `News` gadget's `feed` user preference in the `Gadget` class. Notice that in the previously defined `Gadget` class code there is a hash table that stores a list of values. The list is keyed on `UserPref` objects. The values in the hash table are the values of the user preferences.

The following code from the `GadgetClass` stores the user preference definitions for its gadgets in a list with this code:

```
private ArrayList userprefs = new ArrayList();

public int getUserPrefsCount(){
    return userprefs.size();
}
```

```
public UserPref getUserPref( int pos ){
    return (UserPref)userprefs.get(pos);
}

protected void addUserPref( UserPref up ){
    userprefs.add( up );
}
```

This next code shows the implementation of the `UserPref` class representing the definition of a user preference:

```
public class UserPref {
    private Object defaultvalue;
    private String name;

    public UserPref( String n, Object d ){
        defaultvalue = d;
        name = n;
    }

    public String getName(){
        return name;
    }

    public Object getDefaultValue(){
        return defaultvalue;
    }
}
```

The constructor takes the user preference name and the default value as
parameters in its constructor. This class facilitates the desktop's ability to
generically operate on each gadget's preference values. We'll use these
user preference definitions to display each gadget's edit fields and to per-
sist the state of the gadget.

Building a Columned Container Interface

With the model of the application defined through a gadget's framework,
we can continue by defining the application's view. The view of the application is based on a three-column page of widgets with a top row for a
menu and a row for tabs beneath it, as shown in Figure 6-5. When building
the layout it's helpful to think about it as a hierarchical box model.

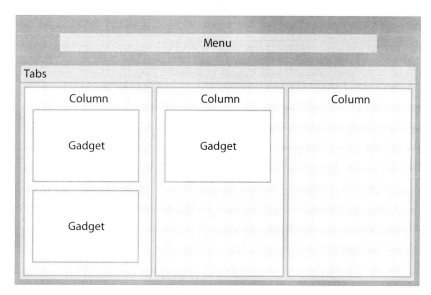

Figure 6-5. A mock-up of the interface

In Figure 6-5 the elements of the application's layout are identified as boxes. The box shading indicates the level in the hierarchy, with the darkest color being the root. In this case the root has a menu at the top and tabs beneath it. Each tab, when clicked, displays a distinct three-column page. Each column can hold a number of gadgets configured by the user and listed vertically.

We will build this layout using GWT widgets and panels. Using GWT panels, the layout in Figure 6-5 can be constructed according to the UML diagram shown in Figure 6-6.

Here we have a `DesktopView` class at the top of the hierarchy, which we'll look at later. It has a `VerticalPanel` as the root of the layout. This is used because the menu and tabs are listed vertically. The menu uses a

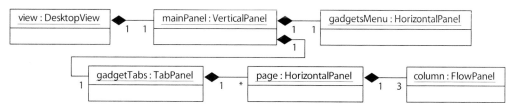

Figure 6-6. The user interface structure

HorizontalPanel to display the menu commands horizontally. GWT's TabPanel class displays the view's tabs. Each tab in the TabPanel has a child widget. In this case it is a page with its layout as a Horizontal Panel, since each page has a horizontal list of columns. The three columns on each page display a vertical list of Gadgets. The vertical list will be implemented as a FlowPanel. We will discuss the use of all of these panels later in this section as we build the layout.

Of course, we could build this layout in the HTML host file, but we want to leverage the more advanced and responsive widgets that come with GWT. Instead, the HTML host file will simply act as a thin wrapper for the application. The application attaches itself to the HTML host file in its entry point method by connecting the DesktopView class to the HTML tag with the ID DesktopView:

```
public class Desktop implements EntryPoint{
    public void onModuleLoad() {
        RootPanel.get("DesktopView").add( new DesktopView() );
    }
}
```

Defining the View

The DesktopView class extends GWT's Composite widget. The Composite is a simple widget that acts as a wrapper for another widget. It's similar to the SimplePanel in that it contains just one child widget, but it does not expose the extra methods a panel would have. Instead, the Composite hides the methods of the contained class to simplify its interface. In this application the Composite widget allows us to abstract the layout away from the rest of the application. The entry point code, acting as the application's controller, does not have any knowledge of the layout. This ensures a loose coupling between these two sections of the application. We want a loose coupling in this situation because it lets us make changes to the view without affecting the controller and vice versa.

We'll start this view by using an empty version of the DesktopView class:

```
public class DesktopView extends Composite {
    public DesktopView(){
    }
}
```

Using a `VerticalPanel` for the Main Layout

The `DesktopView` needs to be able to display the gadget's menu and the tab widget vertically, but since it's a composite it can only have one immediate child. To give the view a more complex layout we need to use a layout panel. Since the gadget's menu should be above the tabs, we'll use the `VerticalPanel`. The following code performs this task in the constructor of the `DesktopView` class:

```
public DesktopView() {
    //initialize the main panel
    VerticalPanel mainPanel = new VerticalPanel();
    initWidget( mainPanel );
    setWidth("100%");
    setHeight("100%");
}
```

The `initWidget` method you see in this code is a method on the `Composite` superclass that sets its child widget. This means that when you run the application, it adds the `DesktopView` to the host HTML page through the `RootPanel` widget and this `VerticalPanel` is displayed. However, there isn't anything visual to indicate that a `VerticalPanel` exists on the page, so let's continue building the layout with more child widgets.

Using `HorizontalPanel` for the Menu

The menu is a simple list of available gadgets. Users can click each item in the list, which causes a new instance of the gadget to be added to the current page. The list displays at the top of the application and is centered as indicated in the layout diagram. The items display next to one another horizontally, so we use a `HorizontalPanel` to perform this layout task. We can add this menu layout by adding a `HorizontalPanel` to the main vertical panel in the `DesktopView` constructor:

```
public DesktopView() {
    //initialize the main panel
    VerticalPanel mainPanel = new VerticalPanel();
    initWidget( mainPanel );
    setWidth("100%");
    setHeight("100%");
```

```
//create the menu
HorizontalPanel gadgetsMenu = new HorizontalPanel();
mainPanel.add( gadgetsMenu );
mainPanel.setCellHorizontalAlignment(
gadgetsMenu, HasHorizontalAlignment.ALIGN_CENTER );

//add items to the menu
gadgetsMenu.add( new Label("gadget 1") );
gadgetsMenu.add( new Label("gadget 2") );
gadgetsMenu.add( new Label("gadget 3") );
}
```

In this code the `HorizontalPanel` is constructed and added to the main `VerticalPanel` with its `add` method. Then the code calls `setCell HorizontalAlignment` on the main `VerticalPanel` to center the menu in the application. The last bit of code adds three `Label` widgets to the `HorizontalPanel` to simulate menu items; we'll add real menu items later. We can now run the application, and Figure 6-7 shows how a browser displays this layout.

Note that the three labels are displayed horizontally and are centered. At this point you can see one of the benefits of using GWT to build layouts: The panels have well-defined behavior for the layout of their child widgets, and the GWT library ensures that the behavior is the same across browsers. The GWT library does this by automatically including different JavaScript code for different browsers when necessary. Compare this to implementing the layout with pure HTML. You may have different behav-

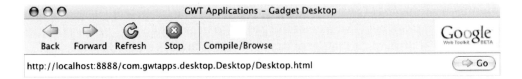

Figure 6–7.   The layout of the Gadget Desktop's menu

ior or looks between different browsers and no clear way to manage the differences.

Using `TabPanel` for Page Selection

Beneath the menu the application will have tabs that let the user select which page of gadgets should be displayed. The GWT `TabPanel` widget can accomplish this. The `TabPanel` is similar to a dialog with tab selection you would commonly see in a Windows application, as shown in Figure 6-8.

Figure 6–8. An example of a TabPanel widget

Let's add this widget to the application and create two sample tabs. Adding the following code to the `DesktopView` constructor performs this:

```
//create the tab panel
TabPanel gadgetTabs = new TabPanel();
mainPanel.add( gadgetTabs );
mainPanel.setCellHeight(gadgetTabs, "100%");
gadgetTabs.setWidth("100%");
gadgetTabs.setHeight("100%");
```

```
//create the tabs and pages
gadgetTabs.add( new Label("Page 1"), "Tab 1");
gadgetTabs.add( new Label("Page 2"), "Tab 2");

//select the first tab
gadgetTabs.selectTab(0);
```

This code creates a new `TabPanel` widget and adds it to the main panel. You should do this after the menu is added so the tabs are displayed below the menu. After the tabs are added, the cell height for the `TabPanel` in the main `VerticalPanel` is set to 100 percent. This ensures that the tabs and their pages take all of the remaining space on the web page. The width and height of the tab panel are also set to 100 percent. This means that the `TabPanel` will take up the entire cell of the parent `VerticalPanel` widget. This is ideal since we want the gadgets and columns to occupy the entire width and height of the browser window.

The code also adds two tabs to the `TabPanel` and selects the first to illustrate the layout when we run the application. The `TabPanel`'s add method takes two parameters. The first is the widget that should be displayed on the tab's page. In this case we are just putting a label in the page to test the layout. We will change this so that it is the rest of the three-column gadget layout for each page. The second parameter is the tab's label. When you click on the tab's label, the tab's page displays. In this code we select the first tab, index 0, using the `selectTab` method, so the first page displays when the application loads. Figure 6-9 shows the menu and tabs that display when running the application at this point.

Figure 6–9. The layout with tabs

This isn't visually impressive. But remember, we are building the application's layout and will work on the style later. This is the default look of the panels we're using. It illustrates an important design point of building GWT applications: The style information is not typically set within Java code. The Java portion of your application is for structure, layout, and behavior. You then connect your widgets and views to CSS style names so that you can change their visual styles through CSS. As described earlier in this book, CSS is a rich style language that is an excellent resource for application development. It is also outside of your application code, so you can have a designer play with styles with simple browser refreshes. The application does not need to be recompiled. It may be hard to visualize the tabs in Figure 6-9, but they are functional. The Java code to handle click events is built into the `TabPanel` class, so clicking on either of these tabs makes their page viewable.

Using `HorizontalPanel` and `FlowPanel` for Columns

Each page within the `TabPanel` will have three columns. The columns will each have an equal share of the width of the page and will extend to its full height. To implement the columns we will use the `HorizontalPanel` widget because it can arrange child widgets horizontally. Since a page can be created dynamically, one for each tab, we will create a new method on the `DesktopView` class to build a page. First, let's change the code in the `DesktopView`'s constructor that creates tabs and call the `createPage` method instead:

```
gadgetTabs.add( createPage(), "Tab 1");
gadgetTabs.add( createPage(), "Tab 2");
```

In this code the `createPage` method returns the widget that represents the tab page. The following code implements this method:

```
public HorizontalPanel createPage(){
    //create horizontal panel to hold columns
    HorizontalPanel page = new HorizontalPanel();
    page.setWidth("100%");
    page.setHeight("100%");
    page.setVerticalAlignment( HasVerticalAlignment.ALIGN_TOP );

    //add columns
    createColumn(page,0);
    createColumn(page,1);
```

```
    createColumn(page,2);
    return page;
}
```

The first part of this method creates the `HorizontalPanel` for the columns, sets its height and width to 100 percent, and sets the alignment of its children to the top of the widget. This means that if child widgets don't extend the full height of the widget, they will be located at the top. Alternatives for this vertical alignment are the middle or the bottom.

The second part of this method uses a new `createColumn` method to add the contents of each of the three columns. The contents are not directly widgets since each cell of a `HorizontalPanel` can only contain one child widget. We need to add a widget to the column that can list widgets vertically. We could use a `VerticalPanel` for this, but its behavior isn't quite what we need. We want the panel to stretch the height of the window (so that we can drag gadgets onto it at any height—more on this later) but have the gadgets all at the top. With a `VerticalPanel` the gadgets are listed evenly over its height (we could set the height of the cells using `setCellHeight`, but this is extra work). A `FlowPanel`, however, can have any height, and its child widgets will just "flow" one after the other from left to right, top to bottom. This will give us the desired behavior of the panel being the full height but having its child widgets sitting as close to the top as possible. You might want to try the `VerticalPanel` just to see what it looks like. It's a good idea to understand the layout nuances of each of the panels. Try playing around with each to see how they behave. Have a look at Figure 6-10, which illustrates the differences for our use case.

Now that we've decided on using the `FlowPanel` for the columns, we can implement the `createColumn` method on the `DesktopView` class. The following is the code for this method:

```
public void createColumn( HorizontalPanel page, int columnNumber ){
    //create the column with a FlowPanel
    FlowPanel column = new FlowPanel();
    page.add( column );
    page.setCellWidth( column, "33%");
    page.setCellHeight( column, "100%");
    column.setHeight("100%");

    column.add( new Label("gadget"));
    column.add( new Label("gadget"));
    column.add( new Label("gadget"));
}
```

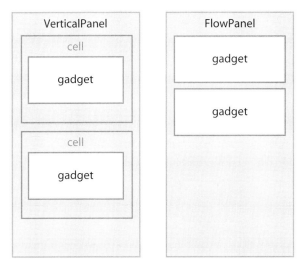

Figure 6–10.   Comparing *VerticalPanel* to *FlowPanel*

This code creates the FlowPanel for the specified column and adds it to the HorizontalPanel parent. We then set its height to take up the full column and its width to take up one-third of the column. In the last line we add a simple label to the column so that we can see the layout of the columns when the application runs. At this point running the application should present something like Figure 6-11 in the hosted mode browser. This is essentially the layout we want for the Gadget Desktop application.

Figure 6–11.   The layout with columns

Putting Gadgets in the View

So far we've looked at building a framework for gadgets and a layout for
the application's view. In this section we'll look at how to combine the two.
We've defined a base class for gadgets that extends `Composite` so they can
be easily added to the view. However, we want to provide a wrapper
around each gadget to display its title, preferences, and other common
gadget widgets. The `GadgetContainer` widget does this task. Before
looking at the container, let's first create a test gadget called Hello World.

The Hello World Gadget

The Hello World gadget simply displays the text *Hello World* and defines a
user preference that represents the text being displayed. Let's create a new
package, called `com.gwtapps.desktop.client.gadgets`, to hold our
gadgets, and then create a class inside this package called `HelloWorld`.
The following code implements this gadget:

```
public class HelloWorld extends Gadget{
    // define the class object with one preference
    static public class Class extends GadgetClass {
        static UserPref text = new UserPref("Text","Hello World");

        public Class(){
            super("HelloWorld");
            addUserPref( text );
        }

        public Gadget newGadget(){
            return new HelloWorld(this);
        }
    }

    // use a label as the main widget
    Label label = new Label();
    protected HelloWorld(Class c){
        super(c);
        initWidget( label );
    }

    // set the label text to the preference text
    public void refresh(){
        label.setText( (String)getUserPrefValue(Class.text) );
    }
}
```

The Hello World gadget integrates itself into the gadget's framework by

- Extending the Gadget class
- Creating a class object that can be added to the list of gadget class objects
- Attaching an interface to Composite superclass using its initWidget method
- Implementing the refresh method to update the interface based on user preference values

You can add this gadget to the gadget's framework by adding its class object to the list of gadget class objects in the Desktop class' onModuleLoad method:

```
ArrayList gadgetClasses = new ArrayList();
   public void onModuleLoad() {
      gadgetClasses.add( new HelloWorld.Class() );
```

This Hello World gadget is complete and uses the gadget's framework features to have a preference value and the ability to be dynamically constructed.

We need to do one last thing before we can run the application to test this first gadget and the gadget's framework. We need to add this gadget to the Gadget menu so new Hello World gadgets can be added to the desktop. To do this we need to properly handle the click event for each menu item in the DesktopView class. In the following code the click handler for a menu item is implemented to insert a new gadget onto the desktop:

```
//handle the click event by inserting a new gadget
gadgetLink.addClickListener( new ClickListener() {
   public void onClick( Widget sender ){
      insertGadget( gadgetClass.newGadget() );
   }
});
```

The insertGadget method is responsible for taking the newly created gadget and inserting it into a column on the desktop. We haven't yet implemented this method. To implement it we need to first define a gadget container which holds the gadget in its place in a column on the desktop.

Making a Gadget Container

Each gadget will have operating system window-like controls such as a Minimize button, a title area, a Refresh button, an Edit button, and a Close button. The implementation of these controls will be put in a separate class called `GadgetContainerView`. These controls could go in `Gadget` instead, but that would also limit where gadgets could be used. Separating `GadgetContainerView` from `Gadget` is a smart move in case we ever want to use gadgets in another structure.

The controls for the gadget container will be listed in a title bar above the gadget. The title will take most of the space and the other controls will be the minimum size for buttons. Figure 6-12 illustrates the layout of the gadget container.

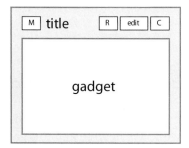

Figure 6–12.   The gadget container's layout

In the title bar, the M button represents the Minimize button. It is followed by the title of the gadget, which is followed by the Refresh button, the Edit button, and the Close button. Beneath the title bar will be the space for the gadget.

Let's begin building this layout by creating the `GadgetContainerView` class in the view package. Then we can add the code to define the class and its constructor like this:

```
public class GadgetContainerView extends SimplePanel {
    private Gadget child;
    private HorizontalPanel titleBar = new HorizontalPanel();
    private VerticalPanel mainLayout = new VerticalPanel();
    private Label title = new Label();
    private Hyperlink edit = new Hyperlink("edit","");
    private Button minimizeButton = new Button("M");
```

```
    private Button closeButton = new Button("C");
    private Button refreshButton = new Button ("R");
    private FlexTable editPanel = new FlexTable();
    private boolean open = true;
    private boolean editopen = false;

    public GadgetContainerView( Gadget c ){
        child = c;
        buildTitleBar();
        buildMainLayout();
        mainLayout.setWidth("100%");
        setWidget(mainLayout);
        child.refresh();
}
```

In this code listing you can see the GWT widgets being used to construct the gadget container, including layout panels, labels, and buttons. The helper methods `buildTitleBar` and `buildMainLayout` construct the layout. Let's first look at the implementation for the `buildMainLayout` method:

```
protected void buildMainLayout(){
    roundTitle.setWidth("100%");

    mainLayout.add(titleBar);
    if( child.getGadgetClass().getUserPrefsCount() > 0 ){
        mainLayout.add( editPanel );
        editPanel.setWidth("100%");
        buildEditPanel();
    }
    mainLayout.add(child);
}
```

This code adds the two child widgets to the `VerticalPanel` widget with the title bar above the gadget. It inserts a third widget between the two widgets if the gadget has any user preferences. This third widget, the edit panel, is viewable after the user clicks the Edit button (see Figure 6-13).

We built the Edit panel layout by looping over each `UserPref` object on the gadget's `GadgetClass` object. A new row is added for each preference along with a label and a `TextBox` widget. This implementation gives us a flexible Edit panel that automatically supports the user preferences defined for any gadget. This is another situation where we see the advantage of using the Abstract Factory pattern.

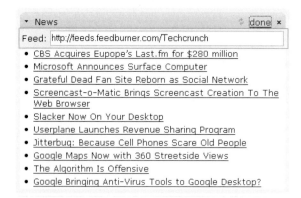

Figure 6–13.   The Edit panel in the gadget container

Now let's look at the `buildTitleBar` method:

```
protected void buildTitleBar(){
    titleBar.add( minimizeButton );
    titleBar.add( title );
    titleBar.add( refreshButton );
    if( child.getGadgetClass().getUserPrefsCount() > 0 )
        titleBar.add( edit );
    titleBar.add( closeButton );
    titleBar.setCellWidth( title, "100%" );
    title.setWidth("100%");
    title.setText(child.getTitle());
    buildClickListeners();
}
```

This code adds each child widget to the `HorizontalPanel` title bar widget. The title label has its cell set to 100 percent, so it takes up all of the space remaining in the `HorizontalPanel`. This pushes the buttons following it to the right side of the panel. At the end of the method the `buildClickListeners` method is called to set up the code that handles the buttons' click events.

At this point we have a gadget container that displays the required buttons in the title along with the gadget itself. We can test this out with the Hello World gadget created earlier by implementing the `insertGadget` method in the `DesktopView` class:

```
public void insertGadget( Gadget gadget ){
    FlowPanel column = (FlowPanel)getCurrentPage().getWidget(0);
```

```
    GadgetContainerView gadgetContainer = new GadgetContainerView( gadget );
    column.add(gadgetContainer);
}
```

The `insertGadget` method is called when the user clicks on a gadget button on the top menu. A new gadget is passed into the method and a `GadgetContainerView` is constructed with it. The currently displayed page is retrieved using methods for the table panel, and the gadget container is added to the first column. Figure 6-14 illustrates running the application and clicking on Hello World's menu item to display the new gadget and its container.

It's still not much to look at, but the application works. You can click the HelloWorld link at the top and it will add the gadget to the first column on the left. You can also switch tabs and insert the gadget on a new tab. Figure 6-14 shows the two gadgets in the first column. The second gadget has the Edit panel open to edit its preferences.

We're still going to wait until later to dig into using CSS for the interface, but we can make a small improvement to the look by using a couple of `Button` widgets that come with GWT to display images for the buttons in the title bar.

Figure 6–14.   Hello World gadgets added to the desktop

Using `ImageBundle`, `ToggleButton`, and `PushButton`

We've used simple buttons with a letter as their label as placeholders until we have better-looking buttons. Most Ajax start pages have images for these buttons instead. This keeps the size of the button small while still being easily identifiable.

Fortunately GWT now ships with two button implementations that allow you to use images: `ToggleButton` and `PushButton`. `ToggleButton` has a state of up or down, similar to a check box. This button is a perfect widget for our Minimize button. Figure 6-15 illustrates the `ToggleButton` used for the Minimize button in its two states. Notice that we're using a down arrow when the gadget is open and a right arrow when the gadget is closed.

Figure 6–15. The toggle button in its two states

In Figure 6-15 you can see the other two buttons on the title bar—the Refresh button and the Close button. These two buttons are not implemented with a `ToggleButton`, but instead with the more common `PushButton` widget. This acts like a regular button and can have different images set for different states.

The application uses an `ImageBundle` to supply the images to the title bar. The first step when using an `ImageBundle` is to collect the images and copy them to a package in your project. Since these are for the `GadgetContainerView` class, we will copy them to its package in `com.gwtapps.desktop.client.view`, as shown in Figure 6-16.

Now we need to define the image bundle in our code. To do this we must implement GWT's `ImageBundle` interface with one method per image.

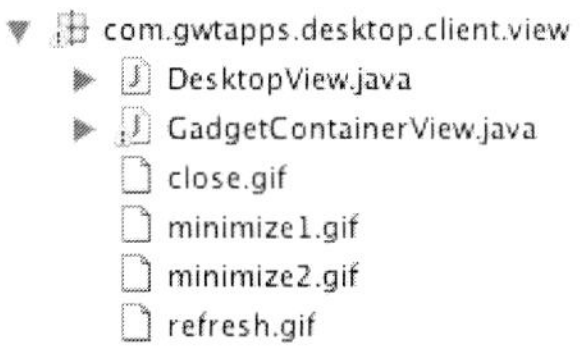

Figure 6–16. Adding the `ImageBundle` images to the view package

Then we use GWT's deferred binding to create an instance of the interface that can point to the individual images:

```
static public interface TitleBarImageBundle extends ImageBundle {
   /**
    * @gwt.resource close.gif
    */
   public AbstractImagePrototype closeIcon();

   /**
    * @gwt.resource minimize1.gif
    */
   public AbstractImagePrototype minimize1Icon();

   /**
    * @gwt.resource minimize2.gif
    */
   public AbstractImagePrototype minimize2Icon();

   /**
    * @gwt.resource refresh.gif
    */
   public AbstractImagePrototype refreshIcon();
}
private static TitleBarImageBundle titleBarImages =
   (TitleBarImageBundle) GWT.create( TitleBarImageBundle.class );
```

Notice that we need to specify a `@gwt.resource` annotation pointing to the image's location for each image method. Since we put the images in the `GadgetContainerView`'s package, we do not need to specify the full package path. After the interface definition, GWT deferred binding is used with the `GWT.create` method to create a single static instance of `Title BarImageBundle` interface at runtime. This instance will be used to call the methods on its interface to load the individual images. The image methods return an `AbstractImagePrototype` object. This object represents a single image and can generate multiple `Image` widgets with its `createImage` method. This allows many images to share a single source.

We can finish this implementation by changing the `Button` widgets used in the title bar to the `ToggleButton` and `PushButton` widgets. These widgets can take `Image` widgets as constructor arguments that set the images to display for the button. Replace the Button declarations in the `GadgetContainerView` class with this:

```
ToggleButton minimizeButton = new ToggleButton(
    titleBarImages.minimize1Icon().createImage(),
    titleBarImages.minimize2Icon().createImage());
PushButton refreshButton = new PushButton(
    titleBarImages.refreshIcon().createImage());
PushButton closeButton = new PushButton(
    titleBarImages.closeIcon().createImage());
```

The `minimizeButton` is set to use a `ToggleButton` so it can handle two states. For its up state it uses the first minimize image and retrieves it from the image bundle; it retrieves the second minimize image for its down state. The Refresh and Close buttons use a `PushButton` widget instead and set a single image to use for every state.

After turning the buttons into identifiable images, the title bar looks a little bit nicer and easier to understand, as you can see now in Figure 6-17. Notice that the images give the title bar a cleaner look. That's where we stop for improving the looks of the desktop until we adjust the interface with CSS. In the next step we add the ability to drag the gadgets around the desktop to new columns or positions.

Figure 6–17.   Gadgets in the gadget container with images

Creating Drag-and-Drop Gadgets

Dockable windows are windows that fit in a parent container and can be dragged using the mouse to a different location in the parent container. Many Windows applications have dockable toolbars, which let users customize their locations. The parent window restricts the locations of the dockable windows in a controlled layout and doesn't let them overlap.

In this section we will make the gadgets dockable. You will be able to drag a gadget by clicking its title bar and moving the mouse. When you let go of the mouse button, the Gadget Desktop will determine the best spot for the gadget to drop into. The best spot is determined as the closest location where the gadget fits in a column. The Gadget Desktop will move other gadgets out of the way if the dragged gadget is being dropped in their location. Figure 6-18 illustrates dragging a gadget from one column to another.

Figure 6–18. Dragging a gadget to another position

The following list outlines the requirements for implementing dockable gadgets.

- The gadgets can be dragged by clicking on the title bar.
- The gadgets can be dropped to another location within their current column, changing their position within the column.
- The gadgets can be moved from their original column and added to another column where they are dropped.
- There should be a signal to the user to tell them where the gadget would be dropped at any time during the drag.
- The code used for docking and dragging should be simple and generic so that it can be used with other widgets, including your own widgets and many panels and the ones shipped with GWT.

To implement this functionality you would typically create a panel to support docking of its child widgets. This application implements docking differently: you add every widget that you'd like to make dockable to a new wrapper widget that provides docking functionality. The advantage of this approach is that you don't need to create new dockable panels for each type of layout you'd like to use. We can write a single implementation for the wrapper widget to generically handle docking in many types of panels.

Docking Widgets Between Panels

The `DockableWidget` is the wrapper widget that makes other widgets dockable . When we put gadgets inside a `DockableWidget`, it makes the gadget dockable to other `DockableWidgets` in the application. When you drag the gadget, it pops out of its `DockableWidget` so that it "floats" with the mouse pointer. When the user releases the gadget, it gets dropped into another `DockableWidget` which has its gadget swapped into the first `DockableWidget`. Using the `DockableWidget` with gadgets in our application causes our gadgets to have a second container, the first being the `GadgetContainerView`. As shown previously, the `GadgetContainerView` provides all gadgets with similar functionality, such as a title bar and buttons. Figure 6-19 illustrates the difference between the `DockableWidget` and the `GadgetContainerView` during a drag operation.

Figure 6–19.   The difference between the `DockableGadget` and the
`GadgetContainerView`

Dragging Widgets Using Mouse Events

Users can drag the gadget with the title bar of the `GadgetContainerView`.
To do this we need to relay mouse events from the `GadgetContainerView`
to the `DockableWidget`. Following GWT's event system design we can
use the `SourcesMouseEvents` for `DockableWidget` to listen to mouse
events from its child widget. This interface is implemented in many GWT
widgets that have mouse events that can be listened to, and it is available
to be used by new widgets defined by our application, including `Gadget`
`ContainerView`. The `SourcesMouseEvents` interface is simple:

```
public interface SourcesMouseEvents {
  void addMouseListener(MouseListener listener);
  void removeMouseListener(MouseListener listener);
}
```

Fortunately the `Label` widget supports this interface, so we can use
`GadgetContainerView`'s title bar, which displays the gadget's title text,
to be the dragable area. To make these events accessible to the `Dockable`
`Widget` class, we need to implement the `SourcesMouseEvents` interface on the `GadgetContainerView` class by forwarding the method calls
to the title label like this:

```
public class GadgetContainerView extends SimplePanel
implements SourcesMouseEvents {

   public void addMouseListener(MouseListener listener){
      title.addMouseListener(listener);
   }
```

```
public void removeMouseListener(MouseListener listener){
   title.removeMouseListener(listener);
   }
}
```

Adding this code causes the mouse events from the `title` label to be relayed to the `GadgetContainerView`'s mouse listener. When you add the `GadgetContainerView` to the `DockableWidget`, the `DockableWidget` can listen to its mouse events that originate from dragging the title label and run the dragging code. This means that the `DockableWidget` must implement GWT's `MouseListener` interface.

From this interface, the `DockableWidget` class needs to define `onMouseDown` to start the dragging code, `onMouseMove` to move the gadget with the mouse pointer, and `onMouseUp` to stop dragging and drop the gadget in its new location.

Before looking at the dragging code we need to describe in a little bit more detail what happens visually when the gadget is dragged. When the user presses the mouse button down, the `GadgetContainer` is detached from `DockableWidget` and starts floating with the mouse. In its place we put a placeholder widget, which is empty but has a border defined in CSS. The placeholder widget will be the same size as the gadget and in a sense will look like its shadow. The application uses this placeholder as a visual marker of where the gadget would be located if it were dropped. This means that as the user drags the gadget around, the application moves the placeholder to different `DockableContainers` and possibly different columns as the drop location changes.

We put the code to start the dragging in the `DockableGadget`'s `onMouseDown` method:

```
public void onMouseDown(Widget sender, int x, int y){
   endDrag(sender);
   dragInfo = new DragInfo();
   dragInfo.dragWidget = getWidget();

   int left = dragInfo.dragWidget.getAbsoluteLeft()-1;
   int top = dragInfo.dragWidget.getAbsoluteTop()-1;
   int width = dragInfo.dragWidget.getOffsetWidth();
   int height = dragInfo.dragWidget.getOffsetHeight();
   dragInfo.dragWidget.setWidth( width+"px");
```

```
      HTML placeholder = new HTML(" ");
      placeholder.setHeight((height+2)+"px");
      setWidget( placeholder);
      RootPanel.get().add(dragInfo.dragWidget);

      Element elem = dragInfo.dragWidget.getElement();
      DOM.setStyleAttribute(elem, "position", "absolute");
      DOM.setStyleAttribute(elem, "left", left + "px");
      DOM.setStyleAttribute(elem, "top", top + "px");
      DOM.setCapture(sender.getElement());
      dragInfo.dragStartX = x;
      dragInfo.dragStartY = y;
      dragInfo.centerX = width/2;
      dragInfo.centerY = height/2;
  }
```

This code does several things.

*   It saves the child widget's location and dimensions.

*   It creates an empty HTML widget as a placeholder and inserts it as the child widget for the class.

*   It removes the child widget from the DockableWidget and adds it to the main RootPanel so that its parent is the page's body.

*   After being added to the RootPanel, the child has its CSS attributes set through GWT's DOM.setStyleAttribute method so that it can float freely on top of the page. Specifically, the CSS position attribute is set to absolute, which means it's positioned on the page based on left and top coordinates relative to the top left of the page. In other words, the child widget does not follow the layout of its parent HTML element. The top and left CSS attributes are set to the top and left location of the widget when it was docked inside the DockableWidget.

*   It captures mouse events with the DOM.setCapture method. Normally mouse events are sent to the widget that that mouse is hovering over or clicking on. The setCapture method will send mouse events to this widget even if they are for another widget. This is required for when the mouse moves quickly to a spot outside of the dragging widget. Without setting the mouse capture, these events would be lost. It's important to call DOM.releaseCapture when the dragging is done so the application can resume normal mouse behavior.

*   It calculates the center of the child widget. The application uses this value to find which new DockableWidget is the closest possible candidate for a drop. It is calculated and saved in this method instead of

on every mouse move event so that the mouse move event can be as fast as possible.

Dragging completes when the user releases the mouse button. This fires the mouse up event and calls the onMouseUp method on the Dockable Widget class. We implement this by calling our endDrag method:

```
public void onMouseUp(Widget sender, int x, int y){
    endDrag(sender);
}
```

Notice that the endDrag method is also called at the start of the onMouseDown method. This ensures that no dragging operation takes place and that a new drag operation starts properly. The following code implements the endDrag method:

```
public void endDrag( Widget sender ){
    if( dragInfo != null ){
        switchWith = null;
        DOM.setStyleAttribute(
            dragInfo.dragWidget.getElement(), "position", "");
        DOM.setStyleAttribute( dragInfo.dragWidget.getElement(), "left", "");
        DOM.setStyleAttribute( dragInfo.dragWidget.getElement(), "top", "");
        dragInfo.dragWidget.setWidth( "100%");
        setWidget( dragInfo.dragWidget );
        DOM.releaseCapture(sender.getElement());
        dragInfo = null;
    }
}
```

This method erases the CSS values that were set in the onMouseDown method that caused the widget to float with the mouse pointer, calls DOM.releaseCapture to set mouse events back to the normal state, and sets the DockableWidget's widget back to the dragging widget, effectively removing the placeholder widget. The dragInfo structure is set to null, which signals that there is no longer a drag operation occurring. There is also a reference here to the switchWith member variable. The class uses this variable when calculating the drop position for the child widget.

Dropping a Widget

The final mouse event that needs to be handled is the mouse move event. It is the onMouseMove method's responsibility to move the dragging window along with the mouse pointer to make the effect of dragging, to calculate if there is a new candidate for a drop location, and to move the placeholder window if any new drop location candidate is determined. The following code implements the onMouseMove method:

```
public void onMouseMove(Widget sender, int x, int y){
   if( dragInfo != null && switchWith == null ) {
      int left = x +
         dragInfo.dragWidget.getAbsoluteLeft()- dragInfo.dragStartX;
      int top = y +
         dragInfo.dragWidget.getAbsoluteTop() - dragInfo.dragStartY;

      Element elem = dragInfo.dragWidget.getElement();
      DOM.setStyleAttribute(elem, "left", left + "px");
      DOM.setStyleAttribute(elem, "top", top + "px");

      findDropContainer( dragInfo.centerX + left, dragInfo.centerY + top );
   }
 }
```

The DockableWidget receives mouse events even when there is no drag procedure taking place, so the method's body only executes during drags. To do this, the code checks the dragInfo member variable to see if it is set. The dragInfo member variable is set only during drag procedures, and this is enforced in the onMouseDown and onMouseUp methods. The first few lines of the method calculate the widget's new location by taking the difference of the mouse pointer location and the location where dragging started. The DOM.setStyleAttribute function sets the new location of the dragging widget using the top and left CSS attributes.

The second part of this method uses the findDropContainer method, which takes the dragging widget's new center coordinates as parameters, to see if there is a new drop position. The findDropContainer method checks if the widget has moved over a new container. For the Gadget Desktop implementation, this checks to see if the gadget has been dragged to a new column.

The code for the DockableWidget is fairly complex, but it sits nicely in an easy-to-use class. You can refer to the source code for its complete implementation.

To add the DockableWidget to the desktop, you just construct it and pass the GadgetContainerView into it. The following code shows how to do this in the DesktopView class' insertGadget method:

```
public void insertGadget( Gadget gadget ){
    GadgetContainer gadgetContainer = new GadgetContainer( gadget );
    FlowPanel column = (FlowPanel)getCurrentPage().getWidget(0);
    column.add( new DockableWidget( gadgetContainer ) );
}
```

Figure 6-20 illustrates what running the application and dragging a `HelloWorld` widget looks like. It may be hard to distinguish without any styles to hint what is happening in the interface, but the third `Hello World` widget is being dragged by the mouse.

The application is starting to take form now, but we still have only one gadget to play with. You'll find a `Calendar` gadget in the source code for this chapter. This gadget is used along with the `Hello World` gadget in the next section.

Figure 6–20.   Dragging a gadget around

Cleaning Up User Interfaces with CSS

The Gadget Desktop gains most of its value from being a fairly rich user experience. This requires having intuitive and satisfying layout, behavior, and style. At this point we have layout and behavior but no style. This not only means that the application is ugly, but it also lacks a lot of the user interface hints that would help make its use intuitive. For example, the tabs on the `TabPanel` widget only display the text label for the tab; nothing tells the user that it is a tab that can be clicked. The user also does not know which tab is current. As you can see, styles are a very important part of user interface design, and we will spend this last step improving the design to move from what you see in Figure 6-21 to Figure 6-22.

Figure 6–21.   User interface before CSS

Figure 6–22.   User interface after CSS

Using CSS with GWT

CSS is completely detached from the Java code, which keeps the style information separate. This allows nonprogrammers to change style information for the application without knowing Java or going through a compile step. CSS for your application consists of a list of style rules. You can place style rules either in the style tag in your HTML host file or in a separate CSS file that is included either using the `link` tag in your host file or the `style` tag in your module file. Let's start with a quick example of changing the application's background color. We would create a CSS style rule for the `body` tag and set its background attribute like this:

```
body{ background-color:#a8b8c3; }
```

The color value is an HTML hexadecimal RGB color code (discussed in Chapter 5).

Since the `body` tag represents the user interface's root inside the browser, this sets the background of the entire application. We can also set style attributes for other HTML tags in the application, such as for fonts and margins. The following code sets these HTML tag styles for this application:

```
body{ margin:0px; padding:0px; background-color:#a8b8c3; }
div,td{ font-size:10pt; font-family: verdana; }
h2{ margin:0px;font-family:arial;}
```

This tells the application that the body does not have any margins or padding, which allows the application to stretch to the edge of the browser window. The attributes set for the `div` and `td` tags apply to most of the text inside the application since the widgets are implemented with these HTML tags. We set the font size to 10 points and the font family to Verdana. Verdana is a sans serif font (this means without *serifs,* the little tips on fonts like Times New Roman) like Arial and Helvetica, but it was specifically designed for web use instead of print. It has a larger base area than Arial and Helvetica, which make it easier to read as small type on screen. For the h2 tag we select Arial, since this font will be large and readable.

 With this CSS we can run our application and get a slightly improved interface, as shown in Figure 6-23.

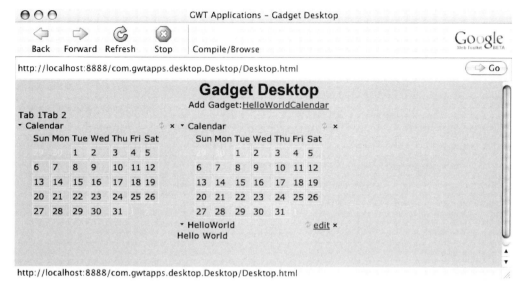

Figure 6–23.   After adding a few lines of CSS

At this point we lose the ability to specify styles for user interface elements based on HTML tag names. For example, we want to specify background images for the tabs, but they use the `div` tag and specifying a background image for this tag in CSS would cause all uses of the `div` tag to have the tab background. Fortunately, CSS is more flexible. With CSS you can also use style names to identify user interface elements and apply style rules to them. GWT integrates with CSS by allowing you to specify style names for each widget in your interface.

Adding Styles to the Tabs

Since the tabs use GWT's `TabPanel` widget, they already have style names defined for them; we just need to add the CSS style rules. The rules we decide upon should accomplish a few things. First, they should make the tabs look somewhat appealing; second, they should make the tabs look like tabs so the user is familiar with their behavior; and third, they should indicate which tab is currently being viewed.

To make them look appealing and similar to tabs found in other applications, we're going to use background images for the tabs. The first image, `tab-selected.gif`, represents a selected tab. It has a light color to indicate that it's in the foreground (see Figure 6-24). The other tabs will use

Figure 6–24. The foreground tab

tab.gif and will have a darker color (see Figure 6-25). Finally, the tabs have a line beneath them as a visual separation from the page. We'll use tab-rest.gif for this (see Figure 6-26). Notice that the line on the bottom seams to join with the selected tab image. This makes the line look connected to the selected tab and enhances the effect that's in the foreground.

Figure 6–25. The background tab

Figure 6–26. The tab base line

Now let's attach these images to the application through CSS. First, these images need to be copied into the desktop module's public directory. This ensures that they are available to the application and included after compilation. To reference the files from CSS we simply need to use these rules:

```
/* TabBar */
.gwt-TabBar{
    background-image:url(tab-rest.gif);
    background-repeat: repeat-x;
    background-position:bottom;
    padding-top:3px;
    width:100%
}
.gwt-TabBar .gwt-TabBarFirst{ width:10px; }
.gwt-TabBar .gwt-TabBarItem {
    background-image:url(tab.gif);
    background-repeat:no-repeat;
    background-position:bottom;
    width:126px;
    height:27px;
    font-size:8pt;
    cursor:hand;
    cursor:pointer;
}
.gwt-TabBar .gwt-TabBarItem-selected {
    background-image:url(tab-selected.gif);
}
.gwt-TabPanelBottom { height: 100%; background-color:#fff; }
```

Let's start with the first rule for the `gwt-TabBar` style name. The rule has three attributes to style the background. The first, `background-image`, is set to a URL with the `tab-rest.gif` filename. This selects the image to be in the background of all `TabBar` widgets in the application. The second attribute, `background-repeat`, is set to `repeat-x`, which causes the browser to render the image repeatedly on the x-axis to fill the width of the widget. Since the image is a horizontal line it will appear seamless. The `background-position` attribute is set to the value `bottom`, which causes the image to be aligned at the bottom of the widget.

The following CSS rules for the `TabBar` specify rules for user interface elements within the widget. The `gwt-TabBarItem` rule is for all tabs and sets the background image to `tab.gif`. It also sets the item's width and height to the width and height of the image so it is fully displayed. This rule also sets attributes for the cursor. The CSS cursor attribute lets you specify which mouse cursor should be used when the mouse hovers over the user interface element selected. In this case we set it to the `hand` and `pointer` values. The `hand` value represents the hand cursor that you would typically see when the mouse hovers over a link. It indicates to the user that the user interface item beneath the cursor is clickable. That is exactly what we want to convey to the user about these tabs. The second cursor attribute is set because Firefox uses the value `pointer` for the hand cursor. Having both attributes set allows the hand cursor to work for the tabs in all browsers.

Finally, the last rule set is for the selected tab. The selected tab also has the `gwt-TabBarItem` style name set, so it will get these rules, including the cursor settings. The rule for the style name `gwt-TabBarItem-selected` has the ability to override any of the previous settings. In this case it overrides the `background-image` attribute to set it to the `tab-selected.gif` image.

These style rules and the tab images changed the tab's appearance shown in Figure 6-27 to its new look in Figure 6-28.

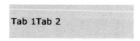

Figure 6–27.   Tabs without images

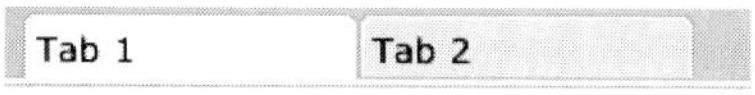

Figure 6–28.   Tabs with images

Adding Styles to the Menu

The menu at the top of the application needs a little bit of work to make it more readable. Currently it looks like Figure 6-29.

Gadget Desktop
Add Gadget: HelloWorldCalendar

Figure 6–29. The unreadable gadget menu

We used a `HorizontalPanel` widget to display this menu, and it is being displayed with its minimum appearance. For example, the lack of spacing between cells makes the gadgets' names unreadable. We can fix this easily with CSS by applying a margin of 10 pixels to the left of the hyperlink. But we don't want to affect hyperlinks elsewhere in the application; we want to specifically target the hyperlinks in the menu. To do this we need to give a style name to the menu using the `setStyleName` on the `gadgetsMenu` widget. When the menu is created in the constructor of the `DesktopView`, we can simply add a line that sets the style name like this:

```
//create the menu
HorizontalPanel gadgetsMenu = new HorizontalPanel();
gadgetsMenu.setStyleName("GadgetsMenu");
mainPanel.add( gadgetsMenu );
```

Now we can reference the menu from CSS and add the left margin like this:

```
/* GadgetsMenu */
.GadgetsMenu .gwt-Hyperlink { margin-left:10px; }
.GadgetsMenu{ margin:10px; }
```

Notice how we can specify the style for only the `gwt-Hyperlink` named widgets within the `GadgetsMenu` named widgets. We've also added a margin to the entire gadget menu to separate it a little bit from the tabs and the title. Now we have the readable menu shown in Figure 6-30.

Gadget Desktop
Add Gadget: HelloWorld Calendar

Figure 6–30. The gadget menu with some CSS

Adding Styles to the `GadgetContainerView`

The `GadgetContainerView` class acts as the container for each gadget and displays a title bar for commands that operate on the gadget. However, nothing indicates that it is a container or that the command buttons apply to the contained gadget. When several gadgets are combined, it can be difficult to determine what is going on, as illustrated in Figure 6-31.

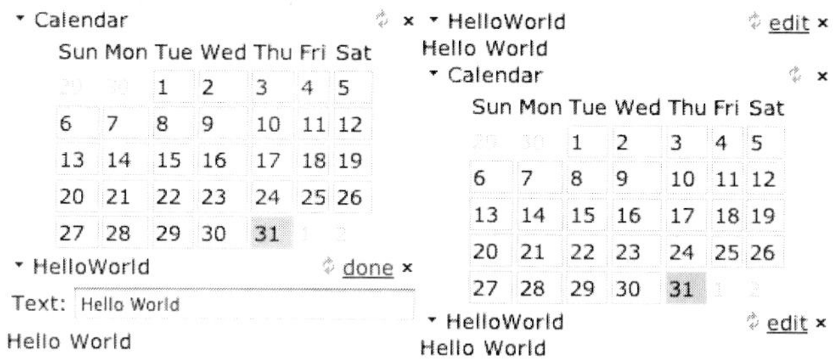

Figure 6–31.   The gadgets without CSS are confusing

We can use CSS to clear up this confusion by setting a border for the `Gadget ContainerView` and setting a background image for the title bar. First we need to set the style names in the Java file for `GadgetContainerView`. The following code shows how to do this in the `GadgetContainerView`'s constructor:

```
public GadgetContainerView( Gadget c ){
    child = c;
    buildTitleBar();
    buildMainLayout();
    mainLayout.setWidth("100%");
    setWidget( mainLayout );
    child.refresh();

    //set style names
    setStyleName("gwtapps-GadgetContainer");
    mainLayout.setStyleName("gwtapps-GadgetContainerPanel");
    titleBar.setStyleName("gwtapps-GadgetContainerTitleBar");
    editPanel.setStyleName("gwtapps-GadgetContainerEditPanel");
    title.setStyleName("gwtapps-GadgetContainerTitle");
}
```

We set style names for many of the panels that make up this view. This lets us be very specific when setting the styles in CSS. Now we can add the following rules to CSS:

```
/* GadgetContainerView */
.gwtapps-GadgetContainerTitle{ cursor: move; color: #262c30;  }
.gwtapps-GadgetContainerTitleBar{
    background-image:url(titleback.gif);
    background-position:bottom;
    background-repeat:repeat-x;
}
.gwtapps-GadgetContainerEditPanel{background-color:#e5e5e5;}
.gwtapps-GadgetContainer{ background-color:#eaecec;padding: 6px; }
```

The first rule sets the text color of the title and the cursor to a move cursor. This tells the user that the gadget is dragable. The next rule, for the full title bar, sets its background image to `titleback.gif`.

Then next two rules set the background colors for the Edit panel and the outside of the container. Since the container has its padding set to 6 pixels, it will appear to have a border in this color. The result is a much more usable interface, as you can see in Figure 6-32.

Compare Figure 6-32 to Figure 6-31 and you can see how a few simple lines of CSS can dramatically improve an application's usability.

Figure 6–32. The gadgets with some CSS

Creating a `RoundedPanel`

As an added bonus we will enhance the styles of the gadgets to give them rounded corners. This softens the application's look, making it more approachable for some users. We've actually used rounded corners already for the tabs in the `TabPanel`. However, we accomplished that by using images. It would be nice to be able to make user interface elements have rounded corners without having to create new image files each time.

We can use a CSS technique to create rounded corners without using images. This technique uses several HTML elements with 1 pixel of height and varying widths to simulate a round corner. We can write this code in a separate `RoundedPanel` widget so its complexity is hidden from the users of this class. Refer to the application source at www.gwtapps.com to see the implementation of the `RoundedPanel` class.

To use the `RoundedPanel` class in this application, we simply need to use it as a wrapper for widgets that we'd like to have rounded corners. For example, the following creates a new `RoundedPanel` that wraps the `mainLayout` widget in the `GadgetContainerView`:

```
RoundedPanel round = new
RoundedPanel("#eaecec",mainLayout,RoundedPanel.ROUND_TOP);
```

Adding rounded corners completes the look for the application. Running it at this point will give us the finished look shown in Figure 6-33.

Figure 6–33.   The finished interface

Adding Persistency

The Gadget Desktop application allows you to build and configure a desktop that has the gadgets that you use the most, and lets you add and arrange the gadgets in columns. However, when we return to the page or refresh the browser, we lose our arrangement. The application starts from the beginning with an empty desktop. This is obviously not ideal. Furthermore, this hinders our ability to design more complex gadgets that need to maintain a state between sessions. We need to add the ability to save the desktop's layout for return visits.

In this extension we will add the ability to save the state of the desktop with the beginnings of a storage framework. We'll start with an implementation based on browser cookies. This is not an ideal solution since cookie size is limited to as little as 4KB on some browsers, but it will eventually act as a last resort for storing information. We will then implement a storage mechanism based on the Google Gears plugin. Google Gears is a browser plugin that allows you to save data on the client side in a lightweight database. We'll provide a storage implementation for the application using Cookies or Gears, but you could create more storage solutions with other plugins or by sending the data to store to the server (we're building this application as one that does not require any server-side code, but it could definitely be added).

Implementing the `CookieStorage` Class

Now let's look at how to implement client-side storage with cookies. The simplest approach would be to save data with GWT's `Cookie` class. This class lets you save and load cookies based on a name. The problem with directly using this class is that it doesn't take into account cookie storage limitations and browser differences.

According to RFC 2109, browsers must support at least 20 cookies per domain, with at least 4,096 bytes available per cookie. Most browser implementations provide this minimum, but Internet Explorer 6 has the limitation of 4,096 bytes total. We will have to provide different implementations of cookies for Internet Explorer.

For other browsers we will extend the size of our storage by having it saved in more than one cookie. The `CookieStorage` class will take care of the details. We will provide an abstract base class called `Storage` that will extend to provide a common interface between storage providers. Let's define the `Storage` class as follows:

```
public abstract class Storage {
   private Map values = new HashMap();

   protected Map getValues(){
      return values;
   }

   public Storage() throws StorageException{
      load();
   }

   public String getValue( String key ){
      return (String)values.get( key );
   }

   public void setValue( String key, String value ){
      values.put( key, value );
   }

   public abstract void save() throws StorageException;
   public abstract void load() throws StorageException;

}
```

This implements the `Storage` class as a key-value `Map` with `save` and `load` methods which its subclasses must implement.

For the cookie storage subclass we will serialize the map of key values to a string and then write the string to cookies. If the map string is larger than one cookie, then we will allow it to span across multiple cookies. Figure 6-34 illustrates this process in three parts:

The application uses this map as a Java map in memory. Then when the application saves its state, it is converted to a string and broken apart into as many cookies as needed. When the application calls the `load` method, the reverse operation occurs: Each cookie is read and appended to form a string, and then the string is deserialized to form a Java map. Now let's look at the implementation for this class starting with how it handles the limitations of different browsers.

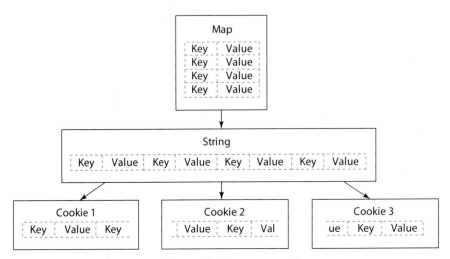

Figure 6–34.   Breaking a map down to fit in browser cookies

Handling Browser Differences

To handle the limitations between browsers we need to use GWT's deferred binding mechanism. This mechanism allows us to have different code that is used for different browsers. One of the benefits of using this mechanism is that only the code needed for the browser in use is downloaded. However, from a maintenance point of view, you want to support the minimum amount of browser specialization code. For the `CookieStorage` class we will have a `CookieConstants` inner class that provides constants. Different browser versions will provide different constants. The following code shows the declaration for the `CookieStorage` class with the `CookieConstants` inner classes:

```
public class CookieStorage extends Storage{
   public CookieStorage() throws StorageException {}

   private static class CookieConstants{
      public String cookiePrefix(){ return "_cs"; }
      public int maxCookies(){ return 20; }
      public int maxCookieLength(){ return 4096; }
      public int maxTotalStorage(){ return maxCookies()*maxCookieLength(); }
   }

   private static class CookieConstantsIE6 extends CookieConstants{
      public int maxCookies(){ return 1; }
   }
   private static CookieConstants constants =
      (CookieConstants)GWT.create( CookieConstants.class );
```

As mentioned earlier, most browsers use the standard limit of 20 cookies with 4,096 bytes each, so most browsers will use the `CookieConstants` inner class as the source for these values. However, Internet Explorer will use the `CookieConstantsIE6` class. It overrides the `maxCookies` method to return 1 instead of 20. IE6 has the limitation of a maximum of 4,096 bytes for all the domain's cookies, limiting us to using only one cookie. Handling this limitation in this way makes saving cookies on Internet Explorer 6 safe.

We've declared a static field called `constants` that the class initializes with the deferred binding result from `GWT.create`. To make this work we need to define when the `CookieConstantsIE6` class should be used instead. This is done in the module XML file using the `replace-with` XML element. The following shows how this element should look for this task:

```
<replace-with class="com.gwtapps.desktop.client.CookieStorage.CookieConstants">
   <when-type-is
class="com.gwtapps.desktop.client.util.CookieStorage.CookieConstantsIE6"/>
   <when-property-is name="user.agent" value="ie6"/>
</replace-with>
```

This XML code tells the GWT compiler to use the `CookieConstantsIE` class for the JavaScript build for Internet Explorer 6. With just this little amount of code we've now provided the `CookieStorage` class with the ability to support full cookie capabilities on all browsers.

Loading and Saving Cookies

To load and save cookies we need to transfer the in-memory map to a string. To do this, we define the `getValuesAsString` and `setValuesFromString` methods. (Refer to the application source code at www.gwtapps.com for how to implement them.) The remaining part of loading and saving code involves breaking the serialized string into chunks that can be saved to cookies. Let's start by looking at how the `CookieStorage` class divides the string among several cookies in the `save` method:

```
public void save() throws StorageException{
   //clear cookies
   Date now = new Date();
   Date expires = new Date( now.getYear(), now.getMonth()-1, now.getDate() );
   for( int i=0; i<constants.maxCookies(); ++i )
      Cookies.setCookie( constants.cookiePrefix()+i,"",expires );
```

```
//get the values as a string and check their length
String valueString = getValuesAsString();
if( valueString.length() > constants.maxTotalStorage() ){
    throw new StorageException( "Out of storage space");
}

//set the expire date to 30 days
expires = new Date(now.getYear(),now.getMonth()+1,now.getDate());

//set the cookies in chunks
int cookiesRequired =
    ((int)valueString.length()/constants.maxCookieLength())+1;
for( int cookieNum=0; cookieNum < cookiesRequired; ++cookieNum ){
    int begin = cookieNum*constants.maxCookieLength();
    int end = Math.min( begin + constants.maxCookieLength(),
        valueString.length() );
    String cookieValue = valueString.substring( begin, end );
    Cookies.setCookie(
        constants.cookiePrefix()+cookieNum, cookieValue, expires );
}
}
```

The `save` method begins by using the `setCookie` method on GWT's `Cookie` class with an expired date to clear any existing cookies from previous uses of the `CookieStorage` class. We need to do this so old cookies don't linger in storage. The second step of the `save` method gets the map of values as a string and verifies that it doesn't exceed the available storage. If it does, an exception is thrown to be handled by the application. The final step of the `save` method calculates how many cookies will be needed, based on the cookie constants defined, and then sets the cookies by breaking apart the string.

The `load` method does the opposite operation: it builds a string from several cookies and then uses the `help` method to deserialize the string to the `Map` for use in the application:

```
public void load(){
    //read the cookies to build the string
    String valueString = "";
    String cookieValue = Cookies.getCookie( constants.cookiePrefix()+"0" );
    for( int cookieNum=0; cookieValue!=null && cookieValue.length()> 0;){
        valueString += cookieValue;
        ++cookieNum;
        cookieValue = Cookies.getCookie(constants.cookiePrefix()+cookieNum );
    }
```

```
    //set up the hash map from the string
    setValuesFromString( valueString );
}
```

To use this in an application you simply need to instantiate the class, use the `setValue` and `getValue` methods to store and retrieve values that should be persistent, and use the `save` and `load` methods to ensure that the values are stored and retrieved.

Using Google Gears for Storage

Using browser cookies for storage is fairly limited. Although we would be able to store many gadgets with this method, it would not scale to larger storage needs. It does, however, provide a safe fallback storage in case other storage options are not available. We built the `CookieStorage` class as part of a `Storage` framework. In this section we'll add a second storage option to the storage framework using Google Gears.

Google Gears is a browser plugin created by Google that allows Ajax applications to store larger sets of data on the client side. Almost immediately after its release, Google provided a GWT module that integrates with the plugin. We will use this module to integrate Google Gears into the storage framework.

To use Google Gears with a GWT application you first need to download Google APIs for GWT from http://code.google.com/p/gwt-google-apis/. Download the `gwt-google-apis.zip` file and extract it to a location on your hard drive. The file that you use is the `gwt-google-apis.jar`. To use it in an application you need to include it in your application's classpath. If you're using Eclipse, select **Java Build Path** from your project's Properties dialog and select the Libraries tab. This tab lists all of the libraries included on the classpath for the project, as shown in Figure 6-35.

Click on the Add External JARs button and select the `gwt-google-apis.jar` file. At this point you can use the Google Gears API Java objects for GWT in your application. The GWT compiler has to know that the Gears module is to be included in the application, so you need to add the following `inherits` tag to the module XML file for your application:

```
<inherits name="com.google.gwt.gears.Gears"/>
```

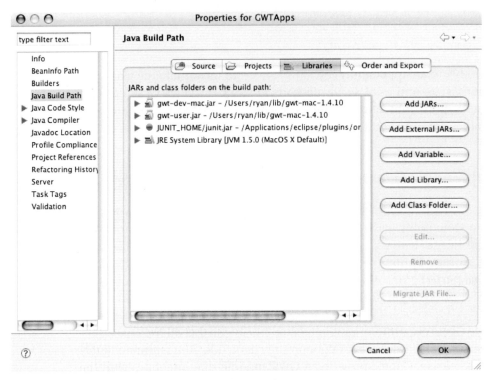

Figure 6–35. Adding a third-party GWT module in Eclipse

To integrate this with the Gadget Desktop storage framework, we will create a `GearsStorage` class that extends `Storage`. This means we will need to implement the `Storage` class' `load` and `save` methods to save and load the map of values.

To implement local storage, Gears provides a `Database` class that supports SQL queries. We'll use a table in the database to store the map values in the `Storage` class. In the `save` method we will run a SQL query to create the table if it doesn't already exist. Then we will iterate over the map and insert values into the table. The following code shows the implementation of the `save` method:

```
public void save() throws StorageException {
    //check for gears installation
    if( ! isGearsInstalled() )
        throw new StorageException("save failed, Gears is not installed");

    try {
        //create the Storage table if it doesn't exist
```

```
      Database db = new Database("Storage");
      db.execute(
         "create table if not exists Storage (key varchar(255), value text)");

      //add the list to the table
      for(Iterator iter=getValues().entrySet().iterator(); iter.hasNext(); ){
         Entry entry = (Entry) iter.next();
         db.execute("insert into Storage values (?, ?)", new String[] {
            (String)entry.getKey(),
            (String)entry.getValue()
         });
      }
   }
   catch (GearsException e) {
      throw new StorageException( "save failed", e );
   }
}
```

First the method checks to see if Gears is installed as a plugin in the currently running browser. If not, the code throws an exception. Generally the
code should not get to this point—the application should check to see if
Gears is installed and, if it isn't, use CookieStorage instead. If Gears is
installed, the save method creates a Database object from the Gears API
and executes a create table query with a column for the key and a column
for the value. Then the code iterates over the values and uses a SQL insert
statement to add each one.

The load method performs the opposite operation: It executes a select
query on the same database table and iterates over a ResultSet object
returned from Gears, and then adds each row in the result set to the map
of values for this Storage class. The following code shows this implementation of the load method:

```
public void load() throws StorageException {
   getValues().clear();

   //check for gears installation
   if( ! isGearsInstalled() )
      throw new StorageException("load failed, Gears is not installed");

   try {
      //select from the database
      Database db = new Database("Storage");
      ResultSet rs = db.execute("select * from Storage");
```

```
        for (int i = 0; rs.isValidRow(); ++i, rs.next()){
            getValues().put( rs.getFieldAsString(0), rs.getFieldAsString(1));
        }
        rs.close();
    }
    catch (GearsException e) {
        throw new StorageException( e.getMessage(), e );
    }
}
```

The isGearsInstalled method is a public static method that we've declared on the GearsStorage to check to see if the Gears plugin is installed. It is implemented as a JSNI method as follows:

```
public static native boolean isGearsInstalled() /*-{
    try {
        return $wnd.google.gears.factory != null;
    }
    catch (e) {
        return false;
    }
}-*/;
```

This method uses GWT's JavaScript Native Interface definition to write JavaScript methods directly in a Java class. These types of methods must be declared native and their implementation must start with /*-{ and end with }-*/.

Now in our application code we can make the decision on whether to use CookieStorage or GearsStorage by first checking if Gears is installed. The following changes to the onModuleLoad method in the Gadget Desktop's Desktop class perform this check and use the appropriate storage class:

```
public void onModuleLoad() {
    //add gadgets
    GadgetClass.addClass( new HelloWorldGadget.Class() );
    GadgetClass.addClass( new CalendarGadget.Class() );
    GadgetClass.addClass( new ToDoListGadget.Class() );

    //create view
    view = new DesktopView(this);
    RootPanel.get("DesktopView").add( view );

    //load layout from storage
    if( GearsStorage.isGearsInstalled() )
        storage = new GearsStorage();
```

```
    else
       storage = new CookieStorage();
    String layout = storage.getValue( "layout" );
    if( layout != null )
       view.setLayoutFromString( layout );
}
```

Now the application has the option of using a more robust storage foundation than cookies, but still has cookies to fall back on if Gears is not installed. You can use this pattern for different storage methods, including using Flash storage or even server-side storage.

Using Other JavaScript Libraries

We could build many more gadgets on our own in Java to provide more functionality for the Gadget Desktop application. However, we can take advantage of the large library of useful JavaScript applications already available on the web. Fortunately, GWT provides JSNI to interoperate with JavaScript, which lets us integrate with other JavaScript libraries.

In this extension we will integrate with two JavaScript libraries, both provided for free by Google. The first is the Google Maps API, which we'll use to build a Google Maps gadget for the desktop. The second is the Google Ajax Feed API, which we'll use to build gadgets that read XML feeds from other servers.

Using Google Maps API

The Google Maps API allows you to integrate a map into your Ajax user interface. The API is provided as a JavaScript library, which we'll use in this example, but there is also third-party GWT implementation of the API available at http://sourceforge.net/projects/gwt, and Google will probably provide support for this as part of their gwt-google-apis package.

To add the JavaScript Google Maps library to our application we first need to get an API key, which helps Google track use and stop misuse of the library. You can get an API key for your domain from www.google.com/apis/maps.

For testing this application we are using the Google Maps API key for localhost:8888. This will probably also work on any machine running the GWT hosted mode browser on the default port.

To add the JavaScript library to a GWT application, we just need to include it using the `script` tag in our host HTML file as follows:

```
<script src="http://maps.google.com/
maps?file=api&amp;v=2&amp;key=ABQIAAAACeDba0As0X6mwbIbUYWv-RTb-
vLQlFZmc2N8bgWI8YDPp5FEVBQUnvmfInJbOoyS2v-qkssc36Z5MA" type="text/javascript"></
script>
```

The API key used is set as the key parameter in the URL for the `script` tag.

Now we can access the JavaScript methods provided by this library using JSNI methods in our application. Let's start by creating a simple widget that displays a Google Map. Then we can use this widget inside a gadget to integrate it with the Gadget Desktop application. The widget will extend GWT's `HTML` widget, since Google Maps needs to attach to an HTML element with a specified ID. The widget will initialize its contents to have a child `HTML` tag with a unique ID. Then it will use JSNI to create a new map object from the Google Maps JavaScript library. Additional JSNI calls will use this JavaScript object to operate on the map object. The following code connects the Google Maps API with a GWT widget:

```
public class GoogleMap extends HTML{
    private static int nextId = 0;
    private JavaScriptObject map;
    public GoogleMap(){
        String id = "map"+(++nextId);
        setHTML("<div id='"+id+"' style='height:100%'></div>");
        RootPanel.get().add( this );
        map = initMap(id);
    }

    public void setCenter( final double lon, final double lat ){
        setCenterImpl( map, lon, lat );
    }

    private native static JavaScriptObject initMap( String id )/*-{
        var map = new $wnd.GMap2( $doc.getElementById(id) );
        return map;
    }-*/;
```

```
   private native static void setCenterImpl(
      JavaScriptObject map, double lon, double lat )/*-{
      map.setCenter(new $wnd.GLatLng(lon, lat), 13);
   }-*/;
}
```

Notice that we first add the widget to the RootPanel. We do this because the HTML tag used by Google Maps needs to be attached to the current document for the map initialization to work properly. Also notice that the initMap method returns a JavaScriptObject object. This opaque object can only be used within JSNI methods, but we can store it as a variable on our Java class. In this case the object represents the newly created Google Map. We use it in the setCenterImpl JSNI method to set the location viewed in the map.

This widget can be used inside a GoogleMapsGadget class to add a Google maps gadget to the desktop, as shown in Figure 6-36.

Figure 6–36.   Google map in a gadget

Using Google Ajax API for Feeds

The Google Ajax API is another nice JavaScript API provided by Google. It gives JavaScript applications the ability to load XML or JSON feeds from other servers. Typically Ajax applications are not able to load data from other servers due to browser security restrictions. Usually solutions involve creating server-side code on the server from which the Ajax application was loaded; this server contacts other servers for data, which it relays back to the Ajax client. Because we've decided that this application is not going to have any server-side code, we will use this Ajax API from Google instead.

The API uses a workaround to the browser security restrictions with a technique that takes advantage of the `script` tags. We'll look at how to implement this type of data retrieval directly in the Multi-Search application in Chapter 7.

To add the Ajax Feed API to our application, we follow the same method we used to include the Maps API. First we need to add a reference to the JavaScript library in a `script` tag in our HTML Host file like this:

```
<script type="text/javascript" src="http://www.google.com/
jsapi?key=ABQIAAAACeDba0As0X6mwbIbUYWv-RTb-
vLQlFZmc2N8bgWI8YDPp5FEVBQUnvmfInJbOoyS2v-qkssc36Z5MA"></script>
<script type="text/javascript">
    google.load("feeds", "1");
</script>
```

You will also need an API key to use this service. You can get one for free on the Ajax Feed API page at http://code.google.com/apis/ajaxfeeds.

Once you've added this script to your host HTML page, you can access the service through JSNI methods. We will create a wrapper Java class called `GoogleFeedRequest` that makes calls to this service. The class will have a static `get` method that accepts a URL to a remote feed and a callback object. The callback object will implement the `GoogleFeedRequest Handler` interface to receive the response from the remote server. This will allow us to retrieve remote data using the `GoogleFeedRequest` from any of the gadgets in the Gadget Desktop.

Let's first look at the `GoogleFeedRequest` class:

```
public class GoogleFeedRequest {
    static public void get( String url, GoogleFeedRequestHandler handler ){
        createCallbackFunction( handler, url );
    }

    private native static void createCallbackFunction(
        GoogleFeedRequestHandler obj, String url )*-{
        var feed = new $wnd.google.feeds.Feed(url);
        feed.setNumEntries(10);
        feed.load( function( result ) {
            if(!result.error)
obj.@com.gwtapps.desktop.client.GoogleFeedRequestHandler::onRequestComplete(Ljav
a/lang/String;)(result.feed.toJSONString());
```

```
        else
obj.@com.gwtapps.desktop.client.GoogleFeedRequestHandler::onRequestFailed(Ljava/
lang/String;)(result.error.message);
      });
    }-*/;
}
```

The static `get` method simply calls the JSNI method `createCallback Function`, which interacts with the Google Ajax Feed API by creating a new `Feed` object and calling its `load` method. The code passes in a JavaScript function as a callback, which is called when the `load` call completes. In this function's implementation the JavaScript code checks the feed result and calls the appropriate method on the `GoogleFeedRequestHandler` object. Figure 6-37 identifies the different parts of the elaborate declaration you need to call a Java method from JavaScript.

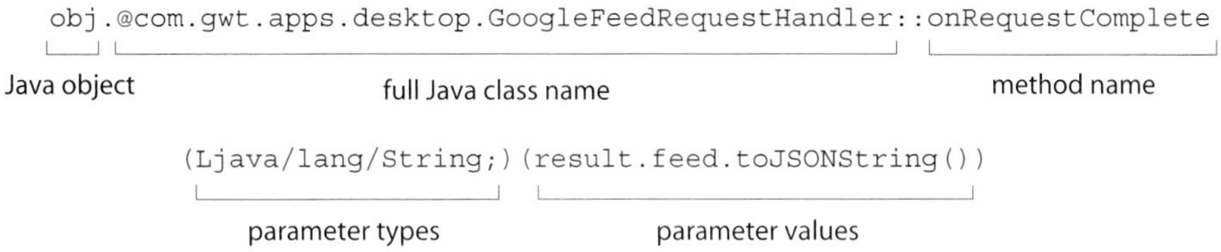

```
obj.@com.gwt.apps.desktop.GoogleFeedRequestHandler::onRequestComplete
```
Java object   full Java class name   method name

```
(Ljava/lang/String;)(result.feed.toJSONString())
```
        parameter types   parameter values

Figure 6–37. The structure of a call from JavaScript to Java

This causes the JavaScript callback to call the Java callback methods on the `GoogleFeedRequestHandler`. The following code shows how we defined this interface:

```
public interface GoogleFeedRequestHandler {
   public void onRequestComplete( String result );
   public void onRequestFailed( String error );
}
```

You will see how to use this interface and the `GoogleFeedRequest` class when we implement the weather gadget and the news gadget.

Building a Weather Gadget

You can choose to use any of several weather services on the Internet, but the easiest one to integrate with the Gadget Desktop to illustrate using the `GoogleFeedRequest` class is the Yahoo! Weather server. This free weather service lets you append a zip code to a URL and retrieve its weather as

XML. We'll base the Weather gadget on this and provide a user preference for the zip code. The service also provides weather information for non-U.S. locations, but to keep this example simple we won't support this functionality with this gadget.

Let's start by looking at the beginning of the Weather gadget definition:

```
public class WeatherGadget
    extends Gadget implements GoogleFeedRequestHandler{
    public static class Class extends GadgetClass {
    static UserPref location = new UserPref("Location","10001");

    public Class(){
        super("Weather",true);
        addUserPref( location );
    }

    public Gadget newGadget(){
        return new WeatherGadget(this);
    }
}

Private HTML body = new HTML();
protected WeatherGadget(Class c){
    super(c);
    initWidget( body );
}
```

The `WeatherGadget` class extends the `Gadget` class and implements a `Gadget` class object so it can be part of the gadget's framework. The `Gadget` class object defines one user preference called Location, which defaults to 10001, the zip code for part of New York City. This causes the gadget's framework to automatically generate an Edit view for the gadget where the location can be set. It also automatically stores the changed location in the storage system for the desktop whether it's `CookieStorage` or `Gears Storage`.

The gadget's constructor sets the main widget to be an HTML widget. When the application adds the gadget to its container, the container calls the gadget's `refresh` method. The `refresh` method is implemented to retrieve the remote data from the Yahoo! Weather service:

```
public void refresh(){
    body.setHTML("");
    String url = "http://xml.weather.yahoo.com/forecastrss?p=" +
        getUserPrefValue( Class.location );
```

```
GoogleFeedRequest.get( url,  this );
}
```

The Yahoo! Weather URL is used with the Location user preference appended as a parameter for the `get` method on the `GoogleFeedRequest`. The code passes the gadget as the second parameter to receive the response from the request. To do this the gadget implements the `GoogleFeedRequest Handler` interface. Two methods need to be implemented on this interface: the `onRequestComplete` method to handle a successful request for remote data, and the `onRequestFailed` method to handle failed requests. The following code implements these methods on the `WeatherGadget` class:

```
public void onRequestComplete( String result ){
   JSONObject feed = (JSONObject) JSONParser.parse( result );
   JSONArray entries = (JSONArray) feed.get("entries");
   if( entries.size() > 0 ){
      JSONObject item = (JSONObject)entries.get(0);
      JSONString content = (JSONString) item.get("content");
      body.setHTML(content.stringValue());
   }
}

public void onRequestFailed( String error ){
   body.setHTML(error);
}
```

When the request is successful, the application calls the `onRequest Complete` method with the requested data. The format of the data is JSON, one of the two formats available for the Google Ajax Feed API. (The other is XML.) This code uses GWT's JSON library to parse the JSON data, extract the content of the data, and add it to the HTML widget. This results in HTML formatted weather information for the specified location from Yahoo! displayed as the contents of the gadget, as shown in Figure 6-38.

Figure 6–38. A gadget based on Yahoo! Weather

Since we are using GWT's JSON library to parse the data, we need to make sure we include the module in our application's module file like this:

```
<inherits name='com.google.gwt.json.JSON'/>
```

Building an RSS News Gadget

We can also use the `GoogleFeedRequest` class to request RSS or Atom news feeds from various news sources. We will do this to create a News gadget for the Gadget Desktop. The following code shows how to define the News gadget:

```
public class NewsGadget
    extends Gadget implements GoogleFeedRequestHandler{
    static public class Class extends GadgetClass {
        static UserPref feed = new UserPref(
            "Feed","http://feeds.feedburner.com/Techcrunch");

        public Class(){
            super("News", true);
            addUserPref(feed);
        }

        public Gadget newGadget(){
            return new News(this);
        }
    }

    Private VerticalPanel list = new VerticalPanel();
    protected NewsGadget( Class c){
        super(c);
        initWidget( list );
}
```

The `NewsGadget` class has one user preference, Feed. This value is the URL to an RSS datafeed. The gadget will display the results of the feed. The default value for the Feed preference is the RSS feed for the TechCrunch blog. In the constructor the gadget's widget is set to a `VerticalPanel` so that each news item displays in a vertical list.

When the application adds the gadget to its container, the container calls the gadget's `refresh` method, which then requests the feed URL from the `GoogleFeedRequest` class:

```
public void refresh(){
    list.clear();
    String url = (String) getUserPrefValue( Class.feed );
    GoogleFeedRequest.get( url,  this );
}
```

When the request is complete, the `onRequestComplete` or `onRequest`
`Failed` method is called on the `NewsGadget`. The `onRequestComplete`
method parses the result using GWT's JSON library. It iterates over the list
of entries and adds a link for each one:

```
public void onRequestComplete( String result ){
    JSONObject feed = (JSONObject) JSONParser.parse( result );
    JSONArray entries = (JSONArray) feed.get("entries");
    for(int i=0;i<entries.size();i++ ){
        JSONObject item = (JSONObject)entries.get(i);
        JSONString title = (JSONString) item.get("title");
        JSONString url = (JSONString) item.get("link");
        HTML html = new HTML("<a href='"+url.stringValue()+
            "' target='_blank'>"+title.stringValue()+"</a>");
        html.setStyleName( "News-Item" );
        list.add( html );
    }
}

public void onRequestFailed( String error ){
    list.add( new HTML(error) );
}
```

Figure 6-39 shows what the Gadget Desktop looks like when we add the
News gadget.

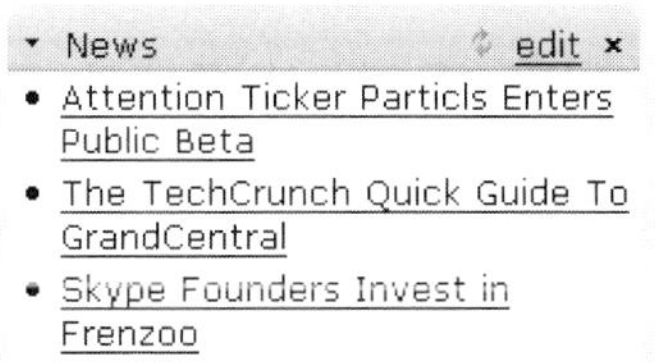

Figure 6–39. An RSS feed gadget

Summary

This chapter looked at the Gadget Desktop sample application, which is a start page application, one of the most common types of Ajax applications. The application uses MVC architecture to organize its components. The model uses an Abstract Factory pattern to provide a solid framework for widgets. Building the view illustrated how to create a complex layout with GWT widgets and panels, how to use CSS to style them, and how to handle mouse events to create a responsive dockable interface. The chapter explored building persistency into the application without relying on a server for the application controller. However, servers were used through JavaScript libraries to build an RSS gadget and a weather gadget.

This application illustrates many of the core concepts of GWT and shows how to organize a nontrivial client-side application. The sample applications in the rest of this book look into communication with servers in greater detail.

7

Multi-Search
Application

The Multi-Search application is a search engine client that submits a single query to several search engines simultaneously and displays the results. This type of task is useful for situations where you need an overview of results from more than one source. It applies the Aggregator Application pattern as a solution.

The application is entirely client side and communicates to remote servers for search data. Typically this wouldn't be possible due to the Same Origin policy in web browsers (discussed in Chapter 3), but this chapter illustrates a way to bypass this restriction. The application uses this technique to get search results from Yahoo! Search, Google Base, Amazon Books, and Flickr. You'll find a running instance of this application at http://multisearch.gwtapps.com.

Using the Aggregator Application Pattern

As the number of services and applications increases, users can become overwhelmed with choices and incapable of organizing all of their options. We have all become familiar with many installed software applications from different providers; these can cause confusion and take up valuable processing power and space on our computers. You can use the Aggregator pattern to build applications that consolidate several streams of data into a single interface.

Typically the name *aggregator* is used on the web to describe a **feed aggregator,** which is a web application that reads multiple RSS or Atom feeds and groups them together in a single interface. The usefulness of a feed aggregator comes from its ability to consolidate a large amount of recent news into a single interface for review. The alternative is to visit each web site that is a feed source and read the news from there. The obvious upsides to the aggregator are:

- You don't need to manually browse to each site, which usually has to be done serially and takes much more time. Also, this manual approach is prone to user errors.
- You don't need to locate the news section on each site you visit. You have a single interface to learn, which is a big time saver.

Although a feed aggregator is probably what most people think of when they hear the term *aggregator* in the context of the web, there are plenty of examples where this type of application has been useful elsewhere. In general we can define an aggregator as the following:

> An aggregator application is an application that applies a unified task and interface to several similar resources.

A real-life example of an aggregator that acts as a good analogy for the Multi-Search application is an audio receiver. An audio receiver fits into our definition of an aggregator since it plugs into several audio components (CD player, MP3 player, radio tuner, DVD player, etc.) and provides a single interface for some of the component's features. In other words, it has a unified task and interface for its resources, the audio components. The usefulness of this aggregator is obvious when looking at the alternative—to have a separate set of speakers and volume controls on each component.

Comparing this real-life aggregator example to a software aggregator built with GWT acts as a useful design guide. First of all, the audio receiver can fit into the MVC architectural pattern. The format of the information that this application applies to, or the model of MVC architecture, is the audio in an analog stereo format. Each component knows how to transmit or receive this format. The interface or view is the speakers, volume control, and component selector. The speakers render the model (audio) and the controls change the model that is rendered and how it's rendered. Finally the controller is the receiver's circuits that respond to the view and manage the model. Figure 7-1 illustrates the MVC components of an audio system.

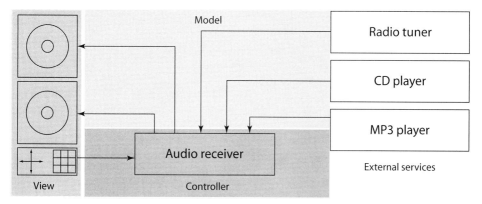

Figure 7–1. An example of the MVC in an audio system

Taking this analogy further, we can define where GWT would fit in. First, let's define the materials (plastics, metals, circuits, etc.) as analogous to web-standard technology in a client web application. The materials are put together to build the receiver. If this were built like a traditional web application, it would be assembled by hand. Obviously, with today's manufacturing technology it would be incredibly inefficient to build a receiver by hand. Receivers are built in sophisticated manufacturing facilities with advanced tools. For web applications, GWT paired with Java is a set of tools that makes manufacturing of client web applications much more efficient.

We can finish this analogy by looking at how modern web architecture follows the audio system design in terms of interdependence and integration. The receiver leverages a vast market of audio components from different manufacturers and has the ability to integrate well with them. The modern web follows the same architecture of integrating components and services through web standards. Fortunately, all of the tools that come with GWT revolve around integrating and interacting with a user interface (the browser) and web services through standard technology. We can be fairly confident that by adopting the general architecture and system design methodology of a mature product like an audio receiver we will also adopt some of the characteristics responsible for its success.

Multi-Search Design

The sequence of events for this application starts with the user entering a search query string and submitting it. Our GWT code takes the string and passes it to each search engine with an asynchronous HTTP call. As each search engine replies to the asynchronous HTTP calls, our GWT code parses the results and displays them to the user. The user can either click a search result to browse to that page or can submit another search. If the user enters another search string, the application clears the old results to make the application's interface ready for new search results.

The application's architecture is very similar to the audio receiver: the search engines are like the audio components and our GWT code is like the receiver. Let's take a closer look at the MVC structure for this application.

The Model

The application's model must represent the data that the rest of the application is going to operate on. In this case the search engine definitions and their results need to be represented in the model. The UML in Figure 7-2 shows this relationship.

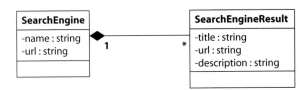

Figure 7-2. The application's model in UML

The `SearchEngine` class holds an engine's name and URL that will be used for asynchronous calls. It has a collection of `SearchEngineResults`. Each instance of a `SearchEngineResult` has a title, which is typically the title of the web page the result points to, the page's URL, and a short description of the page that the search engine has chosen. The Java code to implement this model is simple. For the `SearchEngine` class the code looks like this:

```
public class SearchEngine {
    private String name;
    private String url;
    private List results = new ArrayList();
```

```
public SearchEngine(){ }
public SearchEngine( String name, String url ){
    this.name = name;
    this.url = url;
}

public String getName(){  return name; }
public void setName( String name ){ this.name = name; }

public String getUrl(){  return url; }
public void setUrl( String url ){  this.url = url; }

public List getResults(){  return results; }
public void setResults( List results ){  this.results = results; }
}
```

It is a good idea to keep your model simple like this, with as few dependencies as possible to other code or systems. This allows you to use your model in different scenarios without worrying about bringing in new dependencies.

The SearchEngineResults class is just as simple:

```
public class SearchEngineResult {
    private String title;
    private String url;
    private String description;

    public SearchEngineResult(){ }
    public SearchEngineResult( String title, String url ){
        this.title = title;
        this.url = url;
    }

    public String getTitle(){  return title; }
    public void setTitle( String title ){  this.title = title; }

    public String getUrl(){  return url; }
    public void setUrl( String url ){  this.url = url; }

    public String getDescription(){  return description; }
    public void setDescription( String description ){
        this.description = description;
    }
}
```

The View

The view is a little more complicated than the model in its design. It has the task of presenting the user with a text box and a Submit button to enter a query string and a list of search results for each search engine. Let's start from the top. We'll call the main view `MultiSearchView`. It uses a `HorizontalPanel` to hold the query text box and the search's Submit button. Then it will vertically display a list of `SearchResultsView` instances. The UML in Figure 7-3 illustrates this relationship.

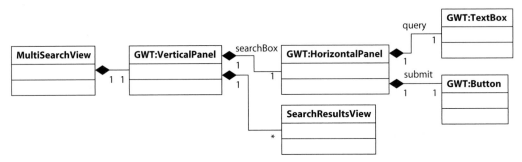

Figure 7–3.   The application's outermost view in UML

Each `SearchResultsView` instance will present the search results from each search engine. It will have a title that displays the search engine's name and a list of search results. Each result will have a title that is a hyperlink pointing to the URL and a description. Figure 7-4 shows the UML for the `SearchResultsView`.

That's it for the entire interface. Of course we will need some CSS later to make things look nice, but these UML diagrams outline the interface's structure. Now let's look at how we implement the view with GWT and Java.

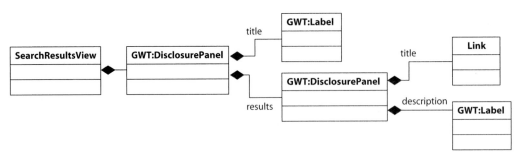

Figure 7–4.   The application's search result view in UML

The `MultiSearchView` Class

Starting from the top, we will define the `MultiSearchView` class to aggregate the topmost `VerticalPanel`. It will add the query text box and Submit button and expose a method to add new `SearchResultsView` instances. As we get into the code, notice that, similar to the model, the view knows little about anything other than itself. Most of the heavy lifting the application does will be done in the controller. The controller will build the view according to the search engines available and it will modify the view when search results arrive. The code we add to the view aims to make the controller's job easier. One thing that was left out of the UML diagrams that is part of the view and makes the controller's job easier is an interface that the controller will implement to respond to events that the view fires. In this case the event that the controller needs to handle is when a user submits a query. An interface of this kind is usually called a *listener*. Let's define the interface for this task as follows:

```
public interface MultiSearchViewListener {
    void onSearch( String query );
}
```

This simple interface allows the view to communicate its events to whatever system is listening. We will make an instance of the `MultiSearch ViewListener` interface a requirement for constructing a `Multi SearchView` by making it a constructor argument. The reference to this instance will be used to call the `onSearch` method when a user submits a query from the search text box.

Now let's look at the code for the `MultiSearchView` class:

```
public class MultiSearchView extends Composite {
    private MultiSearchViewListener listener;
    private VerticalPanel mainPanel = new VerticalPanel();
    private TextBox searchBox = new TextBox();
    private Button submitButton = new Button("Search");

    public MultiSearchView( MultiSearchViewListener listener ){
        this.listener = listener;
        initWidget( mainPanel );
        HorizontalPanel searchPanel = new HorizontalPanel();
        searchPanel.add( searchBox );
        searchPanel.add( submitButton );
        //enter key causes a search
        searchBox.addKeyboardListener(new KeyboardListenerAdapter(){
```

```
        public void onKeyPress( Widget sender, char keyCode, int modifiers){
            if(keyCode == KEY_ENTER )
                onSearch();
        }
    });
    //clicking the submit button causes a search
    submitButton.addClickListener(new ClickListener(){
        public void onClick(Widget sender){
            onSearch();
        }
    });
    mainPanel.add( searchPanel );
}

private void onSearch(){
    String query = searchBox.getText();
    if( query.length() > 0 ){
        listener.onSearch(query);
    }
}

public void addSearchResultsView( SearchResultsView view ){
    mainPanel.add( view );
}
}
```

The class extends GWT's `Composite` widget. The composite is a simple widget that acts as a wrapper for another widget. It's similar to the `SimplePanel` in that it contains just one child widget, but it does not expose the extra methods a panel would have. Instead, the composite hides the methods of the contained class to simplify its interface.

The `MultiSearchView` class has two methods and a constructor. The constructor first takes the listener interface described earlier and stores a reference to it so that the `onSearch` method can use it later. Then the constructor initializes the contained widget with the `initWidget` method on the Composite superclass to a `VerticalPanel` named `mainPanel`. This makes the single child widget for this composite a vertical panel. After this, the search text box and Submit button are added to a `HorizontalPanel`, so that they appear side by side, and the `HorizontalPanel` is added to the `mainPanel`. The search text box and the Submit button have listeners added to them so they can respond to events that the widgets fire using the `addKeyboardListener` method on the `TextBox` widget and the `addClickListener` method on the `Button` widget. These methods add the listener passed in to a `List` of listeners that is iterated over to have a

method called when an event occurs. In this case these methods take a
`KeyboardListener` and a `ClickListener` instance.

The `KeyboardListener` and `ClickListener` interfaces come with
GWT to handle these types of events. The interfaces can be implemented
inside the constructor like this as a Java expression called an *anonymous
local class*. These class implementations don't have names and can't be
used elsewhere. In this case we just need them defined for this one task, so
it is more convenient to write them as an expression like this. It also places
their implementation in a spot that is relevant to their task. In the case of
the `KeyboardListener`, notice that a `KeyboardListenerAdapter` is
used instead because `KeyboardListenerAdapter` is a class GWT provides
to make implementing a `KeyboardListener` interface more convenient.
The class has each method of the `KeyboardListener` implemented as
an empty method. This is done so you do not have to implement every
method. If we implemented the `KeyboardListener` instead, we would
need to provide an implementation for each of its three methods to meet
the `KeyboardListener` interface requirements.

The implementations of the `KeyboardListener` and the `ClickListener`
have the same task. They need to fire the `onSearch` event to the `Multi
SearchViewListener` that we have saved a reference to earlier in the
constructor. Calling `onSearch` on this listener is telling whatever code is
listening that the user has entered information and is sending a search
query. The click and keyboard listeners are able to make this happen by
responding to the user interface events that occur when the Search button
is clicked or the Enter key is pressed in the search text box. In the preceding code the `KeyboardListener` checks for the Enter key, and if it finds
that the Enter key has been pressed, it calls the `onSearch` method. The
`ClickListener` simply calls the `onSearch` method. The `onSearch`
method implemented later in the preceding code checks to see if there is
any text in the search text box, and if so it calls the `onSearch` method on
the `MultiSearchViewListener`.

The final part of the `MultiSearchViewListener` is the `addSearchView`
method. The controller will call this method to add a search view to the
interface, and will do this for each of the search engines used.

This code is the first half of the view for the Multi-Search application and
an implementation of Figure 7-3. Notice how the code is very concise. We
are creating a rich responsive interface with just a little bit of Java code.

GWT gives us widgets that guarantee behavior like a vertical panel. Java's strong organization type structure lets us have confidence that we haven't made a mistake. If we were to write this code in HTML and JavaScript, we wouldn't know about any problems until we ran the code in a browser.

The `SearchResultsView` Class

Now we need to apply the same coding technique to the second half of the interface represented in Figure 7-4. The second half is the presentation of the search results for each search engine defined in the `SearchResults View` class:

```java
public class SearchResultsView extends Composite {
    DisclosurePanel mainPanel = new DisclosurePanel();
    VerticalPanel results = new VerticalPanel();

    public SearchResultsView( SearchEngine engine ){
        initWidget( mainPanel );
        Label title = new Label( engine.getName() );
        mainPanel.setHeader(title);
        mainPanel.setContent(results);
    }

    public void addSearchResult( SearchEngineResult result ){
        VerticalPanel searchResultPanel = new VerticalPanel();
        Link title = new Link( result.getTitle(), result.getUrl() );
        HTML description = new HTML( result.getDescription() );
        searchResultPanel.add( title );
        searchResultPanel.add( description );
        results.add( searchResultPanel );
    }

    public void clearResults(){
        results.clear();
    }
}
```

The controller instantiates the `SearchResultsView` class to add new search engine results to the view. Like the `MultiSearchView`, the `SearchResultsView` class extends `Composite` so that it can simplify its interface. The constructor takes a `SearchEngine` object as a parameter. The `SearchEngine` is a simple class that was described earlier as part of the application's model. It holds general information about a `SearchEngine`. The `SearchResultsView` class represents the presentation of results from the search engine that is passed into its constructor. It uses this object to build a title for this view. The constructor initializes the view by setting a `DisclosurePanel` as its main child widget by calling the `init Widget` method from the `Composite` superclass. The `DislosurePanel` is a GWT widget introduced in GWT 1.4 that allows you to set a header widget and a content widget. Then when the user clicks on the header, the visibility of content is toggled. This is perfect for our list of search results. When the user has finished viewing one set of results, a click on its header will hide the results and thus make room for the results from the next search engine. A `Label` with the search engine's name is added as the header and a `VerticalPanel` is added as the content to display the results of a query.

The first method after the constructor in the `SearchResultsView` class, the `addSearchResult` method, takes a `SearchEngineResult` instance as a parameter and has the job of rendering this result in its view. The `SearchEngineResult` (another simple class that was defined as part of the application's model) holds information for a single result from a query. The result is displayed in a vertical panel with two rows. The first row is a `Link` (which we will implement next) with the title and URL from the search result. The second row is an HTML widget with the description from the search result. The description could go in a `Label` widget, but an HTML widget does the same job as a `Label` and also allows other HTML codes to be part of the text. We may want to display HTML in the descriptions in the future.

The final method on the `SearchResultsView` class is the `clearResults` method. Remember that this is a dynamic interface that can perform more than one query. When a new query is preformed, the old query results need to be removed. In traditional web applications this would be done automatically since the browser would need to refresh the entire page.

Building a `Link` Widget

GWT comes with a `Hyperlink` widget that wraps the HTML anchor tag. The implementation deals with the problem of pressing the back button after clicking a link on Ajax pages. In traditional web applications the link would bring you to a new page and the back button would bring you to the previous page. The application would render the same page when you press the back button. However, with Ajax applications the back button still loads the previous page, but the page will be in its initial state instead of the same state as when the user left it. The `Hyperlink` class solves this problem by making the link display a particular state in your Ajax application. When you click the link you move to a new state. When you click the back button you return to the previous state.

The problem with using the `Hyperlink` widget for our application is that it is intended for internal links within an application, but we want to be able to link to an external site. Unfortunately GWT doesn't have a class that performs this task, so we have to build one. Luckily it is simple to do, and this is a good opportunity to illustrate how to extend GWT.

Let's look at the code for the `Link` class:

```
public class Link extends Label {
   public Link(){
       setElement( DOM.createAnchor() );
       sinkEvents( Event.ONCLICK | Event.MOUSEEVENTS );
       setStyleName("gwtapps-Link");
   }

  public Link(String text, String href) {
       this();
       setText(text);
       setLink(href);
   }

   public void setLink( String link ){
       DOM.setAttribute(getElement(), "href", link );
   }
}
```

The `Link` class extends the `Label` class to get all of the basic features of a `Label` widget. The `Link` class' constructor creates an HTML anchor element and sets it as its element using the `setElement` method. This means that any method that operates on this widget will be working with the anchor element. To receive events for the widget we need to call `sinkEvents` with the list of events we want to receive. The `Label` class already implements the listener code for these events, so we don't have to do any more work for events. The rest of the class sets the text for the link and the URL. The URL is set by directly setting the `href` attribute on the anchor HTML element by using the `DOM.setAttribute` helper method.

You can use the `Link` class anywhere in a GWT interface to represent a link to an external URL.

The Controller

We will write the rest of the application in the controller. At this point the model is defined and gives us a structure for the data that the rest of the code operates on. The view is defined to display this data and respond to user events. Now the controller needs to do the heavy lifting of getting the search results from the search engines and building a model that will be displayed.

The sequence of events that the controller makes possible begins with the user submitting a search query through the text box in the MultiSearch View. The controller acts as a listener to this view by implementing the MultiSearchViewListener defined earlier. In response to the onSearch method call the controller will submit a request to each search engine. The requests are asynchronous, so the response will be handled as another event. The response from each search engine is going to be in a slightly different format, so there will have to be different code for each search engine to translate the format to the application's model. After this code translates the search results to our application's model, they are ready to be displayed in the view.

The UML diagram in Figure 7-5 illustrates the controller's structure.

The MultiSearch class will be our entry point to the application. It will create a list of Searcher objects, one for each search engine type that we want. Each search engine class will extend the Searcher class to implement the formatting code unique to the search engine.

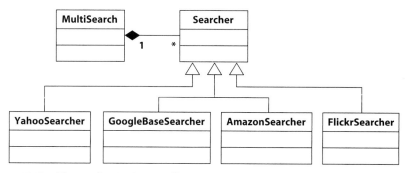

Figure 7–5.   The application's controller in UML

First, let's look at the code for the `Searcher` class:

```
abstract public class Searcher {
    private SearchResultsView view;

    public Searcher( MultiSearchView view, SearchEngine engine ){
        this.view = new SearchResultsView( engine );
        view.addSearchResultsView( this.view   );
    }

    public SearchResultsView getView(){
        return view;
    }

    abstract public void query( String q );
}
```

The `Searcher` class is abstract, which means you cannot create an instance of it. We need the class to be abstract because we've defined an abstract method. An **abstract method** is a method that does not have an implementation and is required by any concrete subclass. This type of design is similar to an interface, but differs in that you can have method implementations. In this class we have a constructor and a `get` method. The constructor takes the main view and a `SearchEngine` instance from the model. Since the `Searcher` class is part of the controller, it is responsible for making sure that the view is set up properly according to the model. This constructor does the task of setting up the view for one search engine. It creates a new `SearchResultsView` with the engine model instance as a parameter and adds it to the main view. A reference to the `SearchResultsView` instance is saved as a member on the class so it can be accessed later via the `getView` method and be modified.

The abstract method on the class, `query`, is the method that the controller will call in response to the user submitting a search request. It is implemented as an abstract method so that the main part of the controller does not need to keep track of each search engine running. It can simply iterate over a collection of objects that implement the `Searcher` class.

The `MultiSearch` class implements the main part of the controller and the entry point to the application:

```
public class MultiSearch implements EntryPoint, MultiSearchViewListener{
    private ArrayList searchers = new ArrayList();
```

```
public void onModuleLoad() {
   MultiSearchView view = new MultiSearchView( this );
   RootPanel.get("multiSearchView").add( view );
   searchers.add( new YahooSearcher( view ) );
   searchers.add( new FlickrSearcher( view ) );
   searchers.add( new AmazonSearcher( view ) );
   searchers.add( new GoogleBaseSearcher( view ) );
}

public void onSearch( String query ){
   for( Iterator it = searchers.iterator(); it.hasNext(); ){
      Searcher searcher = (Searcher)it.next();
      searcher.query( query );
   }
}
}
```

GWT calls the onModuleLoad method when the application starts, so this is where we set up the view and define the search engines we need. A MultiViewSearch instance is created in the onModuleLoad method, and the MultiSearch instance is passed into the constructor as a listener. Then the view is added to the web page through the RootPanel class. The RootPanel is the bridge between GWT widgets and an HTML page. This code gets the element on the page with the ID multiSearchView and inserts the widget inside. The rest of the onModuleLoad method creates a new Searcher for each search engine and adds it to an array so that they can be iterated over in the onSearch method.

The onSearch method implements the MultiSearchViewListener interface. It is called by the view when the user enters a search query and presses Enter or clicks the Search button. It is the controller's job at this point to send the query string to each of the Searcher objects so that they can query the search engines. Since the Searcher objects have references to their SearchResultsView widgets, they are able to independently update the interface when search results arrive.

That wraps up the application's design. While going over the design we've also looked at some of the code that acts as the structure for the design. Thinking about design in this way and providing a solid structure for the application will greatly simplify completing the details of the application and extending the application in the future.

Importing Structured Data Formats

A standard web browser is capable of making HTTP connections using any URL and retrieving the data. Traditionally this was done with page refreshes, and more recently Ajax techniques have loaded the data through JavaScript code asynchronously. Although the browser renders data formatted in HTML well, that's not the only type of data a browser can fetch. There's nothing wrong with HTML in general; it's a simple way to format text. But for our application, fetching HTML would not fit the definition of an aggregator well.

If we were to fetch HTML results from each of the search engines, we would probably be able to display the results as HTML fragments on the page. We could even display them in a frame if we wanted. This, however, is not ideal for the user, since it is not a unified interface. The user is faced with many of the same issues they would have if they were to visit each search engine directly. The search results would be formatted differently and the user would have to learn where to look for information. An alternative is to parse the HTML so that we can extract the data and use it in our own format. There are three problems with doing this. One, GWT does not ship with an HTML parser. Two, we don't know where to look for the data. HTML is not structured well and is not really self-describing. It's hard to understand what certain text means. And three, the data in the HTML can change locations with a small change in web design or simply by using a different browser.

Fortunately, there are two other data formats that GWT understands, are common on the web, and are structured well. The first, and more common, is XML, and the other is JSON. We can use the browser's capability of retrieving data from a URL to retrieve XML data or JSON data. Most web services and search engines provide a feed of data in XML format. Fewer provide the JSON format. This application will use JSON. To understand why we need to use JSON, you need to understand a browser's Same Origin policy.

Bypassing the Same Origin Policy

The web in general is open and not secure. With a browser you can visit any web page you request. Some of these web pages might be malicious, but the browser isn't going to tell you want you can and can't do. Instead, the browser can ensure as much as possible that malicious web sites are contained.

First of all, a browser runs JavaScript code in a sandbox. This means that the scripts it runs doesn't have access to system resources. Everything outside of the browser is safe from malicious JavaScript code. The browser also must put restrictions on what a script can access inside the browser. If it didn't, a malicious script could access other browser tabs, windows, or frames and modify the content. If a malicious script like this were executed, at the very least the web pages you view would have content that didn't originate there. At the worst the script would gain access to some of your private information. However, the browser doesn't completely restrict scripts from accessing content in other windows or frames. There are valid situations where a developer would want this type of access. So, standard browsers implement a simple security policy, called the Same Origin policy, which defines what a script has access to.

The Same Origin policy dictates that a script can only have access to JavaScript objects that were loaded on a page with the same origin as the running script. This effectively prevents a script from accessing a page on another domain while allowing it to access anything that came from the same domain.

This policy also covers loading data asynchronously using JavaScript. That is, data can only be loaded asynchronously from the same domain as the page the script was loaded on. For example, our GWT script running on the page www.gwtapps.com/multisearch is not allowed to load data asynchronously from www.google.com because they are two different domains. However, our GWT script can only load data from www.gwtapps.com.

This is obviously a big drawback for Ajax applications. With the number of web services available increasing, there is a growing desire to integrate a client directly, but the Same Origin policy does not let this happen. There are, of course, ways to work around this restriction to access third-party web services. One workaround is creating a proxy on the server of origin. In this case the proxy would run on the www.gwtapps.com web server. It would be implemented using a web server technology like JSP, a servlet, ASP.NET, Ruby, or PHP, and its job would be to relay requests for a resource to the destination. Because the server does not have the same security restrictions as a browser, it can access data on any server. Once the proxy retrieves the data from another server, it can return the data to the client.

This solution works well, though with a small downside of having the data transmitted twice, but more sophisticated servers can implement caching or other performance improvements. However, for this sample application we don't want to deal with writing a server; we want to keep things relatively simple and have our client independent of a server and access the search engine services directly. Fortunately there is another way to bypass the Same Origin policy with an implementation that exists entirely in the browser.

This client-side solution is possible because the browser isn't subjecting the source of the resources to the Same Origin policy. Take images, for example. The `image` tag can specify an image's URL on another web server. When the page is loaded, the browser retrieves the image from the other web server and displays it on the page. Since the page and the image are from different domains, they don't follow the Same Origin policy. If we were to load an image from www.yahoo.com in our web page, we are effectively communicating with the Yahoo! server.

Another example is with JavaScript files. Using the `script` tag you can specify a script that is stored on another web page to be included in the page. This is a common practice for JavaScript libraries. For example, to put a map from Google Maps on your web page, you would import a Google map script from the Google web server and it would do the work of putting a map on the page. The script runs as if its origin was the origin of the web page and not the server that stored the script. The scripts have total access to your web page, so it is important that you trust where the script comes from. Since JavaScript is a very flexible scripting language, these scripts can include any type of code and even structure data. This is how we will get around the Same Origin policy in this application. We will request data from a web service through a `script` tag, and the web service will return requested data in a JavaScript format. Then our application will interpret that data. Returning data in a JavaScript format is not a feature that all web services have. But Yahoo! and Google have committed to providing this feature for their services, so it should be increasingly popular in the future.

Loading JSON Feeds with JSONP

The standard format used for requesting data as a JavaScript file is JavaScript Object Notation (JSON), and its format is easily readable by JavaScript code. It's a hierarchical structure similar to XML except it matches the JavaScript type structure.

The building blocks of a JSON structure can be an object, an array, and/or a value. A JSON object is a list of name-value pairs, a JSON array is an ordered list of values, and a JSON value is a string, number, object, or array and can be nested within an object or an array. The syntax is a subset of JavaScript syntax and is similar to C++ and Java. For example, let's take a look at a JSON-formatted item returned from Yahoo! Search:

```
{
   "Title":"Ajax for Java developers: Exploring the Google Web Toolkit",
   "Summary":"The recently released Google Web Toolkit (GWT)...",
   "Url":"http:\/\/www-128.ibm.com\/developerworks\/library\...",
   "ClickUrl":"http:\/\/uk.wrs.yahoo.com\/_ylt=...",
   "DisplayUrl":"www-128.ibm.com\/developerworks\/library\/j-...",
   "ModificationDate":1175670000,
   "MimeType":"text\/html",
   "Cache":{
      "Url":"http:\/\/uk.wrs.yahoo.com\/_ylt=A9iby5yIFRVGjcOA...",
      "Size":"81686"
   }
}
```

This result, a JSON object, is surrounded by curly the braces: {}. It has several name-value pairs. The names are strings surrounded by quotes. The values are strings when they're surrounded by quotes, and numbers or numeric text when they aren't surrounded by quotes. The `Cache` name-value pair that you see here has a value that is another object. You don't really need to know this format since GWT comes with a JSON parser, but it will help you to understand the structure when we look at the parsing code.

The piece that GWT doesn't ship with is the ability to load a JSON feed from another URL. It provides the HTTP library to perform remote HTTP requests, but we cannot use this since it would violate a browser's Same Origin policy. We could use the HTTP library to contact our own server if we were using the proxy solution. Instead, we will use the workaround to the Same Origin policy outlined previously, where we load the feed as a resource on the page using the `script` tag.

Essentially we just need to add a `script` tag to the page and set its `src` attribute to the JSON feed's URL. The browser will then retrieve the feed and execute it like it's a script. This is an asynchronous task, so after we add the tag we need some way of knowing when the script has been loaded by the browser and the JSON feed is ready. To accomplish this we can take advantage of a standard feature that most services implement for

JSON feeds: returning the feed in a callback method, commonly called JSON with Padding (JSONP). When the browser finishes loading the remote script, it runs the script. When this is a JSON feed with a callback, the callback method is called with the feed as the first parameter. To make this functionality available to GWT, we need to implement a class that adds a `script` tag to request a JSON feed and provides a callback to bring the feed back into GWT to be parsed.

We'll call the class `JSONRequest`, and its code is as follows:

```
public class JSONRequest{
    public static void get( String url, JSONRequestHandler handler ){
        String callbackName = "JSONCallback"+handler.hashCode();
        get( url+callbackName, callbackName, handler );
    }

    public static void get(
        String url, String callbackName, JSONRequestHandler handler ){
        createCallbackFunction( handler, callbackName );
        addScript(url);
    }

    public static native void addScript(String url) /*-{
        var scr = document.createElement("script");
        scr.setAttribute("language", "JavaScript");
        scr.setAttribute("src", url);
        document.getElementsByTagName("body")[0].appendChild(scr);
    }-*/;

    private native static void createCallbackFunction(
        JSONRequestHandler obj, String callbackName )/*-{
        tmpcallback = function( j ){
            obj.@com.gwtapps.client.util.JSONRequestHandler::onRequestComplete(
                Lcom/google/gwt/core/client/JavaScriptObject;)( j );
        };
        eval( "window."+callbackName+"=tmpcallback" );
    }-*/;
}
```

The class is short and simple, but it is doing some complex things. It provides a static `get` method whose job is to make a request for a JSON feed. The method takes the JSON feed URL as a string and a reference to an implementation of the `JSONRequestHandler` interface, which is responsible for handling the asynchronous result of the `get` call. There are two implementations of the `get` method: one for when a callback name is not specified and will be generated, and another for when a callback name is specified. The reason for this is that some web services that provide a JSON feed require a specific name for the callback function. Most services, however, let you specify the name. When a name is not specified, this class generates a callback name to be used. The get method creates the script tag and sets its type attribute to JavaScript and its src attribute to the requested URL with the callback name appended. The class needs to use a JSNI method implemented as addScript to create the script tag in the same document that the GWT code runs from. This is an important technical point. There are essentially two windows in a GWT application: the window in which your GWT application displays and another window where the GWT code runs. To use GWT's JSON library to operate on a returned JSON object, the object needs to exist in the same window as the GWT code. The JSNI method ensures that the script tag is added to the correct document. After it is added, the browser retrieves the script based on the tag's URL property.

The get method also sets up the JavaScript callback method using the createCallbackFunction method. The createCallbackFunction method is another JSNI method that creates a function in the browser with the callback name. This JavaScript function simply calls the onRequest Complete method on the JSONRequestHandler interface. The code that implements this interface will receive the call with the JSON feed as a JavaScriptObject. The JavaScriptObject can be passed into the constructor of the JSONObject so that its contents can be inspected.

To complete the implementation of the JSONRequest, let's look at the JSONRequestHandler interface:

```
public interface JSONRequestHandler {
    public void onRequestComplete( String json );
}
```

The implementing class simply needs to write the onRequestComplete method and handle the JSON string.

We now have the groundwork complete for our application, including the model, view, and controller. We also have the helper class ready that will allow us to communicate asynchronously with other domains from our client. Now we just need to implement the Searcher's for each search engine and understand how to interact with their service.

Integrating with Yahoo! Search

Yahoo! has a large number of web services that are freely open for integration with other applications. Typically they offer APIs through XML with a REST interface (using GET and POST to URLs), but they also support JSON for quite a few of their services.

To use any of their services in an application you need to sign up for a free application ID from their web site at http://developer.yahoo.com. The application ID is a way that Yahoo! can track the usage of their API per application. In the case of abuse, Yahoo! has the option of shutting down the abusive application. They also limit the number of queries an application can make to a service. The rate limits per service vary, but are typically in the range of thousands of queries per day.

For this application we will use the Yahoo! Search service. The service follows a REST interface, which means we can request specific data based on a URL. The URL points to a Yahoo! resource that knows how to interpret it and find the correct data to return. Let's look at the structure of the URL to request search results from Yahoo!. The following list outlines the parts of a Yahoo! Search request URL.

- http://search.yahooapis.com/

  The URL starts with the Yahoo! Search domain.

- /WebSearchService/V1/

  This part specifies the web service followed by the version number.

- webSearch?

  This part specifies the method to call followed by the parameters for the method.

Before submitting this URL we need to look at the parameters for the `webSearch` method.

- `appid`

  This is the application ID Yahoo! requires so they can keep track of your application requests.

- `query`

  This is the query for which we want to receive search results.

- `output`

  This specifies the format of the returned search results. The default format is XML. We will specify JSON.

- `callback`

  This is the name of the callback function that should be called when the data is returned.

There are several other parameters that you can add to you search request, and they're all documented on the Yahoo! developer site. We need these four parameters to perform our search and integrate the results into our GWT application. If we put these parts together we can construct a full URL:

```
http://search.yahooapis.com/WebSearchService/V1/
webSearch?appid=J6rsiJoB7SAtdbVtTn7djfGD5sdOPF5TXMLD&query=gwt&output=json&callb
ack=callbackFunction
```

The application ID shown here is the one I used to test this application. You can use it as well to test, but you should also apply for one that is exclusive to your application to avoid any problems. The search query in this URL is for *gwt,* the output is JSON, and the callback function is called `callbackFunction`. One of the benefits of REST-like interfaces is that you can test them in a regular browser window. You can copy this URL into your browser window to see the output. The following is a sample of the output's beginning (formatted for readability).

```
callbackFunction({
    "ResultSet":{
        "type":"web",
        "totalResultsAvailable":1540000,
        "totalResultsReturned":10,
        "firstResultPosition":1,
    "moreSearch":"\/WebSearchService\/V1\/
webSearch?query=gwt&amp;appid=J6rO9izV34EhxGtDM14W5Dzj0Hs33LosiJoB7SAtdbVtTn7djf
GD5sdOPF5TXMLD&amp;region=us",
        "Result":[{
            "Title":"Ajax for Java developers: Exploring the Google Web Toolkit",
            "Summary":"The recently released Google Web Toolkit (GWT) is a
comprehensive set of APIs ...
```

This is the beginning of the JSON data returned from the URL. It is exactly as expected. The callback function is called with the parameter being the

JSON result from our query. The `JSONRequest` code will request this data by adding a `script` tag to the document that points to this URL. It will also implement the callback function so the returned data can be passed back to the application.

Now let's look at the code for the `YahooSearcher`:

```
public class YahooSearcher extends Searcher implements JSONRequestHandler{

    public YahooSearcher( MultiSearchView view ){
        super( view, new SearchEngine("Yahoo Search", "http://www.yahoo.com"));
    }

    public void query( String q ){
        JSONRequest.get( "http://search.yahooapis.com/WebSearchService/V1/
webSearch?appid=J6rO9izV34EhxGtDMl4W5Dzj0Hs33LosiJoB7SAtdbVtTn7djfGD5sdOPF5TXMLD
&query="+q+"&output=json&callback=", this );
        getView().clearResults();
    }

    public void onRequestComplete( JavaScriptObject json ){
        JSONObject j = new JSONObject(json);

        //iterate over each Result in the ResultSet
        JSONObject feed = (JSONObject)j.get("ResultSet");
        JSONArray entries = (JSONArray)feed.get("Result");
        for( int i=0; i< entries.size(); ++i ){

            //get the values from the JSON object to create a SearchEngineResult
            JSONObject entry = (JSONObject)entries.get(i);
            JSONString title = (JSONString)entry.get("Title");
            JSONString url = (JSONString)entry.get("Url");
            JSONString summary = (JSONString)entry.get("Summary");
            if( url != null ){
                getView().addSearchResult( new SearchEngineResult(
                    title.stringValue(),url.stringValue(),summary.stringValue()));
            }
        }
    }
}
```

This class extends the `Searcher` class that we defined earlier so that it fits into the application's controller framework. In its constructor it defines a new `SearchEngine` instance with the Yahoo! name and URL and passes that to the `Searcher` superclass. It implements the `query` method from the `Searcher` class. This is the method that's called when the user submits a query from the interface. In this method the class calls the `get` method on the `JSONRequest` and passes in the Yahoo! web search URL with the query added in. The second parameter for the `get` method on the `JSONRequest` class is a `JSONRequestHandler` instance; in this case it is the `YahooSearcher` class. The class implements the `JSONRequestHandler` interface so it can receive events back from a `JSONRequest`. The `onRequestComplete` method handles the events. In this method the `YahooSearcher` parses the JSON result using the GWT JSON library, constructs a `SearchEngineResult` object from each result, and passes it to its view to be rendered.

The structure of the data returned from Yahoo! is similar to an RSS or an Atom XML feed. These types of feeds basically have a feed object with a list of results inside. Figure 7-6 shows the UML structure for the feed.

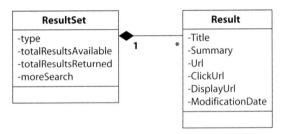

Figure 7–6. The UML structure of the returned Yahoo! feed

For this application we are only interested in each result and their `title`, `url`, and `description`, so the JSON code in the `onRequestComplete` method extracts this information. It first retrieves the `ResultSet` object, and then gets the `Results` as a `JSONArray`. It iterates over the array to get each `Result` object. The `Title`, `Url`, and `Summary` values are extracted from the `Result` object to create the `SeachEngineResult` object for the view.

With this class implemented, we have a runnable application. The application will take a search query and submit it to Yahoo!. Figure 7-7 shows the output.

This application is now at the point where it can be extended quite a bit with just a little effort. Any number of search engines can be supported as long as they provide a web service with a JSON output. The rest of this chapter looks at other services that do this.

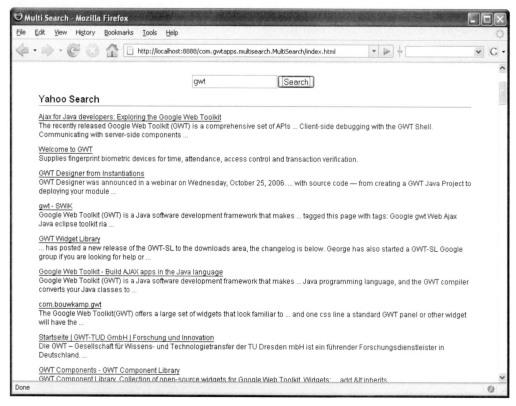

Figure 7–7.   The application displaying a feed returned from Yahoo! Search

Integrating with Google Base

Google, like Yahoo!, also provides open access to many of its services. They are also committed to REST-like interfaces; in fact, they have created their own protocol based on Atom API called GData. The GData protocol has the REST-like features of the Atom API protocol, including getting data using HTTP GET, updating data using HTTP POST, and creating data using HTTP PUT. On top of this it defines a way to query a data set. But the feature that we're interested in with GData is its ability to output feeds in JSON format so we can integrate it into the Multi-Search application.

At this point Google does not provide GData access to its search engine, but it does provide access to its Google Base service. Google Base is a massive database of things on the Internet. Anybody can add items to Google

Base, and generally it is used to sell things. It allows bulk uploads of data; many sites upload their entire inventory so that it is searchable.

We're not going to use the full functionality of Google Base in this application. We will only use the search feature. Using the search feature is similar to the Yahoo! API search. First, we need to construct a URL that encapsulates our request for query results from the server. The URL structure for Google Base is as follows:

- www.google.com/base/feeds

    The URL starts with the Google Base feed URL.

- /snippets?

    This part points to the snippets feeds, which are the public version of Google Base data. It can be accessed without authentication but is read only. You put the parameters for the query after this part.

You can use the following parameters for the query.

- `alt`

    By default, an Atom XML feed will be returned. You can specify an `alt` value to get a different format.

- `max-results`

    This value is optional but you can specify this to limit the number of results returned. The default is 25 and the maximum value is 250.

- `callback`

    This is the name of the callback function that should be called when the data is returned.

To construct the URL that we'll use to send a query to Google Base, we need to put the parts and parameters together. The value that we'll use for the `alt` parameter is `json-in-script`. This tells Google Base that we want the output formatted in JSON, that we are using it in a `script` tag, and that we expect a callback function to be called. The callback function name is specified in the callback parameter. For a search for *gwt* the fully constructed URL looks like this:

```
http://www.google.com/base/feeds/snippets?q=gwt&alt=json-in-
script&callback=callbackFunction
```

Taking advantage of the ability to load data from a REST interface in a regular browser, we can take a look at what the results look like before adding any code. The following is the beginning of the results (formatted for readability):

```
callbackFunction({
    "version":"1.0",
    "encoding":"UTF-8",
    "feed":{ "xmlns":"http://www.w3.org/2005/Atom",
        "xmlns$openSearch":"http://a9.com/-/spec/opensearchrss/1.0/",
        "xmlns$gm":"http://base.google.com/ns-metadata/1.0",
        "xmlns$g":"http://base.google.com/ns/1.0",
        "xmlns$batch":"http://schemas.google.com/gdata/batch ...
```

The results have the same JSON syntax as the Yahoo! Search results but the structure is different. To translate the parsed JSON objects to our model, we need to understand this feed's structure. Basically the structure is a feed object with an array of entries, as shown in Figure 7-8.

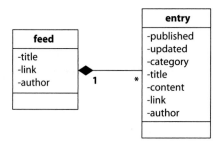

Figure 7–8.   The UML structure of the feed returned from Google Base

Google Base returns quite a bit of extra data not included in Figure 7-8. The service acts as a database, so there is a lot of extra data that describes the result. For example, there may be a price field, a country field, a color field, and so on. For this application we'll extract the feed and then extract the title link and content for each entry.

Now that you understand the Google base Feed format and how to query it, let's look at the code for the `GoogleBaseSearcher`:

```
public class GoogleBaseSearcher
    extends Searcher implements JSONRequestHandler {

    public GoogleBaseSearcher( MultiSearchView view ){
        super( view, new SearchEngine("Google Base","http://base.google.com"));
    }
```

```java
    public void query( String q ){
        JSONRequest.get(
"http://www.google.com/base/feeds/snippets?q="+q+"&alt=json-in-
script&callback=", this  );
        getView().clearResults();
    }

    public void onRequestComplete( JavaScriptObject json ){
        JSONObject j = new JSONObject(json);

        //iterate over each entry in the feed
        JSONObject feed = (JSONObject)j.get("feed");
        JSONArray entries = (JSONArray)feed.get("entry");
        for( int i=0; i< entries.size(); ++i ){
            JSONObject entry = (JSONObject)entries.get(i);

            //get the entry title
            JSONObject titleObj = (JSONObject)entry.get("title");
            JSONString title = (JSONString)titleObj.get("$t");

            //find the link labeled alternate
            JSONArray links = (JSONArray)entry.get("link");
            String link = null;
            for( int k = 0; k < links.size(); ++k ) {
                JSONObject linkObj = (JSONObject)links.get(k);
                JSONString linkType = (JSONString)linkObj.get("rel");
                if( "alternate".equals(linkType.stringValue())){
                    JSONString linkString = (JSONString)linkObj.get("href");
                    link = linkString.stringValue();
                    break;
                }
            }

            //get the content
            JSONObject contentObj = (JSONObject)entry.get("content");
            JSONString content = (JSONString)contentObj.get("$t");

            //create a new SearchEngineResult
            if( link != null ){
                getView().addSearchResult( new SearchEngineResult(
                    title.stringValue(),link, content.stringValue() ) );
            }
        }
    }
}
```

Just like the YahooSearcher, this class extends the Searcher class so that it fits into the controller framework. In its constructor it defines a new

`SearchEngine` instance with the Google Base name and URL, and passes that to the `Searcher` superclass. The `query` method is implemented to send a query to the Google Base service using a combination of the URL described earlier, the search string passed in from the interface, and the `JSONRequest` class to do the work. The `JSONRequest` class returns the requested data to the client through the `onRequestComplete` method. In this method the `GoogleBaseSearcher` parses the JSON result using GWT's JSON library, constructs a `SearchEngineResult` object from each result, and passes the `SearchEngineResult` object to its view to be rendered.

The Google Base format is a little more verbose. Notice how the `title` and `content` values are objects with a child string with the key `$t`. Also, there are multiple URLs listed under a link. There is one link with the `rel` attribute set to `self`, which we ignore but it can be used for managing the entry through the GData REST interface; the other link with the `rel` attribute set to `alternate` represents the destination page for the entry. This code selects the alternate link so that a click on the link in our application takes the user to the original web page.

Adding this class to the application, let's us run a query on both Yahoo! and Google Base at the same time.

Integrating with Flickr Search

Flickr is a community-driven photo organizing and sharing web site that provides many different feeds to its users' photos. Similar to Yahoo! and Google, Flickr exposes its feeds through a REST-based web service. The difference is that the items in the feeds are images instead of textual data. Adding Flickr as a search engine source for our Multi-Search application means that we can also display photos as search results.

To start working with the Flickr REST API, you first need to get an application key. Just like the Yahoo! Search web service, Flickr uses this key to track use and stop abuse. You can get your own ID and find information about Flickr web services at www.flickr.com/services/api/.

Our sample application is going to use a simple keyword search on Flickr to find matching photos. The photos will then be added as search results in the application. The search query is submitted using our `JSONRequest`, and we expect JSON-formatted output from Flickr as a result. First, we need to build a URL to submit with the `JSONRequest` object. The following is the structure of a Flickr REST URL request.

- http://api.flickr.com/services

  The URL starts with the Flickr API domain and the services application.

- /rest?

  Flickr provides many types of interfaces including XML RPC, SOAP, and REST. We will use the REST interface since this is what we are using elsewhere.

Making REST calls on the Flickr web service will require the following parameters for this application.

- `method`

  This is where we specify which method we're calling. For this application we are going to use `flickr.photos.search`.

- `api_key`

  This is the application key that you need to get from Flickr to write applications that use its services. It is required.

- `per_page`

  This is a numeric value specifying the number of search results you'd like.

- `format`

  This parameter specifies the type of output desired. The default is XML, but Flickr supports JSON, which is perfect for client-side JavaScript.

- `text`

  This is the query string. Flickr attempts to match this to a photo's title, description, or tags.

Putting the URL and its parameters together we have the following URL that makes a query to Flickr web services to match photos based on a query string:

```
http://api.flickr.com/services/rest/
?method=flickr.photos.search&api_key=85618ad7d326d8ef93c6bee9ed32706f&per_page=5
&format=json&text=gwt
```

By submitting this URL in a web browser we are able to see what the output of the query looks like:

```
jsonFlickrApi({
    "photos":{
        "page":1,
        "pages":30,
        "perpage":5,
        "total":"148",
        "photo":[{
            "id":"419053246",
            "owner":"99511910@N00",
            "secret":"fc1a5a5e16",
            "server":"165",
            "farm":1,
            "title":"Rockit Room April 20th!",
            "ispublic":1,
            "isfriend":0,
            "isfamily":0
        } , {
            "id":"405149819",
            "owner":"91606623@N00",
            "secret":"281fc71978",
            "server":"143",
            "farm":1,
            "title":"TRINDADE (RJ)",
            "ispublic":1,
            "isfriend":0,
            "isfamily":0} ,…
```

Flickr doesn't let us specify the callback name. Instead, it is hard-coded to the value `jsonFlickrApi`. This could cause problems in our code if we were to run multiple Flickr queries simultaneously. Since we don't plan to do this, we'll be okay. With this query Flickr returns a root-level object called `photos`, which has an array called `photo`. Each item in the array represents one photo. Figure 7-9 illustrates the UML for this structure.

These returned results differ from the results we've retrieved from Google and Yahoo! in that the items do not contain URLs to resources. In other words, we don't have the URL to the images or to a Flickr page hosting the images. Instead, we have several IDs for each photo. From these ID's we can construct the URLs that point to both an image which we can use in an HTML `img` tag and a URL to a Flickr page which hosts the photo, so that we can link to the original page. The only thing that we don't need to modify is the title attribute on the photo.

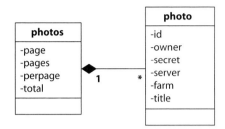

Figure 7–9.   The UML structure of the feed returned from Flickr

To construct a URL to a photo hosted on Flickr based on the returned photo object, we need to observe the following URL structure:

```
http://{farmfarm-id}.static.flickr.com/{server-id}/{id}_{secret}_[mstb].jpg
```

We can obtain each of the parameters found in the URL from the attributes of the photo object returned from the Flickr query. The last option specifies the size of the image, where m is medium, s is small, t is thumbnail, and b is large.

To construct a URL to a Flickr page for a particular photo, use the following URL structure:

```
http://www.flickr.com/photos/{user-id}/{photo-id}
```

The user-id option in this URL is the owner attribute in the photo object returned from the Flickr query, and photo-id is the ID parameter.

At this point we have enough information to construct the FlickrSearcher class to implement the ability to return Flickr image results and integrate them into the query system in the Multi-Search application. The following code implements the FlickrSearcher class:

```
public class FlickrSearcher extends Searcher implements JSONRequestHandler{

    public FlickrSearcher( MultiSearchView view ){
        super(view, new SearchEngine("Flickr Search","http://www.flickr.com"));
    }

    public void query( String q ){
        JSONRequest.get( "http://api.flickr.com/services/rest/
?method=flickr.photos.search&api_key=85618ad7d326d8ef93c6bee9ed32706f&per_page=5
&format=json&text="+q, "jsonFlickrApi", this  );
```

```
        getView().clearResults();
    }

    public void onRequestComplete( JavaScriptObject json ){
        JSONObject j = new JSONObject(json);

        //iterate over each photo
        JSONObject root = (JSONObject)j.get("photos");
        JSONArray entries = (JSONArray)root.get("photo");
        for( int i=0; i< entries.size(); ++i ){

            //get the values required to create the URLs
            JSONObject entry = (JSONObject)entries.get(i);
            JSONString title = (JSONString)entry.get("title");
            JSONNumber farm = (JSONNumber)entry.get("farm");
            JSONString server = (JSONString)entry.get("server");
            JSONString id = (JSONString)entry.get("id");
            JSONString owner = (JSONString)entry.get("owner");
            JSONString secret = (JSONString)entry.get("secret");

            //create the img URL and the link URL
            String imageUrl = "http://farm"+ ((int)farm.getValue())+
                ".static.flickr.com/"+ server.stringValue()+
                "/"+id.stringValue()+ "_"+ secret.stringValue()+ "_m.jpg";
            String htmlUrl = "http://www.flickr.com/photos/"+
                owner.stringValue()+ "/"+id.stringValue();

            //create a new SearchEngineResult
            getView().addSearchResult( new SearchEngineResult(
                title.stringValue(),htmlUrl, "<img src='"+imageUrl+"'/>" ) );
        }
    }
}
```

The class constructor starts by creating a SearchEngine class to add Flickr Search to the model and instruct the Searcher superclass to add Flickr to the view. The query method makes an asynchronous JSON request using the URL described earlier with the query appended. The FlickrSearcher handles the asynchronous JSON request by implementing the JSONReqeustHandler interface and the onRequestComplete method.

The onRequestComplete method parses the returned JSON string using GWT's JSON library. First, the photo's object is retrieved. Then from the photo's object the photo array is retrieved and iterated over. The various IDs required to build the Flickr URLs are extracted from the JSON photo object along with the title. Once the URLs are constructed, a `Search EngineResult` object is created with the title from the photo object as its title, the constructed URL that points to the Flickr HTML page for the photo as its URL, and an `img` HTML tag with the `src` attributed as the constructed URL that points directly to the Flickr image as its description. Each `SearchEngineResult` is passed to the view where they will be rendered.

Adding this class to the application adds the Flickr Search as one of the search engines used for a query. After running a query you will be able to see the Flickr images as search results, as shown in Figure 7-10.

Figure 7–10. The application displaying a feed returned from Flickr

Integrating with Amazon Search

Integrating with Amazon Search is a little more difficult than Google Base and Yahoo! Search because they don't actually have a JSON feed, but they do provide a flexible way of transforming their XML feeds using XSLT.

Extensible Stylesheet Language Transformations (XSLT) is a transformation language based on XML which transforms XML data into any other text-based format, typically another XML document, an HTML document, or plain text. Amazon Web Services (AWS) provide the option to specify an XSLT document as an option to apply to the results of a REST query. Before returning the query's XML result, AWS transforms it on the server using the specified stylesheet. It's okay if you're not familiar with XSLT—we're basically just going to use a document to transform the output from AWS from one format (XML) to another (JSON).

Using AWS requires that you sign up and obtain a developer token that you must use with your queries. This token is used to track use and abuse of your application's interaction with AWS. You can sign up for a token at http://aws.amazon.com.

You may also want to use an associate ID with your queries. An associate ID allows Amazon to track purchases that were made on their site as a result of someone using your application. They provide an affiliate program where they will credit your account for referrals like this.

For our application we are going to make a REST query to Amazon to retrieve a list of books matching the search criteria. Let's take a look at the parts of the URL that are needed for an AWS REST query.

- http://ecs.amazonaws.com

  The URL starts with the Amazon Web Service URL for the E-Commerce Service (ECS).

- /onca/xml?

  This part points to the XML web application that responds to REST queries.

There are a vast number of parameters you can use to query AWS. We use just a few to get a list of books.

- Service

  `AWSECommerceService` is the service name for ECS and the value that we use.

- AWSAccessKeyId

  The access key ID obtained from aws.amazon.com to identify your application.

- AssociateTag

  Specify the value obtained from the Amazon associate program to track purchases.

- Operation

  This is the method that you are requesting to call. It can be one of several methods provided by the ECS. In this application we use the `ItemSearch` operation.

- ResponseGroup

  Reponse groups allow you to specify the type of information that you would like returned. We will use `Small,Offers`. The small group specifies that we just want a small summary for each item. The Offers group specifies that we want pricing information for each item.

- SearchIndex

  Amazon doesn't just sell books. This parameter lets us specify the product index we want to search. For this application we will use `Books`.

- Style

  This specifies the URL of the stylesheet we want to use. For this application we will use http://kokogiak.com/amazon/JSON/ajsonCategorySearch.xsl. This stylesheet was developed by Alan Taylor for the specific use of transforming Amazon XML to JSON.

- ContentType

  This parameter tells AWS to return a specific content type. We use this parameter to force the content type to be `text/javascript`.

- Keywords

  This specifies the keywords we are searching for.

- Callback

  This is the callback method that the JSON output will call.

We will use this single REST request to query for data on Amazon Books. The following is the constructed URL using these parameters:

```
http://ecs.amazonaws.com/onca/
xml?Service=AWSECommerceService&AWSAccessKeyId=1K7P8WX9YVQ28BNZRCG2&AssociateTag
=ryandews-
20&Operation=ItemSearch&ResponseGroup=Small,Offers&SearchIndex=Books&Style=http:
//kokogiak.com/amazon/JSON/ajsonCategorySearch.xsl&ContentType=text/
javascript&Keywords=java&CallBack=callbackFunction
```

The URL is using my access key and associate tag. You may want to use your own values there. Like the other REST URLs, we can use it in a browser to check what the output will look like:

```
callbackFunction({
    "ItemSet":{
        "category":"Books",
        "pagenum":"",
        "TotalResults": "5789",
        "Item" : [  {
            "asin":"0072253606",
"url":"http://www.amazon.com/gp/redirect.html%3FASIN=0072253606%26tag=ryandews-
20%26lcode=xm2%26cID=2025%26ccmID=165953%26location=/o/ASIN/
0072253606%253FSubscriptionId=1K7P8WX9YVQ28BNZRCG2",
            "title":"SCJP Sun Certified Programmer for Java 5 Study Guide (Exam 310-
055) (Certification Press Study Guides)",
            "price":"$32.99",
            "lowestnewprice":"$32.53",
            "lowestusedprice":"$29.90"} ,
```

The AWS servers transformed the XML-formatted data into JSON-formatted data. The structure of the JSON begins with an `ItemSet` object at the root with an array named `Item` that contains the results of the book search. Figure 7-11 shows the UML for this structure.

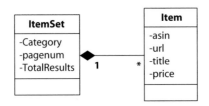

Figure 7–11.   The UML structure of the feed returned from Amazon

Now that you have an understanding of how to get JSON feeds from AWS, we can implement the Searcher interface for our application fairly easily. We follow the pattern of the previous Searcher specializations and plug in the Amazon URL and some code to transform the JSON results structure to our application's model. The code for the `AmazonSearcher` class looks like this:

```
public class AmazonSearcher extends Searcher implements JSONRequestHandler {

    public AmazonSearcher( MultiSearchView view ){
        super( view, new SearchEngine("Amazon Books","http://www.amazon.com"));
    }

    public void query( String q ){
        JSONRequest.get( "http://ecs.amazonaws.com/onca/
xml?Service=AWSECommerceService&AWSAccessKeyId=1K7P8WX9YVQ28BNZRCG2&AssociateTag
=ryandews-
20&Operation=ItemSearch&ResponseGroup=Small,Offers&SearchIndex=Books&Style=http:
//kokogiak.com/amazon/JSON/ajsonCategorySearch.xsl&ContentType=text/
javascript&Keywords="+q+"&CallBack=", this );
        getView().clearResults();
    }

    public void onRequestComplete( JavaScriptObject json ){
        JSONObject j = new JSONObject(json);

        //iterate over each Item
        JSONObject feed = (JSONObject)j.get("ItemSet");
        JSONArray entries = (JSONArray)feed.get("Item");
        for( int i=0; i< entries.size(); ++i ){

            //get the values from JSON and create a new SearchEngineResult
            JSONObject entry = (JSONObject)entries.get(i);
            JSONString title = (JSONString)entry.get("title");
            JSONString link = (JSONString)entry.get("url");
            JSONString price = (JSONString)entry.get("price");
            if( link != null )
                getView().addSearchResult( new SearchEngineResult(
                    title.stringValue(),link.stringValue(), price.stringValue()));
        }
    }
}
```

The `AmazonSearcher` class starts by creating an instance of the `Search Engine` class for the model that specifies the engine's name and URL.

Using this model class the `Searcher` superclass ensures that this search engine is properly presented in the view. The `query` method is implemented to add the query to the URL string (which we've described earlier) and pass it to the asynchronous `get` method on the `JSONRequest` class. The `AmazonSearcher` implements the `JSONRequestHandler` interface to handle the response of the `JSONRequest` get call. When the response is ready, the `onRequestComplete` method is called with the JSON response as the parameter.

The JSON response is parsed using GWT's JSON library. The root object of the feed, `ItemSet`, then has its child array, `Item`, retrieved. The `Item` array is iterated over and three strings are retrieved for each item to build the `SearchEngineResult` model object. The `title` and `url` map to the title and URL on the `SearchEngineResult`, and the price string returned from Amazon is set as the description. Each `SearchEngineResult` is added to the view so it can be rendered.

Simply adding this class to the application adds results from Amazon Books to the Multi-Search queries.

Summary

Although the Multi-Search application can be extended easily by adding more `Searcher` classes, it is fairly complete. We started by deciding that the application use the Aggregator pattern and built a MVC framework to support this. The model is simple, consisting of `SearchEngine` objects and their results, `SearchEngineResults`. The view creates a way for a user to enter a search query and a way to display results from any number of search engines. The controller consists of an extendable list of `Searcher` objects that respond to user interface events, and we built a model to be sent to the view for rendering.

The Google Web Toolkit assisted in building this application by allowing us to build an object-oriented framework in Java that followed an MVC design. It also provided tools to let us create user interface objects, communicate asynchronously over HTTP with remote web services, and compile the application to web-standard technologies so that it can be run in any standard browser.

Using the compile script that was created when the application was created makes performing the compile step simple. It can be found in the
application directory and is named MultiSearch-compile. Inside the command file you can see that the GWTCompiler class is run in a Java virtual
machine with the Multi-Search project specified as a parameter:

```
@java -cp "%~dp0\src;%~dp0\bin;E:/code/gwt/gwt-user.jar;E:/code/gwt/gwt-dev-
windows.jar" com.google.gwt.dev.GWTCompiler -out "%~dp0\www" %*
com.gwtapps.multisearch.MultiSearch
```

The output of this command is placed in the www/com.gwtapps.multi-
search.MultiSearch directory. To deploy this application, simply copy the
files in this directory to your web server. Since there is no server-side code,
you don't have to set up or configure anything else on the server.

8

Blog Editor Application

A **blog** is an informal journal, usually personal, that is published on the web. It has a fairly basic data structure and needs a client application to manage it. Typically a blog service provides the client application as a traditional web application and includes a storage and web publishing system as an easy way for users to manage their blogs. Blog services have also led the way in providing public APIs and have increased the popularity of REST-based interfaces, which allow other applications to integrate with their services.

For this sample application we will create a blog editor that can connect to a blog service and interact with their API to manage blogs and blog entries. This application illustrates how GWT can richly interact with a web service and how an Ajax blog interface can simplify and speed up blog management. We will connect to one blog network but will design the application to allow for other networks to be integrated, effectively making the application follow the Aggregator model, which we also used for the Multi-Search application in Chapter 7.

Using the Workspace Application Pattern

Applications are usually procedural or command based. This means a user typically works with an application by following steps or executing commands. Often as applications become more complex, users get disassociated from the task at hand and the application's usability suffers. A common solution to this problem is to present users with a metaphor for the application. For example, the desktop metaphor used in operating systems helps users manage and organize data the way they would with papers and files on a physical desk. Another metaphor, a generalization of the desktop's workspace, is familiar to most users. They can relate to a clear area for working where they can focus on tasks and have organized tools out of the way but readily available. The workspace metaphor is the foundation of the Workspace Application pattern.

This pattern is typically used in user-centric applications that require a variety of actions in different combinations to build on some type of document. The application is often flexible and the document fairly unstructured when compared to structured data like a calendar or a database. Applications that follow the Workspace pattern include word processors, image editors, and even an operating system desktop.

Workspace-based applications are fairly rare on the Internet due to the limitations of HTML. However, with the growing popularity and expertise of Ajax applications they are becoming more common. For example, Google purchased Writely in 2006 to help create its Ajax word processor, shown in Figure 8-1.

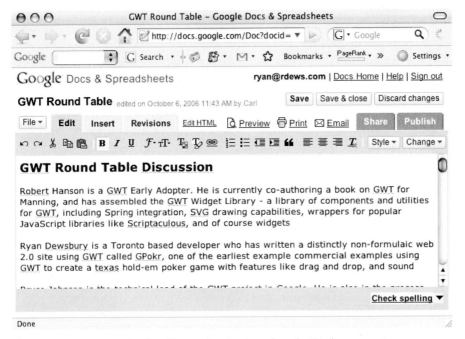

Figure 8–1.   An example of an Ajax application based on the Workspace pattern

In this chapter we'll use the Workspace Application pattern to build a blog editor. Typically you are presented with some sort of text box in a Blog editor to write your post. This is a simple example of a workspace, but in a traditional web application the workflow interrupted by page refreshes diminishes an application's usability. We will build the Blog Editor application based on the Workspace pattern. This allows the user to focus on blog entry management without being distracted by the technical framework. You can find an example of this application running at http://blogeditor.gwtapps.com.

Building a Web Service Client

Interoperable web services act behind the scenes to power much of the web. These services can be provided programmatically by any organization for use by other organizations or the public. Their emergence is a sign of the web evolving. The early web was used by organizations primarily as an information source or for a presence on the web, but now organizations are using the web for much more complex business processes. This emergence comes from a growing knowledge of what services can be performed on the web paired with the increasing understanding and standardization of web interoperation technologies.

What's nice about building a client application to a web service is that we don't need to know how the service was implemented to integrate with it. It actually doesn't matter what type of technology the service is built with as long as it can provide an interface that is accessible using standard technologies.

Many web services support technologies that enable you to programmatically interact with them. The first web services provided an RPC interface to their service, typically using XML as the format for the calls. An early standard to emerge from this style of web service communication, XML RPC, is an XML-based remote procedure call protocol. The more robust SOAP[1] standard was developed based on this standard. SOAP was originally an RPC-based protocol similar to XML RPC, but it has evolved into a

---

1. SOAP originally stood for Simple Object Access Protocol but this acronym was dropped in June 2003 as it was considered misleading. Now the technology is simply known as SOAP.

document-centric protocol that addresses one of the concerns with RPC interfaces—that they are commonly too closely coupled with the software interface. Instead of defining a service interface based on procedure calls, document-centric SOAP uses messages to have a decoupling effect. SOAP is one of the more widely used standards for web service interoperation, although it has the drawback of being complex. A third technology for web service interoperation is based on representational state transfer (REST). REST is a resource-based model that acts as a natural extension to the HTTP protocol. Each resource is identified by a URL that can only have four well-defined methods applied to it; these typically are the four HTTP methods POST, GET, PUT, and DELETE. These methods map to the actions of creating, reading, updating, and deleting data (CRUD). The strength of REST is in its simplicity. Publicly available web services provided by companies such as Amazon.com see their users having a preference for REST interfaces over SOAP interfaces.

These technologies form a solid foundation for web services to build on. They do not prescribe what technology needs to be used to build the service itself, and they don't impose restrictions on how services should be combined or what type of applications should be built on them. This powerful architecture has been proven successful in the past in other industries.

Outside of the web we can find similar service architecture everywhere including, for example, electrical supply. To allow many manufacturers to create devices that will work with an electrical supply service, it needs to implement standards, just like web services. In North America the standard voltage and frequency is 110–120 volts at 60Hz, a standard allowing devices to be built confidently in a consistent way by many manufacturers. The need for the voltage and frequency standard is much like the need for a data format standard like XML for web services. Furthermore, electrical supply has a standard plug for a device to receive a current. This standard plug is akin to the definition of a web service interface. It allows many devices to plug in. It also must follow rules of providing a consistent interface that it cannot change. If change is needed, it must take into account that there are many devices using the old interface.

For example, when the ground contact on a receptacle was introduced to receive current as a safety measure for faults in connected devices, an important design decision had to be made so that older devices could work with grounded plugs. A third contact is provided but not necessary for devices without grounds. A web service interface needs to follow the same consistency to provide integration stability for its consumers. The interface, whether for electrical supply or web services, is a contract between the provider and the consumer and providers must consider the effects before requiring modification. Also note that the standards used for electrical supply do not dictate what the current can be used for. We see simple applications like a light bulb or complex applications that combine multiple services like a television, which uses electrical service and cable service.

It's possible to take advantage of this powerful web architecture to build client applications leveraging web services using GWT. In this chapter we will build a blog editor client application using GWT that integrates with a web service interface.

Blog Editor Design

The blog editor starts with the application being loaded into the browser and connecting to the blog web service. Connecting to the blog web service may involve some security steps, after which the service returns a blog list for an account. The editor loads all of the recent posts from each blog so that they can be displayed in a list for the user. The application provides the user the ability to add a new entry to a blog and edit or delete an existing entry. Once the user has completed entering or modifying a blog entry, the application sends it to the blog web service for creation or updating.

The internal design of the application follows model-view-controller (MVC) architecture. The model represents the objects that the application operates on, the view presents the controls and blog entries to the user, and the controller defines how the application interacts with the web service to build the model and display it in the view.

The Model

The Blog Editor application's model involves two classes: the `Blog` class representing one blog and the `BlogEntry` class representing an entry in a blog. The UML diagram in Figure 8-2 illustrates the structure of the two classes.

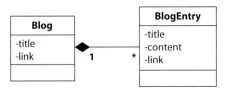

Figure 8–2. UML diagram for the application's model

The Blog class holds the blog's title and its link. The link is a URL that points to the HTML page for the blog hosted by the blogging service. The BlogEntry class has a title, content representing the body of the entry, and a link. The link in this case is a URL that points to the HTML page for the single entry. These objects can be implemented with simple Java code. The code for the Blog class looks like this:

```
public class Blog {
    private String title;
    private String link;
    private List entries = new ArrayList();

    public Blog( String title, String link ) {
        this.title = title;
        this.link = link;
    }
    public String getTitle(){
        return title;
    }
    public String getLink(){
        return link;
    }
    public void addEntry( BlogEntry entry ){
        entries.add( 0, entry);
    }
    public int getEntryCount(){
        return entries.size();
    }
    public BlogEntry getEntry( int index ){
        return (BlogEntry) entries.get(index);
    }
}
```

The Blog class simply holds data and provides get methods for access. It keeps a list of its entries and allows access to them through three methods. The addEntry method adds an entry and puts it at the front of the list, so that entries appear in reverse chronological order as you typically see in blogs. The `getEntryCount` method returns the number of entries, and the `getEntry` method returns an entry based on an index.

The `BlogEntry` class, also a simple Java class, looks like this:

```java
public class BlogEntry {
    private Blog blog;
    private String title;
    private String content;
    private String link;

    public BlogEntry( Blog blog ){
        this.blog = blog;
    }
    public String getTitle(){
        return title;
    }
    public void setTitle( String title ){
        this.title = title;
    }
    public String getContent(){
        return content;
    }
    public void setContent( String content ){
        this.content = content;
    }
    public String getLink(){
        return link;
    }
    public void setLink( String link ){
        this.link = link;
    }
}
```

The `BlogEntry` class implements the `get` and `set` methods for the attributes listed in Figure 8-2.

Building a Multiple Document View

The view is the part of the application that handles the visual presentation of data. Typically a blog service provides a visual presentation through a series of HTML pages. The first page lists blogs that a user can add entries to. The list has several buttons that let users navigate to the management of each blog. Once on a blog page, the user is usually presented with a list

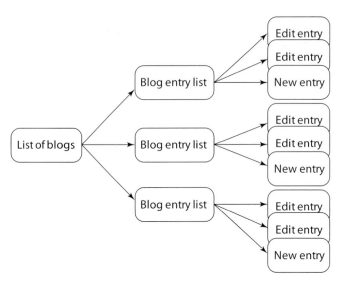

Figure 8–3. Page relationships for a blog manager web application

of existing entries that he can modify. The entries have several options, such as edit and delete, and each takes the user to a new web page. Figure 8-3 illustrates the page relationships.

Each box in Figure 8-3 typically represents a distinct web page. This type of design is functional and works well. However, the spread of functionality over many web pages like this is a great opportunity for an Ajax application to dramatically increase workflow by grouping this functionality on one page and asynchronously load data as needed. Granted, not everyone that runs a blog needs fast workflow, but for those who do, a more advanced view based on GWT will speed up workflow dramatically.

The Blog Editor application is built on an existing web service, so we're not going to change any of the basic relationship structures. Blog services typically follow the structure illustrated in Figure 8-3, where a list of blogs each has a list of entries with a list of operations. We will use this same relationship structure, but instead of spreading its management out over several web pages, we will combine it all into one page. This provides users with a quick overview of all blog entries, fast editing, and easy cutting and pasting between entries.

The class structure to implement this view contains four major classes, as illustrated in the UML diagram in Figure 8-4.

BlogEditorView
BlogView
BlogEntryView
EditEntryView
1
*
1
*
1
*

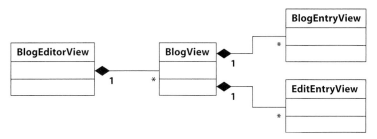

Figure 8–4. UML diagram for the application's view

The `BlogEditorView` class, the container for the application and the main widget added to the HTML page through the `RootPanel` class, renders the application. The `BlogView` class acts as the view of one blog; the `BlogEntryView` class presents the view of one entry; and the `EditEntryView` class presents the view of editing an existing entry or writing a new entry.

For the view's layout we'll take advantage of everyone being familiar and comfortable with browsing content within a web page using the vertical scrollbar or a scroll wheel by displaying content vertically. This will also be intuitive for a blog editor, since blogs are typically listed vertically in reverse chronological order. So the `BlogEditorView` will list `BlogViews` vertically, which will in turn list `BlogEntryViews` vertically. Figure 8-5 shows a screenshot of the `BlogEditorView` with its child views.

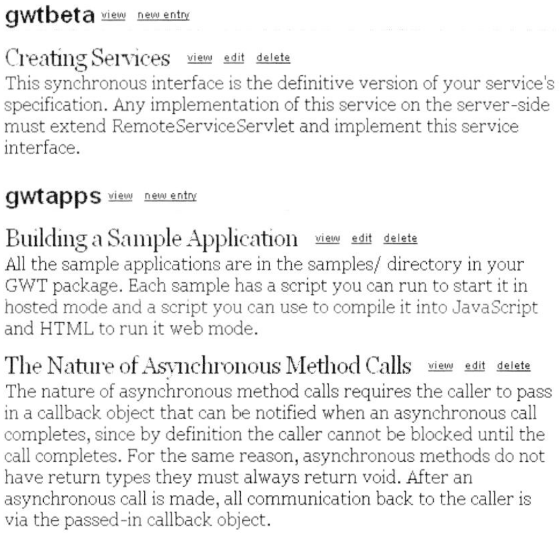

gwtbeta view new entry
Creating Services view edit delete
This synchronous interface is the definitive version of your service's specification. Any implementation of this service on the server-side must extend RemoteServiceServlet and implement this service interface.
gwtapps view new entry
Building a Sample Application view edit delete
All the sample applications are in the samples/ directory in your GWT package. Each sample has a script you can run to start it in hosted mode and a script you can use to compile it into JavaScript and HTML to run it web mode.
The Nature of Asynchronous Method Calls view edit delete
The nature of asynchronous method calls requires the caller to pass in a callback object that can be notified when an asynchronous call completes, since by definition the caller cannot be blocked until the call completes. For the same reason, asynchronous methods do not have return types they must always return void. After an asynchronous call is made, all communication back to the caller is via the passed-in callback object.

Figure 8–5. The `BlogEditorView` showing entries from two blogs

The `BlogEditorView` Class

Let's look at the code for the view, starting with the main view, the `Blog EditorView`:

```
public class BlogEditorView extends Composite {
    private VerticalPanel blogList = new VerticalPanel();
    private HTML status = new HTML();
    private LoadingPanel loadingPanel = new LoadingPanel( new Label("Loading") );
    private LoadingPanel savingPanel = new LoadingPanel( new Label( "Saving" ) );
    private Map blogViews = new HashMap();
    private Map postViews = new HashMap();

    public BlogEditorView(){
        initWidget( blogList );
        blogList.add(status);
        blogList.add(loadingPanel);
        blogList.add(savingPanel);
    }
    public LoadingPanel getLoadingPanel(){
        return loadingPanel;
    }
    public LoadingPanel getSavingPanel(){
        return savingPanel;
    }
    public void addBlog( Blog blog, BlogViewListener listener ){
        BlogView blogView = new BlogView( blog, listener );
        blogList.add( blogView );
        blogViews.put( blog, blogView );
    }
    public BlogView getBlogView( Blog blog ){
        return (BlogView)blogViews.get( blog );
    }
    public void setError( String error ){
        status.setText(error);
    }
}
```

The `BlogEditorView` class extends `Composite` so that it can be used within GWT's widget framework. A `Composite` is a widget and has basic widget functionality, including the ability to have a child widget. The `Composite` class itself does not represent any screen real estate. You would use this class when you want a logical representation of a widget that contains other widgets whose functionality you don't want to expose in your widget's interface through an inheritance relationship.

The `BlogEditorView` has the simple functionality of managing the list of `BlogView` instances and other user interface features that are global to the application. The list of `BlogView` instances is stored in the `blogList` `VerticalPanel`. The `VerticalPanel` is a GWT widget that displays its children vertically. In this case it will display the list of blogs vertically. In this class' constructor the `blogList` is set to be the main widget through the `initWidget` method. The other widgets used in the class include a status `Label`, which will display error information received through the `setError` method, and a `loadingPanel` and a `savingPanel` that will display a message to the user when the application is busy sending or receiving data from the blog service. These last two widgets are instances of the `LoadingPanel`, which displays a loading indication in the browser as shown in Figure 8-6. We will discuss the `LoadingPanel` widget in detail later in this chapter.

Figure 8–6. Indicating asynchronous loading with the `LoadingPanel` widget

The `BlogEditorView` class also keeps a list of `BlogView` instances in a `HashMap` with the key to the `HashMap` being a `Blog` instance from the application's model. This is a mechanism for the application to find a `BlogView` instance that represents the view of a `Blog` instance. The `HashMap` is built when `Blog` instances are added to the view through the `addBlog` method. This method's job is to add a view representing a `Blog` instance to the application. In the method implementation a new `BlogView` class is created and added to the `blogList`'s `VerticalPanel` and to the `HashMap` lookup. The method also takes a listener instance of the class `BlogViewListener`, which is an interface implemented by other parts of the application, specifically the controller, to listen and respond to interface events. The `BlogViewListener` interface looks like this:

```
public interface BlogViewListener {
    void onEntrySaved( BlogEntry entry );
    void onEntryDeleted( BlogEntry entry );
}
```

The application calls the `onEntrySaved` method when the user is done editing or writing an entry and clicks the Save button. The `onEntryDeleted` method is called when the user clicks the Delete button on an entry. The controller implementing these methods must invoke the appropriate actions on the blog service.

The `BlogView` Class

The `BlogView` class is responsible for presenting the view for one blog. It has more responsibility than the `BlogEditorView` class, since it provides management for a blog, for the views for all of the blog's entries, and for each entry's edit views. Figure 8-7 shows each `BlogView` instance surrounded with a border that illustrates the views for two different blogs.

Figure 8–7.   Two blogs listed in the view

To understand the `BlogView` class we will look at it in segments. We'll start with the constructor of the class:

```
public class BlogView extends Composite{
    private Blog blog;
    private Map entryViews = new HashMap();
    private VerticalPanel entries = new VerticalPanel();
    private BlogViewListener listener;
```

```
public BlogView( Blog blog, BlogViewListener listener ){
    this.blog = blog;
    this.listener = listener;

    VerticalPanel container = new VerticalPanel();
    initWidget( container );

    TitleCommandBar titleBar = new TitleCommandBar( blog.getTitle());
    titleBar.addWidget( new Link("view", blog.getLink(),
        Link.TARGET_NEW_WINDOW) );
    titleBar.addCommand( "new entry", new ClickListener(){
        public void onClick( Widget sender ){
            BlogEntry entry = new BlogEntry( BlogView.this.blog);
            EditEntryView editEntryView = new EditEntryView(
                BlogView.this, entry );
            entries.insert( editEntryView , 0 );
            entryViews.put( entry, editEntryView );
        }
    });
    container.add( titleBar );
    container.add( entries );

    setStyleName("blogView");
    titleBar.addStyleName("blogViewTitle");
    entries.setStyleName("blogEntries");
}
```

Like the `BlogEditorView` class, this class is also a `Composite` widget with a `VerticalPanel` as its main widget to display its children vertically. The first child added to the view is a `TitleCommandBar`. This widget displays a title followed horizontally with a list of commands. You can use the widget as a space-saving section heading that has some available commands. Typically this widget looks like the screenshot in Figure 8-8.

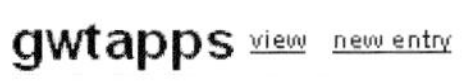

gwtapps view new entry

Figure 8–8. An example of a `TitleCommandBar` widget

The `TitleCommandBar` is described in detail later in this chapter. For now let's look at how it's used in the constructor. The widget has a method named `addCommand` which allows you to add a command built from a string for its label text and a `ClickListener` to respond to a click event. In this constructor we add a **new entry** command using the `addCommand` method and implement its `ClickListener` to create a new `BlogEntry` and a new `BlogEntryView`.

A `Link` widget (described in Chapter 7) is also added to the command bar using its `addWidget` method. The link goes to the HTML page for the blog hosted by the blog server. Clicking this link will open a new window which loads the blog page. This is useful to see how the blog looks to its visitors.

Now let's look at the methods in the `BlogView` class that are responsible for adding `BlogEntry`'s to the view:

```
public void addEntryAtStart( BlogEntry entry ){
    BlogEntryView entryView = new BlogEntryView( this, entry );
    entries.insert( entryView, 0 );
    entryViews.put( entry, entryView );
}

public void addEntryAtEnd( BlogEntry entry ){
    BlogEntryView entryView = new BlogEntryView( this, entry );
    entries.add( entryView );
    entryViews.put( entry, entryView );
}
```

Both methods—addEntryAtStart and addEntryAtEnd—create a new `BlogEntryView` based on the `BlogEntry` instance supplied as a parameter, and add it to the entry's `VerticalPanel` to be displayed. The addEntryAtStart method uses the `VerticalPanel`'s insert method with an index of zero to add the `BlogEntryView` to the start of the list. The addEntryAtEnd method uses the `VerticalPanel`'s add method to include the new `BlogEntryView` to the end of the list. Finally, each method adds the new view to the `entryViews HashMap`. This map is used at other places in the application when a `BlogEntryView` needs to be found based on a `BlogEntry` instance.

The rest of the `BlogView` class deals with managing the child `Blog EntryViews` so that they can be edited in place. This means that when they are edited, the current unchangeable display of the entry is transformed into a changeable one and remains in the same spot on the page. This intuitive technique will not disorient the user with page refreshes. The `BlogView` accomplishes this by switching a `BlogEntryView` and an `EditEntryView` and vice versa depending on the action. When a user edits an entry, the application removes the `BlogEntryView` and puts an `EditEntryView` in its place. When the user finishes with the `Edit EntryView`, it is removed and replaced by a `BlogEntryView`. The following code manages this activity:

```
public void onEntrySaved(
   BlogEntryView entryView, EditEntryView editEntryView, BlogEntry entry ){
   listener.onEntrySaved( entry );
   if( entryView != null ){
      entryView.update();
      entryView.getBlogView().endEdit( editEntryView, entryView);
   }
   else{
      addEntryAtStart( entry );
      editEntryView.removeFromParent();
   }
}

public void startEdit( BlogEntryView entryView ){
   EditEntryView editEntryView = new EditEntryView( entryView );
   swapViews( entryView, editEntryView, entryView.getEntry() );
}

public void endEdit( EditEntryView editEntryView, BlogEntryView entryView ){
   swapViews( editEntryView, entryView, entryView.getEntry() );
}

public void swapViews( Widget oldView, Widget newView, BlogEntry entry){
   int index = entries.getWidgetIndex(oldView);
   oldView.removeFromParent();
   entries.insert( newView, index );
   entryViews.put( entry, newView );
}
```

In this code, the onEntrySaved method is called by an EditEntryView after the user clicks on the Save button. The method passes the entry being saved on to the listener so that it can invoke the appropriate save action on the blog service. Then it replaces the EditEntryView with a BlogEntryView in one of two ways. If the entry being saved is a new entry, denoted by the entryView being null, a new BlogEntryView is created by calling the addEntryAtStart method and the EditEntryView is removed. If the entry being saved is an existing entry, its BlogEntryView is updated with the new edited entry data and the endEdit method is called.

The startEdit and endEdit methods are responsible for doing the swap between the constant BlogEntryView and the changeable EditEntryView. The startEdit method removes the specified BlogEntryView instance and replaces it with a new EditEntryView instance. It does this by getting the index of the BlogEntryView instance in the entry's VerticalPanel, removing the BlogEntryView instance, and inserting the new `EditEntryView` instance at the same index. The `endEdit` method does the reverse operation of removing the `Edit EntryView` instance, replacing it with the `BlogEntryView` instance.

The `BlogEntryView` Class

Now let's look at the `BlogEntryView` class. This class displays a `BlogEntry` to the user and provides buttons for the user to manage the entry. The screenshot in Figure 8-9 shows the `BlogEntryView` instances surrounded by a border to illustrate how and where they are rendered.

gwtbeta view new entry

Creating Services view edit delete
This synchronous interface is the definitive version of your service's specification. Any implementation of this service on the server-side must extend RemoteServiceServlet and implement this service interface.

gwtapps view new entry

Building a Sample Application view edit delete
All the sample applications are in the samples/ directory in your GWT package. Each sample has a script you can run to start it in hosted mode and a script you can use to compile it into JavaScript and HTML to run it web mode.

The Nature of Asynchronous Method Calls view edit delete
The nature of asynchronous method calls requires the caller to pass in a callback object that can be notified when an asynchronous call completes, since by definition the caller cannot be blocked until the call completes. For the same reason, asynchronous methods do not have return types they must always return void. After an asynchronous call is made, all communication back to the caller is via the passed-in callback object.

Figure 8–9.   Instances of the `BlogEntryView` class

The following code for the class implements this view:

```
public class BlogEntryView extends Composite {
    private BlogView blogView;
    private BlogEntry entry;
    private HTML content = new HTML();
    private TitleCommandBar titleBar;
    private Link viewLink;

    private class EditClickListener implements ClickListener {
        public void onClick( Widget sender ) {
            blogView.startEdit( BlogEntryView.this );
        }
    }
}
```

```
   private class DeleteClickListener implements ClickListener {
      public void onClick( Widget sender ) {
         if( Window.confirm( "Are you sure you want to delete '"+
            BlogEntryView.this.entry.getTitle()+"'?") ) {
            blogView.getListener().onEntryDeleted( entry );
            removeFromParent();
         }
      }
   }

   public BlogEntryView( BlogView blogView, BlogEntry entry ){
      this.blogView = blogView;
      this.entry = entry;

      VerticalPanel postPanel = new VerticalPanel();
      initWidget( postPanel );

      titleBar = new TitleCommandBar( entry.getTitle() );
      viewLink = new Link( "view", entry.getLink(), Link.TARGET_NEW_WINDOW );
      titleBar.addWidget( viewLink );
      titleBar.addCommand( "edit", new EditClickListener() );
      titleBar.addCommand( "delete", new DeleteClickListener() );
      postPanel.add( titleBar );
      postPanel.add( content );
      postPanel.setStyleName("postPanel");
      content.setStyleName("postContent");
      titleBar.addStyleName("entryViewTitle");
      update();
   }

   public void update(){
      titleBar.setText( entry.getTitle() );
      content.setHTML( entry.getContent() );
      viewLink.setLink( entry.getLink() );
   }

   public BlogEntry getEntry(){
      return entry;
   }

   public BlogView getBlogView(){
      return blogView;
   }
}
```

This class is also a `Composite` that displays its children vertically using a
`VerticalPanel` as its main widget. It also uses a `TitleCommandBar`
widget to display the entry's title and the commands that are possible for

the entry. First, a view link which points to the entry's blog service web page is added to the command bar. Second, an edit command is added; this has a `ClickListener` that calls the `startEdit` method on the blog view, which causes this view to be removed and replaced with an `Edit EntryView` instance. Third, a delete command is added. This command has a `ClickListener` that uses GWT's `Window.confirm` method to display a dialog box that asks the user if deleting the entry is what was intended. If the user selects yes, the `onEntryDelete` method is called on the `BlogViewListener`, causing the controller to invoke the appropriate delete method on the server, and this `BlogEntryView` instance is removed from the list.

The entry's content is displayed beneath the title bar in an HTML widget. Using GWT's HTML widget allows any HTML codes in the entry to be rendered properly. The entry's content, title, and link are updated into their corresponding widgets with the `update` method.

The `EditEntryView` Class

The final class in the application's view is the `EditEntryView`. This class is responsible for the widgets for editing an existing entry and writing a new one. When rendered in the browser, this class looks like the screenshot in Figure 8-10.

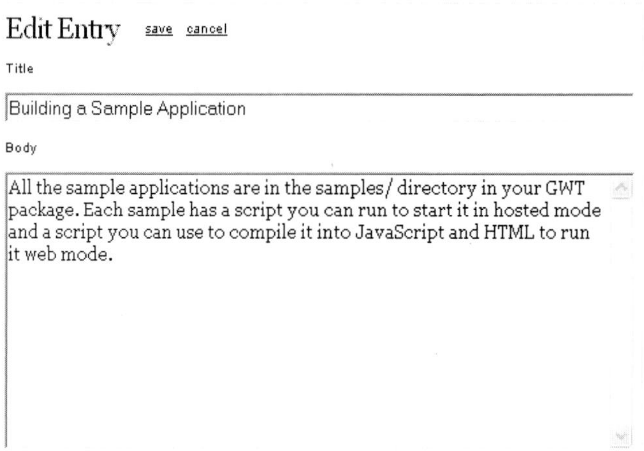

Figure 8–10.   An instance of the `EditEntryView` class

The following code implements the `EditEntryView` class:

```java
public class EditEntryView extends Composite {
    private BlogEntry entry;
    private BlogEntryView entryView;
    private BlogView blogView;
    private TitleCommandBar titleBar = new TitleCommandBar( "New Entry" );
    private TextBox postTitle = new TextBox();
    private TextArea postContent = new TextArea();

    private class SaveClickListener implements ClickListener{
        public void onClick( Widget sender ){
            entry.setTitle( postTitle.getText() );
            entry.setContent( postContent.getText() );
            blogView.onEntrySaved( entryView, EditEntryView.this, entry );
        }
    }

    private class CancelClickListener implements ClickListener{
        public void onClick( Widget sender ){
            if( entryView != null )
                entryView.getBlogView().endEdit( EditEntryView.this, entryView );
            else removeFromParent();
        }
    }

    public EditEntryView( BlogView blogView, BlogEntry entry ){
        this.entry = entry;
        this.blogView = blogView;
        VerticalPanel postPanel = new VerticalPanel();
        initWidget( postPanel );

        titleBar.addCommand( "save", new SaveClickListener() );
        titleBar.addCommand( "cancel", new CancelClickListener() );
        postPanel.add( titleBar );

        Label titleLabel = new Label("Title");
        postPanel.add( titleLabel );
        postPanel.add( postTitle );

        Label contentLabel = new Label("Body");
        postPanel.add( contentLabel );
        postPanel.add( postContent );
    }

    public EditEntryView( BlogEntryView entryView ){
        this( entryView.getBlogView(), entryView.getEntry() );
        this.entryView = entryView;
```

```
        titleBar.setText( "Edit Entry" );
        postTitle.setText( entry.getTitle() );
        postContent.setText( entry.getContent() );
    }
}
```

The `EditEntryView` class has two constructors: one for new posts and the other for existing posts. It also has two `ClickListener` implementations: one to handle a click on the save command and the other to handle a click on the cancel command.

The first constructor, used to create a view to write a new blog entry, starts by setting its main widget to a `VerticalPanel` widget. The `VerticalPanel` layout is used to display the `TitleCommandBar`, the `Label` and `TextBox` for the entry's title, and the `Label` and `TextArea` for the entry's content. The `TitleCommandBar` has the save and cancel commands added to it with the `SaveClickListener` and `CancelClickListener` to handle the click events.

When the user clicks save, the `SaveClickListener` copies the values from the title's `TextBox` widget and the content's `TextArea` widget back to the entry so that the entry has the updated values. Then the `SaveClick Listener` calls the `onEntrySaved` method on its parent `BlogView`, which in turn manages removing this `EditEntryView`, replacing it with a `BlogEntryView` and then passing the `onSave` event to the controller.

When the user clicks cancel, the `CancelClickListener` calls `endEdit` on the parent `BlogView`, which in turn removes this `EditEntryView` instance from the view and replaces it with the original `BlogEntryView`. If the user clicks cancel on a new entry, this `EditEntryView` instance is simply removed from the view.

The second constructor is used to edit an existing entry. This constructor calls the first constructor to share the layout creation code, and also copies the values from the entry passed into the constructor as a parameter to the title's `TextBox` widget and the content's `TextArea` widget so the existing values are displayed initially.

These four classes—`BlogEditorView`, `BlogView`, `BlogEntryView`, and `EditEntryView`—provide the view structure needed to manage the entries on many blogs. When the view is attached to the controller and receives model objects, it looks like the screenshot in Figure 8-11.

Figure 8–11. The application's view when attached to the controller

The next three sections look at additional user interface widgets used in this application: GWT's `RichTextArea` widget, which lets users create and edit more than just plain text in a blog entry's body; the `Loading-Panel` widget, which displays a notification to the user when an asynchronous operation is pending; and the `TitleCommandBar`, which displays a label followed by several commands on a single line.

Adding Rich Text Editing

One of the most difficult cross-browser tasks is creating rich text editing. As of GWT 1.4, the toolkit includes a `RichTextArea` widget, which dramatically reduces the work involved in providing this functionality. Using this widget in our application will allow us to edit rich text in blog entries, as shown in Figure 8-12. The rich text will also be sent to the blog service and will show up as rich text on the hosted blog, which you can see in Figure 8-13.

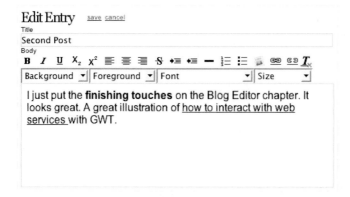

Figure 8–12.   Editing a blog entry in rich text

Figure 8–13.   A rich text blog entry hosted at www.blogger.com

Using `RichTextArea`

We'll use the `RichTextArea` widget as a replacement for the `TextArea` widget used in the `EditEntryView` class. The `RichTextArea` acts in a very similar way, so replacing the `TextArea` widget is fairly straightforward. First, we need to replace the `TextArea` declaration with the `RichTextArea` Declaration:

```
private RichTextArea postContent = new RichTextArea();
```

The `postContent` field variable is used throughout the class in the same way it was used as a `TextArea`. However, one change needs to be made. Currently the `postContent` instance has its text set and read using the setText and getText methods. The RichTextArea has both of these methods, but the text returned does not have the HTML markup that is required to render rich text. We need to change these methods to use the setHTML and getHTML methods on the RichTextArea. In the constructor, the setHTML method is used to transfer the content of the blog entry to the RichTextArea:

```
postContent.setHTML( entry.getContent() );
```

In the SaveClickListener's onClick method, called when the entry is saved, we can retrieve the HTML from the RichTextArea to add to the blog entry object:

```
entry.setContent( postContent.getHTML() );
```

With these simple changes we have installed the RichTextArea widget into the application. This allows us to display HTML in an editable text area, but there is no way for the user to create rich text. The user can only type into the text area and regular text will appear. The control is missing a toolbar with formatting options. However, we can use code for the Rich TextToolbar class from the GWT samples to easily add a toolbar.

Using **ImageBundle**, **Internationalization**, and the **RichTextToolbar**

GWT 1.4 includes a RichTextArea widget but leaves it to you to provide a way for a user to format the text inside. However, there is a great example of a toolbar that is used for formatting text in a RichTextArea in the GWT 1.4 Kitchen Sink sample called RichTextToolbar. The toolbar provides some of the basic formatting options available and is perfectly suitable for the Blog Editor application.

The implementation of the RichTextToolbar is very interesting; it uses some of the more advanced features of GWT, including ImageBundle for the images used in the toolbar buttons and internationalization for the strings in the toolbar's list boxes.

Using an ImageBundle for the toolbar is a technique that improves the application's loading time performance by bundling many individual images into a single image. Downloading a single large image from a server over HTTP is quite a bit faster than downloading many small images. Let's have a quick look at how this toolbar implements an instance of the `ImageBundle`:

```
public interface Images extends ImageBundle {

    /**
     * @gwt.resource bold.gif
     */
    AbstractImagePrototype bold();

    /**
     * @gwt.resource createLink.gif
     */
    AbstractImagePrototype createLink();

    /**
     * @gwt.resource hr.gif
     */
    AbstractImagePrototype hr();

    /**
     * @gwt.resource indent.gif
     */
    AbstractImagePrototype indent();
```

These are only the first few images, but the rest of the interface is similar. The interface extends the GWT `ImageBundle` interface to let the GWT compiler know that this is an image bundle that needs to be constructed during the compilation step. Each method returns an `Abstract ImagePrototype` that is capable of creating instances of the selected image. The GWT compiler knows how to link the image file with each method call through the `@gwt.resource` annotations. The annotations require the value to be the file's location. In this example the location is the filename without a path, so the image files need to be in the same location as this class file. To use this interface you need to create an instance using GWT's deferred binding:

```
private Images images = (Images) GWT.create(Images.class);
```

You can then add the image to a button on the toolbar like this:

```
ToggleButton tb = new ToggleButton(images.bold().createImage());
```

The performance gained from using image bundles is well worth their use. However, there are other reasons to use this GWT feature. For instance, they help you avoid a choppy loading interface that is common with image-heavy Ajax applications. This happens when the browser loads each image independently to construct the interface, but doesn't know the size of the image in advance. The image bundle ensures that the images used are initially sized properly. Also, the images used in the image bundle automatically provide support for PNG transparency in IE6.

The internationalization support with the `RichEditToolbar` follows a similar pattern as the image bundle: it uses the GWT compile step to generate the implementation of an interface as well. In this case the interface returns a string value from each of its methods:

```
public interface Strings extends Constants {

    String black();

    String blue();

    String bold();

    String color();
```

How you implement these methods depends on the local set for the application. The GWT compiler pulls the string values from a properties file for each locale. The default properties file is saved as `RichTextToolbar$Strings.properties`. The file name maps to the `Strings`' inner class on the `RichTextToolbar` class. Inside the file you see a simple list of strings identified by names:

```
black = Black
blue = Blue
bold = Toggle Bold
color = Color
```

The GWT compiler matches the names in the property file to the method names on the interface. You can create an instance of the interface using GWT deferred binding like this:

```
private Strings strings = (Strings) GWT.create(Strings.class);
```

A string can then be retrieved in the application code from this instance when needed:

```
tb.setTitle(strings.bold());
```

There is quite a bit more to internationalization. For more information refer to the discussion on internationalization in Chapter 5.

Adding the `RichEditToolbar` to our application is straightforward. We simply need to create a new instance of the class, passing the `RichTextArea` instance as a parameter to the constructor and then adding the toolbar to the view:

```
postPanel.add( new RichTextToolbar( postContent) );
```

As you can see, it is quite easy to use this toolbar from the GWT sample application. One thing that you should remember to do if you're going to use this widget in another application is to copy the image files and the properties file that are used with the toolbar in the GWT sample.

The `LoadingPanel` Widget

Ajax applications address many usability issues with traditional web pages, but in some situations they introduce new issues. These new issues usually stem from users being familiar with browser features in traditional web pages that might not apply to Ajax web pages. For example, when you click a button or a link on a web page you typically wait for the page to refresh. Several indicators let you know that the browser is busy satisfying your request, including the page going blank, loading messages on the status bar, the cursor changing to indicate progress, and usually an animated image in the browser frame's top, right corner. Unfortunately, when an Ajax application is working on an asynchronous request, the browser doesn't show any of these signs of work being done. This could leave users wondering what's going on or possibly thinking that their action was never registered.

So we should try to solve this potential confusion. The solution is to create indicators to let users know that the application is working on a request. The `LoadingPanel` widget does this by its display in the top, right corner, where the user can look to see if the browser is working on a request (refer back to Figure 8-6). In addition to the indication in the top, right corner, the `LoadingPanel` changes the cursor to the progress cursor, which is actually two cursors in one: It has the pointer cursor, allowing users to still click, and it also displays an hourglass to indicate progress is being made in the background. The cursor typically looks like Figure 8-14.

Figure 8–14. The progress cursor

This is perfect behavior for an asynchronous operation where we want to indicate the user can still interact with the application while waiting for the previous action to complete.

The following code shows the implementation of this class:

```
public class LoadingPanel extends SimplePanel{
   private int loadCount = 0;

   public LoadingPanel(){
      setStyleName( "gwtapps-LoadingPanel" );
      setVisible( false );
   }

   public LoadingPanel( Widget child ){
      this();
      setWidget( child );
   }

   public void loadingBegin(){
      if( loadCount == 0 ){
         setVisible( true );
         DOM.setStyleAttribute(
            RootPanel.getBodyElement(), "cursor", "progress");
         setPosition();
      }
      loadCount++;
   }

   public void loadingEnd(){
      loadCount--;
      if( loadCount == 0 ){
         setVisible( false );
         DOM.setStyleAttribute(RootPanel.getBodyElement(), "cursor", "");
      }
   }
}

   public void setPosition(){
      Widget child = getWidget();
      int top = DOM.getIntAttribute( RootPanel.getBodyElement(),"scrollTop");
      int left = Window.getClientWidth() - child.getOffsetWidth()   +
         DOM.getIntAttribute( RootPanel.getBodyElement(), "scrollLeft");
      DOM.setStyleAttribute(getElement(),"position","absolute" );
```

```
    DOM.setStyleAttribute(getElement(),"top",  Integer.toString( top ) );
    DOM.setStyleAttribute(getElement(),"left",Integer.toString( left ) );
  }
}
```

This code implements the `LoadingPanel` widget as a `SimplePanel`, which means it takes one child widget. Initially it sets itself to not be visible, and waits for the application to tell it something is loading with the `loadingBegin` method. Since the application is capable of more than one asynchronous request at a time, the `loadingBegin` method keeps a count of how many times it has been called so that the class knows to hide the panel when the last asynchronous request completes. The first time the `loadingBegin` method is called, it makes the panel visible, sets the cursor for the body element to the progress cursor using the `setStyle Attribute` from GWT's DOM class, and calls the `setPosition` method to move the panel to the top, right corner. The `loadingEnd` counter is decremented until zero, when it makes the panel invisible again and removes the cursor property from the body element. Adding the cursor to the body element is the easiest way to change the cursor for the entire web page. Of course, this cursor will not display when the cursor hovers over other elements that have a cursor property set (for example, a link).

This widget's behavior is a subtle and familiar indication to users that the application is working on a request.

The `TitleCommandBar` Widget

If you go through the process of creating many user interfaces, you start to bump into areas where you're writing the same code over and over again. In these situations you wrap the code up in a class to make reuse easier in the future. The `TitleCommandBar` is one of these situations. Although it doesn't build any new functionality, it implements a class that handles the common occurrence of needing a section title with a few available commands. With GWT you would typically implement this scenario with a `Label` for the title and then buttons or links for the commands. Then you would throw these widgets into some sort of panel, possibly vertical, maybe horizontal, or maybe a grid. Then you would have to deal with formatting the layout so that it is consistent.

The `TitleCommandBar` is a simple layout for a section title with commands. It aligns the child command widgets in a consistent way so that similar section titles will look the same throughout the application. It's not a terribly exciting widget, but it is a useful one that implements a common task.

This widget was used previously in the Blog Editor application to implement both a blog section title and a blog entry section title, as illustrated in Figure 8-15.

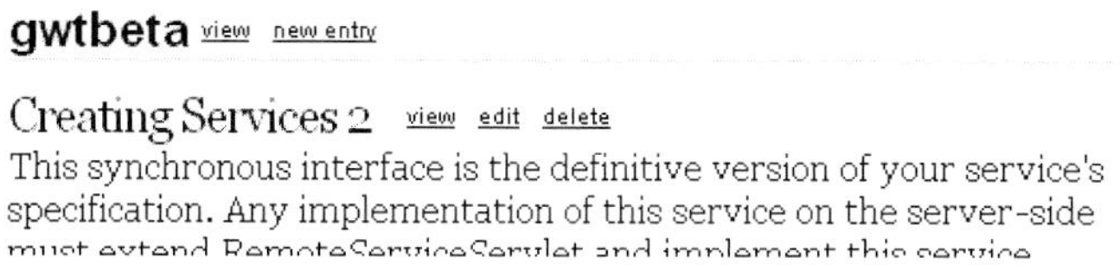

gwtbeta view new entry

Creating Services 2   view edit delete
This synchronous interface is the definitive version of your service's specification. Any implementation of this service on the server-side must extend RemoteServiceServlet and implement this service

Figure 8–15.   Example of the `TitleCommandBar` widget

In Figure 8-15 you can see one `TitleCommandBar` with the title "gwtbeta" and the view and new entry commands, and the second `TitleCommandBar`, "Create Services 2," and its view, edit, and delete commands. Now let's look at the implementation for the `TitleCommandBar` class:

```
public class TitleCommandBar extends Composite{
    private Label titleLabel;
    private HorizontalPanel titlePanel = new HorizontalPanel();
    private Widget lastCommand;

    public TitleCommandBar( String title ){
        initWidget( titlePanel );
        titlePanel.setWidth("100%");
        setStyleName("gwtapps-TitleBar");
        titleLabel = new Label( title );
        titleLabel.setStyleName("gwtapps-TitleBarTitle");
        titleLabel.setWordWrap( false );
        titlePanel.add( titleLabel );
    }

    public void addWidget( Widget widget ){
        if( lastCommand != null )
            titlePanel.setCellWidth(lastCommand, "");
        lastCommand = widget;
        titlePanel.add( lastCommand );
        titlePanel.setCellWidth(lastCommand, "100%");
        titlePanel.setCellVerticalAlignment(
        lastCommand, HasVerticalAlignment.ALIGN_MIDDLE );
    }
```

```
public void addCommand( String name, ClickListener command ){
    Hyperlink hyperlink = new Hyperlink( name, null );
    hyperlink.addClickListener( command );
    hyperlink.setStyleName("gwtapps-TitleBarCommand");
    addWidget( hyperlink );
}

public void setText( String text ){
    titleLabel.setText(text);
}
}
```

The `TitleCommandBar` widget is a `Composite` that sets it main widget to a `HorizontalPanel`. The class does not inherit from `HorizontalPanel` because we don't want to expose all of its methods. Instead, the class provides methods to add commands or widgets next to the title.

The title is displayed in a `Label` widget and has its word wrap property set to false. This ensures that the label will take up as much horizontal space as it needs without wrapping. This is important since the class sets the cell in the `HorizontalPanel` that holds the last command or widget to take up 100 percent of the width. This would push the title `Label` to be wrapped to multiple lines, which is not ideal for readability. Making the final command cell width 100 percent ensures that the title bar can stretch to the entire width of its parent while having the commands pushed to the left side, to the right of the label. Otherwise the commands would be evenly spread throughout the command bar, which could disassociate them from the title. The class has several of these internal layout settings to get the layout looking just right, which can sometimes be a tedious task.

In addition to the layout settings, the code in this class adds widgets and commands in the form of `Hyperlink` widgets to the `HorizontalPanel` to the right of the title. To do this the code calls the `addCommand` method and passes new `Hyperlink` widgets with `ClickListener` defined.

Designing the Application Controller

The controller part of this application has the hefty task of communicating with the blog service, providing model instances for the view to render, and responding to user actions from the view. This chapter has already defined the model and the view, so you already know how the controller needs to plug into these parts of the application. First, the controller needs to connect to the blog service, retrieve the list of blogs available for a particular account, and load the blog entries for each blog. It converts this data to the model objects `Blog` and `BlogEntry` and passes them to the view to be rendered. Once rendered, users can create new entries and edit or delete existing entries. The view passes these actions to the controller so that it can invoke the corresponding action on the web service.

We also want to make it possible to add other blog services to the application, so we need to build a structure to allow that. The view is already capable of displaying multiple blogs, so it will also be able to display multiple blogs from different services without any changes. Each `BlogView` is created with a listener pointer as a parameter, which gives the controller the ability to set a different listener for each blog and to have blog service objects listen to the events that occur from the view on their own blogs only.

The controller implementation begins with the `BlogEditor` class, which has the simple task of implementing GWT's `EntryPoint` interface and its `onModuleLoad` method in which it builds a new `BlogEditorView` and any blog services that will be used:

```
public class BlogEditor implements EntryPoint{
    public void onModuleLoad() {
        BlogEditorView view = new BlogEditorView();
        RootPanel.get("blogEditorView").add( view );
        BloggerService blogger = new BloggerService( view );
        blogger.signin();
    }
}
```

In this code we use just one blog service, `BloggerService`, which connects to the blogger network, but we could create other services by simply instantiating them here and passing them the view. Figure 8-16 illustrates the structural relations between the classes in the controller's architecture.

Figure 8-16 shows what the structure looks like with two blog services. Each blog service instantiates and calls methods on the `BlogViews` that present their blogs, and the `BlogViews` send user interface events back to the blog service instance through the `BlogViewListener` interface.

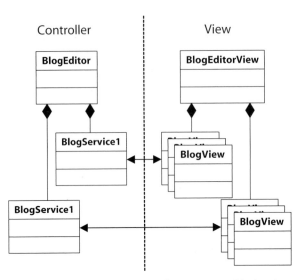

Figure 8–16. UML diagram of how the controller interacts with the view

For this sample application we will just implement one blog service to show you how to communicate with a web service using GWT. We'll use the Blogger blog service since it provides a REST API-based GDdata, which is Google's REST protocol based on the Atom Publishing Protocol. But before getting into how to communicate with Blogger, we need to address the Same Origin policy problem with an HTTP proxy.

Building an HTTP Proxy Servlet

We first discussed the Same Origin policy in Chapter 3, and in the Multi-Search sample application in Chapter 7 you saw a client-based solution implemented to bypass the policy for data feeds (see Chapter 3 for more information about the Same Origin policy). The solution for the Multi-Search example took advantage of the browser's ability to load a script from a different domain through a `script` tag, which allowed the application to load data from other domains in the JSON format as JavaScript files. This solution works well when you need to load data, but isn't sufficient when you need interaction that is richer, such as submitting structured data that has any amount of complexity.

Interacting with a web service typically involves more than just retrieving data from a URL. For the Blogger service we need to be able to get, create, modify, and delete data. We also need access to HTTP headers to provide session tokens for security. This type of interaction is not possible either through a `script` tag or by using Ajax asynchronous requests due to a browser's Same Origin policy. The best alternative is to interact with the Blogger web service on the server side, since it doesn't have a browser's security restrictions.

So, the solution for the Blog Editor application goes like this. The browser sends asynchronous HTTP requests that mirror the requests it would make to Blogger to its own server, (this is what the Same Origin policy allows). We then have a light servlet running on the server which accepts these requests and forwards them to the Blogger web service. The web service's response is then relayed back to the client application. Figure 8-17 illustrates this process.

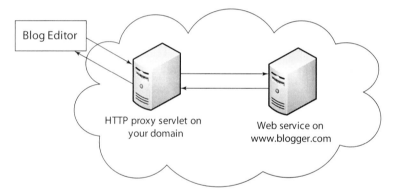

Figure 8–17.   How a proxy server is used to bypass the Same Origin policy

The proxy servlet can run in any servlet container, but for development we will use the Tomcat server that is integrated with the GWT browser. If you're not familiar with Java servlets, the concept is pretty simple. A servlet container is an HTTP server like Apache or IIS with the additional ability to load a Java class called a servlet. The Java class extends the `HttpServlet` class and can implement HTTP methods by overriding the corresponding method from the superclass.

Of course, the HTTP proxy's implementation does not have to be a servlet. You could use pretty much any server-side technology to implement the same functionality. To hide the server implementation from the client we will build a client-side class that interacts with the server and provides methods similar to GWT's HTTP `RequestBuilder` class. The GWT HTTP

`RequestBuilder` class wraps the browser's ability to make asynchronous HTTP calls to the server. We will create an `HTTPProxyRequestBuilder` class that satisfies requests to external domains by using an HTTP `RequestBuilder` instance to communicate with our server proxy, which will make the request to the external domain.

A New Cross-Domain `RequestBuilder`

First let's compare the HTTP `RequestBuilder` class' usage with that of the `HTTPProxyRequestBuilder` class. To load a document asynchronously from our server, you would use the HTTP `RequestBuilder` class like this:

```
//create the request object
RequestBuilder requestBuilder = new RequestBuilder(
   RequestBuilder.GET, "/a_remote_file.xml" );
//send the request, the body of the request is null
requestBuilder.sendRequest( null, new RequestCallback(){
   public void onError(Request request, Throwable exception){
      //handle an error
   }
   public void onResponseReceived( Request request, Response response){
      //handle the response
   }
});
```

In this code an instance of a `RequestBuilder` is created specifying the HTTP method type. In this case the construction parameters are the GET method and the file to get from the server. The request is sent with the `sendRequest` method, passing in a `RequestCallback` instance that handles the asynchronous response. If the call fails the `onError` method is called, and if the call succeeds the `onResponseReceived` method is called.

For our `HTTPProxyRequestBuilder` we want to be able to satisfy requests to other domains with a similar interface so we don't need to learn a new way of making an HTTP request. So using the `HTTPProxyRequest Builder` would be very similar:

```
HTTPProxyRequestBuilder requestBuilder = new HTTPProxyRequestBuilder(
   RequestBuilder.GET, "http://www.otherdomain.com/file.xml");
requestBuilder.sendRequest( null, new RequestCallback(){
   public void onError(Request request, Throwable exception){
```

```
        //handle an error
    }
    public void onResponseReceived( Request request, Response response){
        //handle the response
    }
});
```

This code example highlights the differences. We simply substitute the HTTPProxyRequestBuilder class for the regular RequestBuilder and we can use other domains for the GET parameter.

Now let's look at the implementation code for this class. The following is the basic class with its setter methods implemented to mirror the RequestBuilder class:

```java
public class HTTPProxyRequestBuilder {
    private Map headers;
    private String password;
    private int timeoutMillis;
    private String user;
    private StringBuffer postBuilder = new StringBuffer();

    public void setHeader(String header, String value) {
        if (headers == null) {
            headers = new HashMap();
        }
        headers.put(header, value);
    }

    public void setPassword(String password) {
        this.password = password;
    }

    public void setTimeoutMillis(int timeoutMillis) {
        this.timeoutMillis = timeoutMillis;
    }

    public void setUser(String user) {
        this.user = user;
    }
}
```

These values are saved on the class until the request is sent using the sendRequest method. The sendRequest method will divert the request to our proxy and encode the parameters in the request. The code for the sendRequest method and its helpers looks like this:

```
public HTTPProxyRequestBuilder(String httpMethod, String url ) {
    postBuilder.append( "method=" );
    postBuilder.append( httpMethod );
    setParam("url",url);
}

protected void setParam( String key, String value ){
    postBuilder.append( "&" );
    postBuilder.append( key );
    postBuilder.append( "=" );
    postBuilder.append( URL.encodeComponent( value ) );
}

public Request sendRequest( String requestData, RequestCallback callback )
    throws RequestException {
    if( user != null )
        setParam( "user", user );
    if( password != null )
        setParam( "password", password );
    if( timeoutMillis > 0 )
        setParam( "timeout", Integer.toString( timeoutMillis ) );
    if( headers != null ){
        Set entrySet = headers.entrySet();
        for( Iterator iter = entrySet.iterator(); iter.hasNext(); ){
            Map.Entry header = (Map.Entry) iter.next();
            setParam( (String)header.getKey(), (String)header.getValue() );
        }
    }
    if( requestData != null )
        setParam( "post", requestData );
    RequestBuilder requestBuilder = new RequestBuilder(
        RequestBuilder.POST, GWT.getModuleBaseURL()+"/HTTPProxy" );
    requestBuilder.setHeader(
        "Content-type", "application/x-www-form-urlencoded");
    return requestBuilder.sendRequest( postBuilder.toString(), callback );
}
```

In the class' constructor a `StringBuffer` called `postBuilder` first has the HTTP method appended to it, followed by other variables encoded in a standard format that is usually used for HTML forms. We use this format because it is automatically interpreted and parsed by most server-side environments. It is simply an ampersand-delimited list of name-value pairs in the format `name=value`. The `setParam` method on the class does the work of creating this name-value pair and appending it to the `StringBuffer`. It uses GWT's `URL.encodeComponent` method to encode any control characters in the value. For example, if the value had an ampersand in it, it would get in the way of parsing the variables since an ampersand is used to delimit the variables, so the ampersand would be encoded to another value. Since `URL.encodeComponent` uses standard percent encoding, the server-side will automatically decode that.

In the `sendRequest` method all of the variables are appended to the `StringBuffer`, including all of the HTTP header variables and the requested URL. These values must be encoded as variables and not used in the request to the proxy. Instead we use a predefined URL (`GWT.getModule BaseURL()+"/HTTPProxy"`) and the `Content-type` header to send the variables to the proxy. The proxy will then use the variables to make the request to the desired server.

The request to the proxy is made with the standard HTTP `RequestBuilder` class. This is possible since the request is going to our server, so it does not violate the Same Origin policy. The request's `Content-Type` header to the proxy is set to `application/x-www-form-urlencoded`, which tells the server the format of the variables that are sent. The variables are passed as the post data on the `RequestBuilder.sendRequest` method, and the callback is set to the callback provided by the application, since it will return the result without any extra data. To the application it will seem like a direct request to the remote server.

Writing a Proxy Servlet

Now we need to look at the implementation of the proxy servlet. The class is called `HTTPProxy`, and it basically implements the HTTP POST method. Let's look at this class piece by piece. First the class is defined and extends `HttpServlet` so that it can be a servlet within a servlet container:

```
public class HTTPProxy extends HttpServlet
```

In this case the class implements just one method, `doPost`, to handle the HTTP POST method:

```
protected void doPost( HttpServletRequest req, HttpServletResponse res)
    throws ServletException, IOException
```

The method takes two parameters: a request and a response. The request represents the POST request from the client and contains all of the variables that were sent. The response contains the data that we are going to return to the client. The first thing this method needs to do is to get the variables out of the request:

```
URL url=null;
String user,password,method = "GET",post = null;
int timeout = 0;
Set entrySet = req.getParameterMap().entrySet();
Map headers = new HashMap();
for( Iterator iter = entrySet.iterator(); iter.hasNext(); ){
    Map.Entry header = (Map.Entry) iter.next();
    String key = (String)header.getKey();
    String value = ((String[])header.getValue())[0] ;
    if( key.equals("user") )
        user = value;
    else if( key.equals("password") )
        password = value;
    else if( key.equals("timeout") )
        timeout = Integer.parseInt( value );
    else if( key.equals("method") )
        method = value;
    else if( key,equals("post") )
        post = value;
    else if( key.equals("url") )
        url = new URL( value );
    else
        headers.put( key, value );
}
```

The variables are made available in the request's parameter map. The servlet container has taken the form-encoded variables and placed them in an easy-to-manage map with the variable name as a key and the value as the value. The preceding code iterates over this map and tries to match the variable with some of the parameters that we need for the external HTTP request, such as the HTTP method to use, the URL, and any data that needs to be posted. Any other variables are considered to be headers and are added to a header map.

Once all the variables are ready, the code makes a request to the remote server:

```
//use a loop for handling redirects
boolean complete = false;
while( !complete ){
    //set up the remote connection
    HttpURLConnection urlConnection = (HttpURLConnection)url.openConnection();
```

```
urlConnection.setDoOutput(true);
urlConnection.setDoInput(true);
urlConnection.setUseCaches(false);
urlConnection.setInstanceFollowRedirects(false);
urlConnection.setRequestMethod(method);
if( timeout > 0 ) urlConnection.setConnectTimeout(timeout);

//copy the headers to the new connection
Set headersSet = headers.entrySet();
for( Iterator iter=headersSet.iterator(); iter.hasNext(); ){
   Map.Entry header = (Map.Entry)iter.next();
   urlConnection.setRequestProperty(
      (String)header.getKey(),(String)header.getValue() );
}

//write post body to remote connection
if( post != null){
   OutputStreamWriter outRemote = new
      OutputStreamWriter(urlConnection.getOutputStream());
   outRemote.write( post );
   outRemote.flush();
}

//transfer contentType from remote connection
String contentType = urlConnection.getContentType();
if( contentType != null ) res.setContentType(contentType);

//check for a redirect
int responseCode = urlConnection.getResponseCode();
if( responseCode == 302 ){
   String location = urlConnection.getHeaderField("Location");
   url = new URL( location );
}
else{
   //read from the appropriate stream
   res.setStatus( responseCode );
   BufferedInputStream in;
   if( responseCode == 200 || responseCode == 201 )
      in = new BufferedInputStream(urlConnection.getInputStream());
   else
      in = new BufferedInputStream(urlConnection.getErrorStream());

   //send output to client
   BufferedOutputStream out =
      new BufferedOutputStream(res.getOutputStream());
   int c;
   while((c = in.read()) >= 0 )
      out.write(c);
```

```
        out.flush();
        complete = true;
    }
}
```

This code may seem too much to digest, but if you're interested, it's a good illustration of the basic tasks that need to be done to make an HTTP request. The code sits in a `while` loop since there may be redirects. It's possible for the Java classes used to handle the redirects automatically, but we actually want to provide specific behavior on a redirect. In particular, if the redirect happens when we are posting data, we want to repost the data to the new URL. This is something that is needed for some web services to work properly.

Other than that, the `HttpURLConnection` class handles most of the work. This code transfers the variables that were sent with the request to the new connection, including the HTTP method. If an application sends POST data, the code creates an output stream on the new connection and the POST data is written. The rest of the method deals with the output from the remote connection. The output is relayed to the client connection, so it seems to the client application that the data is being returned directly. This output includes sending the content type, the response code, and any data or error message.

Once the proxy reads the data, it flushes the data and the client side will receive an asynchronous event signaling completion of the external HTTP call. It is important to note that this implementation does not take security into account. It would be possible for other clients to take advantage of this proxy since we are not validating that the client is our client application.

The next step is to get the servlet running inside GWT's hosted mode Tomcat server. This can be done by simply adding a reference to the class in the application's module XML file. For the Blog Editor, this file is located in `com/gwtapps/blogeditor/BlogEditor.gwt.xml`. This is the line that needs to be added:

```
<servlet path="/HTTPProxy" class="com.gwtapps.server.util.HTTPProxy"/>
```

This line tells GWT's hosted browser to load the servlet class called `com.gwtapps.server.util.HTTPProxy`, the class we just looked at, and make it available at the path /HTTPProxy. The path is somewhat arbitrary and can be any name, but the same value must be used by the client class in its sendRequest method:

```
RequestBuilder requestBuilder = new RequestBuilder(
    RequestBuilder.POST, GWT.getModuleBaseURL()+"/HTTPProxy" );
```

To deploy this servlet in a full Java servlet container such as Tomcat (not the GWT server), you would need to create a web.xml file that describes the servlet. This file would look like this:

```
<web-app>
    <servlet>
        <servlet-name>HTTPProxy</servlet-name>
        <servlet-class>com.gwtapps.server.util.HTTPProxy</servlet-class>
    </servlet>
    <servlet-mapping>
        <servlet-name>HTTPProxy</servlet-name>
        <url-pattern>/HTTPProxy</url-pattern>
    </servlet-mapping>
</web-app>
```

With this HTTP proxy defined we are now capable of writing code to interact with an external service directly from the browser.

Integrating with the Blogger API

The Blogger blog service has a relatively long history of support for an API to access its services, though it has changed several times. One change started as a result of Google buying Pyra Labs, the company behind the Blogger service, in 2003. In 2006 Google started the process of moving the Blogger's API over to the Google Data API (GData).

We will use the GData protocol to access Blogger with this application. Although, at the time of writing, the old protocol still works, Blogger will be transitioning it out. The GData protocol is a good protocol to learn since it is not only useful for interacting with Blogger, but Google also makes many other of its services available using this protocol. Furthermore, GData is based on the Atom Publishing Protocol, which is useful for many more web services.

Using Atom Publishing Protocol and GData

Most blog services, including Blogger, started out with a RPC-based API. As new features were added, the API became increasingly complex and hard to manage and learn. Developers identified this as an important problem that needed to be solved. This was the motivation for several blog services and developers to get together to create a universal publishing standard for syndication and authoring of content. The group is called AtomEnabled Alliance and can be found on the web at www.atomenabled.org.

First the AtomEnabled Alliance defined Atom, an XML syndication format aimed at solving problems with RSS. Then the Atom Publishing Protocol extended the syndication format to be used on top of the REST protocol, with the task of managing web content. So, the Atom Publishing Protocol is simply a REST API that uses the HTTP methods to modify data identified by URLs and the Atom XML schema to describe its data. You can find more information about the Atom Publishing Protocol at http://ietfreport.isoc.org/idref/draft-ietf-atompub-protocol/.

GData is based on the Atom Publishing Protocol and provides an extension to allow queries and authentication. The rest of this chapter focuses on implementing a client application to a GData service (Blogger), but you can find more information about the GData protocol at http://code.google.com/apis/gdata/.

Using the GData protocol we will be able to authenticate with Blogger to gain access to read the blogs in users' accounts, and add, modify, and delete blog entries. Now let's start looking at the code that uses the GData protocol.

Defining the `BloggerService` Class

We will perform the work of interacting with the Blogger service using our `HTTPProxy` and updating the application's view in the `BloggerService` class. The class will extend the `BlogService` class.

The `BlogService` abstract base class provides a unified base class for any blog service that is added to the application, and it creates code that can interact with many services at once, such as the simple task of signing in. Also, we can propagate any common code between services to this base class. The following shows how to implement this base class:

```
public abstract class BlogService {
   private BlogEditorView view;

   public BlogService( BlogEditorView view ){
      this.view = view;
   }

   public BlogEditorView getView(){
      return view;
   }

   public abstract void signin();
}
```

As you can see, `BloggerService` is a simple class and there isn't much code that would be reused between services. However, this is because at this point only one service has been developed and it is not clear what code may be shared. So far it is safe to say that all blog services will share the main application view and a `signin` method. The `signin` method tells the service to start the sign-in process.

The `BloggerService` class extends this interface and implements the `signin` method on top of implementing all of the other methods for the blog service. The class is large, so we'll go over it piece by piece starting with the declaration and constructor:

```
public class BloggerService extends BlogService implements BlogViewListener{
   public BloggerService( BlogEditorView view ){
      super(view);
   }
}
```

As you can see, the `BloggerService` class extends the `BlogService` abstract class, implements the `BlogViewListener` interface so that it can receive events from the application's view, and implements the constructor to take the application's view and pass it to the superclass. After the application creates an instance of this class, it calls the `signin` method.

Signing In to a Google Account

Signing in is one of the more complicated tasks for applications that use the GData protocol, although it is considered very simple compared to other authentication mechanisms. For web clients like this Blog Editor application, you use an authentication interface called `AuthSub`. The `AuthSub` interface is a very secure interface that does not require our application to handle user credentials. Instead, our application forwards the user to the `AuthSub` URL to input credentials or verify that that it's okay for this application to have account access. Once the user completes this step, the `AuthSub` interface sends the user back to the Blog Editor application and provides the application with a security token. The token is used for a single request to the web server. However, for our application we need to make multiple requests without going through the authentication mechanism each time. To accomplish this, the `AuthSub` interface provides a **session token,** a token that is capable of being used for multiple requests. Figure 8-18 illustrates the interaction between the user, our application, the Blogger web service, and the `AuthSub` interface.

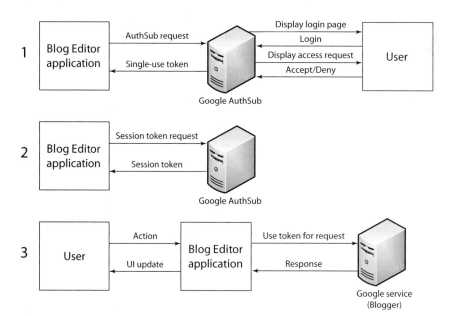

Figure 8–18. The three steps required to sign into a Google account for Blogger

The first step is to get the single-use token from the `AuthSub` interface by forwarding our application to the `AuthSub` URL:

```
https://www.google.com/accounts/AuthSubRequest
```

This displays either the Google Access Request page or a login page. The login page prompts users for Google account credentials and looks like

Figure 8–19. The sign-in screen for a Google account

Figure 8-19. (Users already logged into a Google account will not see this page.)

After signing in, users see the access request page, and for users already signed in this is the first page they see. As shown in Figure 8-20, this page asks users if it is okay for the application to access the web service API through their account.

This page informs the user of the URL that would like access to the requested Google service. In this case you can see that the URL is local-host, since the application was running from the GWT hosted browser on a local machine. The service is Blogger. For this page to work properly we need to send the AuthSub interface our application's URL and the service we're interested in using. This is done with the following parameters in the AuthSubRequest URL.

- next

  Tells AuthSub the URL where it should forward the user after access has been granted.

Figure 8–20.   Google's Access Request screen

- scope

  Specifies the Google service that our application is interested in using. For Blogger, this value is http://www.blogger.com/feeds.

- session

  Determines whether the returned token can be used to obtain a session token. The value can be 1 or 0. For this application we use the value 1 for a session token.

Putting all these parameters together in a URL gives us the following:

```
"http://www.google.com/accounts/
AuthSubRequest?next="+GWT.getModuleBaseURL()+"index.html&scope=http://
www.blogger.com/feeds&session=1"
```

This value is formatted as a Java string to illustrate that the next parameter value can be constructed using GWT's getModuleBaseURL method. This useful method allows GWT application code to ignore its network location. This is helpful for when you need to deploy to different server locations because you will not need to recompile.

The second step, after the user grants access in the `AuthSub` interface and a token is returned to our application, is for our application to use the single-use token to request a second token—we certainly don't want to go through the user confirmation process each time the user makes a change to a blog. To get the session token we need to post the first token to the `AuthSubSessionToken` URL:

```
https://www.google.com/accounts/AuthSubSessionToken
```

The token is posted as a header in the HTTP request under the header name `Authorization` like this:

```
Authorization: AuthSub token="token_value"
```

The `AuthSub` interface then returns an HTTP response with name-value pairs, one of which represents the session token identified with the name token. The following is an example of a response:

```
Token=DQAA...7DCTN
Expiration=20061004T123456Z
```

The third step is to use the token in a request to the Blogger service simply by adding the session token as an HTTP header to each request:

```
Authorization: AuthSub token="session_token_value"
```

These three steps, forwarding the user's browser to Google to receive consent from the user and a single-use token from Google, exchanging the single-use token for a session token, and using the session token in requests to the Blogger service, provide a secure and simple authentication method for the Blogger web service.

Now let's look at the code to implement this process with the `Blogger Service` class:

```
private static final String URL_AUTH_SUB = "http://www.google.com/accounts/
AuthSubRequest?next="+GWT.getModuleBaseURL()+"index.html&scope=http%3A%2F%2Fwww.
blogger.com/feeds&session=1";
```

```
private static final String URL_AUTH_SUB_SESSION =
    "https://www.google.com/accounts/AuthSubSessionToken";

private static final String URL_GET_BLOG_LIST =
    "http://www.blogger.com/feeds/default/blogs";

public void signin(){

    //check for a saved token
    if( sessionToken == null ){
        sessionToken = Cookies.getCookie("BloggerAuthSub");
    }

    //if we have a token get the list of blogs
    if( sessionToken != null ){
        makeRemoteCall( URL_GET_BLOG_LIST, new GetBlogListCallback() );
    }
    else{
        //check for a token in the URL parameters
        String params = BrowserLocation.getURLParameters();
        if( params.length() != 0 ){
            String tokenKey = "token=";
            int tokenIndex = params.indexOf(tokenKey);

            //request a session token using single-use token
            if( tokenIndex != -1  ){
                String token = params.substring( tokenIndex+tokenKey.length());
                makeRemoteCall(
                    URL_AUTH_SUB_SESSION, token, new GetTokenCallback() );
                return;
            }
        }

        //we don't have any tokens so we need to redirect to Google
        BrowserLocation.setLocation( URL_AUTH_SUB );
    }
}
```

First we define a few of the URLs that we need for this process as static strings, and then the signin method is implemented. The signin method first checks for the location of a session token saved in a cookie. Google recommends reusing tokens between sessions. Here we use GWT's Cookie class to save the cookie based on the specified name. If a token is available as a cookie, the signin method continues with the application, which involves making a request for the list of blogs (we will look at this step later).

When there isn't a token saved in a cookie, the `signin` method continues by checking to see if the `AuthSub` interface provided a single-use token in a URL parameter to this application. If this is the case, the token is extracted from the URL and used to make a request for a session token. This method uses another helper method, `makeRemoteCall`, to make this request (we will look at this method later). If a token has not been provided in the URL, which is the case when the user first visits the application, the application forwards the user to the `AuthSub` interface using the `setLocation` command on the `BrowserLocation` class:

```
public static native void setLocation( String url )/*-{
    return $wnd.location = url;
}-*/;
```

This JSNI method changes the current page's URL to the specified URL. In this case the URL is for the `AuthSub` interface and has the next parameter set to return to the application with a token. When the application returns, the `signin` method is called again, but this time the `AuthSub` has added the single-use token to the URL. Then code in the `signin` method that makes a call to get the session token is invoked using the `makeRemoteCall` method:

```
private void makeRemoteCall(
    String url, String contentType, String token, RequestCallback callback ){
    getView().getLoadingPanel().loadingBegin();

    //create a new request and set the authorization header to our token
    HTTPProxyRequestBuilder builder =
        new HTTPProxyRequestBuilder(RequestBuilder.GET, url);
    builder.setHeader("Authorization", "AuthSub token=\""+token+"\"");
    builder.setHeader("Content-type", contentType);
    try {
        //send the request, the body is empty/null
        builder.sendRequest( null, callback );
    }
    catch (RequestException e){ GWT.log( "error", e); }
}
```

This method uses the `HTTPProxyRequestBuilder` class (described earlier in this chapter) to access the remote URL. It adds the GData token as an HTTP header with the name `Authorization`, as prescribed by the GData protocol. The call is invoked using the `sendRequest` method, and the asynchronous result is returned to the callback provided. In this case, the code to get a session token from the `AuthSub` interface uses the local class `GetTokenCallback` for the callback:

```
private class GetTokenCallback implements RequestCallback {

    public void onError(Request request, Throwable exception){
        GWT.log( "error", exception );
    }

    public void onResponseReceived( Request request, Response response){
        getView().getLoadingPanel().loadingEnd();

        //get the response and look for the token
        String responseText = response.getText();
        int equalIndex = responseText.indexOf("=");
        String key = responseText.substring(0,equalIndex);
        if( key.equals("Token") && handleResponse( response ) ){
            sessionToken = responseText.substring(
                equalIndex+1, responseText.indexOf("\n") );

            //save the token in a cookie for another session
            Date today = new Date();
            Cookies.setCookie( "BloggerAuthSub",sessionToken,
                new Date( today.getTime() + 1000*60*60*24 ) );

            //use the token to sign in
            signin();
        }
    }
}
```

When receiving the response, the `GetTokenCallback` implements GWT's `RequestCallback` interface, retrieves the session token name-value pair from the HTTP response, saves it as a cookie for use in other sessions, and calls the `signin` method again. During this invocation of the `signin` method the session token is available, and the application proceeds to load the list of blogs available for the user's account.

Getting the XML List of Blogs for the Account

Once users are signed in and have a session token, they can interact with the Blogger service and manage their blogs. The first thing we need to do is get a list of blogs that are available for the user to manage. Following REST interface style, Blogger makes the list of blogs available for a particular user as a resource identified by a URL. To get the list we simply need to make an HTTP GET request for the URL. It is important to use the user's session token in the HTTP header because this resource is not publicly available. The URL to get the list of blogs is:

```
http://www.blogger.com/feeds/default/blogs
```

When we make a GET request for this URL, Blogger finds the session token we sent in the HTTP headers and is able to identify the user account the token is for. Then it returns a list of blogs available to the user in XML format.

The GET method is invoked in the `signin` method (defined previously) using the `makeRemoteRequest` helper method:

```
makeRemoteCall( URL_GET_BLOG_LIST, new GetBlogListCallback() );
```

This helper method makes the remote call through our `HTTPProxy`, which returns the response from the Blogger service to the callback used. In this case the callback used is the `GetBlogListCallback` local class:

```
private class GetBlogListCallback implements RequestCallback {

   public void onError(Request request, Throwable exception){
      GWT.log( "error", exception );
   }

   public void onResponseReceived( Request request, Response response ){
      getView().getLoadingPanel().loadingEnd();
      if( handleResponse( response ) ){

         //parse the response as XML
         Element document = XMLParser.parse(
            response.getText() ).getDocumentElement();

         //iterate over each entry in the XML
         NodeList items = document.getElementsByTagName("entry");
         for(int i=0;i<items.getLength();i++ ){

            //extract the required data
            Element item = (Element)items.item(i);
            String title = getElementText( item, "title" );
            String link="";
            String postLink="";
            String feedLink="";
```

```
                //get the different kinds of links
                NodeList links = item.getElementsByTagName("link");
                for(int j=0;j<links.getLength();j++ ){
                    Element linkElement = (Element)links.item(j);
                    String rel = linkElement.getAttribute( "rel" );
                    if( rel.equals("alternate") )
                        link = linkElement.getAttribute("href");
                    else if( rel.equals("http://schemas.google.com/g/2005#post") )
                        postLink = linkElement.getAttribute("href");
                    else if( rel.equals("http://schemas.google.com/g/2005#feed") )
                        feedLink = linkElement.getAttribute("href");
                }

                //create a new Blog instance from the XML data
                Blog blog = new Blog( title, link );
                blogPostLinks.put( blog, postLink );
                getView().addBlog( blog, BloggerService.this );

                //request the blog entries for this blog
                makeRemoteCall( feedLink, new GetBlogEntriesCallback( blog ));
            }
        }
    }
}
```

This callback class, implementing GWT's `RequestCallback` interface, handles the server's response and expects a list of blogs in Atom XML format. The body of the `onResponseReceived` method is a good example of XML parsing using GWT's XML parser. The method uses the XML parser to parse the returned string from the Blogger server and then iterate over the content to create new `Blog` instances (this is the class from our application's model) to pass to the view to be rendered.

To understand the parsing code for the XML response, it is helpful to look at what the structure being parsed typically looks like. The following is a simplified example of a blog list feed in Atom format:

```
<?xml version='1.0' encoding='UTF-8'?>
<feed xmlns='http://www.w3.org/2005/Atom'>
   <title type='text'>ryan@rdews.com's Blogs</title>
<author><name>Ryan</name></author>    <entry>        <title type='text'>GWT
Applications</title>       <link rel='alternate' type='text/html'
        href='http://gwtapps.blogspot.com/'>
        </link>
        <link rel='http://schemas.google.com/g/2005#feed'
            type='application/atom+xml'
```

```
        href='http://gwtapps.blogspot.com/feeds/posts/default'>
    </link>      <link rel='http://schemas.google.com/g/2005#post'
      type='application/atom+xml'
     href='http://www.blogger.com/feeds/2573021046464953257/posts/default'>
    </link>      <author><name>Ryan</name></author>    </entry>
</feed>
```

The list of blogs sits inside a `feed` element. Each blog is represented by an `entry` element (just one in this example). The blog name is the text within the `title` element for the entry. Each blog has several links that are provided. The first link represents the URL to the HTML page for the blog hosted by the Blogger service. The second link denotes the link that an application would use to retrieve the feed of entries for the blog. The third link is the link an application would use to post new entries to the blog. The post link, used to post new blog entries, is saved in a hash table on the `BloggerService` class so that it can be used later. It is not saved on the `Blog` model object since it is specific to only this blog service. The feed link, used to retrieve the list of entries for the blog, is immediately used to do just that through the `makeRemoteRequest` method.

Getting the XML List of Entries for Each Blog

The final step in loading information from the Blogger service is to get the entries for each blog. The application starts the request immediately after parsing the XML description for a particular blog and retrieving its feed URL with the `GetBlogListCallback.onResponseReceived` method. This method requests the feed using the `makeRemoteCall` method:

```
makeRemoteCall( feedLink, new GetBlogEntriesCallback( blog ) );
```

The URL for the call uses the feed link provided for the blog in the blog listing as the URL to get an instance of the `GetBlogEntriesCallback` that receives the response. The callback class takes the blog's model object as a parameter so it can properly associate entries to each entry's blog in the model. The `GetBlogEntriesCallback` is implemented like this:

```
private class GetBlogEntriesCallback implements RequestCallback{
    private Blog blog;

    GetBlogEntriesCallback( Blog blog ){
        this.blog = blog;
    }
```

```
public void onError(Request request, Throwable exception){
   GWT.log( "error", exception );
}

public void onResponseReceived(Request request, Response response){
   getView().getLoadingPanel().loadingEnd();
   if( handleResponse( response ) ){
      //parse the XML response
      Element document = XMLParser.parse(
         response.getText() ).getDocumentElement();

      //iterate over each entry in the response
      NodeList items = document.getElementsByTagName("entry");
      for(int i=0;i<items.getLength();i++ ){

         //create a new blog entry and add it to the view
         BlogEntry entry = new BlogEntry( blog );
         blog.addEntry( entry );
         entryFromXml( entry, (Element)items.item(i));
         getView().getBlogView( blog ).addEntryAtEnd( entry );
      }
   }
}
}
```

This class implements GWT's `RequestCallback` interface and handles
the server response in the `onResponseReceived` method. The list of
entries returned as a response is similar to the blog list in that it is formatted as Atom XML, with the outer element being a feed element that has
many child entry elements. The response is parsed using GWT's XML
parser and the list of entries is iterated over. For each entry element a
`BlogEntry` instance is created and added to the view. The data for the
entry is copied from the XML to the model `BlogEntry` instance using
`entryFromXml` as a helper method. This method is defined as follows:

```
private void entryFromXml( BlogEntry entry, Element entryElement ){
   entry.setTitle( getElementText( entryElement, "title" ) );
   entry.setContent( getElementText( entryElement, "content" ) );

   String editLink = "";
   NodeList links = entryElement.getElementsByTagName("link");
   for(int j=0;j<links.getLength();j++ ){
      Element linkElement = (Element)links.item(j);
      String rel = linkElement.getAttribute( "rel" );
      if( rel.equals("alternate") )
         entry.setLink( linkElement.getAttribute("href") );
```

```
    else if( rel.equals("edit") )
        editLink = linkElement.getAttribute("href");
    }
    entryEditLinks.put( entry, editLink );
}

private static String getElementText( Element item, String value ){
    String result = "";
    NodeList itemList = item.getElementsByTagName(value);
    if( itemList.getLength() > 0 && itemList.item(0).hasChildNodes()){
        result = itemList.item(0).getFirstChild().getNodeValue();
    }
    return result;
}
```

A `BlogEntry` instance and an `Element` instance representing the entry element in the XML document are provided as parameters to this method. The `title` and `content` tags are retrieved from the element and copied to the `BlogEntry` instance using its setter methods. Then the link elements are iterated over. The first link, labeled as `alternate` through the `rel` attribute, represents the URL to the HTML page for the entry hosted by Blogger. The second link, labeled as `edit` through the `rel` attribute, represents the URL that we need to use to make modifications to this entry. The edit link is saved in a hash table on the Blogger service class for use in its methods that update this entry. The method uses another helper method, `getElementText`, to retrieve the textual data inside an element based on the element's name. As you can see by this method's implementation, several XML API methods must be called to perform the operation, and it helps to clean up code elsewhere.

These callback methods, retrieving the list of blogs and the list of blog entries for each blog, obtain all of the information needed to display all of the resources for the user's blogger account in the view. The view has already been set up to receive the model instances and display them. Running the application at this point will sign the user into Blogger and then display the list of available blogs and their entries.

The next steps involve reacting to user interactions with the view to manage the blogs' resources.

Sending XML to Create and Save an Entry

The view lets the user create a new entry on a blog and modify an existing entry. When a user creates a new entry, the view creates a new `BlogEntry` instance. When a user modifies an existing entry, the view updates an existing `BlogEntry` instance with the new values from the GWT text editing widgets. When a user saves an entry originating from either of these operations, the view calls the `onEntrySaved` method on the `BlogViewListener` interface. The `BloggerService` class implements this interface, receives this method call, and has the responsibility of invoking the appropriate action on the server for the `BlogEntry` instance provided as parameter.

For the Blogger service, we need to post a new entry to one URL and a modified entry to another URL. This follows REST-style interfaces properly. An existing entry is a resource in the web service, and it should have all of its operations available through HTTP methods to only one URL. In this case we were provided with the URL to use when we received the entry in the list of the blog's entries. The URL was within the link element that had its `rel` attribute set to `edit`. We saved this URL in a hash map so we could use it for operations such as updating the entry. For a new entry we use the post link for the blog we're adding to. This link was provided for the blog when we retrieved the list of blogs. We also saved this URL in a hash map for this situation when we need to add an entry.

These URLs are used to post new and updated entries to the Blogger service through the `BloggerService` class' `onEntrySaved` method:

```
public void onEntrySaved( BlogEntry entry ){
    getView().getSavingPanel().loadingBegin();

    //create the request object
    HTTPProxyRequestBuilder builder;
    String editLink = (String)entryEditLinks.get( entry );
    if( editLink == null ){
        String postLink = (String)blogPostLinks.get( Entry.getBlog() );
        builder = new HTTPProxyRequestBuilder( RequestBuilder.POST, postLink );
    }
    else{
        builder = new HTTPProxyRequestBuilder(RequestBuilder.POST, editLink );
        builder.setHeader("X-HTTP-Method-Override", "PUT");
    }
```

```
//set authorization to our token and set the content type to XML
builder.setHeader("Authorization", "AuthSub token=\""+sessionToken+"\"");
builder.setHeader("Content-type", "application/atom+xml");

//send the request using the entry XML as the body
try {
   builder.sendRequest(
      entryToXml( entry ), new PostEntryCallback( entry ) );
}
catch (RequestException e){ GWT.log( "error", e); }
}
```

Notice that this method's implementation does not use the `makeRemote Call` method that we've used for other requests. This is because we need greater control over what the HTTP request sends. Previously we've only retrieved resource data. In a REST interface, reading data is performed with the HTTP GET method, and updating resource data is typically performed with the HTTP PUT method. Thus, you see we use the PUT method to send the request when implementing the `onEntrySaved` method. Actually, we send the PUT method as an HTTP header to override the actual POST method used. This is a workaround to the Safari browser's problem with sending asynchronous requests with HTTP methods other than GET or POST. GWT acknowledges this limitation and only provides constants for GET and POST methods for use when constructing a `RequestBuilder` instance. Fortunately, HTTP has a method override header that we can add to the request to force a different method. You can see this in the preceding method where the `X-HTTP-Method-Override` `header` is set to the value PUT.

The method is able to tell whether the `BlogEntry` is a new or an existing entry by searching for its edit URL in the hash map. If the edit URL exists in the hash map, the method knows to post to the edit URL. If not, the `BlogEntry` is new and the method posts the entry to the blog's post URL. We use the HTTP POST method to post a new entry to a REST resource. We don't need to use the `X-HTTP-Method-Override` header in this case since POST is supported in all browsers.

Finally, the method makes the request using the `HTTPProxyRequest Builder`'s `sendRequest` method, converting the entry to an XML string (using the helper method `entryToXml`) to use as the HTTP POST data. It then passes in an instance of the `PostEntryCallback` local class to receive the response. Let's take a quick look at the `entryToXml` method:

```
private String entryToXml( BlogEntry entry ){
    Document document = XMLParser.createDocument();
    Element entryElement = document.createElement("entry");
    Element titleElement = document.createElement("title");
    Element contentElement = document.createElement("content");
    Text titleText = document.createTextNode( entry.getTitle());
    Text contentText = document.createTextNode( entry.getContent() );
    document.appendChild(entryElement);
    entryElement.setAttribute("xmlns","http://www.w3.org/2005/Atom");
    entryElement.appendChild(titleElement);
    entryElement.appendChild(contentElement);
    titleElement.appendChild(titleText);
    contentElement.appendChild(contentText);
    contentElement.setAttribute("type","xhtml");
    return document.toString();
}
```

This method is the reverse of the `entryFromXml` method. It takes a
`BlogEntry` instance and produces an XML string in Atom format. It is a
good example of using GWT's XML library to build an XML document. The
code builds the entry elements one by one and adds the appropriate text
nodes as their children. Once the document construction is complete, it is
converted to a string and returned. The output of this method should look
something like this:

```
<entry xmlns="http://www.w3.org/2005/Atom">
    <title>This is an entry title</title>
    <content type="xhtml">This is the content of an entry.</content>
</entry>
```

The Blogger server receives this content after our application posts it over
HTTP. If the blog's post URL is used, the Blogger server will add this as a
new entry. If an entry edit URL was used, the Blogger server will modify
the existing entry. Then the Blogger server returns a response to our application, which handles it in the `PostEntryCallback` local class:

```
private class PostEntryCallback implements RequestCallback{
    BlogEntry entry;

    PostEntryCallback( BlogEntry entry ){
        this.entry = entry;
    }

    public void onError(Request request, Throwable exception){
        GWT.log( "error", exception );
    }
```

```
public void onResponseReceived( Request request, Response response ){
   getView().getSavingPanel().loadingEnd();
   if( handleResponse( response ) ){
      entryFromXml( entry, response.getText() );
      getView().getBlogView( entry.getBlog() )
         .getEntryView( entry ).update();
   }
 }
}
```

Like the other callback class, this class implements GWT's `RequestCall`
`back` interface and its `onResponseReceived` method. This handles the
response of posting an entry to the Blogger server. The response text
returned from the server is the updated entry. The server may have
changed some of the entry's values, so it is important to copy this data
back to the entry we posted. To do this we use the `entryFromXml` method
again, and then we pass the entry to the view so that the view can update
the values that are rendered to the user.

Sending a Delete Request for an Entry

So far we've implemented three of the four REST methods available for
resources on a web service. We used the GET method to retrieve the blog
list and entry list, the POST method to post a new entry to a blog, and the
PUT method to update an entry. The final method that we need to implement to complete the set of REST methods is the DELETE method. We will
use the DELETE method to delete an entry in the implementation for the
`onEntryDeleted` method that the `BloggerService` implements from
the `BlogViewListener` interface. The following code shows how to do
this for the `onEntryDeleted` method:

```
public void onEntryDeleted( BlogEntry entry ){
   //create the request
   HTTPProxyRequestBuilder builder;
   String editLink = (String)entryEditLinks.get( entry );
   if( editLink != null ){
      builder = new HTTPProxyRequestBuilder( RequestBuilder.POST, editLink );

      //set the authorization, content type, and method override headers
      builder.setHeader("X-HTTP-Method-Override", "DELETE");
      builder.setHeader(
         "Authorization", "AuthSub token=\""+sessionToken+"\"");
      builder.setHeader("Content-type", "application/atom+xml");
```

```
        //send the request
        try {
            builder.sendRequest(entryToXml( entry ), new DeleteEntryCallback());
        }
        catch (RequestException e){ GWT.log( "error", e); }
    }
}
```

The `onEntryDelete` method is similar to the `onEntrySaved` method in that it takes a `BlogEntry` instance that will be operated on and invokes an HTTP request on the Blogger server. To delete the entry the method needs to send the delete request to the entry's edit URL. To send the DELETE method the request needs to set the `X-HTTP-Method-Override` header to DELETE, since the method is not supported for asynchronous requests on all browsers. The call is made using the `sendRequest` method on the `HTTPProxyRequestBuilder`, and the response is received in the `DeleteEntryCallback` instance.

We don't need to do much work to implement the callback for the DELETE method. The only thing we should do is report any errors to the view. So the implementation for the `DelteEntryCallback` is minimal:

```
private class DeleteEntryCallback implements RequestCallback {
    public void onError(Request request, Throwable exception){
        GWT.log( "error", exception );
    }

    public void onResponseReceived(Request request, Response response){
        handleResponse( response );
    }
}
```

Notice that there is no verification to the user that an entry is about to be deleted. Since this code is in the controller, it has faith that the view is taking the appropriate actions to verify with the user that he actually wants an entry deleted. Looking back on the view's implementation in the `BlogEntryView` class code for handling a click on the Delete button, we have code that uses the `GWT.confirm` method to present a confirmation dialog to the user verifying whether to delete an entry.

Summary

At this point all of the actions that we made available in the view are implemented and the controller is fully interacting with the Blogger service to retrieve data to populate the view. The only step left to use this application is to log in using your Blogger account or create one if you don't have one (its free!). Figure 8-21 shows how the application should look (this is using my test account).

Also, the application can still be extended further by adding new blog services to plug into the view or adding new functionality to the view for more control over the blogs and their entries.

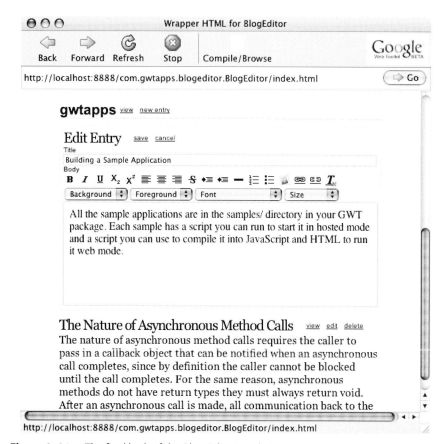

Figure 8–21.   The final look of the Blog Editor application

It is easy to forget about what this application is actually accomplishing. To create a client application that interacts richly with a web service isn't anything to get too excited about. We've followed many of the application design concepts, such as MVC, that make client applications work well and be easily maintained. The big accomplishment here is that this client implementation is running entirely in a browser without any other dependencies. The Google Web Toolkit has made it possible to build a well-designed application using the powerful object-oriented constructs and development tools provided by Java without having Java as a dependency when the application is deployed. And deploying the application is another big accomplishment, taking advantage of the ease of downloading the application code as JavaScript over HTTP. The application is truly cross-platform and cross-browser and will download to the client in seconds. It can be instantly made available to millions with ease.

You can deploy the application by copying the files in the www directory after using the GWT-generated compile script called `BlogEditor-compile`. The files are simple HTML files unique to this version of the application. If you were to update the application, the files would have different filenames and users would have the new version automatically simply by refreshing their browser.

9

Instant Messenger Application

This chapter shows how to build the web-based Instant Messenger application. The application is a good example of building on top of a well-defined GWT-RPC interface. Every client that loads the application will connect to a servlet on the server and make method calls through RPC. Each client connects to the same server, so it is possible for clients to collaborate with each other. The chapter also looks at building an unobtrusive user interface that integrates well with an existing web page and that only presents information to the user when necessary. We close the chapter by seeing how events can be added to HTTP using GWT-RPC and how to integrate with server features that make event-based protocols more efficient. You can work with a running instance of this application at http://messenger.gwtapps.com.

Using the Collaborator Application Pattern

Desktop applications are typically written for people working individually. This makes sense since desktop computers only have one person using them at a time. However, in the real world we tend not to work alone but in teams and multiple people have to collaborate on a single document. For example, many document-based applications are single-user based even when certain documents need to be edited by more than one person. Applications typically don't have a way to manage this type of collaboration.

We resort to passing documents through e-mail or copying them to disk. The Collaborator Application pattern addresses the awkwardness of manual collaboration by building collaboration systems directly into the application.

Building collaborative applications is made substantially easier due to the Internet and its pervasiveness. We can fairly simply transfer data from one source to another. Every person who needs to collaborate just must be able to connect to the Internet and use a web browser. It's important to have low user requirements for collaboration, even more so than for a single-user application, so everyone who needs to be involved can get involved. Traditional web applications have provided a great collaboration platform in this respect, as shown by the popularity of e-mail and other online collaboration applications. The low barrier to entry for Ajax applications can bring richer experiences to web collaboration.

To build an application using the Collaborator pattern you need to define your model as a centralized model that is accessed through a controller, as illustrated in Figure 9-1. Each collaborative client interacts with the controller to operate on the model. The controller is then responsible for informing the remaining clients of the model changes. You may be thinking that using a collaboration pattern like this can be a challenge for applications that have their communication based on HTTP, because HTTP does not let servers send data to clients without a request being sent by the client. We'll look at solutions to this problem later in this chapter.

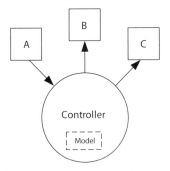

Figure 9–1.   An example of the Collaborator Application pattern

Instant Messenger Design

If you're reading this book you most likely are familiar with what an instant messenger does. You've probably run into them many times and may even use instant messenger services on a daily basis. Their job is to provide instant textual communication between two or more people that is more conversational than e-mail and less intrusive than a phone call. They have been gaining usage with hundreds of millions of users.[1] This is a truly successful desktop Internet application only rivaled by e-mail clients and web browsers. Bringing this type of application into a browser through Ajax provides the added benefits associated with web-based applications: giving people the ability to communicate from anywhere with a web browser without the need to install client software. Furthermore, the ease of running, building, and deploying an Ajax instant messenger means that it can be used easily in many specialized situations without any barriers to entry.

For this sample application we will create a specialized instant messenger for a web page. It will integrate with a web page as an embedded widget complementing the page's existing purpose with presence[2] and instant communication among its users. It will accomplish this by providing a contact list that has, instead of a list of friends or colleagues, a list of visitors to the web page. A visitor will be able to supply his name to be added to the list, and then be able to see other visitors and interact with them through instant messages.

Typically with instant messenger systems the clients do not connect directly to each other; instead, they relay messages through a server. Our application will do the same. Figure 9-2 shows a simplified illustration of how clients communicate with each other through the server.

When the client loads the web page, the GWT application will be loaded as well and will connect to the server. The user can input a name and then receive events from the server, such as other users viewing the page and coming online or leaving the page, and messages sent from another user.

---

1. Based on a February 2006 comScore survey (www.comscore.com/press/release.asp?id=800).

2. **Presence** is an instant messenger feature that provides realtime online status for you and your contacts.

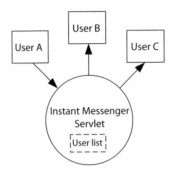

Figure 9–2.   Collaborator Application pattern applied to instant messaging

Users can also send messages to other users. The server receives these requests and provides responses in a typical request-response behavior, and it also sends events based on these requests to other users using event protocol behavior.

The Instant Messenger server will run as a GWT servlet with a GWT-RPC interface. The clients will connect and make method calls to the servlet to support the instant messenger functionality. The servlet will implement the RPC interface and provide an event broadcasting system to each client. We'll discuss the event implementation over GWT-RPC later in this chapter.

The application's internal design follows the Model-View-Controller architecture. The model represents the objects on which the application operates, including the contacts in the contact list and messages. The view presents the contact list and other windows required to render the Instant Messenger on a web page. The controller implements communication with the server and manages model objects to be rendered in the view.

The Model

The Instant Messenger application's model has three classes: ContactList, Contact, and Message. These classes are very simple and it is easy to suggest that they are not needed in this application; however, one goal of this sample application is to illustrate how to organize your code. If we were building more functionality into this application, we would be putting more data into our model and would find it useful to separate the application's components.

Another benefit of the model for this application and for the use of GWT for client applications is that we can share our model objects with server-side code. Since we are implementing the server as a servlet, its implementation is also in Java. Furthermore, GWT-RPC allows transferring of Java objects, which lets us use our model objects again for the structure of our protocol's data.

So let's look at the structure of the model. If you're familiar with instant messenger applications, the UML in Figure 9-3 seems intuitive.

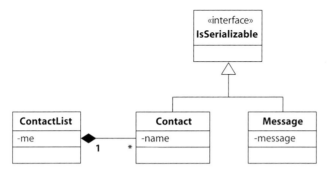

Figure 9–3.   The application's model

The `ContactList` class contains a list of `Contacts` and a me attribute. This attribute is a reference to a `Contact` instance that represents the current user. The `Contact` class has a `name` attribute representing the contact's name, and the `Message` class has a `message` attribute for the body of the message. These classes can easily be expanded to add functionality to the application. Also notice that the `Message` and `Contact` classes implement GWT's `IsSerializable` interface. Implementing this interface and creating a `no-arg` constructor allows their instances to be transferred over the GWT-RPC protocol. As of GWT 1.4 you can use Java's `Serializable` interface instead.

These objects are implemented with simple Java code. The following code shows the implementation for the `ContactList` class:

```
public class ContactList {
   private Contact me;
   private List contacts = new ArrayList();

   public ContactList( String name ){
      me = new Contact( name );
   }
```

```
public Contact getMe(){
    return me;
}

public void addContact( Contact contact){
    contacts.add( contact );
}

public int getContactCount(){
    return contacts.size();
}

public Contact getContact( int index ){
    return (Contact) contacts.get(index);
}
}
```

The class implements what the UML diagram in Figure 9-3 defined. The class provides three methods for the list of contacts: The addContact method inserts a new contact in the list, the getContactCount method returns the number of contacts in the list, and the getContact method returns the contact at a specific index. Now let's look at the Contact class:

```
public class Contact implements IsSerializable{
    private String name;

    public Contact(){}

    public Contact( String name ){
        this.name = name;
    }

    public String getName(){
        return name;
    }
}
```

This is another simple class. It has just one attribute, the contact's name. This class can be extended to provide more functionality. For example, you could add an e-mail address so that it could be displayed as a link for the user on the page to e-mail other users. Here we see the benefit of the model with this change. The change would be easily available to the controller, the server (since the model will still transfer over RPC), and the view.

The final class in the model is the `Message` class:

```
public class Message implements IsSerializable{
   private String message;

   public Message(){}
   public Message( String message ){
      this.message = message;
   }

   public String toString(){
      return message;
   }
}
```

Again, this is another simple class in our model. It has just one attribute, the message body. This class can also be easily extended to provide more information, such as adding a timestamp.

Building a Complementary Interface

This application's view is responsible for presenting users with instant feedback about the presence of other users on the page and their messages. Typically an instant messenger sits hidden in the taskbar of an operating system, or its contact list fits snugly out of the way at the side of the desktop. By contrast, our Instant Messenger application can't interact with the desktop or a taskbar and has to share space in a browser window. We've chosen to implement the messenger as a complement to an existing web page, so it should fit snugly somewhere on the page that does not interfere with the page's main usage. We will insert the application on the web page based on an HTML element with the ID `messengerView`, so it is up to the person who implements the web page to define where this element is displayed. Typically it would be displayed in a page's sidebar, out of the way of the main content, as illustrated in Figure 9-4.

The messenger's contact list would fill the area the arrow points to. This area will also hold a view that lets users sign in with a display name.

Using this defined area for the application is sufficient for logging in with a display name and presenting a list of other users on the page, but we need

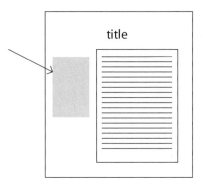

Figure 9–4.   Showing the contact list on the side

another view to display and send messages. Again, it is good to follow the example of a desktop messenger here since people are already familiar with this interface. In a desktop instant messenger, a window pops up when another user sends a message. This can be somewhat intrusive since the user could be working on anything on her computer when the window shows up. Some messengers show a nonintrusive toaster-style pop-up in the bottom, right corner of the screen. This pop-up doesn't take the focus away from what the user is working on, but provides the ability to click it to bring the Chat window to the foreground. In our Ajax version we don't have to worry too much about interrupting work on the desktop since we can only notify users of an incoming message in the browser window, but we can use the idea of a pop-up in the bottom, right corner to make the notification more familiar to users. Our Chat window will pop up in the bottom, right corner with all the widgets needed to display messages from the other user and send messages to him or her. Figure 9-5 illustrates how the Chat window will be displayed in this application.

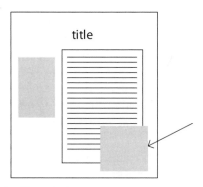

Figure 9–5.   Showing the Chat window as a pop-up

The pop-up appears in the bottom, right corner and overlaps whatever content is currently at that location. The user can have more than one conversation. When more than one pop-up appears, we will make it appear to the left of the previous one.

The sequence of events that occurs in the application's view starts with the sign-in view being displayed in the contact list's location and asking for the user's display name. After the user provides a sign-in name, the contact list displays, the application starts receiving events from the server, and the view responds to these events by rendering the model. The first events that the application may receive are new contacts to be displayed in the contact list. Then the view may receive new messages it will display in a Chat window, one per contact. The view can also receive events from the user, including opening a Chat window by clicking on a contact. The user can enter messages into a Chat window, which the view sends to the controller to send to the server so that the recipient will receive the message.

To provide this functionality we need four view classes. The `MessengerView` class manages the views in the application, and the `SignInView` class provides a view for the user to enter a display name. The `ContactListView` class shows a list of `Contacts` on the page and allows the user to open Chat windows with each. The `ChatWindowView` class provides the list of messages for a chat between two contacts and allows the user to send messages. The UML diagram in Figure 9-6 shows these classes.

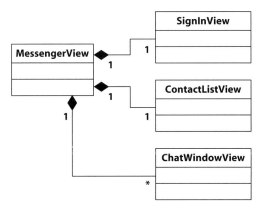

Figure 9–6. UML diagram for the application's view

The `MessengerView` Class

The `MessengerView` class is the main view for the application. Its responsibilities include managing the Chat windows, providing their layout in the bottom right of the browser, displaying a `SignInView` instance and a `ContactListView` instance, and responding to messages from the controller.

This class performs a lot of tasks, so let's start looking at the code piece by piece starting with the class declaration and its constructor:

```
public class MessengerView extends Composite
    implements WindowCloseListener, WindowResizeListener{
    private DeckPanel mainPanel = new DeckPanel();
    private ContactListView contactListView;
    private SignInView signIn;
    private ContactList contactList;
    private List openChatWindows = new ArrayList();
    private Map allChatWindows = new HashMap();
    private MessengerViewListener listener;

    public MessengerView( MessengerViewListener listener ){
        initWidget( mainPanel );
        this.listener = listener;

        signIn = new SignInView( this );

        mainPanel.add( signIn );
        mainPanel.showWidget(0);

        Window.addWindowCloseListener(this);
        Window.addWindowResizeListener(this);
    }
```

The class extends the GWT `Composite` class, similar to many other views discussed in this book. This allows us to define a custom public interface for our view without exposing another widget's unneeded methods. The class also implements the `WindowCloseListener` and the `Window ResizeListener` interfaces. These two interfaces require the class to implement methods that will receive events from the browser to handle resizing and closing events. This handling arranges the Chat windows, and we'll look at their implementations later. After the class' declaration, its private member variables are declared, including our other views, a main panel using GWT's `DeckPanel` widget, a reference to the `ContactList` instance from our model, and a reference to a `MessengerViewListener`. The reference to a `MessengerViewListener` instance is required to construct the class, and the controller implements this class to receive interface events. The following is the `MessengerViewListener`'s interface:

```
public interface MessengerViewListener {
    void onSignIn( String name );
    void onSignOut();
    void onSendMessage( Contact toContact, Message message );
}
```

The application's controller needs to implement the `onSignIn` method to handle when a user enters a display name and signs in to the messenger, the `onSignOut` method to handle when the user leaves the page and therefore signs out of the messenger, and the `onSendMessage` method to handle when the user sends a message to another contact. In this case the implementer will be the controller for our application, which we'll describe later.

Continuing with the `MessengerView` constructor, you can see that the next thing that happens is an instance of the `SignInView` is created and added to the `DeckPanel` widget, which has its `showWidget` method called. (We will look into the implementation for the `SignInView` later.) The `DeckPanel` used is a GWT panel widget that can have many child widgets but displays only one widget at a time. It is also the panel used to implement a `TabPanel` widget's body. We are using it here in a similar way but without the tabs. The `SignInView` will be displayed first, and then we will add the `ContactListView` to the panel so that it can be displayed in the same spot. We could switch back and forth between the `SignInView` and the `ContactListView` if, for example, we wanted to provide a sign-out option.

Handling Window Close and Resize Events

After the `mainPanel` has the `SignInView` class added to it in the constructor, two lines add this class as a listener for events. The first uses the GWT method `Window.addWindowCloseListener`, which tells GWT to send window close events to this class. This class must implement the `WindowCloseListener` interface to receive these events. Similarly, the second line calls the `Window.addWindowResizeListener` method and tells GWT to send the browser's resizing events to the `SignInView` class. This class must implement the `WindowResizeListener` interface.

The `SignInView` class implements the `WindowCloseListener` events like this:

```
public String onWindowClosing(){
    listener.onSignOut();
    return null;
}

public void onWindowClosed(){
}
```

GWT calls the `onWindowClosing` method before the window starts closing. It calls the `onWindowClosed` method after the window has closed or when the user navigates to a different site. The `SignInView` class implements the first method to call `onSignOut` on the listener. The listener will then take the appropriate measures with the server to tell it that this contact is no longer on the page. The return value of this method can be a string message to confirm the page's closure to the user. This method returns null, which tells the browser that no confirmation should be displayed. The class does not need to implement the `onWindowClosed` method.

The other window listener interface that the `MessengerView` class implements, `WindowResizeListener`, defines its single method like this:

```
public void onWindowResized( int width, int height ){
    resetChatWindowPositions();
}
```

This method is called when the browser window is resized. The method uses the browser's window new width and height as parameters. The `MessengerView` class implements this method for calling the `resetChatWindowPositions` helper method, which is responsible for aligning all of the visible Chat windows at the bottom right of the browser window. When the browser window resizes, the Chat windows follow the location of the bottom, right corner. The implementation of the `reset ChatWindowPositions` method looks like this:

```
protected void resetChatWindowPositions(){
    for( int i=0; i< openChatWindows.size(); ++i ){
        ChatWindowView chatWindow = (ChatWindowView)openChatWindows.get(i);
        chatWindow.setPosition(i);
    }
}
```

The method iterates over the list of open Chat windows and calls the setPosition method on each one. The setPosition method on the ChatWindowView is responsible for positioning the view at a particular position along the browser's bottom from right to left. We'll look at the implementation of the setPosition method later when we look at the ChatWindowView class.

Handling Chat Windows

The application also calls the resetChatWindowPositions method when a Chat window closes in the closeChatWindow method:

```
public void closeChatWindow( ChatWindowView windowToClose ){
   openChatWindows.remove( windowToClose.position );
   windowToClose.setVisible(false);
   windowToClose.position = -1;
   resetChatWindowPositions();
}
```

The application calls the closeChatWindow method after the user clicks the close button on the ChatWindowView. Then the MessengerView removes the window from the list of open windows and makes it invisible by calling the setVisible method—which every GWT widget has—with the value of false. Then it calls resetChatWindowPositions to line up the remaining open windows along the bottom.

The getChatWindowView method opens the Chat window:

```
public ChatWindowView getChatWindowView( Contact contact ){
   ChatWindowView chatWindow =
       (ChatWindowView)allChatWindows.get( contact.getName() );
   if( chatWindow == null ){
      chatWindow = new ChatWindowView( this, contact );
      allChatWindows.put( contact.getName(), chatWindow );
   }
   if( chatWindow.position == -1 ){
      chatWindow.position = openChatWindows.size();
      openChatWindows.add( chatWindow );
   }
   chatWindow.show();
   return chatWindow;
}
```

This method takes a `Contact` object from the model and has the job of either creating a new Chat window for communicating with the contact or showing an existing Chat window. To perform this operation, the `Messenger View` class stores a map of `ChatViewWindows` keyed on the contact name. The method checks for an existing Chat window for a contact using this map. If there is no existing window, a new `ChatWindowView` is created and added to the map. The method also checks to see if the Chat window is in the open window list. Each Chat window has a position variable that indicates its position in the list. If the value is `-1`, then this method knows it is not yet in the list and adds it. Finally, the `show` method is called to display the window and the `ChatWindowView` instance is returned.

The final method in this class involves the switch from the `SignInView` to the `ContactListView` when the `ContactList` is ready:

```
public void setContactList( ContactList contactList ){
   this.contactList = contactList;
   if( contactListView == null ){
      contactListView = new ContactListView( this );
      mainPanel.add( contactListView );
   }
   mainPanel.showWidget(1);
}
```

The `setContactList` method is called by the controller when a contact list is available, which will be after the user signs in. This method saves the contact list as a reference on this class, adds the `ContactList` view, and shows it on the main `DeckPanel` widget, effectively hiding the `SignInView`.

The `SignInView` Class

The first view users see is the `SignInView`. This view sits in the spot selected in the HTML for the application. It simply shows a `Label` with the value **Sign in name:**, a `TextBox` widget for input, and a `Button` widget to submit and sign in. Figure 9-7 shows a screenshot of the sign-in view. As you can see, the view is out of the way and doesn't intrude on the page's main task.

If the user decides to sign in, the view hides its widgets and changes the label to indicate that the sign-in process is occurring. Figure 9-8 shows the view during this state.

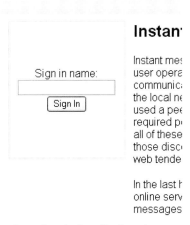

Figure 9–7. The `SignInView` class being displayed

Figure 9–8. The `SignInView` pending signing in

Both of these states are handled in the single view since their layout is very similar. The following code implements this view:

```
public class SignInView extends Composite {
   private VerticalPanel mainPanel = new VerticalPanel();
   private TextBox nameBox = new TextBox();
   private MessengerView view;

   public SignInView( MessengerView view ){
      initWidget( mainPanel );
      this.view = view;
      mainPanel.setVerticalAlignment(HasVerticalAlignment.ALIGN_MIDDLE);
      mainPanel.setHorizontalAlignment(HasHorizontalAlignment.ALIGN_CENTER);
```

```
Button signInButton = new Button( "Sign In" );
VerticalPanel vpanel = new VerticalPanel();
vpanel.setHorizontalAlignment(HasHorizontalAlignment.ALIGN_CENTER);
vpanel.add( new Label( "Sign in name:") );
vpanel.add( nameBox );
vpanel.add( signInButton );
mainPanel.add( vpanel );
nameBox.addKeyboardListener(new KeyboardListenerAdapter() {
    public void onKeyPress(Widget sender, char keyCode, int modifiers){
        if(keyCode == KEY_ENTER )
            signIn();
    }
});

signInButton.addClickListener(new ClickListener() {
    public void onClick(Widget sender){
        signIn();
    }
});
}

public void signIn(){
    String name = nameBox.getText();
    if( name.length() > 0 ){
        mainPanel.clear();
        mainPanel.add( new Label("Signing in...") );
        view.getListener().onSignIn(name);
    }
}
}
}
```

The `SignInView` class extends GWT's `Composite` widget and sets the main widget to a `VerticalPanel`. The class actually uses two `VerticalPanels`. The first, which acts as a container that centers its contents vertically, calls the `setVerticalAlignment` method on the `VerticalPanel` with the parameter value of `HasVerticalAlignment.ALIGN_MIDDLE`. Then the second `VerticalPanel` is added, which has the `Label`, `TextBox`, and `Button` widgets added as children. A `KeyboardListener` is added to the `TextBox` widget so that it can listen for an Enter key press in the keyboard events. Also, a click listener is added to the button. If the user presses the Enter key or clicks the button, the `signIn` method is called. The `signIn` method is implemented to ensure that the user has entered a name, and if so, clears the main vertical panel and adds a label to indicate that the application is signing into the messenger server. Then the `onSignIn` method is called on the `MessengerViewListener` instance so that the controller can handle this event.

The `ContactListView` Class

The `ContactListView` class takes the same spot on the page as the `SignInView`. Their parent view, `MessengerView`, uses a `DeckPanel` to handle the switching between the `SignInView` and `ContactListView`. After a user has signed in has successfully, the `ContactListView` displays, but it doesn't have any contacts listed except for the current user listed at the top. Figure 9-9 shows the contact list at this point.

Figure 9–9. Showing the contact list

As other users visit the page and log into the messenger, the controller and server will do the work to create new `Contact` instances and distribute them to each client. The `Contact` instances are sent to this view from the controller. Figure 9-10 shows the view after several other contacts come online.

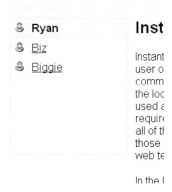

Figure 9–10. Showing the updated contact list

Each contact is listed vertically down the view as a clickable link with a little icon[3] to hint that this represents another person. Let's take a look at the code that's needed to build this view:

```
public class ContactListView extends SimplePanel {

    private class ContactClickListener implements ClickListener{
        Contact contact;

        ContactClickListener( Contact contact ){
            this.contact = contact;
        }

        public void onClick( Widget sender ){
            view.getChatWindowView( contact );
        }
    }

    private FlexTable listTable = new FlexTable();
    private MessengerView view;

    public ContactListView( MessengerView view ){
        setWidget( listTable );
        this.view = view;
        listTable.setCellPadding(0);
        listTable.setCellSpacing(0);
        addContact( view.getContactList().getMe() );
        listTable.getRowFormatter().addStyleName(0, "myContactItem" );
        listTable.getColumnFormatter().setWidth(1,"100%");
    }

    public void addContact( Contact contact ){
        int row = listTable.getRowCount();
        Hyperlink link = new Hyperlink( contact.getName(), null );
        listTable.getRowFormatter().setVerticalAlign(
            row,HasVerticalAlignment.ALIGN_TOP);
        listTable.setWidget(row,0,new Image("icon_user.gif"));
        listTable.getRowFormatter().setStyleName(row, "contactItem" );
        if( row != 0 ) listTable.setWidget(row,1,link);
        else listTable.setText(row,1, contact.getName() );
        link.addClickListener( new ContactClickListener(contact) );
    }
```

---

3. This icon is from www.famfamfam.com/lab/icons/silk/.

```
    public void removeContact( Contact contact ){
        for( int i=1; i<listTable.getRowCount();   ){
            Hyperlink link = (Hyperlink)listTable.getWidget(i,1);
            if( link.getText().equals( contact.getName() ) )
                listTable.removeRow(i);
            else ++i;
        }
    }
}
```

This class implements GWT's `SimplePanel` instead of the `Composite` widget that we've used for our other views. The reason for this is we don't want the contained widget to stretch the entire height of the view. In this case the contained widget is a `FlexTable`, which if stretched to the entire height would distribute the height evenly to each row. Using a `Simple Panel`, the contained widget sits at the top left of the panel and only grows based on its contents, or explicit calls to `setHeight`, and makes the rows only as big as their contents, which is the look we want. This illustrates a subtle difference between the `SimplePanel` and `Composite` widgets. A `SimplePanel` wraps its child panel in an HTML `div` tag, while a `Composite` contains the child widget directly. Any CSS or sizing applied to the `SimplePanel` gets applied to its `div` tag, but not to the contained widget as it would with a `Composite`.

The constructor for the `ContactListView` class takes the `MessengerView` as a parameter and saves a reference to it for use later in the class. GWT's `FlexTable` widget is responsible for the layout of each contact's rows in the `ContactListView`, and it is set as the `SimplePanel`'s child widget. The first contact added is the current user. It has a style name set for it, so we can make it look different than the other contacts. In particular, we will change its background color. The contact is added by calling the `addContact` method on the class.

The `addContact` method is responsible for inserting a new contact into the list of contacts for the view. It is called once for the current user and again for each new contact that comes online. In the method, a new `Image` widget pointing to the person icon is created and added to the first column of a new row in the list. Also, a `Hyperlink` widget is created and added to the second column. The `Hyperlink` widget has a `ClickListener` implementation added to handle its click events. The listener is implemented as an inner class called `ContactClickListener`, which responds to a click event by calling `getChatWindowView` on the

`MessengerView` instance. This method on the `MessengerView`, as described previously, will create a new `ChatWindowView` or make an invisible one visible.

The controller calls the final method on the `ContactListView`, `remove Contact`, when a contact leaves the page or goes offline. This method searches the `FlexTable` for a matching contact and, if found, removes it.

The `ChatWindowView` Class

The `ChatWindowView` class is responsible for rendering a view that allows the user to send messages to another `Contact`. It also displays the message history between the two contacts in a vertically scrolling list with the newest messages at the bottom. Figure 9-11 shows an example of a rendered `ChatWindowView` instance with a couple messages sent between two contacts.

Figure 9–11.   A Chat window

The view is divided vertically into three sections. The first section represents the title and is similar to title bars in operating system windows. The title's string value is the name of the `Contact` who is on the other end of this conversation. Next to this name is a **close** link that will hide the window when clicked. The second section represents the chat history. Any new messages from the other contact and new messages sent to the contact are displayed here. The third section, at the bottom of the view, is a text box where the user can type and then press Enter to send a message.

The code to implement this view can also be divided into three sections: The first constructs the view and creates its widgets and layout, the second responds to message input from the user and adds new messages to the message list; and the third aligns the view with the bottom right of the browser window.

Let's look at the first section of code, which constructs the view and creates its widgets and layout:

```
public class ChatWindowView extends Composite{
    private MessengerView view;
    private Contact contactTo;
    private ScrollPanel conversationScroller = new ScrollPanel();
    private VerticalPanel conversationPanel = new VerticalPanel();
    private TextBox input = new TextBox();
    int position = -1;

    public ChatWindowView( MessengerView view, Contact contactTo ){
        this.view = view;
        this.contactTo = contactTo;

        VerticalPanel mainPanel = new VerticalPanel();
        initWidget( mainPanel );

        TitleCommandBar titleBar;
        titleBar = new TitleCommandBar( contactTo.getName() );
        titleBar.addCommand("close", new ClickListener(){
            public void onClick( Widget sender ){
                ChatWindowView.this.view.closeChatWindow( ChatWindowView.this );
            }
        });
        mainPanel.add(titleBar);

        VerticalPanel vpanel = new VerticalPanel();
        vpanel.setHeight("100%");
        vpanel.setWidth("100%");
        mainPanel.add( vpanel );
        mainPanel.setCellHeight(vpanel, "100%");

        conversationScroller.setHeight("100%");
        vpanel.add( conversationScroller );
        vpanel.setCellHeight(conversationScroller, "100%");

        conversationScroller.setWidget( conversationPanel );
        vpanel.add( input );
        input.setWidth("100%");
        input.addKeyboardListener( new InputListener() );
        RootPanel.get().add( this );
    }
```

Again, this view extends GWT's `Composite` class. It is constructed with two parameters: the `MessengerView` for the application and the `Contact` instance that represents the other person in this conversation. The main widget for the `Composite` is set to a `VerticalPanel`, since it will be able to build the layout just described. The first row of the `VerticalPanel` is set to an instance of a `TitleCommandBar` widget (described in Chapter 8). The title bar has its label set to the value of the other contact and has a close command added that handles a click event by calling the `closeChatWindow` method on the `MessengerView`. The `MessengerView` implements this method to set this view to invisible, and rearranges other `ChatWindowViews`, if available, to fill the space left by this one. After the title bar another `VerticalPanel` is added to hold the message list and the message input. The message list is built with two widgets. The outer widget is an instance of GWT's `ScrollPanel` widget, which lets us set its height to a constant value that can be exceeded by its child widget. When the child widget grows larger than its parent, `ScrollPanel`, the parent provides scroll bars for the user to scroll over the child content.

The widget used inside the `ScrollPanel` is the container for the messages and is implemented as a `VerticalPanel`. The application will add messages directly to this panel. Underneath the message list is the message input, which is implemented as an instance of GWT's `TextBox` widget. The message input has a `KeyboardListener` added to it to check for the Enter key being pressed. The `KeyboardListener` implementation is an inner class on this view called `InputListener`.

This leads us to the second part of this view implementation: responding to message input from the user and adding new messages to the message list. This includes the implementation for the `InputListener` class and the `addMessage` method:

```
private class InputListener extends KeyboardListenerAdapter{
    public void onKeyPress(Widget sender, char keyCode, int modifiers){
        if( keyCode == KEY_ENTER ){
            String text = input.getText();
            if( text.length()>0 ){
                Message message = new Message(text);
                addMessage( view.getContactList().getMe(), message );
                view.getListener().onSendMessage( contactTo, message );
                input.setText("");
            }
        }
    }
}
```

```
public void addMessage( Message message ){
    addMessage( contactTo, message );
}

public void addMessage( Contact contact, Message message ){
    HTML messageLabel = new HTML(
        "<b>" + contact.getName() + "</b>: " + message);
    conversationPanel.add( messageLabel );
    conversationScroller.setScrollPosition(
        conversationPanel.getOffsetHeight());
    messageLabel.setStyleName("convMessage");
}
```

The `InputListener` extends GWT's `KeyboardListenerAdapter`, so it doesn't have to implement each method of the `KeyboardListener` interface. It implements the `onKeyPress` method to receive key press events and listens for the Enter key. When the user presses the Enter key, signaling that he wants to send a message, the method creates a new `Message` object, adds it to this view using the `addMessage` method, and calls the `onSendMessage` method on the `MessageViewListener`.

The controller, implementing the `MessengerViewListener` interface, implements the `onSendMessage` method by communicating with the server so that the other contact receives this new message. The `addMessage` method updates the view with the new message. The `addMessage` has two method signatures, one relying on the other. The first method signature takes a message and assumes the message is from the other contact. The second method signature adds a message from any contact to the list by creating a new `HTML` widget and adding the message prefixed by a bolded contact name. After the message is added, the `ScrollPanel` that scrolls the message list has its position set to the end of the list so the newly appended message is visible. If the application didn't scroll after adding new messages, the scroll panel would continue to show the messages at the top while the new messages would be added to the end, and continue out of view. The `addMessage` methods are called from two different spots: The first we see in the preceding code after the user sends a message, and the second will be called by the controller when a new message arrives from the other contact.

The third part of the code to implement the `ChatWindowView` involves aligning the view with the bottom right of the browser window. This is achieved with two public methods and a few constant values:

```
static final int CHAT_WINDOW_WIDTH = 250;
static final int CHAT_WINDOW_HEIGHT = 200;
static final int CHAT_WINDOW_MARGIN = 5;
static final int CHAT_WINDOW_OFFSET = 20;

public void show(){
   setWidth( CHAT_WINDOW_WIDTH + "px" );
   setHeight(CHAT_WINDOW_HEIGHT + "px");
   setVisible( true );
   setPosition( position );
   input.setFocus( true );
}

public void setPosition( int position ){
   this.position = position;
   int top = Window.getClientHeight() + DOM.getIntAttribute(
      RootPanel.getBodyElement(), "scrollTop") -
      getOffsetHeight() - CHAT_WINDOW_MARGIN;
   int left = Window.getClientWidth() + DOM.getIntAttribute(
      RootPanel.getBodyElement(), "scrollLeft") -
      CHAT_WINDOW_WIDTH*(position+1) - CHAT_WINDOW_MARGIN*(position+1) -
      CHAT_WINDOW_OFFSET;
   DOM.setStyleAttribute(getElement(),"position","absolute" );
   DOM.setStyleAttribute(getElement(),"top",Integer.toString(top));
   DOM.setStyleAttribute(getElement(),"left",Integer.toString(left) );
   conversationScroller.setScrollPosition(
      conversationPanel.getOffsetHeight());
}
```

The constant values define the size of each `ChatWindowView` instance, along with the spacing between each and the offset from the right side of the browser window. These values are used in the `setPosition` method to position the view in one of several positions, indicated by the `position` parameter, starting from the bottom right of the browser window and moving left.

The bottom right of the browser window is calculated by using GWT's `Window.getClientHeight` and `Window.getClientWidth` methods. The code also takes into account that the browser window may be scrolled down the page. We need to get the scroll position to properly calculate the position of this view. GWT does not have methods that directly allow us to get the scroll positions, but we can use methods from the DOM class to operate on the page's body element to return the scroll position values. In the preceding code this is done by calling GWT's `RootPanel.get BodyElement` to get the element that represents the body of the page and then calling `DOM.getIntAttribute` for the attributes named `scrollTop` and `scrollLeft`.

Once the application calculates top and left locations of the window, they are set using the CSS properties `top` and `left`. For the browser to properly render the CSS `top` and `left` properties we also need to set the CSS `position` property to `absolute`. This tells the browser that the position values set for `top` and `left` are relative to the page's top left position.

The `MessengerView` calls the `setPosition` method when it is rearranging the `ChatWindowView` instances and also when a `ChatWindowView` instance is set to be visible using the `show` method. The `show` method sets the view's width, height, and coordinates using the `setPosition` method, and sets visibility to true. It also sets the keyboard focus to the message input `TextBox` widget so the user can immediately start typing without needing to click in the text box first.

The application's four views build an interface that presents the application's model to the user and allows the model to be transferred to other users on the same page. The `MessengerView` manages the child views, including the `SignInView`, which takes the display name for the user; the `ContactListView`, which displays a list of contacts for the users currently on the page; and the `ChatWindowView`, which allows users to send and receive messages from each other. The aim of the views is to complement other web page functionality by displaying a minimal interface. Together the views create the interface shown in Figure 9-12.

The Controller Overview

The Instant Messenger application's controller has the job of receiving events from the view, communicating with the server, and operating on the application's model objects. The interaction with the view and model is fairly straightforward, and you can probably easily derive it from what we've already defined. The more difficult part of implementing the controller will be creating the RPC interface for the Instant Messaging server. In addition to this we will need to create the event-based protocol on top of technology that does not directly support this. Fortunately, we will be using the GWT-RPC implementation, which saves quite a bit of time by letting us avoid designing a protocol and providing a method of server communication that is intuitive to Java developers.

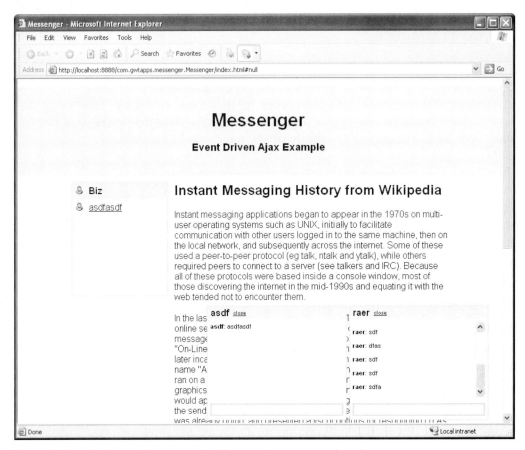

Figure 9–12. The Instant Messenger interface running on a sample web page

To start to understand the controller, let's look at the sequence of events that it handles in the lifetime of the application. It starts the application by setting up the main views. As you saw earlier, the `MessengerView` displays the `SignInView` to start, so the application waits for the user to sign in. Once the user has entered a sign-in name, the controller creates the `ContactList` model object and sends the sign-in name to the server so the server can broadcast to all the other connected clients that this user has come online. Once this sign-in step is complete, the controller tells the view and the view displays the contact list. At this point the controller is set up to receive events from the server, so as other contacts come online or go offline, the controller gets these events and processes them to be reflected in the view. The user also has the opportunity to send a message. In this case the controller receives the event from the application's view and relays the message to the server, which will then send it to the message's recipient. The opposite happens when another client sends a message to the current user: The controller receives the message as an event and passes it to the view to render.

Implementing the controller can be divided into three parts. First is the entry point responsible for handling the start-up call by creating the connection to the server and attaching the view to the HTML host document. The second part implements the client-side RPC interface for remote communication in response to events from the view. The third part, the server-side implementation of the RPC interface, handles connections from many clients and relays events.

The class structure for the controller is fairly simple but may require some knowledge of RPC to fully understand. Looking at the structure illustrated in Figure 9-3 before considering the RPC might be helpful.

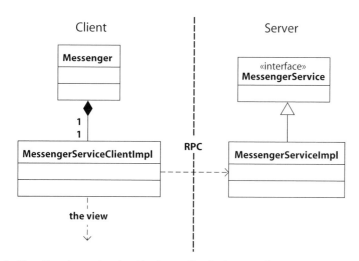

Figure 9–13.   The classes involved in the application's controller

Let's start by looking at the entry point as it's implemented in the Messenger class. The Messenger class simply creates an instance of an RPC client class and inserts the view into the host web page using the messengerView ID:

```
public class Messenger implements EntryPoint{
    public void onModuleLoad() {
        MessengerServiceClientImpl messengerService =
            new MessengerServiceClientImpl(GWT.getModuleBaseURL()+"messenger");
        RootPanel.get("messengerView").add( messengerService.getView() );
    }
}
```

This class implements GWT's `EntryPoint` interface and its `onModule Load` method. When GWT loads this application, this method is called first. The code in the method creates an instance of the `MessengerService ClientImpl` class, which has the job of interacting with the messenger server and the application's view. The `MessengerView` instance, responsible for managing the application's view, is instantiated as a member of the `MessengerServiceClientImpl` class. In the application's `EntryPoint` method in the `Messenger` class, the view is retrieved from the `Messenger ServiceClientImpl` instance and inserted into the host HTML page using GWT's `RootPanel` class. The `MessengerServiceClientImpl` class deals with interacting with the application's view and the server. The communication with the server is done using the GWT-RPC library.

Using GWT-RPC

The Google Web Toolkit provides many tools to programmatically make calls to servers, as you've seen in previous sample applications. All of them rely on web-standard technology or are open enough for you to decide on the format used. This allows the maximum amount of flexibility when deciding on communication technology for an application. GWT does not try to prescribe how to use the technologies that are available in the browser, but GWT provides Remote Procedure Call (RPC) as an additional technology for network communication. Built on standard browser functionality, it provides a high level of abstraction away from network protocols and is exclusive to GWT. The goal of RPC implementations is to provide callable methods in the client, which eventually call a similar method on the server. This facilitates network communication so that the protocol details are hidden from application developers. Since application developers are familiar with calling methods in their code, they do not have to learn much new technology and will not make as many coding errors as they would using a protocol directly.

The GWT-RPC implementation works by automatically providing a proxy object for a server interface. The client application uses the proxy object to communicate with the server by calling methods. The server handles calls from the proxy and dispatches them to the corresponding Java method implementations. Any return values are sent back to the client's proxy. The client application making the call provides the proxy with a callback object that receives any return value from the server or any failure messages. Figure 9-14 illustrates how GWT-RPC works.

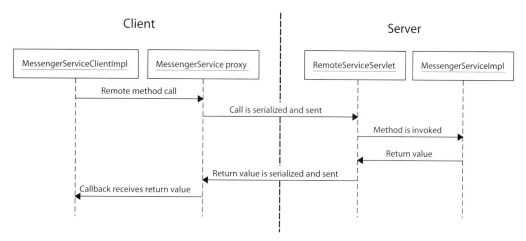

Figure 9–14. How GWT-RPC works

In Figure 9-14, the `MessengerServiceClientImpl` is our controller code that makes RPC method calls to the server and handles the results in a callback. The `MessengerService` proxy is an object GWT generates to implement an asynchronous version of the `MessengerService` interface and as well as GWT's `ServiceDefTarget` interface. (We'll describe the asynchronous version of the `MessengerService` interface, called `MessengerServiceAsync`, a little later.) On the server an instance of GWT's `RemoteServiceServlet` class handles the serialized request and invokes the requested method on the `MessengerServerImpl` instance, which uses the `RemoteServiceServlet` as its superclass. The UML diagram in Figure 9-15 illustrates the relationships between the interfaces and classes involved in this RPC system.

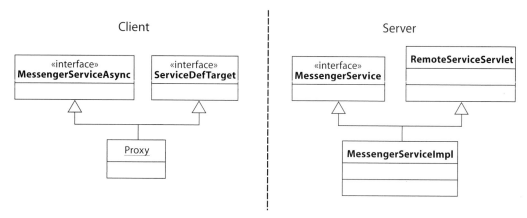

Figure 9–15. Relationships between RPC interfaces and classes

On the client-side, the generated proxy object implements both the `MessengerServiceAsync` interface and the `ServiceDefTarget` interface. On the server-side, the `MessengerServiceImpl` instances implement the `MessengerService` interface and extend GWT's `Remote ServiceServlet`.

The `RemoteService` Interface

Now let's look at this system's implementation starting with the `Messenger Service` interface. `MessengerService` is a regular Java interface that defines the methods we want to use for remote communication to our server. The following is the definition of the `MessengerService` interface:

```
public interface MessengerService extends RemoteService {
    void signIn( String name );
    void signOut();
    void sendMessage( Contact to, Message message );
}
```

GWT remote interfaces must extend GWT's `RemoteService` interface. The `RemoteService` interface is empty and simply acts as a tag to tell the GWT compiler that this interface will be used for RPC communication.

For our application, the interface defines three methods that will be used as the signatures for three different calls to the server. First, the controller will call the `signIn` method when the user provides a display name in the view. The server will implement this method, and when it is invoked will announce to other connected clients that this user has come online. The second is the `signOut` method, which has the opposite behavior of the `signIn` method: all connected clients are notified that this user has gone offline. The third method, `sendMessage`, will be implemented on the server to send a message to the specified contact. Notice that this method takes regular Java objects as parameters. It could also return a regular Java object or primitive value. This is one of the nice features of GWT-RPC—we can send Java objects and translation to a wire format performed by GWT. The only thing we need to do to support this is to implement GWT's `IsSerializable` interface or Java's `Serializable` interface along with a `no-arg` constructor on the classes we want to send. For example, the following code shows the `Contact` class defined in our model implementing the `IsSerializable` interface:

```
public class Contact implements IsSerializable{
```

When the GWT compiler sees this interface on a class, it knows to generate the required code that will serialize an instance of this class for use in its RPC implementation.

The `RemoteServiceServlet` Class

A server-side class implements the `MessengerService` interface. In our implementation we have a servlet called `MessengerServiceImpl` that implements the `MessengerService` interface, and instead of extending `HttpServlet` to get the functionality to run in a servlet container, the class extends GWT's `RemoveServiceServlet`. The `RemoteServiceServlet` class is an `HttpServlet` that does some extra work to translate the RPC calls from a client to invoke method implementations on the class. This class makes implementing the `MessengerService` on the server very simple and clean without any RPC code. The following example shows an empty server-side RPC implementation:

```
public class MessengerServiceImpl
extends RemoteServiceServlet implements MessengerService {
    public void signIn( String name ){
    }

    public void signOut(){
    }

    public void sendMessage( Contact to, Message message ){
    }
}
```

As you can see, there are empty implementations for the `MessengerService` methods, and the only trace of RPC is the mention of superclass `Remote ServiceServlet`. When this servlet is deployed in a servlet container, it is ready to receive GWT-RPC. Adding the following line to the application's module file will register the servlet with GWT's embedded Tomcat server:

```
<servlet path="/messenger"
class="com.gwtapps.messenger.server.MessengerServiceImpl"/>
```

Notice that the path to the servlet is set to `/messenger`. This is the path that the client-side code needs to reference to connect. Similarly, you must use a matching path when deploying to a servlet container in the `web.xml` file (see Chapter 3 for an example of a web.xml file).

Using an Asynchronous Interface

It would be nice if we could use the server's `MessengerService` interface to make our calls in the client. The one problem that prohibits this is that our method calls must be asynchronous. If they were blocking calls[4], they would stop the single thread used for JavaScript in a browser and the application would appear to freeze. Also, a callback is needed to inform the client if the method failed or succeeded and whether there is a return value. So, the asynchronous interface matches the `MessengerService` interface except each method cannot provide a return value and must accept a callback object as the last parameter. When the client makes a call to the server over one of the interface methods, the method returns immediately. The return value for the method is passed as an object to the callback. To implement a callback for an RPC method you need to provide an implementation of GWT's `AsyncCallback` interface:

```
public interface AsyncCallback {
    void onFailure(Throwable caught);
    void onSuccess(Object result);
}
```

The single parameter of the `onSuccess` method represents the return value of the method called. The `onFailure` method's parameter is an exception thrown either by GWT due to a communication failure or from code on our server side.

The implementation of the `MessengerService` interface's asynchronous version is called `MessengerServiceAsync`, and it has a method for each method on the `MessengerService` interface with the same signature, except each method does not have a return value and has an extra parameter of the type `AsyncCallback`. The following is the asynchronous version of the `MessengerService` interface:

```
public interface MessengerServiceAsync {
    void signIn( String name, AsyncCallback callback );
    void signOut( AsyncCallback callback );
    void sendMessage(Contact to, Message message, AsyncCallback callback );
}
```

---

4. A blocking call is a method call that does not return immediately but instead waits for a resource to be available.

The client code can make calls on this interface to communicate with the server, but first it must create a proxy object that will run on the client and automatically translate these calls to HTTP requests to be sent to the server. A proxy object can be created like this:

```
MessengerServiceAsync messengerService =
(MessengerServiceAsync) GWT.create( MessengerService.class );
```

In this code the GWT.create method instantiates a class through its deferred binding mechanism. This GWT feature allows different imple-mentations to be chosen at runtime depending on the browser being used or other criteria. In this case GWT notices that the MessengerService class implements RemoteService, so it knows to create a proxy instance implementing the MessengerServiceAsync interface. When the client makes calls to the methods of this interface, the proxy translates them to the RPC format and makes a call on the server. At this point the proxy is not connected and the server URL still needs to be specified. The follow-ing code connects the proxy instance to the server specified at the given URL:

```
ServiceDefTarget endpoint = (ServiceDefTarget) messengerService;
endpoint.setServiceEntryPoint( GWT.getModuleBaseURL() + "messenger" );
```

The proxy also implements the ServiceDefTarget interface, which pro-vides a method to set the remote URL. Once the URL is set, method calls can be made from the client using the asynchronous interface. The follow-ing is an example of calling the signIn method on the server from the client:

```
messengerService.signIn( name, new AsyncCallback(){
    public void onFailure(Throwable throwable){
        GWT.log("error sign in",throwable);
    }

    public void onSuccess(Object obj){
        /* TODO: change view to acknowledge success */
    }
});
```

To the client this looks like a regular method call with an added callback instance. The proxy handles this method by serializing the parameters and sending the call to the server. When the server completes the method call, it sends a response back. If the remote call is successful, the proxy calls the onSuccess method on the callback instance passing the return value, if any, from the server as the `Object` parameter. If the call fails, the `onFailure` method is called on the callback instance.

At this point we've looked at what it takes to make a complete implementation with GWT-RPC. This includes creating an interface that represents the interface exposed by the server to accept calls from a client. In this case this is the `MessengerService` interface. The server implements this interface and extends GWT's `RemoteServiceServlet` to handle incoming HTTP requests and translate them to invoke Java methods on the servlet. The calls are made by a proxy object that implements an asynchronous version of the remote interface and is created using the `GWT.create` method. With this complete, we can start to look at how our application implements these remote calls in the client.

Connecting to the Server

The `MessengerServiceClientImpl` class handles the bulk of the controller's work. This class handles the interaction with the view and makes method calls to the server through GWT-RPC. To interact with the view it implements the `MessengerViewListener` interface and its required methods. It also creates a `MessengerView` and stores its reference. The following is the declaration for this class and its methods that allow it to interact with the view:

```
public class MessengerServiceClientImpl implements MessengerViewListener{

    private MessengerServiceAsync messengerService;
    private ContactList contactList;
    private MessengerView view = new MessengerView( this );

    public MessengerServiceClientImpl( String url ){
        messengerService = (MessengerServiceAsync) GWT.create(
            MessengerService.class );
        ServiceDefTarget endpoint = (ServiceDefTarget) messengerService;
        endpoint.setServiceEntryPoint( url );
    }

    public MessengerView getView(){
        return view;
    }

    public void onSignIn( String name ){
        contactList = new ContactList( name );
```

```
   messengerService.signIn( name, new SignInCallback() );
}

public void onSignOut(){
   messengerService.signOut( new EmptyCallback() );
}

public void onSendMessage( Contact toContact, Message message ){
   messengerService.sendMessage( toContact, message, new EmptyCallback());
}
```

The constructor implements the creation of the RPC proxy using
GWT.create as described earlier. Also, the MessengerViewListener
implements the onSignIn, onSignOut, and onSendMessage methods
to respond to events from the application's view.

The onSignIn method creates a new ContactList object based on the
name provided from the view and then calls the RPC method signIn to
let the server know that a user has signed in. The application handles the
response with the SignInCallback inner class:

```
private class SignInCallback implements AsyncCallback{
   public void onFailure(Throwable throwable){
      GWT.log("error sign in",throwable);
   }

   public void onSuccess(Object obj){
      view.setContactList( contactList );
   }
}
```

When the signIn call succeeds on the server, the onSuccess method is
called on this callback, which sets the contact list on the view. The view in
turn switches from the sign-in view to the contact list view.

The view calls the onSignOut method when the browser window is closing or the user navigates to another URL. The implementation simply calls
the signOut method on the server. The application handles the response
with the EmptyCallback inner class:

```
private class EmptyCallback implements AsyncCallback{
   public void onFailure(Throwable throwable){
      GWT.log("error",throwable);
   }
```

```
    public void onSuccess(Object obj){
    }
}
```

This callback reports errors and is used as the callback for the `sendMessage` call to the server.

Finally, the view calls the `MessengerServiceClientImpl`'s `onSend Message` method after the user enters a message and presses Enter. The `Contact` and `Message` objects can be passed directly through the `send Message` call to the server since they implement the `IsSerializable` interface.

Adding RPC Events

Instant messaging requires an event-based protocol. This is something that may be easy for a desktop application since it can be based on a TCP/IP sockets implementation, but Ajax applications rely on HTTP, which does not support event broadcasting. HTTP only supports sending a response to a client-initiated request, and the server can't send data without a request.

Not all RPC implementations require RPC events, only certain applications. For example, let's look at an e-mail client, since it is both popularly implemented on the desktop and on the web and typically does not use an event-based protocol. E-mail client applications are implemented to retrieve e-mail data from a server in batches through periodic checks and display e-mails to the user. Users are accustomed to e-mail being retrieved in batches, and we even see user interface features for this behavior in the form of an application's button to bypass the wait and initiate a check. Ajax applications can easily replicate this behavior, as you've seen in previous chapters, by making an asynchronous HTTP request to the server.

Polling Protocols

The technique to retrieve data in e-mail applications and many Ajax applications is called **polling.** Polling is easy to implement both in a client and as a network protocol. It has been successfully used for e-mail protocols for a long time, and it is easy to implement in an Ajax application. The downside to polling is that there is latency for the message delivery. For

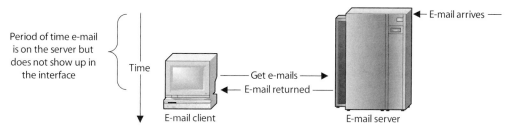

Figure 9–16.   E-mail latency

example, as a result of this periodic check in an e-mail client, e-mail is not received the instant it arrives on the server, but only after the client requests new e-mails from the server, as illustrated in Figure 9-16.

As you can see, the e-mail client experiences latency in receiving an e-mail. Of course the latency isn't too bad, because we don't expect e-mails immediately, and because its maximum delay is its polling interval, which is usually only a few minutes.

With e-mail clients and many other applications, users accept that data is not instantaneous or realtime and use a refresh or data retrieval button without much hassle. However, there are some applications where this latency would not be acceptable. For example, in an instant messenger we expect to see presence and message events the instant they happen. Let's look at the different ways we could implement an application which receives instant events.

Starting with an e-mail client application's polling implementation, we could simply reduce the period for checks to a small enough number where the responses become quick enough that they seem instantaneous. This solution would work but would not scale. For example, if we reduced the period to one second, each client connected would receive events seemingly instantly, but would also make a new request each second regardless of whether any e-mails were available on the server. If 1,000 clients used e-mail on the server, you can easily see that the server resources would need to support 1,000 requests per second. This is not very economical given such a simple task. For any application that will have more than a few users, a polling implementation will not work to provide instantaneous or realtime data to its clients.

A better solution is to receive events from the server only when new data or updates are available. The client would have no way of knowing when new data is available, so with this method the server must send the client data without any matching request. The difference between this method and the polling method is that data is only transferred when it's available, which would increase performance and save bandwidth.

Event-Based Protocols

Event-based protocols benefit from the Observer design pattern, a popular pattern in software development that allows the state of an object to be observed. The pattern is typically used to prevent coupling between two distinct components. The subject of the observer in the pattern provides an interface for the observer that must be implemented to be notified of state changes in the subject. Use of this pattern in software development has been around quite a while. Examples in early computer software include receiving events from the operating system in the form of interrupts. The operating system would handle these interrupts, such as typed data arriving from the keyboard, at the time they were called instead of having the application poll a device for information. This technique saved CPU cycles for a computer in the same way an event model used over a network saves bandwidth. We also see a similar solution within GWT's UI event system, where our application can register to receive events from widgets. In this situation the client code registers itself as a listener so it can be called when an event occurs.

In a network environment the server is the subject and the client is the observer. If a network protocol were to actually implement the Observer pattern, we would see the subject/server calling an interface on the client. We do not see this with the mail client and, as we noted before, the mail client does not use an event-based protocol. With an instant messenger protocol being event-based, the client does respond to calls from the server and therefore follows the Observer pattern.

To understand the benefit from an event protocol, let's look at how an instant messenger communicates with its server compared to the e-mail client. The instant messenger client starts by connecting to the server and then waits for events. When a contact comes online or when a message arrives, the server sends a message over the already established connection to the client, as illustrated in Figure 9-17.

As you can see in Figure 9-17, when compared to the diagram of the e-mail protocol in Figure 9-16, there isn't the same latency between events arriv-

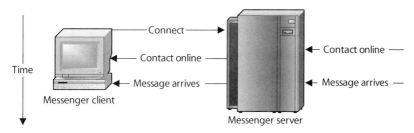

Figure 9–17.   Low latency with instant messaging

ing on the server and events arriving on the client. The only latency would
be the time it takes to send a short notification message over the existing
connection. To the user, on a normal connection, this will seem instantaneous. This solution also requires far less resources than the polling
method.

Creating a protocol that allows this behavior is actually fairly simple with a
standard TCP/IP connection, since it allows bidirectional communication
in any format. We could format each event as a message and send this
data from the server over the connection to the client at any time. These
types of connections, commonly called **sockets,** are usually provided by
the operating system with a supporting library in the language of choice.
They are typically used for desktop applications that need to communicate with a server. Unfortunately, since Ajax applications are limited to the
features a web browser provides, we don't have the luxury of this type of
connection. We can only rely on, and are limited by, HTTP for network
communication. This is why creating event-based Ajax applications is
somewhat rare and difficult.

As you've seen previously, Ajax applications are able to asynchronously
communicate to a server using a browser facility called XMLHttpRequest.
Although using this object does not dictate that you need to be requesting
XML data, it does not allow any protocol other than HTTP. HTTP, unfortunately, is strictly based on requests and responses, like the e-mail protocol,
and does not offer the ability to receive messages from the server that were
not paired with a request. The HTTP connection fails to act as a transport
for an event-based protocol.

However, to build the Instant Messenger application with GWT in this
chapter, we will overcome this limitation of Ajax applications. We will use
the HTTP request functionality that is provided by a browser to gain the

responsiveness of desktop applications based on event-based protocols and avoid the latency and scalability issues of a polling solution.

Implementing Events

The RPC implementation that comes with GWT does not provide any sort of event mechanism. That is, we can only receive data back from the server as a direct request from a method call. To support notifying other clients about a contact's online status or to send a message to another client, we need to be able to support events. At the beginning of this section we looked at a polling alternative; we could implement polling through GWT-RPC by periodically checking the server for new messages or contacts over a small interval. However, this solution proves to be too costly on server resources. An alternative is to support an event-based protocol where the server only sends data to clients when it's available. This is the ideal solution, but due to HTTP limitations and, therefore, GWT-RPC, we cannot build an interface that requires a pure event-based protocol. We can, however, obtain a close approximation.

The solution, a hanging RPC call, is a mix between polling and server events. It has the advantage of instant events from the server and does not suffer from the same performance problems a polling implementation would.

The sequence involved in a hanging RPC call starts with the client calling the hanging RPC method; for this application we call that method `getEvents`. The server handles this call by identifying the user and checking to see if there are any pending events for him. If there are, the method returns a list of events. If there aren't any events, the server blocks the thread with a maximum wait time; for our application we set this to 30 seconds. If no events are available after 30 seconds, the method returns and the client calls `getEvents` again. If an event does arrive while the thread is hanging, the thread is woken up and returns the event to the client immediately. This solution provides instant event notification and reduces polling frequency to 30 seconds. The downside of this technique is that a thread on the server is held up for each client that is waiting for events. For this technique to scale, you would need to use a very large thread pool or a server that provides a way to release a thread in these situations (we handle this problem later in this chapter).

The implementation on the client is fairly straightforward. First we need to add a new method to the `MessengerService` and `MessengerService Async` interfaces to represent the hanging RPC call:

```
public interface MessengerService extends RemoteService {
    void signIn( String name );
    void signOut();
    void sendMessage( Contact to, Message message );
    /**
     * @gwt.typeArgs <com.gwtapps.messenger.client.Event>
     */
    List getEvents();
}
```

Notice that we're specifying the `gwt.typeArgs` Javadoc annotation. The GWT compiler uses this as a hint when generating the serialization code for this interface. In this case the code tells the GWT compiler that the returned collection of the `getEvents` method can only contain instances of the `Event` class. This lets the compiler reduce the amount of code that needs to be generated since it knows only `Event` instances need to be serialized for this method. You can use this type of annotation for fields on serializable classes and also for RPC interface parameters. For example, you could write the following code to send events to the server in a list:

```
/**
 * @gwt.typeArgs events <com.gwtapps.messenger.client.Event>
 * @gwt.typeArgs <com.gwtapps.messenger.client.Event>
 */
List sendAndGetEvents( List events );
```

Getting back to the application, next we need to make a call to `getEvents` after we've signed in the `SignInCallback` inner class for `Messenger ServiceClientImpl`:

```
private class SignInCallback implements AsyncCallback{
    public void onFailure(Throwable throwable){
        GWT.log("error sign in",throwable);
    }

    public void onSuccess(Object obj){
        view.setContactList( contactList );
        messengerService.getEvents( new GetEventsCallback() );
    }
}
```

The callback used for the `getEvents` call, `GetEventsCallback`, iterates over the call's return value, in this case a list of events:

```
private class GetEventsCallback implements AsyncCallback {
   public void onFailure(Throwable throwable){
      GWT.log("error get events",throwable);
   }

   public void onSuccess(Object obj){
      List events = (List)obj;
      for( int i=0; i< events.size(); ++i ){
         Object event = events.get(i);
         handleEvent( event );
      }
      messengerService.getEvents( this );
   }
}
```

After handling each event, the callback calls the `getEvents` method on the server again. This is an endless cycle that mimics an event loop.

Each event in the list of events is a simple object with attributes that act as parameters for the event. For the Instant Messenger application we define three events: `SignOnEvent`, `SignOffEvent`, and `SendMessageEvent`:

```
public class Event implements IsSerializable{
}

public class SignOnEvent implements Event{
   public Contact contact;
}

public class SignOffEvent implements Event {
   public Contact contact;
}

public class SendMessageEvent implements Event {
   public Contact sender;
   public Message message;
}
```

The server generates these events in response to other clients' actions. When the `MessengerServiceClientImpl` instance receives them, they are handled to invoke the appropriate actions on the view. This work is done in the `handleEvent` method:

```
protected void handleEvent( Object event ){
    if( event instanceof SendMessageEvent ){
        SendMessageEvent sendMessageEvent = (SendMessageEvent)event;
        view.getChatWindowView( sendMessageEvent.sender ).addMessage(
            sendMessageEvent.message );
    }
    else if( event instanceof SignOnEvent ){
        SignOnEvent signOnEvent = (SignOnEvent)event;
        view.getContactListView().addContact(signOnEvent.contact);
    }
    else if( event instanceof SignOffEvent ){
        SignOffEvent signOffEvent = (SignOffEvent)event;
        view.getContactListView().removeContact(signOffEvent.contact);
    }
}
```

If the event is a `SendMessageEvent` instance, the application retrieves the `ChatWindowView` and adds the message to it using the `addMessage` method. If the event is a `SignOnEvent` instance, the application retrieves the `ContactListView` and adds the contact to it. Finally, if the event is a `SignOffEvent` instance, the application retrieves the `ContactListView` and removes the contact from it.

The server side handles implementing the rest of the GWT-RPC events.

The Instant Messenger Server

Now let's look at what is required to build the instant messenger functionality into the server. The GWT-RPC servlet's superclass `RemoteServiceServlet` already does all the work of translating the asynchronous HTTP calls to method calls. We need to implement each of the methods defined in the `MessengerService` interface (described earlier) and the event broadcasting functionality.

First, let's look at implementing the event broadcasting. To do this we will need to keep track of each client that is connected and hold a list of pending events. When a new event needs to be delivered to a client, it will be added to her list; if there is a thread waiting, then it will be released. The following is the declaration for the `MessengerServiceImpl` class along with its private variables and the `getCurrentUser` helper method:

```
public class MessengerServiceImpl
    extends RemoteServiceServlet implements MessengerService {
```

```
protected static final int MAX_MESSAGE_LENGTH = 256;
protected static final int MAX_NAME_LENGTH = 10;
private Map users = new HashMap();

private class UserInfo{
    Contact contact;
    List events = new ArrayList();
}

protected UserInfo getCurrentUser(){
    String id = getThreadLocalRequest().getSession().getId();
    synchronized( this ){
        //the user's map gets populated in the signin method
        //it is synchronized because multiple clients will be using it
        return (UserInfo)users.get(id);
    }
}
```

The first two constant values represent some limitations to message and contact name length (we will use them later). The `UserInfo` inner class is used as the structure to represent a connected user. It has a `Contact` instance, which is the model object for the connected user and a list of events. Each connected client has its `UserInfo` instance stored in the user's map keyed on its session ID.

If you're not familiar with what a session is, that's okay—we use it briefly here and will provide a brief explanation. A **session** is a server-side concept representing a connection with one client, and it usually lasts as long as the client keeps his browser open. It allows server-side code to set variables unique to the user that can be used between requests and provides an ID to identify the user. For the messenger server we use the ID as the key for `UserInfo` instances in the user's map. At the start of each method call we need to identify which user is making the call. We could require that the client provide its sign-in name for each method call, but this would be vulnerable to impersonation attacks. Instead, we identify the user at the beginning of each method call by its session ID. The `getCurrentUser` method in the preceding code can get the `UserInfo` object for the current user.

Now let's look at the implementation for the `getEvents` method:

```
public ArrayList getEvents(){
    ArrayList events = null;
    UserInfo user = getCurrentUser();
    if( user != null ){
        if( user.events.size() == 0 ){
```

```
        try{
            synchronized( user ){
                user.wait( 30*1000 );
            }
        }
        catch (InterruptedException ignored){}
    }
    synchronized( user ){
        events = user.events;
        user.events = new ArrayList();
    }
  }
  return events;
}
```

The goal of this method is to return a list of events if they're available. If there are no events available, the method calls the `wait` method on the user object. The `wait` method is a thread synchronization method that is available on all Java objects. It causes the current thread to stop processing for a maximum amount of time specified by the parameter in milliseconds. In this case we use 30,000 milliseconds, or 30 seconds. The thread can continue if another thread calls the `notifyAll` method on the object. In this case the `notifyAll` method will be called on this user object when an event has been added to its list. The method completes by returning the event list and resetting the event list on the user object so that it is ready to accept new events.

To understand how the `getEvents` thread is released, let's look at the implementation of the `sendMessage` method:

```
public void sendMessage( Contact to, Message message ){
    String cleanMessage = cleanString( message.toString(),MAX_MESSAGE_LENGTH);

    UserInfo sender = getCurrentUser();
    UserInfo receiver = getUserByName( to.getName() );

    if( receiver != null ){
        SendMessageEvent event = new SendMessageEvent();
        event.sender = sender.contact;
        event.message = new Message( cleanMessage );

        synchronized( receiver ){
            receiver.events.add( event );
            receiver.notifyAll();
        }
    }
}
```

This method is supposed to receive a message from one user and send it as an event to the Contact specified in the parameter (see the source code for the implementation of the cleanString method). The message receiver's UserInfo instance is obtained, and if the user is connected, a new SendMessageEvent is created. The new event has its attributes set to the message value and the sender's identification, and the new event is added to the receiver's list of events. Then the notifyAll method is called on the receiver, causing the receiver's thread waiting in the getEvents method to wake up and return the new event. Figure 9-18 illustrates this process.

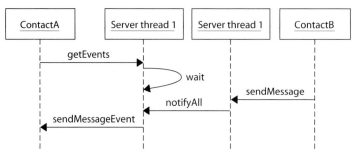

Figure 9–18.   Thread synchronization for events

The SendMessageEvent sent back to the client in this scenario is unique since it is only sent to one client. The notifyAll method is only called on the UserInfo instance that belongs to the message's recipient. Any other clients connected with threads waiting for getEvents are not notified.

For the SignOnEvent and SignOffEvent we must deliver the events to each connected client so everyone receives these presence updates. To implement this we need to write a broadcastEvent helper method:

```
protected void broadcastEvent( Object event, UserInfo except ){
    synchronized( this ){
        Set entrySet = users.entrySet();
        for( Iterator it = entrySet.iterator(); it.hasNext(); ){
            Map.Entry entry = (Map.Entry)it.next();
            UserInfo user = (UserInfo)entry.getValue();
            if( user != except ){
                synchronized( user ){
                    user.events.add( event );
                    user.notifyAll();
                }
            }
        }
    }
}
```

This method takes an event instance and broadcasts it to every connected client except for the client represented by the `UserInfo` instance provided in the method's parameters. The reason for an exception is that the event's sender does not need to be notified. Sending the event to each connected client is simple. The code iterates over the map of `UserInfo` instances, adds the event to their event list, and calls the object's `notifyAll` method to wake up any waiting threads.

The `broadcastEvent` method is used in implementing both the `signOut` and the `signIn` methods. Let's look at the `signOut` implementation first since it is simpler:

```
public void signOut(){
   Contact contact;
   String id = getThreadLocalRequest().getSession().getId();
   synchronized( this ){
      UserInfo user = (UserInfo)users.get(id);
      contact = user.contact;
      users.remove(id);
   }

   //create sign-off event
   SignOffEvent event = new SignOffEvent();
   event.contact = contact;
   broadcastEvent( event, null );
}
```

This implementation simply removes the `UserInfo` that represents this connection from the user's map and then broadcasts a `SignOffEvent` to every other contact.

The `signIn` method does the opposite and a bit more: It creates a new `UserInfo` object to add to the user's map, broadcasts the `SignOnEvent` to every other user, and then sends a `SignOnEvent` for each user to the user signing on. The reason that sign-on events are sent for each connecting user is to provide the client with the `Contacts` to fill its contact list. The following shows the implementation for this method:

```
public void signIn( String name ){
   name = cleanString( name, MAX_NAME_LENGTH );

   //add user to list
   String id = getThreadLocalRequest().getSession().getId();
   UserInfo user = new UserInfo();
   user.contact = new Contact( name );
```

```
   synchronized( this ){
      users.put( id, user );
   }

   //create sign-on event
   SignOnEvent event = new SignOnEvent();
   event.contact = user.contact;
   broadcastEvent( event, user );

   //add sign-on events for current contact list
   synchronized( this ){
      Set entrySet = users.entrySet();
      for( Iterator it = entrySet.iterator(); it.hasNext(); ){
         Map.Entry entry = (Map.Entry)it.next();
         UserInfo userTemp = (UserInfo)entry.getValue();
         if( userTemp != user ){
            SignOnEvent eventTemp = new SignOnEvent();
            eventTemp.contact = userTemp.contact;
            user.events.add( eventTemp );
         }
      }
   }
}
```

The three methods on the `MessengerService` interface are now imple-mented along with the event functionality. Running the application with the servlet at this point will allow multiple users to sign into the server to see who else is online and exchange messages.

Using Server-Side Advanced IO

It's great that with the techniques presented in this chapter we've been able to receive events from the server without resorting to pure polling. Performance is greatly improved compared to polling since each request waits up to 30 seconds before trying again, and the clients still receive instant responses. To accomplish this with polling, we would have to poll at the most every second, which would put an impractical strain on the server.

Although performance is fairly good with this solution, it's not quite ideal. The problem is that each client waiting for an event is blocking a thread on the server. Servlet containers always have a maximum number of concur-rent threads that can be running at one time, which means that this thread maximum is the maximum number of clients that can use your application at one time. If you have a small application audience this might not be a big deal; default thread count maximums are usually 100 to 200. But what happens if you expect 1,000 or even 10,000 concurrent users, which is reasonable for a single-server application?

Running 10,000 threads at once takes a lot of memory and opens the door to massive processing spikes that would bring your server to a halt. Typically event-based threading is fairly idle, but a malicious client could open 10,000 connections to make nonidle calls. Your server would slow down for quite a while. This is the reason for lower maximum thread counts. If you do get flooded, some clients will have to wait a little longer to get a thread. Furthermore, thread switching between 10,000 threads becomes a noticeable drop in performance.

In most HTTP servers there is a 1:1 relationship between a connection and a thread. This means if a client is connected, that connection gets a dedicated thread. Figure 9-19 shows the 1:1 relationship between connections and threads on the server. For each client request there is a dedicated connection and a dedicated thread.

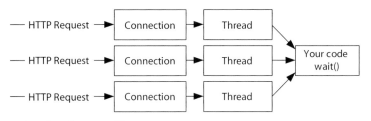

Figure 9–19.   Regular server IO

Why isn't this a problem for regular use of HTTP? Because regular use of HTTP doesn't have the thread wait call. When the server processes a request and returns a response to the client, the thread is freed for other connections, even if the original connection remains open. This allows an HTTP server to have many more connections than threads. A typical server's operating system, while having difficulty with 10,000 threads, doesn't have any problems handling 10,000 connections. Connections scale much better.

Fortunately, a couple of solutions to this problem have been developed specifically for Ajax-based events. The solutions require more advanced IO to be performed on connections involving nonblocking calls, which allows the server to free up threads even while a connection is pending.

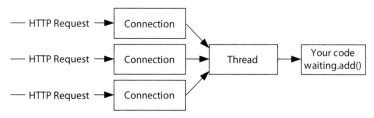

Figure 9–20.   Advanced server IO

The result is the relationship illustrated in Figure 9-20. In this situation several active connections share a single thread. Instead of having the thread block, the pending request is added to a list of pending requests. When the application has data to satisfy the request, it sends a response—most likely on a different thread.

Next we'll look at two methods of providing this advanced IO: one from Tomcat 6 and up called Comet, and one from Jetty 6 and up called Continuations.

Using Comet on Tomcat

Apache Tomcat version 6 and later supports the `CometProcessor` interface on its servlets. The interface has one method, `event`, that needs to be implemented. It takes a `CometEvent` as a parameter and is called for each asynchronous event that occurs on the connection. Your servlet receives BEGIN, END, ERROR, and READ events, and once it's done with the event it calls the `CometEvent`'s `close` method. The event represents one request-response cycle and replaces `doPost` and `doGet` method implementations. You can retrieve the `HttpServletRequest` and `HTTPServletResponse` instances from the event to read and write.

Using this feature we can handle READ events on a servlet to read the pay-load and use the pluggable RPC from GWT 1.4 and up to handle the request. Once the request is handled, we call `close` on the event. A special case needs to be made for the `getEvents` method, which in the previous implementation blocked the current thread. Instead, we will call `getEvents` only if there are events for the current user; otherwise, the servlet saves the response in a list until events arrive and the current thread moves on to process other requests. Let's look at the event method that accomplishes this:

```
class PendingRequest{
   RPCRequest rpcRequest;
   CometEvent event;
   public PendingRequest(RPCRequest rpcRequest, CometEvent event) {
      this.rpcRequest = rpcRequest;
      this.event = event;
   }
}

Map pendingRequests = new HashMap();
CometMessengerService messengerService =  new CometMessengerService();
public void event(CometEvent event) throws IOException, ServletException {
   if (event.getEventType() == CometEvent.EventType.READ) {
      //get the RPC request
      RPCRequest rpcRequest = RPC.decodeRequest( readRequest( event ) );
      Method targetMethod = rpcRequest.getMethod();

      //if it's the event request, then wait for events
      synchronized(pendingRequests){
      messengerService.perThreadRequest.set( event.getHttpServletRequest() );
      if( targetMethod.getName().equals("getEvents") &&
         !messengerService.hasEvents() ){
         //save this request for processing later
         pendingRequests.put( messengerService.getCurrentId(),
            new PendingRequest( rpcRequest, event ) );
      }
      else{
         //otherwise process the RPC call as usual
         sendResponse( event, rpcRequest );
      }
      }
   }
}
```

This code also includes the `PendingRequest` inner class, which is saved in a map keyed on the user's session ID. The `PendingRequest` inner class holds a reference to the GWT-RPC `Request` object and the Tomcat `CometEvent` object. The servlet needs these two objects to send a response to the client in the `sendResponse` method:

```
public void sendResponse( CometEvent event, RPCRequest rpcRequest ) {
   try{
      try{
         messengerService.perThreadRequest.set(
            event.getHttpServletRequest() );
         String result = RPC.invokeAndEncodeResponse( messengerService,
            rpcRequest.getMethod(), rpcRequest.getParameters());
```

```
        writeResponse(event.getHttpServletResponse(), result);
        event.close();
    }
    catch (IncompatibleRemoteServiceException e) {
        writeResponse( event.getHttpServletResponse(),
            RPC.encodeResponseForFailure(null, e) );
    }
}
catch (Throwable e) {
    writeResponse( event.getHttpServletResponse(), "Server Error" );
}
}
```

In this code we use the `messengerService` as the instance for the GWT-RPC call. This instance implements the `MessengerService` interface's methods nearly the same way as the previous implementation. The difference is that the `getEvents` method no longer blocks and an `onEvent` method is called instead of waking up blocking threads with `notifyAll`. The preceding code simply executes the RPC methods as usual, including deserializing parameters and serializing the result.

To finish this implementation we have to look at the specialization of the `AbstractMessengerService` for Comet:

```
class CometMessengerService extends AbstractMessengerService{

    final ThreadLocal perThreadRequest = new ThreadLocal();
    public String getCurrentId() {
        return
((HttpServletRequest)perThreadRequest.get()).getSession(true).getId();
    }

    public void onEvents(String id) {
        synchronized(pendingRequests){
            PendingRequest pr = (PendingRequest)pendingRequests.get( id );
            if( pr != null ){
                pendingRequests.remove(id);
                sendResponse( pr.event, pr.rpcRequest );
            }
        }
    }
}
```

The important part of this specialization, the `onEvents` method, is called when the messenger service implementation has events for the client. The method checks for pending requests on for the user identified by ID. If there are, the servlet calls the `sendResponse` method, which performs the RPC call to the `getEvents` method to satisfy the user's request and serializes the response. This most likely happens on the thread from another user. For example, suppose there are three users online and a fourth signs in. The fourth calls the `signIn` RPC method. Sign-in events are put in the other three users' event queues. Then the `onEvents` method is called for each of the three users; if they have pending requests, then responses are sent. This all happens on the single thread from the fourth user but writes to three other connections.

To run this properly in Tomcat, you need to set up this servlet like any other server and refer to it from the client application. Make sure you use the `CometProcessor` interface like this:

```
public class MessengerServiceCometImpl
   extends HttpServlet implements CometProcessor {
```

You also must use either the APR or NIO connector since they are connectors that have closer integration with the networking support in your operating system and are capable of asynchronous IO. To do this you need to edit your `server.xml` file for your Tomcat installation. The following is an example of specifying a connector for NIO:

```
<Connector
   connectionTimeout="20000"
   port="8081"
   protocol="org.apache.coyote.http11.Http11NioProtocol"
   maxThreads="1"
   acceptorThreadCount="2"
   redirectPort="8443"
   socket.directBuffer="false" />
```

Also notice that this sets the `maxThreads` to 1. This value is not meant for a production application but just to test Comet with Tomcat. The Instant Messenger application ran successfully with many clients with just one server thread. Also, if you're using NIO on OS X, you need to add the following to the command line startup:

```
-Djava.net.preferIPv4Stack=true
```

Using Continuations on Jetty

Jetty was the first servlet container to provide support for Ajax events. It does so through a technique called Continuations. To use Continuations you need to create a `Continuation` object when you want to block a thread. Then you call `suspend` on the `Continuation` object. This causes an exception to be thrown and the stack to unwind out of the current servlet method. Jetty then handles this exception to free up that thread to use it for other connections. Then when a response needs to be sent to the connection that has been suspended, the `Continuation` object is retrieved and the `resume` method called. Jetty handles the `resume` method by getting an available thread and running the servlet request through the servlet again.

There are a couple of problems when using Continuations with GWT-RPC. First, you can only read the payload from the HTTP request input stream once. The second call to the RPC method will fail because there is no payload available to deserialize it. Second, when `suspend` is called and the exception is thrown, the GWT-RPC implementation catches the exception before it gets to Jetty and returns it to the GWT client application. Fortunately, with GWT 1.4 the RPC implementation is pluggable. We can use a similar solution to the one used for Tomcat.

A regular `HttpServlet` will be used that implements the `doPost` method. It reads the payload and saves it as a request attribute in case Jetty calls the RPC call again. Then the servlet uses the payload to execute the RPC request. Exception handling in the `doPost` method takes into account the exception thrown from using a `Continuation.suspend` call and rethrows it to Jetty:

```
public void doPost(HttpServletRequest httpRequest,
   HttpServletResponse httpResponse) throws ServletException, IOException {

   //get the payload
   String payload=(String)httpRequest.getAttribute("payload");
   if (payload==null){
      payload = readPayloadAsUtf8(httpRequest);
      httpRequest.setAttribute("payload",payload);
   }

   try {
      try {
         //make the RPC call
```

```
          RPCRequest rpcRequest = RPC.decodeRequest(payload);
          messengerService.perThreadRequest.set( httpRequest );
          String result = RPC.invokeAndEncodeResponse(messengerService,
             rpcRequest.getMethod(), rpcRequest.getParameters());
          writeResponse(httpResponse, result);
       }
       catch (IncompatibleRemoteServiceException e) {
          writeResponse(httpResponse, RPC.encodeResponseForFailure(null, e) );
       }
    }
    catch (Throwable e) {
       if (e instanceof RuntimeException &&
          "org.mortbay.jetty.RetryRequest".equals(e.getClass().getName())){
          throw (RuntimeException) e;
       }
    }
 }
}
```

Notice that this code is also using a specialization of the messenger service for the RPC call. It shares the `AbstractMessengerService` class that the Tomcat implementation used but overrides the `getEvents` and `onEvents` methods to use Jetty `Continuations`:

```
class ContinuationsMessengerService extends AbstractMessengerService{

   final ThreadLocal perThreadRequest = new ThreadLocal();
   public String getCurrentId() {
      return
((HttpServletRequest)perThreadRequest.get()).getSession(true).getId();
   }

   public void onEvents(String id) {
      synchronized(pendingRequests){
         Continuation c = (Continuation)pendingRequests.get( id );
         if( c != null ){
            pendingRequests.remove(id);
            c.resume();
         }
      }
   }

   public ArrayList getEvents(){
      ArrayList events = null;
      UserInfo user = getCurrentUser();
      if( user != null  ){
         if( user.events.size() == 0){
            Continuation continuation = ContinuationSupport.getContinuation(
               ((HttpServletRequest)perThreadRequest.get()),this);
```

```
            pendingRequests.put(user.id,continuation);
            continuation.suspend(30000);
        }
        synchronized( user ){
            events = user.events;
            user.events = new ArrayList();
        }
    }
    return events;
}
}
```

Support for both Jetty Continuations and Tomcat's Comet implementation is relatively new at the time of writing this book. Hopefully, development will mature and libraries will be made that make events a part of GWT-RPC.

Summary

Creating the Instant Messenger application helps illustrate the construction of a nonintrusive web application that uses GWT-RPC and HTTP events. The application's model provides a simple representation of the data involved with the application. The view is able to integrate and complement an existing web page or application. The application takes into account well-known instant messenger UI conventions, including notifying the user of messages in the bottom, right corner. The application's controller ties the model and view together and communicates with the server to send and receive model objects between clients of the same application.

The application also illustrates how to use GWT-RPC to build a Java service based on an interface, and the interface is extended to provide functionality for instant events. Although GWT-RPC won't work with non-JEE servers, it speeds up development of client-server communication by providing a nice Java interface-based abstraction.

The only things left to do with the application at this point are to extend it, add more instant messaging functionality, and deploy it. To deploy the application you need to compile it using the `Messenger-compile` script and copy the generated files to your web server. To deploy the messenger servlet you need to copy the servlet class to your servlet container implementation along with the GWT servlet JAR file, or create and deploy a WAR file (typically using Ant or Maven).

10

Database Editor Application

When deciding what type of technology to use for a new web application, it doesn't always make sense to go with the latest Ajax technology. Building web applications as traditional web pages has the advantage of simplicity and mature infrastructure. However, you may find that some tasks with a traditional web application would benefit from an Ajax utility. One common example is a web site administration tool that allows you to manage your application resources. In this chapter we will build the Database Editor application that gives fast access to web application data to facilitate its management.

The Database Editor application is based on a fictional social news web application similar to Digg (http://digg.com), where users decide the front page news. Users submit stories which are then voted on, and the stories with the most votes make it to the front page. This type of site would typically have a traditional web-based front end for its users. This interface is designed so users can easily read and submit news, but it would be cumbersome as an interface for administration. For administration, administrators could go directly to a SQL client to manage the data, but this could be dangerous: A simple mistake could have dramatic effects.

A good option is to have a client that is aware of the domain model and can accomplish administrative tasks quickly. The solution presented in this chapter is an Ajax database editor that allows fast asynchronous browsing and editing of application data.

The application illustrates many advanced topics for application development with GWT. It uses MVC architecture similar to the other sample applications, but it also uses Data Access Objects (DAOs) to access complex data structures on the server. The DAOs also provide an abstraction to the wire-data format, communication method, and server implementation. This application illustrates how to translate objects and collections of objects to XML and JSON. To relieve some of the tedium of translating Java objects to a document object model, we create and use a code generator. The application also illustrates three methods of communicating with the server: using RPC through GWT-RPC, traditional actions, and REST. On http://databaseeditor.gwtapps.com you'll find examples provided as Java for RPC, PHP for actions, and Ruby on Rails for REST.

Using the Manager Application Pattern

This application follows the Manager Application pattern. You use a manager application to manage a large set of data. It typically provides an interface that makes it straightforward to locate data and then proceed to operate on it. Operations can simply be the basic creating, reading, updating, and deleting (CRUD) data operations, or they can be more advanced application processes. Familiar manager style applications include file system explorers, e-mail clients, and media libraries like iTunes, as shown in Figure 10-1.

This sample application, based on the Manager pattern, acts as an administrator for a traditional web application. It will operate on the application's data model by providing a simple interface that dynamically loads data from the application's server.

The traditional web application chosen for this example is a social news web site similar to Digg (see http://digg.com). A social news web site allows its members to submit a link to a news story along with a short description. Other members of the site who read the story can choose whether they like it or not (a digg). When a story gets a certain number of diggs, it gets displayed on the front page. The utility of the site is that you see the most popular news, as decided by members, on the front page. The example in this chapter doesn't build this traditional web application, only a server-side implementation that supports communication with the client-side manager application and a database with a schema required to support the traditional web application. Figure 10-2 illustrates how the

Figure 10–1. Applications based on the Manager pattern

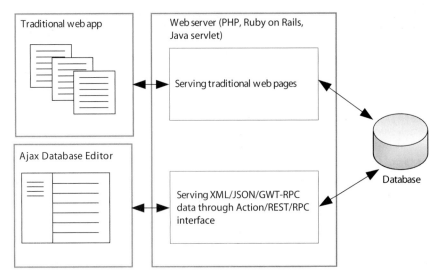

Figure 10–2. The Database Editor as part of a larger web application

Database Editor application fits into the tranditional web application architecture.

In this chapter we look at how to implement the bottom half of Figure 10-2, including the Database Editor as a GWT application, the server side as PHP scripts, a Ruby on Rails application, a Java servlet, and the database implementation.

Designing the Model

The application's model is shared between a traditional web application and a database editor since they need to operate on the same data in a shared database. The entities in the model are a User, which represents a person using the web application, and a Story, which represents one story that a User submits. The entity relationships are:

- Posted by: Each story is posted by a user
- Digs: Each story can have many users who have dug it (voted for it)

Figure 10-3 illustrates these relationships and the entities' simple fields.

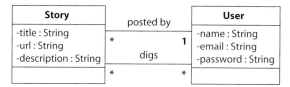

Figure 10–3.   The application's model

In the Java code, the Story class will hold a reference to an instance of User for the posted-by relationship, and it will hold a list of User instances for the digs relationship. The following is the implementation of the Story class:

```
public class Story extends BaseObject {
    private String title;
    private String url;
    private String description;
    private String user_id;

    /**
     * @gwt.typeArgs <com.gwtapps.databaseeditor.client.model.User>
     */
    private List digs;

    public String getDescription() { return description; }
    public void setDescription(String description) {
        this.description = description; }
    public List getDigs() { return digs; }
    public void setDigs(List digs) { this.digs = digs; }
    public String getTitle() { return title; }
    public void setTitle(String title) { this.title = title; }
    public String getUrl() { return url; }
    public void setUrl(String url) { this.url = url; }
    public String getUser_id() { return user_id; }
    public void setUser_id(String user_id) { this.user_id = user_id; }
}
```

This class is a simple Java object with private string members for fields and getter/setter methods. The relationships are represented by the user_id value for the posted-by relationship and the digs' List for the digs relationship. An extra comment above the digs' List field specifies the type of object that the list contains. This specification is meant as a hint to the GWT-RPC code generator as to the type of objects in the list. The code generator can generate less code for the RPC implementation (we'll look into the RPC implementation later in this chapter). You may also notice that the class extends the BaseObject class, which allows our application to use all objects in the system in a generic manner. For example, all Story and User objects have an ID field that is used for client-server communication. The following shows the implementation of the BaseObject class:

```
public class BaseObject implements Serializable {
    protected String id;
    public String getId() { return id; }
    public void setId(String id) { this.id = id; }
}
```

Notice that this class implements the Serializable interface. This interface is required for objects that will be used as arguments or return values with GWT-RPC. The GWT-RPC code generator produces serialization code for each class that supports this interface. We will also create a code generator that creates serialization code for classes with this interface to support easy serialization to XML and JSON.

Finally, let's look at the User class:

```
public class User extends BaseObject {
    private String name;
    private String email;
    private String password;

    public String getEmail() { return email; }
    public void setEmail(String email) { this.email = email; }
    public String getName() { return name; }
    public void setName(String name) { this.name = name; }
    public String getPassword() { return password; }
    public void setPassword(String password) { this.password = password; }
}
```

Like the Story class, the User class also extends the BaseObject class. This class provides getter and setter methods for its three fields.

These Java classes will be used by our client-side Database Editor application and can also be used on the server side for the Java servlet implementation with GWT-RPC. For the PHP and Ruby on Rails implementations we will handle these classes on the server side in their respective languages. The database implementation, however, can use the same schema regardless of the server-side language used. The following is the schema in SQL that we'll use for the database:

```
DROP TABLE IF EXISTS 'stories';
CREATE TABLE 'stories' (
   'id' int(11) NOT NULL auto_increment,
   'title' varchar(255) default NULL,
   'url' varchar(255) default NULL,
   'description' varchar(255) default NULL,
   'user_id' int(11) default NULL,
   PRIMARY KEY ('id')
);

DROP TABLE IF EXISTS 'user_dug';
CREATE TABLE 'user_dug' (
   'user_id' int(11) default NULL,
   'story_id' int(11) default NULL
);

DROP TABLE IF EXISTS 'users';
CREATE TABLE 'users' (
   'id' int(11) NOT NULL auto_increment,
   'name' varchar(255) default NULL,
   'email' varchar(255) default NULL,
   'password' varchar(255) default NULL,
   PRIMARY KEY (`id`)
);
```

You'll notice that the users and stories tables match the Java classes defined in this schema. The `posted-by` relationship is represented by the `user_id` foreign key in the stories table. This means that each story in the stories table will reference one user. The digs relationship is more complex since it is **many-to-many**, which means that each story can have many digs and each user can dig many stories. We cannot satisfy this relationship with a column on either the users or stories table since the relationship would need to span many rows. The solution is to create a join table for the relationship that has one foreign key for a story and one for a user. A **join table** is a table in a relational database that creates a relationship between rows in two tables by pairing their IDs in a row. In this case, every time a user digs a story, a new row gets put into this table with the user ID and the story ID.

Using Asynchronous Data Access Objects

It is good practice to separate your entity objects from the code that retrieves the entities. One way to keep access code from the entity objects is to create Data Access Objects (DAOs). Creating these objects allows us to reuse the entities elsewhere without coupling the data access code. It also allows us to easily switch between data access methods. We will see their value in this sample application because we will reuse the entity classes on the server for the GWT-RPC implementation, but we will not use the DAOs. Furthermore, the DAOs will provide a level of abstraction from the three data access methods (action, REST, and RPC) that we use in the application. The application's view will use an `ObjectDAO` interface to retrieve data and will not know the underlying implementation. If the access method does change, then no code in the view needs to change. The UML diagram in Figure 10-4 illustrates this relationship.

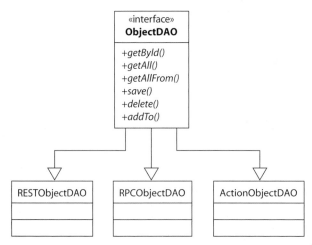

Figure 10–4.   The Data Access Objects abstraction

Each object access method will have its own DAO implementation. You'll notice that Figure 10-4 has six methods on the `ObjectDAO` interface. These are the six methods that the application's view uses to perform administrative tasks on the server data. The following list outlines what each method does.

- `getById( String id, ObjectListener handler )`

  Asks the server for an object based on its ID. The method takes an ID as the first parameter and an `ObjectListener` as a second parameter. Since these method calls to the server are always asynchronous, the return value is passed back through the `ObjectListener` interface.

- `getAll( CollectionListener handler )`

  Asks the server for all objects for this type. The results are returned to the `CollectionListener` handler.

- `getAllFrom( BaseObject object, String member, Collection Listener handler )`

  Asks the server for all of the objects on an object's specified field. For example, to get all of the digs for a story you would call this method, passing the story object and the value `digs` for the member variable. The return value is returned to the `CollectionListener`.

- `save( BaseObject object )`

  Sends an object to the server. If the object has not yet been saved, then a new object is created; otherwise, an existing object is updated.

- `delete( BaseObject object )`

  Deletes the specified object from the server.

- `addTo( BaseObject object, String string, BaseObject objectToAdd)`

  Adds an object to the specified member on another object. For example, to add a user to the digs list on a story, you would call this method with the first parameter as the story, the second parameter as `digs`, and the third parameter as the user you want to add.

The DAOs are the view's point of integration with the rest of the application and the server side. The view gets references to these DAOs through an `ObjectFactory` interface. The application creates an `ObjectFactory` for each method of interacting with the server. Its interface used in the application's view looks like this:

```
public interface ObjectFactory {
   ObjectDAO getUserDAO();
   ObjectDAO getStoryDAO();
   void setListener( ObjectFactoryListener listener );
}
```

The interface provides a method to access each class of objects on the server, as well as a method to set the `ObjectFactoryListener` so that events can be received that would assist the view's implementation:

```
public interface ObjectFactoryListener {
   void onRefresh();
   void onError(String error);
```

```
    void onLoadingStart();
    void onLoadingFinish();
}
```

With these interfaces defined, we can build the application's view, implement these interfaces, and then implement the server.

Building a Two-Paned Editor Interface

The application's interface, like the interfaces of other applications that use the Manager Application pattern, is two-paned: the left pane typically lists categories or folders, often in a hierarchical view, and the right pane has a detailed view of the selected item.

In the Database Editor application the left pane has a hierarchical view of the data in the system. It is dynamic, and as the user opens nodes in the list, more data is downloaded from the server, and the user can select items on it. When users select an item, a detailed view of the item appears in the space to its right. Figure 10-5 shows the Database Editor interface with the Stories item selected in the left pane and its contents displayed in the right pane.

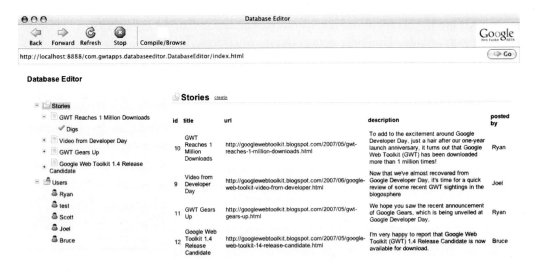

Figure 10–5. The two-paned editor interface

Using the `Tree` and `SplitPanel` Widgets

The application's main view is defined in the `DatabaseEditorView` class. This class extends GWT's `Composite` widget and builds the two-paned view shown in Figure 10-5. It is the root view for the application and is added to the HTML host page through the `RootPanel` class:

```
public class DatabaseEditor implements EntryPoint{
   public void onModuleLoad(){
      //create view
      DatabaseEditorView view = new DatabaseEditorView();
      RootPanel.get("databaseEditorView").add( view );
   }
}
```

The `DatabaseEditorView` builds the application interface by using a `HorizontalSplitPanel` widget with a `Tree` widget on the left and various other views on the right. You can see how this class does this by looking at its class declaration and constructor:

```
public class DatabaseEditorView extends Composite
   implements TreeListener, ObjectFactoryListener{

   //widgets
   private HorizontalSplitPanel mainPanel = new HorizontalSplitPanel();
   private Tree treeList = new Tree();
   private LoadingPanel loading = new LoadingPanel(new Label("loading..."));

   //tree items
   private UsersTreeItem userItems = new UsersTreeItem(this);
   private StoriesTreeItem storyItems = new StoriesTreeItem(this);

   //object factory
   private ObjectFactory objectFactory;

   public DatabaseEditorView(){
   initWidget( mainPanel );
   setStyleName("databaseEditorView");
   RoundedPanel rounded = new RoundedPanel( "#f0f4f8" );
   rounded.setWidget(treeList);
   rounded.setWidth("100%");
   mainPanel.add( rounded );
   mainPanel.setSplitPosition("250px");
   treeList.addItem( storyItems );
   treeList.addItem( userItems );
```

```
    treeList.addTreeListener(this);
    RootPanel.get().add( loading);
}
```

This class starts by extending the `Composite` widget and implements two interfaces. The first interface, `TreeListener`, allows this class to respond to events from its `Tree` child widget (we'll discuss these events later). The class implements the second interface, the `ObjectFactoryListener`, to provide feedback to the user about what is happening on the server. In particular, the class uses the `LoadingPanel` widget, defined in the Blog Editor application in Chapter 8, to let the user know that an asynchronous request is pending on the server. The other two widgets listed as fields are the `HorizontalSplitPanel` and the `Tree` widget. In the constructor the view is built by initializing the main widget for this `Composite` class to the `HorizontalSplitPanel`, then adding the `Tree` widget to the left side of the split panel. You'll notice that a `RoundedPanel` is used as the `Tree`'s container. The `RoundedPanel` widget does not come with GWT; we defined it as part of the Gadget Desktop application in Chapter 6. It is not necessary for this application but helps visually separate the two views and adds a friendly look to the application, as shown in Figure 10-6.

Figure 10–6.   The `Tree` widget in a `RoundedPanel`

The class initially creates two tree items and adds them to the `Tree` in the constructor. One is an instance of the `UsersTreeItem` class and the other is an instance of the `StoriesTreeItem` class. They represent the two root nodes on the tree that the user sees and is able to interact with when the application starts. Typically you would add instances of `TreeItem` to the tree. These two classes extend `TreeItems` but add more functionality.

Extending and Dynamically Loading Tree Items

Extending the `TreeItem` class allows you to provide extra functionality for each item in the tree and perform polymorphic operations on each item. In this application we will be passing the tree events that the `Database Editor` view sees to each tree item so that it can be handled differently.

The alternative to extending the TreeItem class is to use an if/else structure to handle events for different tree items. Extending the TreeItem
class gives your application slightly better performance and makes the
code more organized and easier to read.

The application uses two abstract base classes, BaseTreeItem and
DynamicTreeItem, to provide functionality that is shared between other
tree items. The UML diagram in Figure 10-7 shows the inheritance structure of the tree item classes in this application.

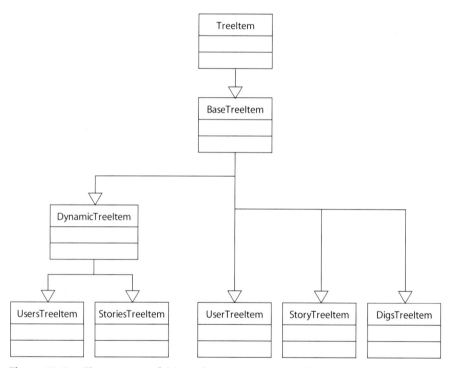

Figure 10–7.   The structure of this application's TreeItem hierarchy

The BaseTreeItem holds a reference to the main application view so
each tree item can obtain context information. It also contains empty
implementations of the event methods that the Tree widget sends to its
listener. The following is its implementation:

```
public class BaseTreeItem extends TreeItem {
    private final DatabaseEditorView view;
    public BaseTreeItem(String html, DatabaseEditorView view) {
        super(html);
```

```
      this.view = view;
   }

   public DatabaseEditorView getView() {
      return view;
   }

   public boolean isSelected(){
      return getTree().getSelectedItem() == this;
   }

   public void onTreeItemSelected(){}
   public void onTreeItemStateChanged(){}
   public void onRefresh(){}
}
```

There are three empty event methods in this implementation, each of which the `DatabaseEditorView` calls in response to events from the `Tree` widget. In the `DatabaseEditorView` class, the class relays these calls to the `TreeItems` to be handled polymorphically (handled differently depending on the concrete class):

```
public void onTreeItemSelected(TreeItem item) {
   if( item instanceof BaseTreeItem ){
      BaseTreeItem eventsItem = (BaseTreeItem)item;
      eventsItem.onTreeItemSelected();
   }
}

public void onTreeItemStateChanged(TreeItem item) {
   if( item instanceof BaseTreeItem ){
      BaseTreeItem eventsItem = (BaseTreeItem)item;
      eventsItem.onTreeItemStateChanged();
   }
}
```

Each concrete tree item implementation will handle these tree events to provide custom functionality. For example, when the user clicks on the Users tree item, the `onTreeItemSelected` method is called and the `UsersTreeItem` class fetches the collection of users through the user DAO object:

```
private void onTreeItemStateChanged () {
   onTreeItemSelected();
}
```

```
private void onTreeItemSelected() {
   getView().getObjectFactory().getUserDAO().getAll(this);
}
```

The `UsersTreeItem` class implements both the `onTreeItemState Changed` event and the `onTreeItemSelected` event as doing the same thing. However, these events are not necessarily the same. The `onTree ItemStateChanged` event occurs when the user opens or closes a tree item. The `onTreeItemSelected` occurs when the user clicks on the item or selects the item using the keyboard.

Also notice that the `onTreeItemSelected` implementation in this code passes a reference to itself in the `getAll` method on the user DAO. This passed reference is the `CollectionListener` interface described previously. This means that the `UsersTreeItem` class also implements the `CollectionListener` interface and its `onCollection` method to receive the collection of users when the collection is retrieved from the server. When the tree item receives this list, it can add new child items to itself that represent each `User` instance returned. If you're thinking about performance, you may wonder whether it is efficient for the tree item to request new data each time it is selected. However, the `ObjectFactory` has the responsibility of caching data from the server. We'll look at how this is done later in this chapter.

Handling the tree events and requesting data asynchronously from the `ObjectFactory` in this application provides the user with a `Tree` view that the application loads dynamically as it is browsed. There is one final piece to the puzzle for support of a dynamic `Tree`. Tree items such as the `UsersTreeItem` initially do not have any child items, and therefore they do not have any indication that there are dynamically loadable child items in the tree. In terms of visual clues, they will not have the plus symbol next to them to indicate they can be expanded. Visually they will look like a leaf of the tree. To solve this problem we need to build the `DynamicTreeItem` class for use by tree nodes that have dynamically loadable children. This class adds a single child item with the label *loading....* When the item is initially closed, it will have the plus symbol to indicate it can be expanded. When it is expanded, it will handle the `onTreeItemSelected` event and load the child items asynchronously. While the user waits for them to be loaded, the "loading..." child tree item is displayed. When the application receives the objects from the server, the "loading..." child tree item is removed. The following shows the implementation for the `Dynamic TreeItem` class:

```
public class DynamicTreeItem extends BaseTreeItem {
    final int STATE_EMPTY=0;
    final int STATE_LOADING=1;
    final int STATE_LOADED=2;
    private int state;

    public DynamicTreeItem(String html, DatabaseEditorView view){
        super(html, view);
        setEmpty();
    }

    public void addItem( TreeItem item ){
        if( !isLoaded() ){
            state = STATE_LOADED;
            removeItems();
        }
        super.addItem(item);
    }

    public boolean isLoaded(){ return state == STATE_LOADED; }
    public boolean isLoading(){ return state == STATE_LOADING; }
    public boolean isEmpty(){ return state == STATE_EMPTY; }
    public void setToLoading(){ state = STATE_LOADING; }
    public void setEmpty(){
        removeItems();
        addItem("loading...");
        state = STATE_EMPTY;
    }
}
```

As you can see in this code, the `DynamicTreeItem` class handles the loading state of the tree item and adds and removes the "loading…" child item.

In addition to loading child items, the tree items are responsible for determining what is displayed in the right side of the application's view when the item is selected.

Creating Workspace Views

The right side view, or workspace view, is the view added to the right pane of the `DatabaseEditorView`. It represents a more detailed view of the currently selected tree item. Workspace views are displayed every time the user selects a new tree item and replace the previously displayed view. These views can be divided into two categories: a list view for tree items that represent a collection of data such as the `UsersTreeNode`, and an object view for tree items that represent a single object. Every view in the list view category extends the `ListView` class to share functionality, and every view in the object view category extends the `ObjectView` class. Each view displays a title and one or more commands using the `Title CommandBar` widget that we built in the Blog Editor application in Chapter 8. For the `ListView`, underneath the `TitleCommandBar` widget will be a table listing the field values of each object in the list. The `ListView` follows the layout shown in Figure 10-8.

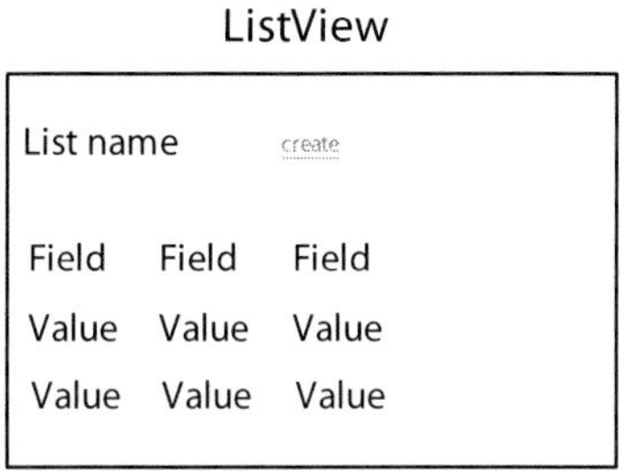

ListView

Figure 10–8.   The layout for the `ListView`

In this layout you can see the **create** command next to the list name. This command adds a new object to the list. Figure 10-9 shows an example of the `StoryListView`, which extends the `ListView` class:

Stories create

id	title	url	description	posted by
10	GWT Reaches 1 Million Downloads	http://googlewebtoolkit.blogspot.com/2007/05/gwt-reaches-1-million-downloads.html	To add to the excitement around Google Developer Day, just a hair after our one-year launch anniversary, it turns out that Google Web Toolkit (GWT) has been downloaded more than 1 million times!	Ryan
9	Video from Developer Day	http://googlewebtoolkit.blogspot.com/2007/06/google-web-toolkit-video-from-developer.html	Now that we've almost recovered from Google Developer Day, it's time for a quick review of some recent GWT sightings in the blogosphere	Joel
11	GWT Gears Up	http://googlewebtoolkit.blogspot.com/2007/05/gwt-gears-up.html	We hope you saw the recent announcement of Google Gears, which is being unveiled at Google Developer Day.	Ryan
12	Google Web Toolkit 1.4 Release Candidate	http://googlewebtoolkit.blogspot.com/2007/05/google-web-toolkit-14-release-candidate.html	I'm very happy to report that Google Web Toolkit (GWT) 1.4 Release Candidate is now available for download.	Bruce

Figure 10–9.   An example of the `StoryListView`

Classes that extend the list view include the `StoryListView` to list all of the stories, the `UserListView` to list all of the users, and the `DigsListView` to list all of the users that dug a story. Let's look at the implementation of the `StoryListView` to see how the `ListView` class is used in the application:

```
public class StoryListView extends ListView {
   //object listener callback for the posted-by request
   private class GetPostedByListener implements ObjectListener{
      private final int row;
      public GetPostedByListener( int row ){
         this.row = row;
      }

      public void onObject(BaseObject object) {
         User user = (User)object;
         addField(row,user.getName());
      }
   }

   public StoryListView( List stories, DatabaseEditorView view) {
      //pass the html title to the superclass
      super("<img src='item-stories.png' hspace='3'>Stories", view );

      //create the fields headings for the list
      addColumn( "id" );
      addColumn( "title" );
      addColumn( "url" );
      addColumn( "description" );
      addColumn( "posted by" );

      //iterate over the list of stories and add their fields
      int row = 0;
      for( Iterator it = stories.iterator(); it.hasNext();){
         Story story = (Story)it.next();
         addField(row,story.getId());
         addField(row,story.getTitle());
         addField(row,story.getUrl());
         addField(row,story.getDescription());

         //make an async request for the posted-by user
         if( story.getUser_id().length()>0)
            getView().getObjectFactory().getUserDAO().getById(
               story.getUser_id(), new GetPostedByListener(row) );
         row++;
      }
   }
}
```

```
   //load the StoryDialog when the user clicks create
   protected void onCreate(){
      new StoryDialog( getView() );
   }
}
```

The layout for the `StoryListView` is handled by the superclass in its constructor. The `StoryListView` simply passes the HTML title to the superclass to render it at the top of the view. The rest of the constructor for the `StoryListView` class uses the `ListView`'s `addColumn` and `addField` methods to build the table of values. The `addColumn` method adds a column and takes the column header value as a parameter and the `addField` adds one field value in the specified row. For the posted-by relationship that each `Story` object has with a `User` object, the class requests the `User` object from the user's DAO. Since the request is asynchronous, it needs to wait for a response by implementing an instance of the `ObjectListener` interface. At the top of the class definition you'll see this handler as the `GetPostedByListener` inner class. The class handles the `onObject` event by adjusting the field value to the user's name that was retrieved. The `ObjectFactory` is responsible for fulfilling this request. It could be an instant response if the `ObjectFactory` has the object cached, or it could require a request to the server, in which case the application displays the `LoadingPanel` to the user to indicate that more data is being loaded.

At the end of the class definition is the `onCreate` method. The `ListView` superclass calls this method when the **create** command is clicked. The `StoryListView` class implements this method and creates a new `StoryDialog` instance. This dialog, described later, provides the user with the fields necessary to build a new `Story` object.

The implementation of the `ListView` superclass uses a `TitleCommandBar` widget for the title and a `FlexTable` widget for the table of objects. The following code implements the `ListView` class:

```
public class ListView extends Composite {
   private final DatabaseEditorView view;
   private final TitleCommandBar title;
   private final FlexTable rows = new FlexTable();

   public ListView( String titleValue, DatabaseEditorView view ){
      this( titleValue, view, "create" );
   }
```

```
public ListView(
   String titleValue, DatabaseEditorView view, String createLabel ){
   this.view = view;
   VerticalPanel mainPanel = new VerticalPanel();
   initWidget( mainPanel );
   mainPanel.setWidth("100%");
   rows.setWidth("100%");
   title = new TitleCommandBar(titleValue);
   mainPanel.add( title );
   mainPanel.add(rows);
   rows.getRowFormatter().setStyleName(0, "gwtapps-ListHeaderRow");
   title.addCommand(createLabel, new ClickListener(){
      public void onClick( Widget sender ) {
         onCreate();
      }
   });
}

protected void addColumn( String name ){
   int column = rows.getRowCount()>0?rows.getCellCount(0):0;
   rows.setWidget(0, column, new Label(name));
}

protected void addField( int row, String value ){
   row = row + 1;
   int column = 0;
   if( rows.getRowCount()==row ){
      if( row%2 == 0)
         rows.getRowFormatter().setStyleName(row,"gwtapps-Even");
   }
   else{
      column = rows.getCellCount(row);
   }
   Label fieldValue = new Label(value);
   fieldValue.setStyleName("gwtapps-FieldValue");
   rows.setWidget(row, column, fieldValue);

}

protected void onCreate(){}
public DatabaseEditorView getView() {
   return view;
}
}
```

One thing to note in this code is how the table is styled using CSS. If you look at Figure 10-9, you'll notice that the FlexTable has bold column headers and that the row color alternates between a color, shown as gray in Figure 10-9, and white to help make rows look distinct. For the headers, the header row has its CSS style name set in the constructor using the `RowFormatter` object from the flex table. The `RowFormatter` allows you to specify certain format options for any particular row in the table. Here it is set to `gwtapps-ListHeaderRow`, which is later changed in the HTML host page's style section to the following:

```
.gwtapps-ListHeaderRow{ font-weight:bold;  }
```

To create the alternating row colors, the code checks to see if the row number is even or odd using `row%2`, which either evaluates to 0 or 1. If it is 0, it means the row number is even and the `gwtapps-Even` style name is added. Then in CSS we define this style as the following:

```
.gwtapps-Even{ background-color:#f0f4f8; }
```

Since only the even rows will have this style name, they are the only rows to have this color background.

The `ObjectView` class layout is slightly different than the `ListView` layout. It only needs to display one object and it supports an **edit** and a **delete** command. The object's fields are displayed horizontally instead of vertically to use the horizontal space more efficiently and make it easier to read the fields. The `ObjectView` follows the layout shown in Figure 10-10.

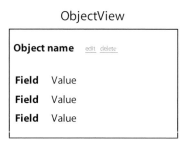

Figure 10–10.   The layout of the `ObjectView`

As you can see, the layout also uses a `TitleCommandBar` widget for the title. Figure 10-11 illustrates the `StoryView`, which extends the `ObjectView` class.

GWT Reaches 1 Million Downloads edit delete

id	10
title	GWT Reaches 1 Million Downloads
url	http://googlewebtoolkit.blogspot.com/2007/05/gwt-reaches-1-million-downloads.html
description	To add to the excitement around Google Developer Day, just a hair after our one-year launch anniversary, it turns out that Google Web Toolkit (GWT) has been downloaded more than 1 million times!
posted by	Ryan

Figure 10–11.   An example of the `StoryView`

Now let's look at the code required for the `StoryView`:

```
public class StoryView extends ObjectView {

    //called when the posted-by user has been loaded
    private class GetPostedByListener implements ObjectListener{
        public void onObject(BaseObject object) {
            User user = (User)object;
            addField("posted by",user.getName());
        }
    }

    private final Story story;
    public StoryView( Story story1, DatabaseEditorView view ){
        //pass the html title to the superclass
        super(
            "<img src='item-story.png' hspace='3'>" + story1.getTitle(), view );
        this.story = story1;

        //set the fields in the view
        addField( "id", story.getId() );
        addField( "title", story.getTitle() );
        addField( "url", story.getUrl() );
        addField( "description", story.getDescription() );

        //request the posted-by user object
        if( story.getUser_id().length()>0)
            getView().getObjectFactory().getUserDAO().getById(
                story.getUser_id(), new GetPostedByListener());
    }

    //handle the delete command by calling delete on the DAO
    protected void onDelete() {
        getView().getObjectFactory().getStoryDAO().delete(story);
    }
```

```
    //handle the edit command by loading the story dialog
    protected void onEdit() {
       new StoryDialog( story, getView() );
    }
}
```

At the top of the class definition is the GetPostedByListener inner class, which gets the response for a request for this Story's posted-by User instance. In the StoryView constructor the superclass constructor is called with the HTML text that goes in the TitleCommandBar widget. Then the superclass' addField method is called to add a new field name and value to the view. The final field in the view is the **posted by** field, which displays the name of the user who posted the story. The User object needs to be retrieved using the user's DAO getById method. The final two methods on this class respond to the **delete** and **edit** commands. The onDelete method handles the **delete** command by calling the delete method on the story DAO, and the onEdit method handles the **edit** command by creating a new StoryDialog instance.

The StoryView's superclass, ObjectView, implements the addField method and constructs its layout similar to the ListView. It uses a TitleCommandBar for the title and commands and the FlexTable widget to display the field data. The following is the implementation of the ObjectView class:

```
public class ObjectView extends Composite {
    private FlexTable fields = new FlexTable();
    private TitleCommandBar title;
    private final DatabaseEditorView view;
    public ObjectView( String titleValue, DatabaseEditorView view ){
        this.view = view;
        VerticalPanel mainPanel = new VerticalPanel();
        initWidget( mainPanel );
        mainPanel.setWidth("100%");
        fields.setWidth("100%");
        title = new TitleCommandBar(titleValue);
        mainPanel.add( title );
        mainPanel.add(fields);

        title.addCommand("edit", new ClickListener(){
            public void onClick( Widget sender ) {
                onEdit();
            }
        });
```

```
        title.addCommand("delete", new ClickListener(){
            public void onClick( Widget sender ) {
                if( Window.confirm(
                "Are you sure that you want to delete this object?") ){
                    onDelete();
                    getView().getTree().getSelectedItem().remove();
                }
            }
        });
    }

    protected void onDelete() { }
    protected void onEdit() { }

    protected void addField(String name, String value ) {
        int row = fields.getRowCount();
        Label fieldName = new Label( name );
        Label fieldValue = new Label( value );
        fieldName.setStyleName("gwtapps-FieldName");
        fieldValue.setStyleName("gwtapps-FieldValue");
        fields.getCellFormatter().setWidth(row,1,"100%");
        fields.setWidget(row, 0, fieldName);
        fields.setWidget(row, 1, fieldValue);
        if( row%2 == 0)
            fieldValue.addStyleName("gwtapps-Even");
    }

    public DatabaseEditorView getView() {
        return view;
    }
}
```

Notice that in this code, like the `ListView` class, even-numbered fields
have the `gwtapps-Even` style name set so field backgrounds have alternating colors. It is also important to note that the `remove` command is
implemented to use GWT's `Window.confirm` method to display a confirmation dialog box to the user to help prevent accidental deletion of data.

Using Dialogs for Editing and Creating Objects

Both the `User` and `Story` objects have dialogs defined for editing and creating objects, called `UserDialog` and `StoryDialog`, respectively. The
`UserDialog` displays when users click on the **edit** command in the `User`
`View` and the **create** command in the `UserListView`. The `StoryDialog`
displays when users click on the **edit** command in the `StoryView` and on

the create command in the `StoryListView`. These same dialogs are used for creating and editing since they both need to provide the same editable fields. When the dialogs display they hover over the rest of the application, and users must click the **Ok** or **Cancel** button to return to the application. For example, the Create Story dialog (`StoryDialog`) shown in Figure 10-12 displays when users click the **create** command.

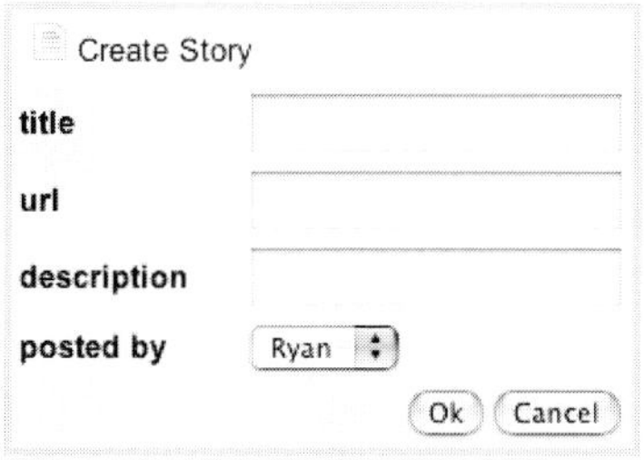

Figure 10–12. The Create Story dialog (`StoryDialog`)

Notice that each field in this dialog has a label on the left and a text box on the right except for the **posted by** field. Instead, the **posted by** field uses a list box to let users select from the list of available `User` objects. After the user fills in the fields and clicks the **Ok** button, the `StoryDialog` calls the `save` method on the story's DAO. The same process is followed for editing, and the application also calls the `save` method. The DAO determines if the object needs to be created or updated. Let's look at the implementation of the `StoryDialog` class:

```
public class StoryDialog extends ObjectDialogBox {

    private Story story;
    private ListBox userList = new ListBox();

    //construct a dialog for creating a Story
    public StoryDialog( DatabaseEditorView view ) {
        super("<img src='item-story.png' hspace='3'>Create Story", view );
        story = new Story();
        init();
    }

    //construct a dialog for editing a Story
    public StoryDialog(Story story, DatabaseEditorView view) {
        super( "<img src='item-story.png' hspace='3'>Edit Story", view );
        this.story = story;
        init();
    }
```

```
//initialize the dialog fields
private void init() {
    addField( "title", story.getTitle() );
    addField( "url", story.getUrl() );
    addField( "description", story.getDescription() );
    addField( "posted by", userList );

    addButtons();

    //fill posted-by list box
    final String postedby_id = story.getUser_id();
    getView().getObjectFactory().getUserDAO().getAll(
        new CollectionListener(){
        public void onCollection(List list) {
            for( Iterator it = list.iterator(); it.hasNext(); ){
                User user = (User)it.next();
                userList.addItem( user.getName(), user.getId() );
                if( postedby_id != null &&
                    postedby_id.compareTo(user.getId())==0)
                    userList.setSelectedIndex(userList.getItemCount()-1);
            }
        }
    });
}

//copy the values from the widgets to the objects and call save
public void onSubmit(){
    story.setTitle( getField(0) );
    story.setUrl( getField(1) );
    story.setDescription( getField(2) );
    story.setUser_id( userList.getValue( userList.getSelectedIndex() ) );
    getView().getObjectFactory().getStoryDAO().save( story );
}

}
```

The StoryDialog class does not directly extend GWT's DialogBox class; instead, it extends the ObjectDialogBox class. The ObjectDialogBox class has some helper methods, such as addField, that can be shared by the UserDialog. This simplifies the construction of the StoryDialog. There are actually two constructors in the StoryDialog class: The first constructor is used when the dialog creates a new object, and the second constructor takes a reference to a Story object and is used for editing the object. Both constructors call the init method to initialize the fields on the dialog box. For the **posted by** field a request for the list of users is sent to the user's DAO. An anonymous inner class is instantiated to receive the response from this asynchronous request. When the response is received, the anonymous inner class populates the list box with the users' names. The final method on the class, onSubmit, is called by the superclass when the user clicks the **Ok** button. The method is implemented to get the field data from the widgets and set the corresponding values on the story's object. Once all the values are set, the onSubmit calls the save method on the story's DAO.

The ObjectDialogBox class extends GWT's DialogBox widget, builds the layout inside the dialog with a FlexTable and two Button widgets, and provides the derived classes with the addField method to customize the editable fields. The following code shows the implementation of this class:

```
public class ObjectDialogBox extends DialogBox {
   private FlexTable fields = new FlexTable();
   private final DatabaseEditorView view;

   //construct the dialog with an html caption
   public ObjectDialogBox(String string, DatabaseEditorView view) {
      this.view = view;
      setHTML( string );
      setWidget( fields );
      show();
      center();
   }

   //add a text field and value
   public void addField(String name, String value) {
      TextBox fieldValue = new TextBox();
      fieldValue.setText(value);
      addField( name, fieldValue );
   }

   //add a field based on any widget
   public  void addField(String name, Widget fieldValue) {
      int row = fields.getRowCount();
      Label fieldName = new Label( name );
      fieldName.setStyleName("gwtapps-FieldName");
      fieldValue.setStyleName("gwtapps-FieldValue");
      fields.getCellFormatter().setWidth(row,1,"100%");
      fields.setWidget(row, 0, fieldName);
      fields.setWidget(row, 1, fieldValue);
   }
```

```
//add the ok and cancel buttons
public void addButtons(){
    int row = fields.getRowCount();
    HorizontalPanel buttons = new HorizontalPanel();
    fields.setWidget(row, 1, buttons );
    //handle ok by calling onSubmit and hiding
    buttons.add( new Button( "Ok", new ClickListener(){
        public void onClick( Widget sender ){
            onSubmit();
            hide();
        }
    }));
    //handle cancel by hiding
    buttons.add( new Button("Cancel", new ClickListener(){
        public void onClick( Widget sender ){
            hide();
        }
    }));
    fields.getCellFormatter().setHorizontalAlignment(
        row, 1, HasHorizontalAlignment.ALIGN_RIGHT );
}

public String getField(int row){
    TextBox field = (TextBox)fields.getWidget(row, 1);
    return field.getText();
}

public void onSubmit(){}
public DatabaseEditorView getView() {
    return view;
}
}
```

One important method to note in this implementation of a `DialogBox` widget is that the `center` method is called in the constructor. This method centers the dialog in the middle of the browser. If it is not used, you would need to set the dialog's position using the `setPosition` method; otherwise, the dialog will be appended to the end of the document and the user may need to scroll down to see it.

We've gone through the four parts of the application's user interface. The two-paned tree-based view at the root presents the user with a dynamic way to navigate through data for CRUD operations. The `TreeItem` implementations give the tree a polymorphic way to respond to user events, including displaying views unique to the selected item in the workspace pane. The workspace views provide distinct ways of displaying the data for the selected item. Finally, the dialog boxes provide ways for users to create and edit objects and commit them to the server. Next we'll look at how to integrate the application with various types of servers.

Server Integration Overview

So far we've constructed a manager-style interface that integrates with DAOs. On the other side of the DAO interface is where the client application sends messages to and receives messages from a server. There is a seemingly endless array of choices for how to implement the server, but your decision is most likely going to come down to what you or your development team is most familiar with.

To satisfy as many server-side skill sets as possible, this sample application divides the type of server integration techniques into three categories. Out of the thousands of server-side technologies you could use, the one you choose will most likely fall into one of these three categories: Actions, REST, or RPC.

Using Actions

The most traditional way to build web applications is using Actions on HTML forms. The name comes from the `action` attribute on the HTML `form` tag that points to the URL that will accept the form's submission. Typically the URL points to a script on the server that will read the submitted parameters and perform some sort of action, and then the server returns a response to the user. You would construct a traditional web application with a series of these action scripts,[1] along with HTML pages that provide the `form` tags to invoke them. Many web developers have developed efficient techniques for building web applications through actions, and fortunately these techniques can be reused for GWT Ajax applications.

Actions can actually provide a fairly flexible interface to our Ajax application. The flexibility comes from the `form` tag's additional `method` and

---

1. This is not referring to the Flash scripting language called ActionScript, but rather any server-side script that handles an HTML form action.

encoding attributes. The `method` attribute tells the browser which HTTP method should be used to submit the data, and the encoding parameter tells the action how the submitted data is encoded. In traditional web applications the encoding is set to `application/x-www-form-urlencoded`, which concatenates name-value pairs and delimits them with the ampersand character. We won't use this encoding for our application's action implementation since it does not give us the ability to encode more complex hierarchical data or object data. Instead we will use JSON or XML as the encoding. There won't be any `form` tags in our implementation, but we will follow the action technique that a form uses for the server-side code, which may be familiar to you.

To illustrate action-based server integration, we implement actions in PHP to handle the DAO operations. We'll use JSON as the encoding format and the `json_encode` and `json_decode` PHP methods to translate the encoding to and from PHP structures.

Figure 10-13 illustrates how the `Story`'s DAO will integrate with the server side through an `Action` interface.

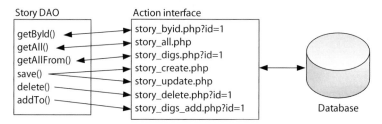

Figure 10–13.   Mapping DAO methods to an `Action` interface

Using REST

Using REST APIs has become more popular recently due to its relative simplicity. It's a back-to-basics approach for server integration that uses the HTTP protocol more closely in tune to the way it was designed to be used. Instead of writing the server-side web interface as a set of actions identified by URLs, the server side is a set of stateless resources identified by URLs that can be operated on using four HTTP methods: GET, POST, PUT, and DELETE. These methods mirror the traditional CRUD operations that are typically required for objects. Since the server-side resources are considered stateless and there are only four operations possible, the server-side implementation is often much simpler and the API that the client needs to learn is much less complex. Also, two different REST implementations share more similarities with each other than two different Action implementations would, making REST skills more transferable between implementations.

We've actual already integrated with a REST-based API in the Blog Editor application in Chapter 8. In this chapter you'll see a little bit further into the server-side implementation of a REST API. We'll use Ruby on Rails as the server-side application interface and XML as the transport format.

Figure 10-14 illustrates how the story DAO will integrate with the server side through a REST interface.

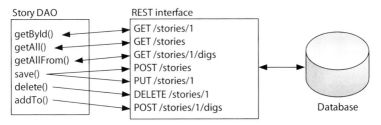

Figure 10-14.   Mapping DAO methods to a REST interface

Using RPC

Remote Procedure Calls is the third server integration technique that this application handles. RPC provides a programmatic approach to defining an interface with a server that attempts to mimic module integration in a nondistributed application. This makes the interface familiar to software developers already accustomed with programming to a well-defined interface.

Several RPC technologies can be used over HTTP, including XML-RPC and SOAP, but this application is going to use GWT's RPC implementation. You've already seen how to use GWT-RPC in the Instant Messenger application in Chapter 8, so this chapter will just use this integration technique as a comparison to Action-based integration and REST integration.

Figure 10-15 illustrates how the story DAO will integrate with the server side through an RPC interface.

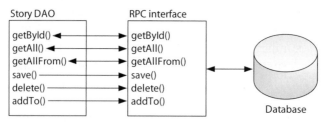

Figure 10–15.   Mapping DAO methods to an RPC interface

As an application developer this diagram probably looks the most appealing, and it may be the best decision if you don't need to rely on an existing skill set or server-side infrastructure in non-Java languages.

Writing a Generic GWT Code Generator

Before we look into implementing the server interaction, we will handle one complexity in the implementation: serializing to and from the JSON or XML data formats. In previous chapters we've done manual transformation, where we've built a JSON or XML Document Object Model or populated an object from a DOM manually. This can be a tedious and error-prone process, especially as your application's model grows. This type of code is the perfect candidate to use GWT's code generation capability.

There are several approaches that can be taken to generate code to provide automatic serialization of the classes. One approach would be to have the generator run for each object that implements the serialization interface. Then we would use GWT's deferred binding mechanism through the GWT.create method to create the entity objects with the new serialization methods on them. The methods could be called toXML/fromXML or toJSON/fromJSON. This approach would work, but it would mean that the user must use the GWT.create method each time an entity object is instantiated, which leaves a lot of room for a forgetful mistake.

Another approach would be to run the generator for a single interface that acts a factory for serialization. You would only need to call GWT.create once on the serialization interface to trigger the code generation. The code generation would then generate a new serializer class for each class that implements the Serializable interface and add an instance to the serializer factory. Then in the application you would just need to call the toXML/fromXML or toJSON/fromJSON methods on the factory passing the object to serialize/deserialize as a parameter. This approach allows you to instantiate the entity objects without relying on GWT deferred binding.

We can actually make the code generator one step better than the previous approach. Since we want to serialize/deserialize both JSON and XML, we will need to provide code generation for both formats. This is unfortunate, since we are essentially performing the same task of populating a DOM from a Java object and vice versa. The only reason we need to generate different code for each format is because they do not share a common DOM. To simplify our code generator, we'll first create a common DOM wrapper for GWT's XML-DOM and JSON-DOM and then create a code generator that uses the common DOM. This approach allows us to generate one set of classes that perform serialization and deserialization with both JSON and XML formats.

Using this approach, the serialization code that would be used in an application becomes very simple:

```
//use deferred binding to create a serializer
//this triggers code generation for all Serializable objects
//only one serializer is needed for the application lifetime
Serializer serializer = (Serializer)GWT.create( Serializer.class );

//create JSON and XML documents using the common DOM
JSONDocument jsonDocument = new JSONDocument();
XMLDocument xmlDocument = new XMLDocument();

 //serialize a story object to JSON and then to XML
 serializer.serializeToDocumentObject(
story, jsonDocument.createObject() );
serializer.serializeToDocumentObject(
story, xmlDocument.createObject() );

//get the string values
String storyAsJSON = jsonDocument.toString();
String storyAsXML = xmlDocument.toString();
```

This example illustrates the components involved in making this serialization happen. In this application we would only use one of the formats, and we would only create the document and serializer once. The format used can be configured in the application's entry point. For example, when running the application with REST server integration using XML, we would use the following code to create the `ObjectFactory` for the view:

```
RESTObjectFactory objectFactory = new RESTObjectFactory( new XMLDocument() );
```

You can also see the benefit of the common DOM in this example, since the data format can be switched with JSONDocument easily.

Before looking at the code generator implementation, let's look at the common DOM interfaces for this serialization task. First is the Document Adapter object, which provides a common interface to the DOM's Document:

```
public interface DocumentAdapter {
    public String getFormatName();
    public DocumentObject createObject();
    public DocumentObject[] createCollection( String name, int size );
    public String toString();

    public void parse( String value );
    public DocumentObject getObject();
    public DocumentObject[] getCollection();
}
```

The interface supports several methods that can be used for reading and writing to the document. The toString method transfers the document to a string, and the parse method parses a string to a document. The document aggregates a hierarchy of DocumentObject instances. The DocumentObject interface is as follows:

```
public interface DocumentObject {
    public void setAttribute( String name, String value );
    public String getAttribute( String value );
    public void setName( String name );
    public String getName();
}
```

The DocumentObject supports a simplified view of an Object in a DOM, but it is sufficient for the serialization of Java objects.

Writing the Code Generator

With these interfaces defined we can focus on the serialization code that transfers a Java object to a DocumentObject and vice versa. Let's look at the how the code generation process works for this serialization approach.

1. The GWT compiler finds that the Serializer interface is instantiated using GWT.create and invokes the SerializationGenerate code generator by calling its generate method.

2. The code generator begins to build a new class, `Serializer_TypeSerializer`, that extends `Serializer` as the returned instance from the `GWT.create` call.

3. Inner classes implementing the `ObjectSerializer` interface are added to `Serializer_TypeSerializer` for each class in the code that implements the `Serializable interface`. In this application this is the `Story` and `User` objects. The inner classes are named `Story_SerializableImppl` and `User_SerializableImpl`. Each one has a custom serialize and deserialize method implemented which can populate a common DOM object from a Java object and vice versa.

4. In the constructor for `Serializer_TypeSerializer`, a new instance of each generated implementation of `ObjectSerializer` is added to a map of `ObjectSerializers` with the class name as a key. This allows the `Serializer` to find the right `ObjectSerializer` for any `Serializable` object.

5. The generation code completes and the `GWT.create` method returns a new `Serializer` instance.

6. When either the `serializerToDocumentObject` or `deserialize FromDocumentObject` methods are called, the `Serializer` implementation is able to locate the appropriate `ObjectSerializer` instance and calls either serialize or deserialize on it.

At this point you probably realize that code generation can become confusing when you're using code to write code. In certain situations the effort to understand pays off quite a bit. For this instance we will be able to reuse this code generator to automatically serialize and deserialize JSON or XML with very little effect. The payoff for building this code generator can be substantial even for a single project.

To help you understand this in a different way, Figure 10-16 illustrates the components involved in this code generation process.

Out of all the classes in this diagram, our application only needs to pay attention to the `User` and `Story` entity objects and the `Serializer` interface to serialize the entities. The rest of the classes are hidden and act as the engine to serialization. With this approach the serialization complexity is factored out of the application.

One important thing to note about Figure 10-16 is the divisions between runtime code, generated code, and compile-time code. The runtime code

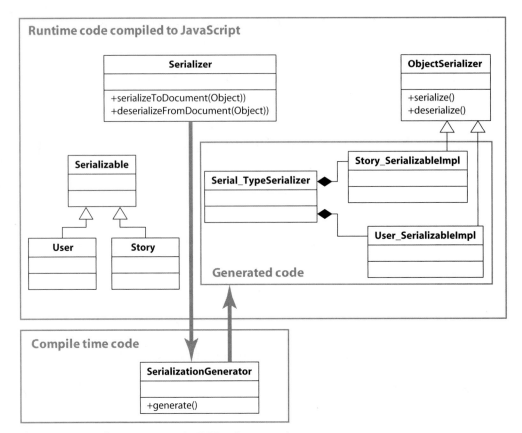

Figure 10–16.   The components in GWT code generation

is part of the application and will be compiled by the GWT compiler to Java-Script to run in a browser. The generated code becomes part of the run-time code, but is not available during development. The compile-time code is only run during GWT's compilation process and is not included in the compiled application. It is important not to put the compile-time code in the client package for your application; otherwise, GWT will consider it part of the runtime code and try to compile it to JavaScript.

Now let's look at the implementation of the `SerializationGenerator` class. First of all, for this class to integrate with GWT's compilation process it needs to extend GWT's `Generator` class and implement its `generate` method. Then it needs to use GWT's type information and class genera-tion tools to read the types being compiled and generate new classes. The class implementation can be divided into three parts. The first part is the declaration and the implementation of the `generate` method. The `generate` method calls two helper methods on the class, `writeSerialize` and `writeDeserialize`, which are the other two parts of this class implementation. For the first part, the code is as follows (get ready):

```
public class SerializationGenerator extends Generator {
   private JClassType serializeInterface;
   private JClassType stringClass;
   private SourceWriter srcWriter;
   private String className;
   public String generate( TreeLogger logger, GeneratorContext ctx,
      String requestedClass) throws UnableToCompleteException {

      //get the type oracle
      TypeOracle typeOracle = ctx.getTypeOracle();
      assert (typeOracle != null);
      serializeInterface = typeOracle.findType(Serializable.class.getName());
      assert( serializeInterface!= null );
      stringClass = typeOracle.findType(String.class.getName());
      assert( stringClass!= null );

      //get class from type oracle
      JClassType serializeClass = typeOracle.findType(requestedClass);
      if (serializeClass == null) {
         logger.log(TreeLogger.ERROR, "Unable to find metadata for type '"
            + requestedClass + "'", null);
         throw new UnableToCompleteException();
      }

      //create source writer
      String packageName = serializeClass.getPackage().getName();
      className = serializeClass.getSimpleSourceName()+ "_TypeSerializer";
      PrintWriter printWriter = ctx.tryCreate(
         logger, packageName, className);
      if (printWriter == null) {
         return packageName+"."+className;
      }
      ClassSourceFileComposerFactory composerFactory =
         new ClassSourceFileComposerFactory( packageName, className );
      composerFactory.addImport(DocumentObject.class.getName());
      composerFactory.addImport(ObjectSerializer.class.getName());
      composerFactory.addImport(Serializable.class.getName());
      composerFactory.setSuperclass("Serializer");
      srcWriter = composerFactory.createSourceWriter(ctx, printWriter);
      if (srcWriter == null) {
         return packageName+"."+className;
      }
```

```
//create a serializer for each interface that supports Serializable
JClassType[] subTypes = serializeInterface.getSubtypes();
for( int i=0; i< subTypes.length; ++i )
{
    srcWriter.println("public class "+ subTypes[i].getName()+
        "_SerializableImpl implements ObjectSerializer{");
    srcWriter.indent();
    srcWriter.println("public "+
        subTypes[i].getName()+"_SerializableImpl(){}");
    writeSerialize(logger,subTypes[i]);
    writeDeserialize(logger,subTypes[i]);
    srcWriter.outdent();
    srcWriter.println("}");
}


//in the class constructor, add each serializer
srcWriter.println("public "+className+"(){");
srcWriter.indent();
for( int i=0; i< subTypes.length; ++i )
{
    srcWriter.println("addObjectSerializer(\""+ subTypes[i].getName()+
        "\", new "+subTypes[i].getName()+"_SerializableImpl() );");
}
srcWriter.outdent();
srcWriter.println("}");

srcWriter.commit(logger);
return packageName+"."+className;
}
```

This `generate` method has some complex code in it. It can be tough to
think about generating code. If you're feeling less ambitious, you can rely
on this code generator's interface to simply use JSON and XML serialization and skip these intricate details by continuing to the next section. If
you are more ambitious and really want to understand how a fairly complex GWT code generator is built, read on!

Let's start by looking at the first block of code in the `generate` method. It uses
the `GeneratorContext` variable that is passed into the `generate` method
from the GWT compiler to retrieve the `TypeOracle`, which is an object
that has a list of every type that is being compiled by GWT. It provides
access to these types in a way that is very similar to the way Java provides
reflection to its types. You can retrieve a type from the `TypeOracle` using
its class name, as the preceding code does, and call methods on it to get

information about it. This type information can be used by a generator to make decisions on what type of code should be generated. In this method we're going to use the type information from the `TypeOracle` to get a list of all the objects that implement the `Serializable` interface. We need this list to generate an `ObjectSerializer` for each item in the list.

The second block of code in the `generate` method builds an instance of GWT's `SourceWriter`. The `SourceWriter` class is used to write Java code for one class. In this case we're creating a `SourceWriter` for a new class that extends the `Serializable` class and will be called `Serializable_TypeSerializer`. First an instance of `PrintWriter` is created using the `tryCreate` method on the `GeneratorContext`. This method attempts to create a new file. If the file exists or has already been generated, then this call fails; the code handles this by immediately returning. If a `PrintWriter` can be created, then a `ClassSourceFile ComposerFactory` is created. The `ClassSourceFileComposerFactory` starts the construction of the new class file by setting up the required imports, implemented interfaces, and superclass. Once this is done its `createSourceWriter` method is called and passes in the `PrintWriter` reference to create the `SourceWriter`. Creating the `SourceWriter` object is not very intuitive, but writing code generators is not a well-advertised or documented feature of GWT.

Once we have the `SourceWriter` for the class we can begin writing the class body. We want to write one inner class for each class that implements `Serializable` that we can find in the `TypeOracle`. The `Serializable` interface type was retrieved form the `TypeOracle` previously, and in the third block of code its `getSubtypes` method is called to get an array of all of the classes that implement this interface. The array is iterated over to generate one inner class per type. These inner classes implement our `ObjectSerializer` interface and its two methods, `serialize` and `deserialize`. These methods will transfer fields from Java objects to the common DOM and vice versa. The method implementations are written to the `SourceWriter` in this generator's `writeSerialize` and `write Deserialize` helper methods. We'll look at these methods after we look at the remaining code in the `generate` method.

The remaining code in the `generate` method implements the class' constructor. Inside the constructor an instance of each `ObjectSerializer` is created and added to a map for use at runtime. When an object needs to be serialized or `deserialized`, the `Serializer` will find the appropriate `ObjectSerializer` instance.

Finally, the `commit` method is called on the `SourceWriter` to write the file to disk, and the full class name of the generated class is returned from the method. We haven't yet looked at the generated class name in detail. The generated class name is for the class that this generator returns. It uses the original class name and appends `_TypeSerializer`. It also uses the same package as the original class. The package chosen is important for using the correct imports in the generated class. In our application only one class causes this generator to be invoked. We use the following line once:

```
Serializer serializer = (Serializer)GWT.create( Serializer.class );
```

But the generator could also be invoked for other instances that extend the serializer instance. This is why we need to generate the name from the original class—we should be able to generate code for more than one class.

We also haven't specified how GWT knows to use the code generator. To do this we add a simple instruction to the module that the code generator's code is part of. In this application it is separated into the `com.gwtapps` `.serialization.Serialization` module. Inside the module's XML we need to add the following instruction to connect the `Serialization` `Generator` with the deferred binding of the `Serializer` class:

```
<generate-with class="com.gwtapps.serialization.SerializationGenerator">
<when-type-assignable class="com.gwtapps.serialization.client.Serializer"/>
</generate-with>
```

As you can see here, the `when-type-assignable` instruction is given to the GWT compiler, which causes the deferred binding of any derived implementation of `Serializer` to trigger the `SerializationGenerator` as well.

Now let's look at the implementation for the code generation of the `serialize` and `deserialization` methods on the `ObjectSerializer` instances. The following is the implementation to the `writeSerialize` method on the `SerializationGenerator` class:

```java
public void writeSerialize( TreeLogger logger, JClassType classType)
   throws UnableToCompleteException {

   String fullName = classType.getQualifiedSourceName();
   srcWriter.println(
      "public void serialize( Serializable obj, DocumentObject document ){");
   srcWriter.indent();

   //cast the object to the concrete class
   srcWriter.println(fullName+" objImpl = ("+fullName+")obj;");

   //iterate over the get methods
   JMethod[] methods = classType.getMethods();
   for( int i=0; i < methods.length; i++ ){

      String methodName = methods[i].getName();
      if( "get".equals( methodName.substring(0,3) )&& methods[i].isPublic()){
         //call the setAttribute method on the document object
         JType returnType = methods[i].getReturnType();
         if( returnType.isClass() != null  &&
            returnType.isClass().isAssignableTo( stringClass ) ){
            String attributeName = methodName.substring(3);
            srcWriter.println( "document.setAttribute(\""+
               attributeName.toLowerCase()+ "\",
               objImpl."+methodName+"());");
         }
      }
   }
   srcWriter.outdent();
   srcWriter.println("}");
   srcWriter.println();
}
```

The method starts by writing the serialize method declaration to the SourceWriter. Then it writes code that will cast the object to serialize to the concrete class in order to call its field getter methods. Using the type information from the TypeOracle for this class, an array of its methods is retrieved and then iterated over to find all the getter methods. When the code finds a getter method that has a String return type (only strings are supported but code can be generated to support more field types), it writes out code that calls the DocumentObject's setAttribute method with the return value from a call to the getter method. This may sound complicated, but essentially the generated code is a list of calls to document.setAttribute with the attribute name and value as returned from the field's getter method.

The `writeDeserialize` helper method on the `SerializationGenerator` performs the opposite operation. It creates a new concrete class and then iterates over the setter methods on the class to find setter methods that have a `String` as their parameter type. Code is generated to call the setter on the new concrete class with the return value from the `Document Object`'s `getAttribute` method. The following is the code for the `write Deserialize` method:

```
public void writeDeserialize( TreeLogger logger,JClassType classType)
    throws UnableToCompleteException {

    String fullName = classType.getQualifiedSourceName();
    srcWriter.println(
        "public Serializable deserialize( DocumentObject document ){");
    srcWriter.indent();

    //create a new concrete object
    srcWriter.println(fullName+" obj = new "+fullName+"();");

    //iterate over the set methods
    JMethod[] methods = classType.getMethods();
    for( int i=0; i < methods.length; i++ ){

        String methodName = methods[i].getName();
        if( "set".equals( methodName.substring(0,3) ) && methods[i].isPublic()){

            //make sure there is only one parameter
            JParameter[] parameters = methods[i].getParameters();
            if( parameters.length == 1 &&
                parameters[0].getType().isClass() != null &&
parameters[0].getType().isClass().isAssignableTo( stringClass ) ){

                //get the attribute's string value
                String attributeName = methodName.substring(3);
                srcWriter.println("obj."+methodName+"( document.getAttribute(\""+
                    attributeName.toLowerCase()+"\") );");
            }
        }
    }
    srcWriter.println("return obj;");
    srcWriter.outdent();
    srcWriter.println("}");
    srcWriter.println();
}
```

Automatically Serializing to XML

We've looked at the common DOM interfaces and how the generated code translates Java objects to and from them automatically, but we haven't yet looked at the implementations for the common DOM interfaces in the data formats we require for the application.

For XML's common DOM implementation, the `DocumentAdapter` interface is implemented as `XMLDocument` and holds a reference to GWT's `Document` class from its XML module. The code acts as a bridge between the common DOM we've defined and GWT's DOM. For the implementation of the `XMLDocument` and `XMLDocumentObject` classes, refer to the application's source code (at www.gwtapps.com).

With this implementation we can write code in our application that can automatically serialize an object to XML like this:

```
Serializer serializer = (Serializer)GWT.create( Serializer.class );
XMLDocument xmlDocument = new XMLDocument();
serializer.serializeToDocumentObject( story, xmlDocument.createObject() );
String storyAsXML = xmlDocument.toString();
```

Automatically Serializing to JSON

Implementing the common DOM interfaces with JSON is similar to the XML implementation. It uses GWT's JSON library to provide the DOM parsing and construction. There is no `Document` object with the JSON API; instead, the root object can be any of the JSON value types. Since we are providing a serialization implementation for objects, this implementation will use a `JSONObject` as the root object. When the document consists of a collection of objects, the serializer uses a `JSONObject` with one named member, with the name of the collection as a `JSONArray` of `JSONObjects`. For the implementation of the `JSONDocument` and `JSONDocumentObject` classes, refer to the application's source code.

By adding this code we can now automatically produce JSON strings for any class that implements `Serializable` in our application. The following is an example of serializing a `story` object to a JSON string:

```
Serializer serializer = (Serializer)GWT.create( Serializer.class );
JSONDocument jsonDocument = new JSONDocument();
```

```
serializer.serializeToDocumentObject( story, jsonDocument.createObject() );
String storyAsJSON = jsonDocument.toString();
```

We can continue this pattern for more data formats than JSON and XML by implementing the `DocumentAdapter` and `DocumentObject` interfaces for the new format. Furthermore, the code for the code generator does not need to be adjusted when new formats are added.

Integrating with Action-Based PHP Scripts

Using the `Serialization` package we can easily translate Java objects to and from any format, which makes implementing server integration substantially easier. We can focus primarily on how the client using asynchronous HTTP requests to interact with the application on the server.

For Action-based integration, we'll use several PHP scripts on the server that will be called by an `ActionObjectFactory`. The `ActionObjectFactory` implements the `ObjectFactory` interface and the story and user DAOs with which the view interacts.

Let's first look at how the DAOs' methods map to PHP actions on the server. Six methods need to be implemented on the `ObjectDAO` interface to support its use by the application's view, and each method must map to a PHP action. Some of the methods accept a handler instance that will receive the requested data asynchronously when the method call returns. Figure 10-17 illustrates this process with a sample call to the `getById` method on the story DAO with the ID of 1.

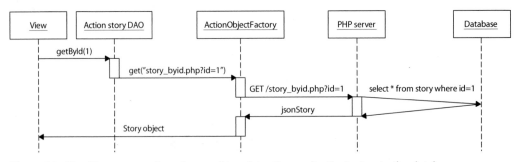

Figure 10–17. The process of getting an object from the application's view to the database

The story DAO translates the request into an action-based request string that can be used with an HTTP request. It passes this to the `Action ObjectFactory`, which uses GWT's HTTP package to send an asynchronous HTTP request to the PHP server. The PHP server accepts the request and runs the requested script, which is written to send a query to the database. It uses the data returned from the query to form a JSON response. Our client receives the JSON response in a `RequestCallback` that was supplied when the request was made. In the callback the JSON response is parsed to create a new `Story` object. The `Story` object is then sent to the view through the `ObjectListener` interface the view supplied when it made the `getById` method call.

Using PHP to Build the Action API

Let's start looking at how an Action API can be implemented beginning with the server. A database needs to be accessible from the server and the SQL schema presented earlier needs to be created. We'll use a common PHP script that we'll include with each action PHP script to connect to the database. The file, `common.php`, looks like this:

```php
<?
$user="ryan";
$password="";
$database="socialnews";
mysql_connect("localhost",$user,$password);
@mysql_select_db($database) or die( "Unable to select database");

function cleanValue( $value ){
  return mysql_real_escape_string( strip_tags( $value ) );
}
function cleanArray( $array ){
  $result = Array();
  foreach( $array as $key => $value ){
      $result[ cleanValue( $key ) ] = cleanValue( $value );
  }
  return $result;
}
?>
```

The first few lines connect to a MySQL database. MySQL is a fast and freely available database commonly used with PHP applications. However, if you have another SQL database that you typically use, you should be able to use it here too. You'll notice that there are two extra functions in this file, `cleanValue` and `cleanArray`. These two functions simply remove any HTML tags and values that may interfere in a SQL query (this is to guard against SQL injection attacks that could harm your database). We'll use these functions in the Action PHP scripts to clean any values that are submitted over HTTP.

We need 12 PHP scripts to implement the methods on the user and story DAOs for our application:

- `story_all.php`
- `story_byid.php`
- `story_delete.php`
- `story_create.php`
- `story_update.php`
- `story_digs.php`
- `story_digs_add.php`
- `user_all.php`
- `user_byid.php`
- `user_create.php`
- `user_update.php`
- `user_delete.php`

We won't go into the details of each one here, but we'll look at four to satisfy each of the CRUD operations for the `Story` entity.

For the create operation, the `story_create.php` script needs to be requested using an HTTP POST method with the new `Story` object submitted as the body in JSON format. The script reads the posted data and decodes it to a PHP structure so that its values can be used in a SQL INSERT query. The following shows the contents of the `story_create.php` script:

```
<?
include("common.php");
$jsonArray = json_decode($HTTP_RAW_POST_DATA);
$result = cleanArray( $jsonArray->story );
$keys = implode(array_keys($result), ',');
$values = "'".implode(array_values($result), "','")."'";
$q = mysql_query( "insert into stories($keys) values($values)" );
?>
```

The script starts by including the common.php script that connects to the database. Then it uses the $HTTP_RAW_POST_DATA global variable, which represents the submitted POST data and parses it using PHP's json_decode[2] method. The decoded values are placed into a PHP associative array, where the object's field names are keys and the field values are the values. The SQL INSERT statement is constructed using these values and run using the mysql_query function.

To illustrate reading from the database, we have the story_byid.php script and the story_all.php script. These scripts differ in that one returns one object and the other returns a collection of objects. Let's look at returning a collection of objects in the story_all.php script. The following is the code for this script:

```
<?
include("common.php");
$result = Array();
$q = mysql_query( "select * from stories" );
while( $a = mysql_fetch_array( $q, MYSQL_ASSOC ) ){
  array_push( $result, $a );
}
print json_encode( Array( "story" => $result ) );
?>
```

This script runs a SQL SELECT query to retrieve a list of all stories in the database using the mysql_query function. The function returns a result set that most likely has many rows. The while loop iterates over each row and adds the associative array result for the row into an array of all objects. When each returned row has been added to the array, the json_encode method is called to translate the structure into a JSON-encoded format. The result is sent back to our client using the print method.

Next we'll look at updating a Story object. This is very similar to inserting, in that the object being updated is submitted over the HTTP POST method and encoded in JSON, but it differs in that the SQL command used is UPDATE. The UPDATE SQL command must also have a WHERE clause that specifies the object ID to update. The following is the contents of the story_update.php script:

---

2. json_decode and json_encode are available in PHP 5.2 and above.

```
<?
include("common.php");
$jsonArray = json_decode($HTTP_RAW_POST_DATA);
$result = cleanArray( $jsonArray->story );
$query = "update stories set ";
$first = true;
foreach( $result as $key => $value ){
  if(!$first)$query.=",";
  $query.= $key." = '".$value."'";
  $first = false;
}
$query.=" where id=".$result['id'];
$q = mysql_query( $query );
?>
```

Notice that the values from the submitted JSON object are used to make the UPDATE query and a WHERE clause is added at the end before the query is executed.

The last operation that we'll look at on the server is deleting an object. To delete, the client sends an HTTP GET request to the `story_delete.php` script with an `id` parameter. For example, the story with `id` 1 would be deleted by requesting `story_delete.php?id=1`. On the server this is the simplest of the PHP scripts:

```
<?
include("common.php");
$id = cleanValue( $_GET['id'] );
$q = mysql_query( "delete from stories where id=".$id );
?>
```

This script simply retrieves the submitted ID and executes the `delete` query, The rest of the scripts are very similar to these four scripts and are included in the source code download for this book at www.gwtapps.com.

Writing the Action Data Access Layer in the Client

Now, with all 12 scripts running on the server, we can build the DAO layer of our application to integrate with them. The UML diagram in Figure 10-18 illustrates how this DAO layer is organized.

The view interacts with the `ObjectFactory` and `ObjectDAO` interfaces. The `AbstractHTTPObjectFactory` is a helper class that provides an object cache and handlers for the HTTP requests. It is also a superclass for

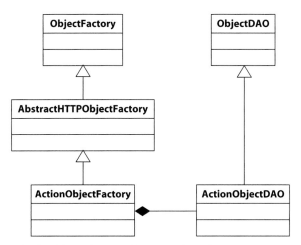

Figure 10–18.   The DAO layer for an action server interface

the `RESTObjectFactory` used in the next section. The `ActionObject Factory` and `ActionObjectDAO` classes are the implementation for integrating with an Action-based server.

First let's look at the implementation for the `ActionObjectDAO`:

```
public class ActionObjectDAO implements ObjectDAO {
    private final String prefix;

    public ActionObjectDAO( String prefix ){
        this.prefix = prefix;
    }

    public void getAll(CollectionListener handler) {
        getCollectionResource( prefix+"all"+ext, handler );
    }

    public void getAllFrom( BaseObject object, String member,
        CollectionListener handler) {
        getCollectionResource(prefix+member+ext+"?id="+object.getId(),handler);
    }

    public void getById(String id, ObjectListener handler) {
        getObjectResource( prefix+"byid"+ext+"?id="+id, handler );
    }

    public void save(BaseObject object) {
        if( object.getId() == null )
            updateObjectResource( prefix+"create"+ext, prefix+"all"+ext,object);
```

```
    else
        updateObjectResource ( prefix+"update"+ext,prefix+"all"+ext,object);
}

public void delete(BaseObject object) {
    deleteObjectResource ( prefix+"delete"+ext+"?id="+object.getId(),
        prefix+"all"+ext);
}

public void addTo( BaseObject object, String member, BaseObject
    objectToAdd) {
    updateObjectResource ( prefix+member+"_add"+ext+"?id="+object.getId(),
        prefix+member+ext+"?id="+object.getId(),objectToAdd );
}
}
```

The `ActionObjectDAO` takes a prefix as a parameter, which will be "story" for the story DAO and "user" for the user DAO, and uses it in each of the six DAO methods to construct the PHP script that should be called to execute the method on the server. This class is an inner class of the `ActionObjectFactory`, so it shares its scope and calls four of its methods: `getCollectionResource`, `getObjectRequest`, `updateObject Resource`, and `deleteObjectResource`. Each of these methods is implemented to use asynchronous HTTP to perform one of the CRUD operations on the script that it passes as a parameter.

The `ActionObjectFactory` class implements the methods needed for the `ActionObjectDAO` class as well as the `getUserDAO` and `getStoryDAO` methods from the `ObjectFactory` interface:

```
public class ActionObjectFactory extends AbstractHTTPObjectFactory {
    private ActionObjectDAO userDAO = new ActionObjectDAO("user_" );
    private ActionObjectDAO storyDAO = new ActionObjectDAO("story_");
    private final String ext;

    public ActionObjectFactory( String ext, DocumentAdapter document ) {
        super(document );
        this.ext = "."+ext;
    }

    public ObjectDAO getStoryDAO() {
        return storyDAO;
    }
```

```
    public ObjectDAO getUserDAO() {
        return userDAO;
    }

    public void getCollectionResource(String path,CollectionListener handler){
        Object object = getCachedObject(path);
        if( object != null )
            handler.onCollection((List)object);
        else
            get( path, new CollectionCallback( path, handler ) );
    }

    public void getObjectResource(String path, ObjectListener handler) {
        BaseObject object = (BaseObject)getCachedObject(path);
        if( object != null )
            handler.onObject(object);
        else
            get( path, new ObjectCallback( path, handler ) );
    }

    public void updateObjectResource(String path,String refresh,
        BaseObject object){
        post( path, object, new RefreshCallback(refresh) );
    }

    public void deleteObjectResource(String path, String refresh) {
        post( path, null, new RefreshCallback(refresh) );

    }

    public String getExt() {
        return ext;
    }
}
```

You can see a bit of the use of the superclass' object cache in the `getObjectResource` and `getCollectionResource` methods. If the object exists in cache, the callbacks receive an immediate response; otherwise, this class makes a request to the server for the object.

Notice that this class takes an extension and a `DocumentAdapter` as constructor parameters. The extension used for this example is `php`, but if you're using a different scripting language to support this action-based server integration approach you can use a different extension. The `Document Adapter` is from the common DOM that we defined earlier. We created a

JSONDocument and an XMLDocument that implement the Document Adapter interface, and we can use them here to define the encoding for the objects as they are sent to and received from the server.

With the PHP scripts running on the server, our view set up to use the ObjectDAO interface, the SerializationGeneration running to create ObjectSerializers for every Serializable object, and the ActionObjectFactory set up to transfer the ObjectDAO calls to the server, we edit the application's entry point to have it run with full integration with the server:

```
public class DatabaseEditor implements EntryPoint{
    public void onModuleLoad() {
        //create view
        DatabaseEditorView view = new DatabaseEditorView();
        RootPanel.get("databaseEditorView").add( view );

        //create objectFactory
        ActionObjectFactory objectFactory =
            new ActionObjectFactory( "php", new JSONDocument() );

        //give the view the object factory
        view.setObjectFactory( objectFactory );
    }
}
```

Integrating with a RESTful Ruby on Rails Application

Ruby on Rails is a popular framework that can be used to build database-driven web applications. It enforces solid software engineering techniques inherently by using MVC design on the server, testing, and migration. It's best known for its use of programming through convention, where most application configuration is implicit in your application code. To further increase development speed, it provides **scaffolding,** which is essentially code generation to get parts of your project running in the application quickly. For example, you could use scaffolding to create a new entity called Story, and the script will generate a Story controller, several Story views, the Story model object, a Story test file, and database migration code.

We will integrate the Database Editor application with a Ruby on Rails application using a REST-based interface. We used REST in the Blog Editor application in Chapter 8 and briefly described it earlier in this chapter. REST is basically a simple way to provide an API for a web application. REST organizes itself into several stateless resources that can be accessed and managed by the POST, GET, PUT, and DELETE commands. Figure 10-19 illustrates the sequence that our application uses to get a `Story` object from a RESTful Ruby on Rails application:

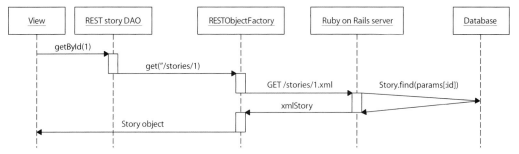

Figure 10–19.   The process of getting an object from the application's view to the database

This is a very similar sequence to the process we used when integrating with PHP. The difference is largely organizational. In this REST example the URL requested refers to a resource and does not have any indication of an action to be taken. In Figure 10-19 the URL is `/stories/1.xml`. This simply points to the story resource with an ID of 1. The action that should be taken is determined by the HTTP method used. In Figure 10-19 the GET method is used. The Ruby on Rails server interprets this as a request to read the selected resource, so it looks up the `Story` object with the requested ID and returns it. The `.xml` extension tells Rails to return an XML version of the resource instead of displaying an HTML view. We can use the same URL with the PUT command to update the object, supplying the new object values in XML format, and we could use the DELETE command to delete the resource.

Using Ruby on Rails to Build a REST API

Instead of using the SQL that we've decided upon, we can rely on Rails to generate the database schema automatically for us. It will, however, be nearly identical. So let's start by building a Rails web application called

SocialNews. You'll need to have Rails installed along with a database. If you need to install Rails you can find it at www.rubyonrails.org/down.

If you need to install a database, you can get MySQL at http://dev.mysql.com/downloads/mysql/5.0.html.

When you have a database and Rails installed, you'll be able to generate a new Rails project by typing the following at a command prompt in the parent directory of where you'd like the project in your file system:

```
rails socialnews
```

You should see Rails generate the application, as shown in Figure 10-20.

All of the directories and files set up the foundations for a Rails web application. It may look like a lot, but it provides a great structure that promotes good code organization and software development practices.

Next we need to create the `Story` and `User` model objects. Typically you would use the following to generate your model objects along with their controller and view:

Figure 10-20.   Rails generating an application

```
ruby script\generate scaffold user user
```

In this command the first user parameter determines the model's name and the second determines the controller's name. This scaffolding is used for a regular Ruby on Rails application. We are going to build a REST Ruby on Rails application, which is slightly different. As of Rails 1.2, which was released in early 2007, REST is fully supported. So instead of using the preceding scaffolding command we use scaffold_resource instead:

```
ruby script\generate scaffold_resource user name:string email:string
password:string
```

This command generates the user model as a resource in the application. We also need to do this with the story model:

```
ruby script\generate scaffold_resource story title:string url:string
description:string user_id:integer
```

When you run these commands you should see something similar to Figure 10-21, where Rails generates the required files for the resource.

One of the major differences between a REST Rails application and a regular Rails application is how the URL routing is handled, since identifying

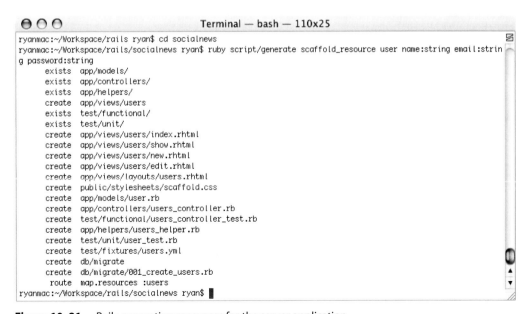

Figure 10–21.   Rails generating resources for the server application

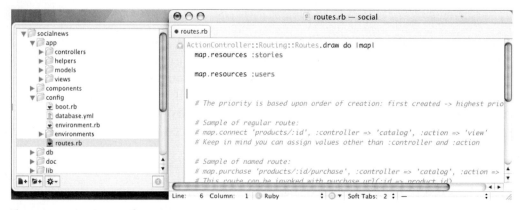

Figure 10–22. Routing for Rails resources

resources with URLs is a big part of REST. You can see this difference in the `config/routes.rb` file, shown in Figure 10-22.

The other difference is how these routes connect to the methods in the generated controllers. Each of the four HTTP commands used for REST interfaces maps to a different method in each controller. Table 10-1 outlines the mappings.

Table 10–1   Mapping REST Methods to Rails Methods

REST request	Rails method	CRUD operation
GET /stories	StoriesController.index()	Reads all story objects
GET /stories/1	StoriesController.show()	Reads the story object with ID 1
POST /stories	StoriesController.create()	Adds a new posted story
PUT /stories/1	StoriesController.update()	Updates the posted story
DELETE /stories/1	StoriesController.destroy()	Deletes the story with ID 1

You should see that these methods were automatically generated when the `scaffold_resource` script was run, as shown in Figure 10-23.

At this point we have a RESTful Rails application and we've only run three command line scripts. There are only two things that we need to do to customize the application so it has the model that we've defined for the Social News web site: We need to add the posted-by relationship, where each story is posted-by one user and the digs relationship, where users can dig a story.

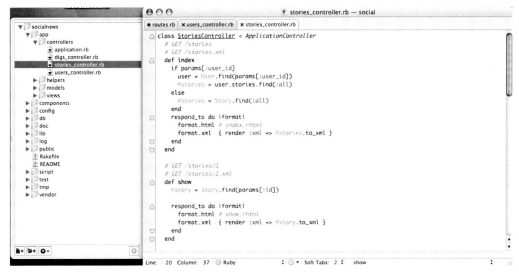

Figure 10–23. Rails automatically generates implementations for the REST methods

Adding the posted-by relationship is fairly straightforward. We've already generated the `Story` model object with a `user_id` integer field. This will act as the foreign key to the user who posted the story. To tell Rails about this relationship we need to add one line to the `Story` model class and one line to the `User` model class. The `Story` should have the following line added:

```
class Story < ActiveRecord::Base
   belongs_to :user
end
```

This tells Rails that the `Story` belongs to one `User`. Rails knows to automatically link this relationship to the `user_id` column from the stories table in the database (an example of configuration by convention).

For the `User` side of the relationship we need to add this line:

```
class User < ActiveRecord::Base
   has_many :stories
end
```

This allows a `User` object to reference the list of stories that it has posted.

The second relationship that we need to add is the digs relation, which is somewhat more complex. When we looked at the SQL for our application earlier we decided that to store this many-to-many relationship in the database we needed another table called `user_digs`, where each row would have a story ID and a user ID. We need to implement the same table in Rails like this:

```
create_table "user_dug", :force => true do |t|
    t.column "user_id", :integer
    t.column "story_id", :integer
end
```

This table allows us to get a list of all the stories one user has dug or all the users that have dug one story. To get Rails to support this relationship we need to add a new line to the `Story` model class and one to the `User` model class. For the `Story` class we need to add the following line:

```
class Story < ActiveRecord::Base
    belongs_to :user
    has_and_belongs_to_many :digs,
        :class_name => "User", :join_table => "user_dug"
end
```

In this line `digs` is declared using the `has_and_belongs_to_many` relationship. This is how you tell Rails that it is a many-to-many relationship. Since there is no model object called `dig`, we need to specify which class is on the other end of this relationship using the `class_name` attribute. We also need to specify the table that is being used, since Rails cannot automatically derive the name.

For the `User` model class we need to add a similar line:

```
class User < ActiveRecord::Base
    has_many :stories
    has_and_belongs_to_many :dug,
        :class_name => "Story", :join_table => "user_dug"
end
```

This line is nearly identical except we tell Rails that `Story` is on the other end of the relationship. Note that we could have called this relationship "stories" to avoid specifying the `class_name`, but there is already a stories relationship.

In terms of implementing the REST interface, we want these relationships set up so we can support more complex REST queries. For example, we want to be able to support a REST query like GET /stories/1/digs to get a list of all the users who have dug the story. By setting up the digs relationship on the Story model class, we have done half of what we need to do to support this type of query. The other part is to set up the routing for the URL properly.

We've seen that REST routes were automatically generated when we ran the scaffolding, but after adding relationships we lack any URL routing to them. To support a REST request like GET /stories/1/digs, we need to add a new routing:

```
ActionController::Routing::Routes.draw do |map|
   map.resources :stories
   map.resources :stories
   map.resources :stories do |stories|
      stories.resources :digs
   end
```

Adding these lines to the config/routes.rb file tells Rails to route requests to the digs relationship on a story to the DigsController. In the digs controller we need to implement the methods that we'll support for our REST API. The DAO's six methods we support include getting and posting to the digs relationship, so these are the minimum two methods that we'll need to implement. The getAllFrom() DAO method maps to the GET /stories/1/digs REST request, which will map to the index method on the DigsController. The index method can be implemented like this on the DigsController:

```
class DigsController < ApplicationController
   # GET /stories/1/digs
   # GET /stories/1/digs.xml
   def index
      story = Story.find(params[:story_id])
      @digs = story.digs.find(:all)

      respond_to do |format|
         format.html # index.rhtml
         format.xml { render :xml => @digs.to_xml }
      end
   end
end
```

Notice that in the first two lines of the method the `story_id` is used to retrieve the story object requested as part of the REST URL, then the digs relationship is used to get a list of all users who have dug the story. The list is then returned encoded as XML.

For adding to the digs relationship the `addTo` DAO method is called, which maps to the `PUT /stories/1/digs` REST request, which maps to the `update` method on the `DigsController`:

```
# PUT /stories/1/digs
# PUT /stories/1/digs.xml
def update
    story = Story.find(params[:story_id])
    @digs = story.digs.find(:all)
    story.digs << User.find(params[:id])

    respond_to do |format|
        format.xml { head :ok }
    end
end
```

In this method the `story_id` from the REST URL is used to retrieve the requested story, then the digs relationship is retrieved, which has the posted user added to it.

Writing the REST Data Access Layer in the Client

With the proper relationships and routes set up in the Rails application, we can build the DAO layer of our application and integrate with the server. The implementation can be done similarly to the Action implementation since we just need to implement a REST version of the `ObjectFactory` and `ObjectDAO` interfaces, and we can use the `AbstractHTTPObject Factory` class to help with HTTP requests and object caching. The UML diagram in Figure 10-24 illustrates how the `RESTObjectFactory` and `RESTObjectDAO` interfaces fit into this structure.

These two new classes have the job of transforming the `ObjectDAO` methods that the view calls into REST requests and sending them asynchronously over HTTP. Let's start by looking at the `RESTObjectDAO` implementation:

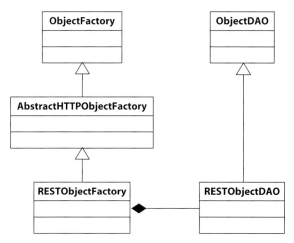

Figure 10–24.   The DAO structure for a REST server interface

```
protected class RESTObjectDAO implements ObjectDAO {
   private final String resource;

   public RESTObjectDAO( String resource ){
      this.resource = resource;
   }

   public void getAll(CollectionListener handler) {
      getCollectionResource( resource, handler );
   }

   public void getAllFrom( BaseObject object, String member,
      CollectionListener handler) {
      getCollectionResource(resource+"/"+object.getId()+"/"+member, handler);
   }

   public void getById(String id, ObjectListener handler) {
      getObjectResource( resource+"/"+id, handler );
   }

   public void save(BaseObject object) {
      updateObjectResource( resource, object );
   }

   public void delete(BaseObject object) {
      deleteObjectResource( resource, object );
   }

   public void addTo( BaseObject object, String member, BaseObject
      objectToAdd) {
```

```
        updateObjectResource(
            resource+"/"+object.getId()+"/"+member, objectToAdd );
    }
}
```

This class is constructed taking a resource name as a parameter, which it will use to construct REST URLs when the view calls its methods. You can see that each method consists of constructing a REST URL and then calling one of the methods on the outer class. The outer class in this case is the RESTObjectFactory, and it implements these methods by sending the REST URL to the server or checking for any cached objects and immediately returning. The following code implements the RESTObjectFactory class:

```
public class RESTObjectFactory extends AbstractHTTPObjectFactory {

    private RESTObjectDAO userDAO = new RESTObjectDAO( "/users" );
    private RESTObjectDAO storyDAO = new RESTObjectDAO( "/stories" );
    private String ext;

    public RESTObjectFactory(DocumentAdapter document ) {
        super( document );
        ext = "."+document.getFormatName();
    }

    public ObjectDAO getUserDAO(){
        return userDAO;
    }

    public ObjectDAO getStoryDAO() {
        return storyDAO;
    }

    protected void put( String url, BaseObject object, RequestCallback
        callback ){
        post( url+"?_method=PUT", object, callback );
    }

    protected void delete( String url, RequestCallback callback ){
        post( url+"?_method=DELETE", null, callback );
    }

    public void getObjectResource(String resource, ObjectListener handler) {
        BaseObject object = (BaseObject)getCachedObject(resource);
        if( object != null )
            handler.onObject(object);
```

```
       else
          get( resource+ext, new ObjectCallback( resource, handler ) );
   }

   public void getCollectionResource( String resource, CollectionListener
       handler) {
       Object object = getCachedObject(resource);
       if( object != null )
          handler.onCollection((List)object);
       else
          get( resource+ext, new CollectionCallback( resource, handler ) );
   }

   public void updateObjectResource(String resource, BaseObject object) {
       if( object.getId() == null ){
          post( resource+ext, object, new RefreshCallback(resource) );
       }
       else{
          String objectResource = resource+"/"+object.getId();
          put( objectResource+ext, object,
             new RefreshCallback(resource, objectResource) );
       }
   }

   public void deleteObjectResource(String resource, BaseObject object) {
       String objectResource = resource+"/"+object.getId();
       delete( objectResource+ext,
          new RefreshCallback(resource,objectResource));
   }
}
```

There are a couple of things to note in this code that make it different from the Action implementation of the `ObjectFactory` interface. First there is an `ext` variable that is appended to each REST URL. The variable is initialized to the document format name. When we use the `XMLDocument` the extension will be XML, and when we use the JSON document the extension will be JSON. This is the method that our Rails application uses to decide on the format that should be returned after a request is made. An alternative to this is to use the `Accepts:` HTTP header. We could set the header to the value `application/xml` or `application/json` to achieve the same result as long as the application's server properly handled the Accepts header.

Also note in the preceding code that the `put()` and `delete()` methods are used differently from the Action implementation. In REST implementations

PUT and DELETE are required for updating and deleting resources, but in Ajax applications we are not always able to send PUT and DELETE requests. In particular, Safari browsers will not send these requests to the server. In the Blog Editor application in Chapter 8, the Blogger API provides a workaround for this limitation by supporting a header that overrides the HTTP method. Rails, however, does not support a header but does support an additional parameter to force the HTTP method. You'll notice that the put() method appends "?_method=PUT" to the URL and calls post(), and the delete method appends "?_method=DELETE" before calling post(). When the request reaches the server, Rails reads the _method parameter and switches the HTTP method, ensuring that the proper controller method is called.

Now, with our Rails application running as a server, our view set up to use the ObjectDAO interface, the SerializationGeneration running to create ObjectSerializers for every Serializable object, and the RESTObjectFactory set up to transfer the RESTObjectDAO calls to the server as REST requests, we can edit the application's entry point to have it run with full integration with Rails:

```
public class DatabaseEditor implements EntryPoint{
   public void onModuleLoad()
   {
      //create view
      DatabaseEditorView view = new DatabaseEditorView();
      RootPanel.get("databaseEditorView").add( view );

      //create objectFactory
      RESTObjectFactory objectFactory =
         new RESTObjectFactory( new XMLDocument() );

      //give the view the object factory
      view.setObjectFactory( objectFactory );
   }
}
```

Integrating with a GWT-RPC Servlet

In the Instant Messenger application in Chapter 9 we built a web page instant messenger that allows visitors to send messages to each other using a GWT-RPC servlet, so in this section we won't go into too much detail about how to build a GWT-RPC servlet, but you can see how the DAOs map to the servlet and to the database using Hibernate.

Writing the RPC Service

Using GWT-RPC, our model objects are automatically serialized when they are used as parameters to a RPC call. The only restrictions are that they must implement the Serializable interface, which they do, and they must have a zero argument constructor, which they also have. On the server we can reuse these classes, and we can even map them directly to the database using Hibernate, an object-relational mapping (ORM) tool for Java.

The first step in implementing the RPC service is to declare the service interface and have it extend GWT's RemoveService interface:

```
public interface RPCObjectFactoryService extends RemoteService{
    /**
     * @gwt.typeArgs <com.gwtapps.databaseeditor.client.model.BaseObject>
     */
    List getAll( String type );
    /**
     * @gwt.typeArgs <com.gwtapps.databaseeditor.client.model.BaseObject>
     */
    List getAllFrom( String type, String Id, String member );
    BaseObject getById( String type, String Id );
    void save( BaseObject object );
    void delete( String type, String id );
    void addTo(String type, String Id, String member, BaseObject objectToAdd);
}
```

This interface has the same six methods that we need to implement from the DAOs, but adds a first parameter to each method to indicate the type of object that should be used. This will either be Story or User for this application. Notice the gwt.typeArgs annotation that has been added. This tells the GWT compiler that the objects in the returned list must be of the type BaseObject. Both the Story and User classes extend BaseObject, so they can be transported in this list. This annotation is required to reduce the amount of code generated by the RPC code generator. If we didn't specify this, it would have to generate serialization code for every object that could be in the list.

Next, the interface's asynchronous version needs to be implemented for the client application since each method call must be asynchronous:

```
public interface RPCObjectFactoryServiceAsync{
   void getAll( String type, AsyncCallback callback );
   void getAllFrom( String type, String Id, String member,
      AsyncCallback callback );
   void getById( String type, String Id, AsyncCallback callback );
   void save( BaseObject object, AsyncCallback callback );
   void delete( String type, String id, AsyncCallback callback );
   void addTo(String type, String Id, String member, BaseObject objectToAdd,
      AsyncCallback callback );
}
```

This is almost the same as the previous interface except any return value is set to `void` and an extra `AsyncCallback` parameter is added to each method. The `AsyncCallback` implementation receives the return value, if any.

To implement the service on the server we need to implement the `RPCObjectFactoryService` interface and GWT's `RemoteServiceServlet`:

```
public class RPCObjectFactoryServiceImpl
   extends RemoteServiceServlet
   implements RPCObjectFactoryService {

   public void addTo( String type, String Id, String member, BaseObject
      objectToAdd) {
   }

   public List getAll(String type) {
      List result = null;
      return result;
   }

   public List getAllFrom(String type, String Id, String member) {
      List result = null;
      return result;
   }

   public BaseObject getById(String type, String Id) {
      BaseObject result = null;
      return result;
   }

   public void save(BaseObject object) {
   }
```

```
public void delete(String type, String id) {
    }
}
```

This code leaves the implementation of these methods empty until the Hibernate mappings are built and the servlet can load and save objects from a database.

To run the servlet in GWT's hosted browser you need to add the following line to the module XML file:

```
<servlet path="/objectFactory"
class="com.gwtapps.databaseeditor.server.RPCObjectFactoryServiceImpl"/>
```

Now that we have an RPC service set up, we need to connect it to the DAO implementation so it can be used by the application's view. Fortunately, the ObjectDAO interface is a close match to the service interface, and the model objects can be automatically used with the service, so this work is fairly straightforward. The following implements the ObjectDAO interface for RPC:

```
protected class RPCObjectDAO implements ObjectDAO {
    private final String type;
    public RPCObjectDAO( String type ){
        this.type = type;
    }

    public void getAll(CollectionListener handler) {
        service.getAll(type, new CollectionCallback( handler ) );
    }

    public void getAllFrom( BaseObject object, String member,
        CollectionListener handler) {
        service.getAllFrom(type, object.getId(), member,
            new CollectionCallback( handler ) );
    }

    public void getById(String id, ObjectListener handler) {
        service.getById(type, id, new ObjectCallback( handler ) );
    }

    public void save(BaseObject object) {
        service.save( object , new RefreshCallback() );
    }

    public void delete(BaseObject object) {
        service.delete( type, object.getId(), new RefreshCallback() );
    }
```

```
public void addTo( BaseObject object, String member, BaseObject
   objectToAdd) {
   service.addTo( type, object.getId(), member, objectToAdd,
      new RefreshCallback() );
   }
}
```

The DAO takes a string as a parameter, which for this application is either
Story or User, and uses the parameter in each call to the service. The service
is a member variable on the outer class, which is the RPCObjectFactory:

```
public class RPCObjectFactory implements ObjectFactory{

   protected class CollectionCallback implements AsyncCallback{
      private CollectionListener handler;
      public CollectionCallback(CollectionListener handler) {
         this.handler = handler;
      }
      public void onFailure(Throwable exception)
         { GWT.log( "error", exception );}
      public void onSuccess(Object result) {
         handler.onCollection((List)result);
      }
   }

   protected class ObjectCallback implements AsyncCallback{
      private ObjectListener handler;
      public ObjectCallback(ObjectListener handler) {
         this.handler = handler;
      }
      public void onFailure(Throwable exception)
         { GWT.log( "error", exception ); }
      public void onSuccess(Object result) {
         handler.onObject((BaseObject)result);
      }
   }

   protected class RefreshCallback implements AsyncCallback{
      public void onFailure(Throwable exception)
         { GWT.log( "error", exception ); }
      public void onSuccess(Object result) {
         listener.onRefresh();
      }
   }

   private RPCObjectDAO storyDAO = new RPCObjectDAO("Story");
   private RPCObjectDAO userDAO = new RPCObjectDAO("User");
```

```
private RPCObjectFactoryServiceAsync service;
public RPCObjectFactory(String baseUrl) {
    service = (RPCObjectFactoryServiceAsync)
      GWT.create( RPCObjectFactoryService.class );
    ServiceDefTarget endpoint = (ServiceDefTarget) service;
    endpoint.setServiceEntryPoint( baseUrl );
}

public ObjectDAO getStoryDAO() {
    return storyDAO;
}

public ObjectDAO getUserDAO() {
    return userDAO;
}

public void setListener(ObjectFactoryListener listener) {
    this.listener = listener;
}
}
```

To handle the callbacks from the RPC calls, the RPCObjectFactory class implements three callback inner classes that extend GWT's AsyncCallback interface. The CollectionCallback class is used for RPC calls that expect a list of objects as a return value. It relays the list to the CollectionListener interface implemented in the application's view. The ObjectCallback class is used for RPC calls that expect a single object return value, and it relays the returned object to an ObjectListener interface implemented in the view. The third callback, Refresh, is used when the currently viewed item in the interface will need to be refreshed. In this application the save and delete DAO methods use this callback.

In the constructor, you can see the client-side object for the service being created using GWT's deferred binding. The ServiceDefTarget interface is used to connect the client-side service object to the service servlet.

With the servlet set up and the RPCObjectFactory connecting the DAO layer with the service, we can run the application on RPC by adding the RPCObjectFactory to the application's entry point like this:

```
public class DatabaseEditor implements EntryPoint{
    public void onModuleLoad() {
        //create view
        DatabaseEditorView view = new DatabaseEditorView();
        RootPanel.get("databaseEditorView").add( view );
```

```
    //create objectFactory
    RPCObjectFactory objectFactory =
       new RPCObjectFactory( "/objectFactory" );

    //give the view the object factory
    view.setObjectFactory( objectFactory );
  }
}
```

At this point, however, we haven't connected the servlet with the database. That is handled in the next section using Hibernate.

Using Hibernate to Store the Model

Hibernate, an object-relational mapping tool for Java applications, lets you map object-oriented Java classes and relationships to a relational database. This application uses Hibernate to map the fields from the Story and User objects to the database tables described earlier.

To get started with Hibernate, download the Hibernate package from www.hibernate.org and put the Hibernate JAR files on your classpath. Once you have Hibernate installed and on your classpath, you can begin to use it in your GWT services. Note that you can't use Hibernate in your client application since the client code is run in a browser and does not have access to a database.

To use Hibernate in the Database Editor RPC servlet, we first need to create the Hibernate configuration file called hibernate.cfg.xml and store it in the root of our package. In this file you configure Hibernate to connect to your database. The following is an example of the Hibernate configuration file:

```
<?xml version='1.0' encoding='utf-8'?>
<!DOCTYPE hibernate-configuration PUBLIC
        "-//Hibernate/Hibernate Configuration DTD 3.0//EN"
        "http://hibernate.sourceforge.net/hibernate-configuration-3.0.dtd">

<hibernate-configuration>

    <session-factory>
    <property name="connection.url">jdbc:mysql://localhost/
socialnews?autoReconnect=true</property>
    <property name="connection.username">root</property>
```

```
<property name="connection.driver_class">com.mysql.jdbc.Driver</property>
<property name="dialect">org.hibernate.dialect.MySQLDialect</property>
<property name="connection.password"></property>
<property name="transaction.factory_class">
org.hibernate.transaction.JDBCTransactionFactory</property>


        <!-- JDBC connection pool (use the built-in) -->
        <property name="connection.pool_size">1</property>

        <!-- Enable Hibernate's automatic session context management -->
        <property name="current_session_context_class">thread</property>

        <!-- Disable the second-level cache  -->
        <property name="cache.provider_class">
        org.hibernate.cache.NoCacheProvider</property>

        <!-- Echo all executed SQL to stdout -->
        <property name="show_sql">true</property>

        <mapping
        resource="com/gwtapps/databaseeditor/client/model/User.hbm.xml"/>
        <mapping
        resource="com/gwtapps/databaseeditor/client/model/Story.hbm.xml"/>

    </session-factory>

</hibernate-configuration>
```

You should refer to the Hibernate documentation for information about the configuration options in this file. A brief overview of the file shows that a MySQL database called "socialnews" is chosen and the root user is used to connect. Two other important lines in this file for this application are the mapping elements at the end. Each one points to a mapping XML file that defines how one class should be mapped in the database. There is one mapping file for the User class called User.hbm.xml and one mapping file for the Story class called Story.hbm.xml.

The User.hbm.xml file is as follows:

```
<?xml version="1.0"?>
<!DOCTYPE hibernate-mapping  PUBLIC "-//Hibernate/Hibernate Mapping DTD 3.0//EN"
"http://hibernate.sourceforge.net/hibernate-mapping-3.0.dtd">
```

```
<hibernate-mapping>
    <class name="com.gwtapps.databaseeditor.client.model.User" table="users">
        <id name="id" column="id" type="long">
            <generator class="native"/>
        </id>
        <property name="name"/>
        <property name="email"/>
        <property name="password"/>
    </class>
</hibernate-mapping>
```

The mapping sits inside a `hibernate-mapping` element. The first child
element is a `class` element that indicates the full class name of the class
that is being mapped. Inside the `class` element is first the ID mapping,
which is set to the type `long` and has a generator set to automatically generate a new ID when new `User` objects are saved. The remaining three elements in the `class` element are property elements that indicate the other
fields that should be mapped. This mapping essentially tells Hibernate to
map `User` objects to a table called `users`, as we've described earlier in
this chapter.

The `Story.hbm.xml` file is implemented like this:

```
<?xml version="1.0"?>
<!DOCTYPE hibernate-mapping  PUBLIC "-//Hibernate/Hibernate Mapping DTD 3.0//EN"
"http://hibernate.sourceforge.net/hibernate-mapping-3.0.dtd">

<hibernate-mapping>
    <class name="com.gwtapps.databaseeditor.client.model.Story" table="stories">
        <id name="id" column="id" type="long">
            <generator class="native"/>
        </id>
        <property name="title"/>
        <property name="url"/>
        <property name="description"/>
        <set name="digs" table="user_dug" cascade="save-update">
                <key column="story_id"/>
    <many-to-many
class="com.gwtapps.databaseeditor.client.model.User"
column="user_id"/>
        </set>
    </class>
</hibernate-mapping>
```

This file has a layout similar to the `User.hbm.xml` file, in which the class
and table name are defined along with the autogenerated ID and three

fields. In addition, there is a set defined that maps the digs `List` on the `Story` class to the `user_dug` table. It sets the key to the `story_id` column in the `user_dug` table and defines a many-to-many relationship to `User` objects for the `user_id` column in the `user_dug` table. This mapping allows us to add and delete `User` objects from the digs `List` on a `Story` object and have the changes automatically reflected in the database when the Hibernate transaction is committed.

With the mappings set up, Hibernate can be used inside the `RPCObject FactoryServiceImpl` to implement the service's methods. To use Hibernate in this class we need to get a Hibernate `Session` object. The common way to get a `Session` object is to set up a Hibernate `Session Factory` in a `HibernateUtils` class:

```
public class HibernateUtil {
    private static SessionFactory sessionFactory;
    static {
        try {
            sessionFactory=new Configuration()
            .configure()
            .buildSessionFactory();
        } catch (Throwable ex) {
            throw new ExceptionInInitializerError(ex);
        }
    }
    public static SessionFactory getSessionFactory() {
        // Alternatively, you could look up in JNDI here
        return sessionFactory;
    }
    public static void shutdown() {
        // Close caches and connection pools
        getSessionFactory().close();
    }
}
```

In this helper class a global `SessionFactory` object is statically initialized for use by all clients that connect to the servlet. Each client that connects to the servlet gets `sessionFactory` and calls the `getCurrentSession()` method to retrieve a `Session` object. The `Session` returned from this call will return the same `Session` each time it is called on the current thread (this was set up as an option in the Hibernate configuration file).

Using the `HibernateUtils` class in the `RPCObjectFactoryServiceImpl` class, we are able to implement the service methods to interact with the

database. For example, the following is the implementation of the `getAll`
method:

```
public List getAll(String type) {
    List result = null;
    Session session = HibernateUtil.getSessionFactory().getCurrentSession();
    session.beginTransaction();
    result = session.createQuery("from "+type).list();
    session.getTransaction().commit();
    return result;
}
```

This code illustrates the steps involved with using a Hibernate session to
interact with the database. First, the current session is retrieved from the
`SessionFactory`, and then the `beginTransaction` method is called to
indicate a unit of work. After a transaction is started, various method calls
can be made on the session to read from and write to the database. In this
example a query is created to get a list of all objects of a certain type. Once
all of the work is done with the database, the `commit` method is called to
save any changes that may have occurred.

The rest of the methods in the `RPCObjectFactoryServiceImpl` follow
this pattern. The following code implements each of the methods, which
illustrates how to use Hibernate to perform all of the DAO's methods
needed for the Database Editor application:

```
public class RPCObjectFactoryServiceImpl
    extends RemoteServiceServlet
    implements RPCObjectFactoryService {

    public void addTo(
String type, String Id, String member, BaseObject objectToAdd) {
        if( type.equals("Story") && member.equals("digs") ){
            Session session =
HibernateUtil.getSessionFactory().getCurrentSession();
            session.beginTransaction();
            Story story = (Story) session.get(Story.class, Id);
            story.getDigs().add( objectToAdd );
            session.getTransaction().commit();
        }
    }

    public List getAll(String type) {
        List result = null;
        Session session =
HibernateUtil.getSessionFactory().getCurrentSession();
```

```
        session.beginTransaction();
        result = session.createQuery("from "+type).list();
        session.getTransaction().commit();
        return result;
    }

    public List getAllFrom(String type, String Id, String member) {
        List result = null;
        if( type.equalsl("Story") && member.equals("digs") ){
            Session session =
HibernateUtil.getSessionFactory().getCurrentSession();
            session.beginTransaction();
            Story story = (Story)session.get(Story.class, Id);
            result = story.getDigs();
            session.getTransaction().commit();
        }
        return result;
    }

    public BaseObject getById(String type, String Id) {
        BaseObject result = null;
        Session session =
HibernateUtil.getSessionFactory().getCurrentSession();
        session.beginTransaction();
        result = (BaseObject)session.get(Story.class, Id);
        session.getTransaction().commit();
        return result;
    }

    public void save(BaseObject object) {
        Session session =
HibernateUtil.getSessionFactory().getCurrentSession();
        session.beginTransaction();
        session.save(object);
        session.getTransaction().commit();
    }

    public void delete(String type, String id) {
        Session session =
HibernateUtil.getSessionFactory().getCurrentSession();
        session.beginTransaction();
        session.delete(session.get(Story.class, id));
        session.getTransaction().commit();
    }

}
```

Summary

In this chapter we've covered a two-paned interface manager-style application along with many complex situations that you may encounter with GWT. We looked at three methods of communicating with the server, and used an action interface and JSON to communicate with PHP scripts. We used a REST interface and XML to communicate with a Ruby on Rails application, and we used GWT-RPC to communicate with a Java servlet and Hibernate. We also looked at building a code generator, which in this application saved a lot of tedious and error-prone code that would need to be written to transfer Java objects to and from JSON and XML.

Index

Tools for Mastering the GWT

Google™ Web Toolkit Solutions
(Digital Short Cut)

David Geary

Some of the more advanced aspects of the Google Web Toolkit (GWT) are explored in this Short Cut using two applications: an address book and a Yahoo! trip viewer. Both applications use remote procedure calls to access information on the server or an online web service. The Yahoo! Trips application also shows how you can incorporate Scriptaculous, a powerful JavaScript toolkit, to apply a useful effect for displaying results. Other cool and useful techniques, including how to implement drag and drop and how to integrate with a database using Hibernate are demonstrated, along with coverage on how to move a GWT application to a servlet container, such as Tomcat or Resin, and the process of deploying a GWT application to Tomcat with Ant.

Digital Short Cuts are in Adobe® Reader® format
www.informit.com/title/0131584650

ALSO AVAILABLE
Mobi Pocket: 0768671027

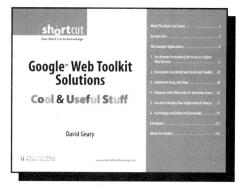

ISBN: 978-0-13-158465-5

Google™ Web Toolkit Solutions:
More Cool & Useful Stuff

David Geary with Rob Gordon

With this book, Java guru David Geary explores the more advanced aspects of Google Web Toolkit (GWT), which you will need to implement real world applications with rich user interfaces. Each solution in this practical, hands-on book is more than a recipe. The sample programs are carefully explained in detail to help you quickly master advanced GWT techniques, such as implementing drag and drop, integrating JavaScript libraries, using deferred commands, and advanced event handling methodologies. Solutions in this book are in response to the most common yet complex obstacles developers run into with GWT.

www.informit.com/title/0132344185
www.safari.informit.com/9780132344814   Safari Edition

ALSO AVAILABLE
book: 013234534X

ISBN: 978-0-13-234481-4

For more information on these titles and to read sample material, visit
www.informit.com/ph

PRENTICE HALL

LearnIT at InformIT

Go Beyond the Book

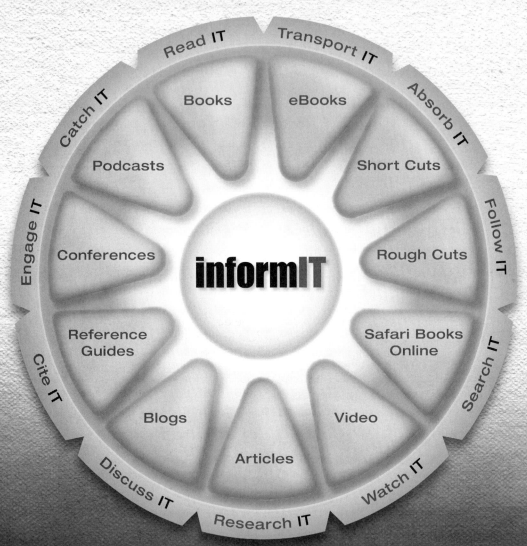

Read IT — Books

Transport IT — eBooks

Absorb IT — Short Cuts

Catch IT — Podcasts

Follow IT — Rough Cuts

Engage IT — Conferences

informIT

Search IT — Safari Books Online

Cite IT — Reference Guides

Discuss IT — Blogs

Research IT — Articles

Video — Watch IT

11 WAYS TO LEARN IT at www.informIT.com/learn

The online portal of the information technology
publishing imprints of Pearson Education